LUCKNOW & OUDE
IN THE MUTINY

LUCKNOW & OUDE IN THE MUTINY

A NARRATIVE AND A STUDY

LIEUT. -GENERAL MCLEOD INNES
R. E., V. C.

GYAN

Published by

Gyan Publishing House
5, Ansari Road
Daryaganj, New Delhi-110002
Phone: 011-47034999, 9811692060
E-mail: books@gyanbooks.com

Distribution Network
gyanbooks.com
India, USA, Canada, UK, Australia, France

ISBN: 978-81-212-8568-1 (PB)
First Published, 1895

2nd Impression 2023

Printed at: Gyan Press, Delhi.

LUCKNOW & OUDE IN THE MUTINY
Author: McLeod Innes

LUCKNOW AND OUDE

IN THE MUTINY

MUTCHI BHAWN.

Western Gate.

LUCKNOW & OUDE

IN THE MUTINY

A NARRATIVE AND A STUDY

BY

LIEUT.-GENERAL McLEOD INNES
R.E., V.C.

LONDON
A. D. INNES AND CO.
BEDFORD STREET
1895

PREFACE

THIS account of the part played by Lucknow and Oude in the Bengal mutiny is not meant to be anything more than what it is called—a narrative and a study; and it has been written with the desire to show, in their true proportion and colour, some of the important points of that convulsion and contest; including its antecedents, its characteristics and its issues, as well as its actual incidents.

Much of what I have recorded came within my own personal knowledge; but the book is not an account of my private experiences or reminiscences, except to the extent requisite to support or illustrate my various statements and views. And I entirely disclaim for it the title of History, which would demand a completeness of narrative, and a fullness of details in incidents and personal references that I have not attempted, and that would have tended to interfere with the clearness that I have aimed at in the narrative and the argument.

In order to show the relative share that Oude and Lucknow had in the conflict generally, I have included a brief sketch of the Mutiny as an introduction, dealing with its origin and development, as well as with its course.

My leading object throughout has been to describe the true military characteristics of the defence and the succour of the Residency, and to lead to a just appreciation of the part played and the influence exercised by Henry Lawrence and Henry Havelock in checking and mastering the

Mutiny at its darkest crisis, and thereby ensuring our ultimate success.

At the Residency, Sir Henry Lawrence's foresight and resolute attitude on the outbreak, with his judicious arrangements, and careful and thorough preparations, formed the foundation for its defence; of which the eventual success was due to our defeating all the ceaseless efforts of the enemy to effect the one definite object at which they aimed, the sudden formation of a practicable breach in our defences.

As to the general contest; Sir Henry's beneficent rule of the Punjab, on its annexation, created the hearty good-will in which lay the influence that kept the Sikhs on our side in the dark days of the siege of Delhi. It was his attitude at Lucknow that chained to the contest there the rebel army of Oude, which would otherwise have joined the one at Delhi, and would without doubt have turned the odds there against us. Havelock for his part, by his brilliant leadership, met with unvarying success; inspiring in his own troops a confidence and spirit, and in the enemy a dread, which minimized the gravity of the struggle in the days of our greatest straits; apart from which the boldness of his venture in invading Oude, and his skill in withdrawing to Cawnpore, stand unrivalled as feats of war. His succour of the Residency saved it from an inevitable catastrophe, since it was effected just in time to anticipate the arrival of the Delhi mutineers, whose accession to the investing force would have doubled the dangers of the defence, and the difficulties of the relief.

These are the points to which I have specially endeavoured to give their due prominence.

For those particulars in which my narrative is at variance with other published accounts of Sir Henry Lawrence's policy and measures while preparing for the defence of the Residency, my authority lies in the record I made in my note-book of the direct instructions and information which he gave to me personally—a record which was habitually read out to him, and to which he constantly referred.

The account of the Engineer operations in the defence is based on my personal knowledge of them, the share I took in them, and the records I kept of them, supplemented by the information supplied to me by my brother officers; at whose request I drew up the official report of them.

For information on other points I have been greatly indebted to Sir James Outram and Lord Napier of Magdala, to Sir Henry Havelock-Allen, General Dodgson, Sir William Olpherts, and other friends.

The account of the Talookdars and people of Oude, and of their fluctuating demeanour, has been based on the descriptions given me by Sir James Outram, Captain Alexander Orr his "Intelligence" officer, and Mr. Patrick Carnegy; and on the records of the trials of the State prisoners on the close of the Mutiny.

In the Appendices will be found extracts from official documents respecting the annexation and administration of Oude, and the treatment of the Talookdars. One of them is a translation of a very singular letter by the Rajah Maun Singh to the other Talookdars, written at the darkest stage of the convulsion, and conveying the criticisms on the situation of one of the cleverest natives of India.

The maps, plans, and views will, I hope, help to make the narrative clear.

For the panoramic views of the Residency Entrenchments, and for the drawing of the Mutchi Bhown, I am under special obligations to my friend Miss Alma Hodge. The former are based on a series of photographs of a model of the position, constructed by the Rev. T. Moore; and the latter on an excellent photograph of the Mutchi Bhown, kindly lent me by Captain Charles Hill, R.A.

J. J. M. I.

CONTENTS

INTRODUCTION

GENERAL SKETCH OF THE MUTINY

CHAPTER I

ITS ORIGIN

CHAPTER II

ITS DEVELOPMENT

CHAPTER III

THE CAMPAIGN IN THREE STAGES

THE VITAL STRUGGLE

CHAPTER V

THE SUPPRESSION OF THE REVOLT

BOOK I

OUDE BEFORE THE SIEGE OF THE RESIDENCY

CHAPTER I

BEFORE THE ANNEXATION

CHAPTER II

THE FIRST YEAR AFTER ANNEXATION

CHAPTER III

UNDER SIR HENRY LAWRENCE

CHAPTER IV

LAWRENCE'S POLICY ON THE OUTBREAK

CHAPTER V

MEASURES BEFORE THE MUTINY AT LUCKNOW

CHAPTER VI

THE MUTINIES AT THE OUT-STATIONS

CHAPTER VII

LUCKNOW FROM THE MUTINY TO CHINHUT

BOOK II

THE FIRST DEFENCE OF THE RESIDENCY

CHAPTER I

CHINHUT AND THE CONCENTRATION

CHAPTER II

DESCRIPTION OF THE ENTRENCHMENTS

CHAPTER III

ARRANGEMENTS FOR THE DEFENCE

CHAPTER IV

THE PROCEEDINGS OF THE ENEMY

CHAPTER V

FIRST STAGE OF THE DEFENCE

CHAPTER VI

SECOND STAGE OF THE DEFENCE

CHAPTER VII

THIRD STAGE OF THE DEFENCE—THE MINING

CHAPTER VIII

THIRD STAGE OF THE DEFENCE—GENERAL INCIDENTS

CHAPTER XI

MINOR INCIDENTS OF THE DEFENCE

BOOK III

HAVELOCK'S CAMPAIGN

CHAPTER I

NEILL'S ADVANCE TO ALLAHABAD

CHAPTER II

HAVELOCK'S ADVANCE TO CAWNPORE

CHAPTER III

HAVELOCK'S FIRST ADVANCE INTO OUDE

CHAPTER IV

HAVELOCK'S WITHDRAWAL TO CAWNPORE

CHAPTER V

HAVELOCK'S FINAL ADVANCE TO LUCKNOW

CHAPTER VI

SUCCOUR OF THE RESIDENCY

BOOK IV

THE SECOND DEFENCE OF THE RESIDENCY

CHAPTER I

EFFORTS TO WITHDRAW THE GARRISON

CHAPTER II

THE BLOCKADE

CHAPTER III

RELIEF BY SIR COLIN CAMPBELL

BOOK V

CAPTURE OF THE CITY OF LUCKNOW

CHAPTER I

PRELIMINARY OPERATIONS ON THE GANGES

CHAPTER II

PRELIMINARY OPERATIONS IN OUDE

CHAPTER III

SIEGE AND CAPTURE OF LUCKNOW

APPENDICES

VIEWS, MAPS, AND PLANS

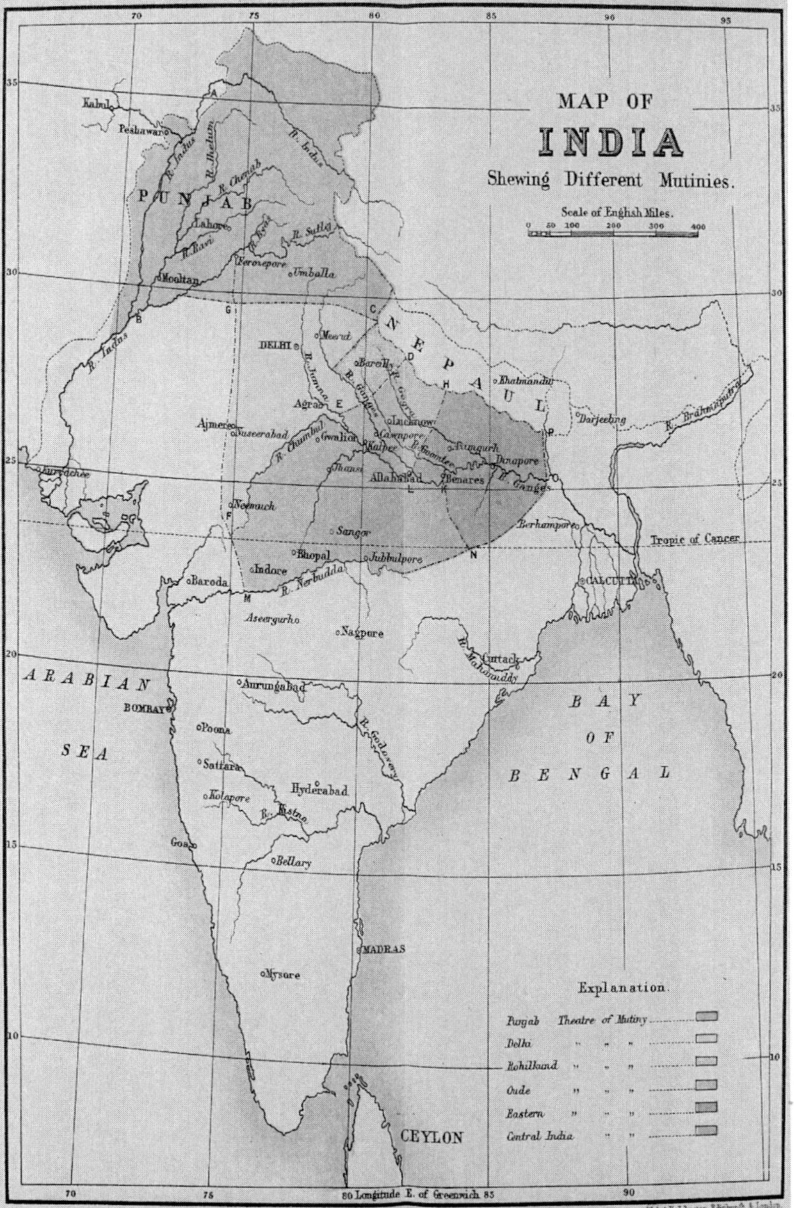
MAP OF
INDIA
Shewing Different Mutinies.
Scale of English Miles.
Explanation.
Punjab Theatre of Mutiny
Delhi " " "
Rohilkand " " "
Oude " " "
Eastern " " "
Central India " "
PUNJAB
NEPAUL
ARABIAN SEA
BAY OF BENGAL
CEYLON
Tropic of Cancer
Kabul
Peshawar
Lahore
Mooltan
Ferozepore
Umballa
DELHI
Meerut
Bareilly
Agra
Lucknow
Cawnpore
Gwalior
Kalpee
Jhansi
Allahabad
Benares
Dinapore
Ajmere
Nuseerabad
Neemuch
Saugor
Bhopal
Indore
Jubbulpore
Baroda
Aseergurh
Nagpore
Cuttack
Aurungabad
BOMBAY
Poona
Sattara
Kolapore
Hyderabad
Goa
Bellary
MADRAS
Mysore
Berhampore
CALCUTTA
Darjeeling
Khatmandu
Longitude E. of Greenwich
W. & A.K. Johnston, Edinburgh & London.

LUCKNOW AND OUDE
IN THE MUTINY

INTRODUCTION

GENERAL SKETCH OF THE MUTINY

CHAPTER I

ITS ORIGIN

THE great convulsion known as the Indian Mutiny broke out in May 1857, consequent directly on the excitement and ill-feeling engendered in the Bengal army by the well-known cartridge incident. Any such military outbreak would naturally cause much civil disturbance and find numerous supporters outside the army, but the wide range and virulence of the general commotion that ensued were exceptional, and the rising was throughout marked by a variety of phases and by singular episodes, for which the disaffection of the troops and the cartridge incident do not, of themselves, adequately account. A reasonable explanation of them, however, is indispensable for a clear insight into the subject, and fortunately it is readily found on turning to antecedent events and circumstances, and to the state of public feeling prevalent among various sections of the community. Investigation in those directions provides us with facts and points to conclusions and probabilities which seem to indicate obviously and amply the several influences that led to the origin of the outbreak, swayed and chequered its development, and further served materially to affect the progress and shape the course of the contest that ensued.

The first matter for consideration is the *chronic* state of public feeling, that is, its general state when not affected by any temporary exceptional excitement or agitation. Up to 1856, the year before the outbreak, there had been for a whole century a continuous, aggressive advance of the British Power till it completed the ring-fence of the Empire by the annexation of Oude. During all that time, it had either been engaged in actual conflict or had been forming dominant relations with the several races of the country, and had reduced them, one after another, to subjection; some provinces being brought under its direct administration, and others being left as feudatory or vassal States under their native rulers. At the start, the old Moghul Dominion had been in a hopeless state of decay, leading to all the horrors of internecine war, and some of the native principalities had gladly turned for safety to the shelter of English protection and supremacy. But the great mass of the people had been brought under our rule by conquest, or by forcible annexation. With ruling dynasties thus set aside, reduced, or crushed, with great races humiliated, and bitterness and misery spread broadcast by the loss of power and place and property, it would be an outrage on common sense to doubt that we had created a host of enemies. Moreover, there had been no rest, no time to reduce their numbers or their irritation. The benefits of civilized rule, of the Pax Britannica, were felt only skin-deep, and the old fierce instincts, the outcome of centuries of strife and oppression, were still in the ascendant. The memory of injuries was still keen and vivid, the newer cases helping to recall the old ones to mind, and to reopen sores that might otherwise have been getting healed: so that, briefly, the mood and temper which prevailed were those of a conquered people who had wrongs and humiliations to remember, and were chafing at having to endure the sway of aliens in race and creed. There existed, in fact, under the best circumstances, a mass of constant disaffection, and whole hosts of malcontents.

Of these, the most powerful and dangerous were the Mussulmans. The entire Mahomedan population were, as a body, rebels at heart, and resented the Christian supremacy, if only on religious grounds and from fanatical pride. And the Moghuls of the Upper Provinces had, in addition, a natural longing to revive their old predominance, and restore their old Empire.

Next may be mentioned the Mahrattas, a warlike and unscrupulous Hindoo race, who, though now split up into rival states, had been most powerful as a confederacy, and felt that, but for the British, they would have been the masters of India.

Another extensive body of malcontents consisted of those who were actual sufferers from British conquest or annexation, or from the action of British Land Policy.

And a fourth group, specially dangerous from their spirit and energy, was formed by those who fretted at the closing of those outlets for ambition, and the loss of those opportunities for aggrandizement through political intrigue or military prowess, that had been current of old.

Such a mass of disaffection, however latent or suppressed, was obviously a standing menace to the tranquillity of the country, constituting a solid basis, and providing a powerful agency, for the rousing of evil passions and the promotion of seditious enterprise—a sure factor in any movement or question involving the peace or security of the State.

At the same time, any tendency to give vent to this ill-feeling in serious action against the British was checked by the universal sense that our presence constituted the only real safeguard against a recurrence of the internecine wars of old, with all their attendant horrors, of which the memories and traditions were still in force: whilst also each of the great races—Rajpoot or Mahratta, Mahomedan or Sikh or Jat—felt that the British rule was preferable to that of any of its native rivals, by whom it might possibly be overcome in a contest for the supremacy.

Under the counteracting influence of this feeling, the chronic disaffection usually remained latent or suppressed; but with any undue temptation or increase of discontent, it was apt to awake into activity, with its agents ready to intensify and inflame any exceptional causes for irritation that might arise.

For too much stress must not be laid on the fact that the races of India are numerous and have conflicting interests and aspirations, and on the resulting theory that they cannot be regarded as one people—as the people of India. It is not to be gainsaid, and it ought not to be ignored, that they are one people in the very important sense of having, in common, characteristics and interests which are opposed to those of the British. They belong to the soil, while the British are aliens, *feringhees.* They are dark-skinned, *kala admi,* while the British are fair. Their creeds are not those of the English. Their social habits and usages, their traditional rights and points of honour to which they cling passionately, and their modes of thought, are Oriental and not European. They are subjects, and practically barred from rule, while the British are rulers, and virtually autocratic. If the English even apparently though not actually ignore or slight—much more if they treat with insult, or outrage—these points of difference, it is folly to suppose that the several races will not tend to combine and act as one people in hostility to the English. And this combination, based on a unity of excited feeling overriding reason and sense, will not be readily checked or thwarted; except by the wanton action of some section, reminding the rest, with the force of a shock, of the other interests at stake.

And this was precisely the course of events in the revolt of 1857. For, as will be seen, the chronic ill-feeling had become intensified, and gave an exceptional colour and weight to the cartridge incident, causing it to develope into a general mutiny. But many of the disaffected sections of the people wavered and stopped short, on their eyes being opened by the partisan aggressiveness of the Moghul section.

From the chronic state of public feeling, and its liability to fluctuation, we pass on to the facts and incidents that affected it. During Lord Dalhousie's rule, which closed in 1856, the boundaries of British Dominion were very greatly extended, so as eventually to include the whole of India; and, in addition to this, many feudatory States which, though included within British Dominion and subject to its suzerainty, had hitherto been left under the sway of their own dynastic chiefs, were removed from such native rule and brought directly under British administration.

These annexations in the aggregate greatly affected the native mind, impressing it with the sense that the greed of the English was insatiable, and troubling it as to the further steps that might follow.

The earliest of the annexations was that of the Punjab. This was a happy one. It saved the empire in 1857. For Sir Henry Lawrence was placed at the head of the administration of the province immediately after its conquest, and, through a carefully selected staff, most of whom he imbued with his own spirit, he carried out such a liberal policy, and showed such a genial demeanour to the proud and warlike race who were smarting under the sense of defeat, that he turned them from enemies into friends, and won their confidence for their English rulers. This good-will had its foundations laid deep ; and, though somewhat affected by the colder and harder rule that replaced Sir Henry's on his transfer to another post, it lasted, under the staff which he left behind him, till the time of trial came and put it successfully to the test.

Of the other annexations, only two were of any particular importance, those of Jhansi and of Oude. But both these cases startled the native community, because the rulers of both provinces were held to have ever been thoroughly loyal and true to British interests. If such fidelity, it was argued, could not avert annexation, what State was there that could consider itself safe ? They were also mischievous, each of them, in other respects.

Jhansi was annexed because the last Rajah had died leaving no lineal heir, but only an adopted one, whom Lord Dalhousie had declined to accept. This refusal was doubtless legal and probably justifiable, but its necessity was questionable. If avoidable, it was impolitic ; and under any circumstances, it was unfortunate, because it set at nought a much cherished custom, and was regarded, in conjunction with other cases, as significant of annexation, being, under similar circumstances, the settled policy of the future.

This caused serious anxiety and irritation in the feudatory States, and especially affected the good-will of the great princes of Rajpootana, hitherto markedly loyal and contented.

The annexation of Oude had been somewhat anxiously regarded by Government with respect to its possible effect on the turbulent Talookdars of the province, and on the

Sepoys, of most of whom it was the fatherland. The latter however did not seem to take it seriously amiss ; while the Talookdars accepted it contentedly, being satisfied with the terms held out to them by the proclamation that was then issued. So the mischief which immediately ensued was not in that direction. But the Mussulman community were affronted by the insult to their religion in the reduction of a Mahomedan power.

Following on the annexations, and resulting directly from them, was the most momentous matter of all. As territory extended, the *native* army was proportionately increased, but without any corresponding augmentation being made of the *British* troops. The consequence was that the Sepoy force attained to overwhelming preponderance over the British, their infantry in Bengal being at one time in the proportion of 20 to 1. This destroyed the equilibrium of the military organization, and thereby endangered its stability and the security of the State.

The risk thus involved was enhanced by the fact—well known—that the Bengal Sepoys had been showing signs of laxity in tone and discipline. Besides one positive mutiny, a group of regiments in the Punjab had been checked in a tendency to combination about an alleged grievance. And, worst of all, there had been successful resistance to orders when troops had been required to proceed on service which entailed a sea voyage. Further, the danger of the temptation which their overwhelming strength held out to a force in which such a tone prevailed, was increased by the absence of any effort, on the part of the Government, to conceal or to counteract by improved military arrangements the weakness of the British troops. For these were mainly massed in the Punjab, leaving huge stretches of country and positions of the first importance, such as Allahabad and Delhi, absolutely denuded of their presence, and with only three regiments to garrison the 900 miles between Calcutta and Meerut. This was the case in Lord Dalhousie's time ; and it was not altered by Lord Canning, who was probably lulled into security by the favourable opinion which he had received from Lord Dalhousie of the state of the native army.

Before passing on from the events during Lord Dalhousie's rule, another point has to be touched on—the effects of his own personality. Able, energetic, and bold, and withal devotedly bent on fulfilling his duty to the country, he conferred lasting benefits upon it. But he was essentially an autocrat, exceptionally imperious, self-willed, and self-sufficient. So he rode rough-shod over all difficulties, among them the prejudices, feelings, habits, traditions, and modes of thought of the native community; and would brook no advice. Formerly local rulers and other responsible authorities were expected to convey information, and to tender suggestions, advice, and opinions freely and frankly—and also to act upon their own judgment in minor matters and in cases of urgency. These were the traditional principles of administration by which the empire had been built up. But Lord Dalhousie practically changed all this. Instead of acting promptly and resolutely on their own judgment, officers had to wait for orders; and advice or suggestion, except from a favoured few, was apt to be regarded as unparalleled presumption; so that many valuable sources of observation and information naturally became closed, independent thought and promptitude of action were checked, and public and official spirit were greatly deadened.

We now come to Lord Canning's rule, under which this tone of administration naturally continued, whilst, as a matter of course, he was personally quite unequal to the task of concentrating all springs of action in himself.

At the same time another and almost opposite result was, that with the withdrawal of Lord Dalhousie's personal sway, real vigorous control on the part of the supreme Government seemed to cease altogether, and administrative discipline was greatly weakened. Hence, though the old tone among the higher officials was not restored, strong-willed subordinates, feeling the relaxation, became inclined to kick over the traces, ignore orders, and disregard authority.

An instance of this occurred at once in Oude with very mischievous results. Lord Dalhousie had, in his proclamation of the annexation, made certain promises which protected the interests of the Talookdars of the Province, of the Royal Family, and of the dependants of the deposed king; and consequently, as has been already mentioned, contentment at first prevailed. But very soon some of the officials, who were at variance with the Chief Commissioner, disregarded orders, and in their judgments and actions violated the terms of the proclamation, and brought much loss and misery on the influential classes. Hence the Talookdars, naturally a turbulent body, were gradually roused during the latter half of 1856 into a state of exasperation that threatened evil results, and was indirectly the first important outcome of Lord Canning's rule.

Of equal gravity, especially with respect to the coming mutiny, was a measure which Lord Canning himself carried out during his first year, called the General Service Enlistment Act. This made an entire revolution in the future terms of service of the Sepoy army, as they would have to be prepared to cross the Blackwater (as they called the ocean), despite caste or religious obligations. Would Brahmins and Rajpoots enlist under such terms, or would they give up military service as their career? This apparent attack on caste privileges seemed to fit in but too well with the sinister rumours which had, by this time, begun to spread respecting the aggressive intentions of Government against the creeds of the country. The matter became an all-absorbing and agitating topic in the regimental lines and in the families and homes of the Sepoys, and was the first actual and tangible strain on the loyalty of the men and their sense of their relations to the State.

Then in January 1857 came the cartridge incident.

These several circumstances may now be usefully summarized before proceeding to show their chief results and the action to which they gave rise on the part of the malcontents.

I. There had been extensive annexations under Lord Dalhousie, leading in the aggregate to a sinister impression, in the native mind, of the greedy and grasping tendency of Government, especially as the claims of loyalty and fidelity appeared to carry no weight.

II. One of the annexations, that of the Punjab, was happy and fortunate, because wisely managed.

III. The annexation of Jhansi was mischievous from the

anxiety and irritation it created in the feudatory States, in regard to the practice of adoption of heirs.

IV. The annexation of Oude was mischievous because it angered the Mahomedan community.

V. The native army had been allowed to attain to overwhelming preponderance, and had been subjected to undue temptation.

VI. It had latterly been irritated, and its loyalty strained by the General Service Enlistment Act.

VII. Lord Dalhousie had, throughout his rule, discouraged independent thought and action, and had exercised a very powerful personal and concentrated control. Hence, on his departure, there was a reaction, leading to insubordinate proceedings on the part of officials in Oude, which exasperated the influential classes of the province.

We now come to the effect of these antecedents on the chronic disaffection, and the action to which they led on the part of the malcontents.

The annexations in general, though they produced anxiety in the feudatory States, did not act much on those already disaffected, beyond rousing their watchfulness and increasing their suspicion and the discussion of the acts and intentions of Government. The annexation of Jhansi, however, from the excitement and ill-feeling it created among the feudatory princes, led the disaffected at once to take energetic measures.

The Mahomedans, always on the alert, were now excited with hopes of the consequent support of the native States and of the country generally; and the malcontents proceeded vigorously to spread sinister and seditious rumours, and to intrigue with the army. On the one hand, they pointed to the conquests and annexations of the British, to their railways, telegraphs, and scientific—if not magical—innovations, and alleged that they had reached to such a pitch of pride and arrogance that they meant to ride rough-shod over the rights, the castes, and the religions of the country; on the other, they declared that the British Power was a myth, that we had really been worsted by the Russians in the Crimea, that our army was insignificant, and that the Sepoys were ready to join in subverting our rule. Such were the stories disseminated broadcast by the fakirs and other picked agents of the malcontent party.

After this, the annexation of Oude roused still further the activity of the Mussulmans. And the troops, which had apparently been indifferent to the temptations held out to them, but whose loyalty had latterly been strained by the General Service Act, now listened with more attention to the whispers of sedition, which quickly became more loud and outspoken.

And then occurred in January 1857 what is known as the cartridge incident. The musket with which the native troops had been heretofore armed was about to be discarded and replaced by a rifle. This rifle required a new kind of cartridge; and these were accordingly being made up in the Government factories near Calcutta. The utmost care had heretofore been customary in preventing the use of objectionable ingredients; but in the present case the contractor had managed, without detection by the authorities, to introduce as one of the lubricants, cows' fat, the use of which would have involved contamination to a Hindoo; though no lard or any other material that would have contaminated Mussulmans had been used.

One day however in January, a factory workman was having a squabble with a Sepoy, and taunted him with the impending loss of all caste throughout the army, as the cartridges they were about to use contained both hogs' lard and cows' fat. As the story was partly correct, and therefore could not be *absolutely* denied, it was believed and adopted in full, and circulated swiftly through the army. And thus a chance spark, but a very fiery one, fell upon combustible material, and caught at once.

At this very time we were about to enter on a war with Persia. Hence the state of public feeling seems to have been this.

I. The Mahomedan community were specially excited owing to the annexation of Oude, and the impending attack on Persia, and were now further counting on the certain accession to the malcontent party of the angry Talookdars of Oude.

II. The native States were uneasy about the tendency to annexation and the question of the adoption of heirs, but less so than before, owing to Lord Dalhousie's departure, and the influence of such men as Henry and George Lawrence, and such native statesmen as Salar Jung of Hyderabad and Dinkur Rao of Gwalior.

III. The country generally was agitated by the circulation of various rumours; and for all of them there had appeared to be plausible grounds, except for those about interference with caste and religion, for which heretofore there had been no foundation save such as lay in the General Service Act.

IV. The army had been specially agitated by this Act after having been already worked up to a vivid sense of its preponderating power.

Under such circumstances there could not have occurred any more astounding fatuity than this cartridge blunder; made in a matter usually seen to with especial care; and appearing to confirm the truth of the gravest charges of the disaffected, rousing the malcontents to the fiercest activity, staggering the loyal, and destroying the fidelity of the army.

Between the cartridge incident in January and the Meerut outbreak in May 1857, events naturally became more marked. The Persian war was carried on, and practically came to an end just as the mutiny broke out. In Oude the tension became acute. The irritation of the influential classes increased more and more. Dacoity spread. Gangs of robbers infested the jungles and roads, and in one case killed an English officer who tried to capture them. And lastly, a fanatic Moulvie (or priest) at Fyzabad defied the Government, and advanced towards Lucknow proclaiming a *jehad* or religious war against the English. Fortunately however in March, Sir Henry Lawrence was transferred from Rajpootana, and appeared on the scene in Oude. Assuming the Government, he captured and imprisoned the Moulvie, dispersed the dacoits, and killed their leader, Fuzl Ali. He then summoned the nobles and Talookdars to a Durbar or meeting, where he addressed them respecting their grievances; and from the promises he gave and the confidence he inspired by his high character and reputation, he succeeded in sending them back to their homes fairly contented and loyally disposed.

While all this was going on and the excitement among the Sepoys was markedly increasing, nothing of moment was done by the Calcutta Government to reduce it or to counteract its possible results; or even to clear up the cartridge blunder. Its only resource seemed to lie in worthless proclamations, which were merely laughed at, and did more harm than good. It even neglected, or avoided to take advantage of, the marching season from January to April to arrange for a better disposition of the forces, the protection of important positions, or the retention of carriage for British troops in case it should become necessary to move them. Allahabad was still unprotected, although Sir James Outram had in the previous May entreated both the Governor-General and the Commander-in-Chief to garrison it with British troops.

This apathy or inertness was simply bewildering. It is impossible to assume that the Government did not receive ample warning of the mischief that was brewing. Much was patent, beyond all question, to the ordinary public. The Calcutta secretariats must have known from the English merchants and traders at their very doors that up-country business was at a standstill, and that the political outlook was alarming. The only possible excuse that can be suggested is, that Lord Canning was suffering from the result of Lord Dalhousie's autocracy,—having to lean on the class of Calcutta officials he had received as his counsellors in preference to statesmen of eminence and repute elsewhere, such as Sir Henry Lawrence. It may also be conceded that the absence of any man of mark among the leaders of rebellion made it less easy to detect the actual plots at work, or their instigators. But, whatever Lord Canning's motive, his policy was obviously that of absolute inaction and abstention from precautionary measures; probably from the fear that they would only tend to precipitate the crisis, and the hope that, if let alone, the ferment might die out of itself.

As to the Sepoys, the flame lighted by the cartridge incident, though it spread widely, did not flare up rapidly. During January, February, and March, the only ebullitions were in the direction of Calcutta, where regiments mutinied at Barrackpore and Berhampore. Next, incendiarism appeared in the camp of exercise at Umballa, to the north of Delhi. The mutiny of a local regiment followed on May 3 at Lucknow, and then on the 10th came the great outbreak at Meerut. These places are all significant. Barrackpore was close to the residence of the deposed King of Oude in Calcutta, where a sort of Alsatia had been created. Berhampore was at the seat of the representatives of the Moghul Viceroy of Bengal; Umballa was near Delhi, the Moghul capital; and Lucknow was the capital of the Moghul viceroys of Oude. These all pointed to Moghul influence rather than to any spontaneous action of the Sepoys themselves.

Of the outbreak itself, the incidents are so well known that they hardly need to be given here. Some cavalry troopers at Meerut, forty miles from Delhi, had been imprisoned for insubordination. On May 10th, their comrades, roused by the taunts of the Bazar, riotously broke into the jail, liberated the prisoners, and being then joined by the rest of the Sepoys, went off in a body for Delhi. The ruffians of the Bazar rose at the same time, and murder and violence ensued; but the British garrison of Meerut remained passive throughout, neither attacking nor pursuing the mutineers; who, next day, reached Delhi, and were welcomed by the Sepoys there and by the city population. Then the palace of the puppet Emperor was forcibly entered, and *the restoration of the Moghul rule was proclaimed.*

The reasonable inference from the course of events so far seems to be that the leading spirits of the rebellion lay in the Moghul faction, and that the Sepoy army was used as a catspaw through the operation of the cartridge incident. Moreover this inference is corroborated by the seditious correspondence that was being watched and detected. At first it was mainly Mahomedan, very cautious and in cipher. Afterwards when it spread among the Sepoys it was more diffuse and readily detected, being in ordinary language with crudely veiled allusions.

CHAPTER II

ITS DEVELOPMENT

THE revolt then began in force on the 10th and 11th May, 1857, with the mutinies at Meerut and Delhi, and the Proclamation of the Restoration of the Moghul Empire. But the mutiny did not spread or extend further for three weeks. The only immediate result of the revolt was the cessation of the Pax Britannica, and the entire disorganization of civil administration in those upper provinces; the criminal classes and predatory tribes there at once showing their teeth, and making life and property unsafe. This halt of three weeks in the spread of the mutiny proved incontestably that the Meerut outbreak was not a specific or pre-arranged part of any concerted programme or matured plan; and that if it was actually connected with any such scheme in preparation, it had been precipitated by undue influences, and the scheme itself disconcerted and more or less upset. No leaders came forward to guide the revolt generally, or even to command in the concentration and operations at Delhi.

The Army, in fact, was not yet prepared for the rising. Its chiefs had not settled their plans, however busy they may have been in arranging them. With the Moghul party, on the other hand, the selection of Delhi as the seat and centre of the rebellion was obviously a fundamental point to be ensured, regardless of any other considerations; and it had doubtless been pressed on all parties as the first step to be taken in the revolt. It certainly was not taken haphazard or on the spur of the moment; it had probably been agreed on universally, and, except for the precipitation, was a masterly move. The strength and political importance of Delhi made its seizure a challenge which forced the hand of the English, and fixed the vital struggle at the site where the only large body of English troops in India could be most easily dealt with. Here they would be hemmed in and cut off from their resources, and ought soon to disappear, from sheer absence of means for replacing the losses which would befall them in fighting and from other causes. The insurgents, on the other hand, might easily count on an ever-increasing accession of numbers, and the eventual concentration of a gigantic army.

During the three weeks then from the 10th to the end of May no further troops joined the mutineers at Delhi except from the immediate neighbourhood; nor did any revolts take place elsewhere in response to the signal given at Meerut. Let us see what advantage the Government and the British took of this precious opportunity. Roused out of their ostrich-like inertness, the Calcutta authorities acted vigorously. They summoned troops from Burmah and Madras, and forwarded all whom they could spare to Benares and Allahabad. They sent for assistance to Ceylon and the Mauritius. They hurried back the army which had been employed in the Persian war, and also took steps to stop and direct to India the expeditionary force which had already started for China. Aid and reinforcements from England were of course urgently applied for, and General Anson, the Commander-in-Chief, was pressed to operate at once against the enemy at Delhi. At the same time the commanding guidance which would have come into force under Lord Dalhousie was wholly wanting. Not merely was every local chief left entirely to his own devices, or want of device, but no specific orders were given on matters of imperial necessity, such as the security of Dinapore, Allahabad, Cawnpore, or Agra.

The Commander-in-Chief endeavoured to collect a force at Umballa for a move against Delhi, but he was paralysed by the absolute want of transport of any kind—the result of his own blindness to the disaffection that was raging, and his own neglect of the precautions and preparations that might consequently be required. And it therefore took him nearly a month to collect a force of even 3,800 men, including native contingents, with which to begin operations against Delhi.

Exceptionally energetic action was taken in two of the

provinces; in the Punjab where John Lawrence ruled, and in Oude where his brother Henry was at the helm.

In the Punjab the British force was large, and the measure which it was therefore natural and easy to adopt there was to coerce and disarm the Hindoostanee troops, to whom the mutiny was thought to be confined. And this was carried out forthwith wherever there were British troops cantoned. Where native troops were isolated by themselves, this could not be done, and they generally mutinied; but they were soon attacked by British troops and destroyed or dispersed. The great Ferozapore arsenal was promptly secured; a matter of great moment, as it possessed the only means for supplying the siege-train and equipment needed for Delhi. Moreover the powerful Sikh chiefs of Puttiala, Jheend, and Nabha, States on the Delhi borders, were influenced into supporting the Government with their contingents, and holding the country in our interest. The Punjabees were roused into siding with the British against the Hindoostanees, but it was not till a later date that it was thought prudent to raise fresh local levies.

In Oude there was but the head-quarters of one weak British regiment at Lucknow, in the midst of some twenty native battalions, and in the heart of the Fatherland of the Sepoy race. Sir Henry Lawrence, therefore, held aloof from any coercive measures against the native soldiery, but prepared promptly for vigorous defence against any that might prove hostile. He redistributed the troops, telegraphed for and obtained the chief command, took measures to retain the services of the Sikhs and the more loyal men among the Sepoys, and, while securing the Mutchi Bhown as a temporary place of refuge against *émeutes*, started the construction of the Residency entrenchments, and the storage of supplies in view of defence against the attack of a powerful enemy.

In Agra, where there was a strong fortress, and a British regiment, the native troops were disarmed. Nowhere else in Upper India were there any steps taken that showed any special and resolute recognition of the crisis. Allahabad was not occupied or even strengthened. At Cawnpore, Sir Hugh Wheler abstained from any serious defensive preparations, though he had an excellent site at hand in the magazine position, and was strongly urged by Sir Henry Lawrence to utilize it, and to take other simple precautions.

The Governments of Madras, Bombay, and Scinde at once took measures for a careful watch over their own provinces, and for assisting Bengal.

Such was the state of matters at the end of May, when the spread of the mutiny really began. But the method of its spread showed as little concert as the outbreak itself. It occurred in five distinct groups,[1] each of which, instead of co-operating with the others, took its own course and line of action.

I. In the *Punjab*, the Sepoys were checkmated by the British taking the initiative, as has been already shown; only those on its southern borders succeeding in escaping to join the enemy at Delhi.

II. In the north-west, all from Rohilkund in the east, to Neemuch and Nusseerabad on the west and northwards from that line, concentrated at *Delhi*, which constituted a distinct theatre of operations.[2]

III. All in *Oude*, and to its immediate south and east as far as Benares, remained in the Oude theatre of operations, to besiege Lucknow and oppose the advance of the British army from the Calcutta base.

IV. *East* and south of Benares, down to Bengal proper, the Sepoys mutinied at intervals and hung about Dinapore and Azimgurh, on the flank of the British advance, generally avoiding any real fighting during 1857.

V. *South* of the Jumna, the mutineers, including the Gwalior Contingent, remained in those districts comparatively inactive, as there were no English troops there for them to contend with. They kept hovering, however, on the bank of the Jumna, and threatening the flank of the British on its north till towards the end of the year.

In all these five theatres, except the Punjab and the eastern, most of the mutinies occurred in the first fort-

[1] See map of India.

[2] This north-west or Delhi group of mutinies included Rohilkund, the mutineers from which joined in the Delhi theatre of operations, and after our capture of Delhi streamed off with the rest of the Delhi rebel force into Oude. But Rohilkund is, in the map, coloured by itself, because in the *third* stage of the war it constituted a distinct theatre of operations.

night of June. In the eastern or the Dinapore group the rising was later, not breaking out till towards the end of July. In the Punjab the coercion of the Sepoys had been effected in May.

Of these five groups then, or corps, of the Bengal native army—one, the Punjab group, had been disposed of locally; two, the eastern and the southern, held aloof at this stage from joining in the contest. Only the remaining two, the north-west and the Oude groups, engaged in the struggle; and they kept each to its own theatre of operations, instead of uniting at Delhi, the vital point.

So that the British force operating against Delhi had only one corps instead of five to contend with. That corps or group eventually numbered about 30,000 men; but, in consequence of the halt in the spread of the mutiny, when the British troops arrived before Delhi, the Sepoys who had arrived and who then fought with them were only about 8,000 (supported, however by a crowd of unorganized detachments and a large number of guns). The rest of the 30,000 men did not join till later on.

The contest at Delhi began on June 8th with the battle of Badli Ke Serai, seven miles off. The British force, which the Commander-in-Chief had managed to collect by that time, amounted to only 3,800 men, including native contingents, and twenty-four guns. But they charged the enemy drawn up on their front, defeated them, capturing twenty-six guns, drove them into the city, and began its siege by occupying the famous ridge that faces it on its north. For two or three days designs were entertained of taking the city by assault; but they were found impracticable, and the force settled down to a prolonged siege; a singular siege, however, for the enemy were gradually reinforced during the month to their full eventual strength of 30,000, while the British force was augmented by supports from the Punjab to only 6,500 men; and this left such a disproportion in the relative strength of the two contending bodies that the British, instead of being the assailants, were practically standing on the defensive. Such then was the development of the mutiny at the end of June in the Delhi theatre of operations.

In the Oude theatre, the contest began and developed on

the 8th and the 30th June, the same dates as at Delhi. The series of Mutinies began at Lucknow on May 30th, followed by risings at Azimgurh, Benares, Allahabad, and Cawnpore, outside of Oude; and at Seetapore, Fyzabad, Sultanpore, and the other stations within it. At Lucknow and Benares the mutineers were driven off, and all, except at Cawnpore, hovered about till they began to concentrate towards the east of Lucknow. At Allahabad the English scored their first important success; a great stroke, which has never been properly appreciated. It is the key of the north-west, the site of a powerful fortress of the European type, which was garrisoned by Brasyer's regiment of Sikhs. There were no English troops. The Sepoy regiment outside rose on June 6th, and essayed to seize the fort. But the Sikhs, under Brasyer's influence, opposed them, and held it for the British until supported a few days later by Neill's Madras Fusiliers from Benares. Allahabad, thus secured, practically formed an advanced base of operations, and gave a very different turn to the future of the war from what it would have been but for Brasyer's intrepidity.

The contest itself began at Cawnpore. The troops there, on mutinying, started for Delhi without molesting the English residents; but the Nana Sahib persuaded them to return on June 8th to beleaguer and destroy the British detachment and residents. The story is too well known to need repetition. It suffices to say that, as soon as the fall of Cawnpore towards the end of the month became known to them, the body of mutineers who had been collecting eastward of Lucknow concentrated on June 28th at Nuwabgunge. They were joined by various adherents of the late Oude dynasty, but by only three of the Talookdars. On the 30th they advanced on Lucknow, met a small force of the garrison that had gone out to reconnoitre towards Chinhut, defeated it, and drove it in with heavy loss; and began the siege of the Residency entrenchments, which Sir Henry Lawrence had by this time constructed and armed and stored.

Thus it was that the mutiny developed in the Oude theatre of operations; the British being the besieged, in contrast to the Delhi theatre, in which they were the besiegers. And, as already mentioned, it was only in these two theatres of operations, or with these two groups of mutineers out of the whole five, that, at this stage, the rising developed in active conflict.

But, in saying that the mutiny of the Bengal army had developed in five groups, it is not to be understood that the whole of the native troops in these five groups or theatres of revolt had mutinied. The Sikhs, the Punjabees, and the Ghoorkas, as a rule, held aloof—both as regiments, and also individually. The rising was almost entirely confined to the Hindoostanees. And even of them many did not join. Thus the 31st N. I. drove off the 42nd, and held Saugor for the Government. The 13th at Lucknow remained staunch. The 43rd at Barrackpore held the other troops in check; Renny's native battery of horse artillery served on the ridge at Delhi throughout the siege; and numerous instances could be cited to show that by no means the whole of even the Hindoostanees of the Bengal army had joined in the revolt. Nor did the mutiny spread beyond the Bengal army at all, though for a short time there was some uneasiness in Bombay.

The Sepoys took unquestionably the lion's share in the contest; practically they bore the whole brunt of it until towards the end. In the five theatres of operations, the civil administration being virtually at an end, the criminal and predatory classes, the town ruffians, the retainers of disloyal landholders, and occasionally Mahomedan zealots, took part in the local conflicts; not doing so much, however, in the fighting line, as proving mischievous in harassing the communications.

No rising occurred in any part of Bengal except in the five theatres of mutiny. The only rising that took place outside Bengal was in the southern Mahratta country, and it was speedily suppressed.

No members of reduced dynasties joined the enemy, except the Nana Sahib and the Ranee of Jhansi. The Nana held himself ill-used as the lineal representative of the head of the great Mahratta Confederacy, and had come under the influence of the notorious Azimoolla. The Ranee was rankling under the sense of wrongs from the British annexation of Jhansi under the adoption question, in spite of the unswerving loyalty of the House. None of the great native rulers, Mahomedan, Mahratta, or Rajpoot, joined the revolt at all, though Scindia's and Holkar's people rose against the local British residents and troops. The puppet Emperor at Delhi was merely a handle for the Moghul party, and not really a leader of the rebellion.

Hence, as a fact, the great Rebellion, which this rising was intended to be, and was on the verge of becoming, had drifted into a war in which the Hindoostanees of the Bengal army alone played any important part, while the Moghul party had sunk almost into insignificance, and none of the great races or chiefs joined in it at all.

At the same time, it is quite certain that only a few months before there had been unusual and bitter disaffection among the latter. The explanation of this apparently paradoxical attitude and conduct, and of the failure of the rising to develope into a great rebellion, lies in the consequences of the aggressive action of the Moghul party at Delhi. They showed their hand too soon, and too eagerly, regardless of results. They evinced their determination to recover their rule and take the lead; to assert their supremacy and set aside all other interests; not merely to subvert the British rule, but to replace it by their own. And this forcibly reminded those other races of that past which they had been forgetting under the pressure of the more recent causes of irritation. To resent the masterful and imperious policy of the British was one thing. To exchange it for what they remembered of the lawless tyranny and brutal rule of the Moghul was quite another matter. So their thoughts of joining in a blow at the English were at once checked, and they remained passive. But their temper toward the English was shown by that passiveness. None of them came loyally and actively to the support of the Government, as the Sikh chiefs did. Had there not been this bitterness and dislike to the English rule, would not the great Mahratta leaders, such as Scindia, Holkar, and the Guicowar, the great Rajpoot chiefs such as Oudeypore, Jeypore, Jodhpore, and others, have aided the Government against any efforts at supremacy on the part of a Hindoostanee army which they cordially hated?

As to that army, and its mutiny, there is every indication that its rising had neither been long premeditated nor matured. The isolated groups into which the mutineers collected, their delays, their halts, their inaction for many months in some cases, their absolute want of concert, the absence of any leaders, real or nominal—all this showed that they rose without any plan or programme; nor was there any sign that they were imbued with any real hostility to the Government before the cartridge incident. They had long been a spoilt body, their discipline had been impaired and become lax, and they had doubtless become aware of their preponderating power. Then in 1856 the General Service Act had caused annoyance and disquietude, but had not directly angered the existing army, as it affected only the future recruits. In January 1857, however, the cartridge question had really roused their fears and their animosity, but hardly gave time before May for organizing a conspiracy.

Before quitting the subject of the part taken by the army in the organization and development of the revolt, it may be as well to point out some other general influences which affected its conduct, and also some characteristics of the individual mutinies.

In the first place, the Sepoys were the one body of natives who had never suffered, but always benefited from British rule. They were identified with it and its power and its triumphs during the whole of its rise. They were linked to it by these relations and by the fidelity of a hundred years. They looked to its service as the career for themselves and their sons after them. They were assured of pensions in their later years, and their fathers and relations were dependent on the pensions they were already enjoying. These formed ties which could not be lightly broken or easily replaced. Besides this, the men were as a rule attached—in some cases greatly attached—to their officers, and under their influence; while there also prevailed the old traditional claim of fidelity to the salt, and loyalty to the oath, which, with Rajpoots, if properly kept in view, could be counted on almost with certainty. The world has shown no nobler examples of military fidelity than that of the Sepoys of the Lucknow garrison.

Many of the Hindoostanee regiments, it has been shown, did not join in the mutiny. It is quite open to question whether the delay of the British for three whole weeks in operating against Delhi did not encourage and lead many regiments to break out, which were wavering and might otherwise have kept loyal.

Further, there is every reason to believe that, in most cases, the bulk of the men, though angry and bewildered, were not disposed to mutiny; they were, however, excited and easily led by the more energetic spirits, who were the agents of the party of sedition. These were mostly the high caste men, the pulwans (the wrestlers and athletes), and those who were personally of a restless, ambitious, and discontented character. And when the time for rising came, these leaders generally had to shoot an officer or to perform some similar act by which the regiment would be led to believe that it had no option left it, and was committed to mutiny. It was well known that the best and the most popular officers were thus sacrificed, to prevent the check which might have resulted from their influence. On the other hand, where the necessity for this was not felt, the men not only avoided molesting their officers, but escorted or helped them to places of safety. And there are numerous well-known, well-authenticated cases where they rescued ladies in difficulties, escorted them in all honour and safety to their friends, and then, deaf to all entreaties, saluted and returned to their comrades, where they said their proper place was.

As to the counter influences, the principal one was that the claim of the State to their fidelity had been weakened if not annulled by the treachery of the British, and their designs against caste; while their pride and patriotism were touched by the tale that their own tribal chiefs and the whole country were with them and expecting them to lead the way. The incitements and taunts of the Bazars then added their weight; and latterly, in no small degree, the doubting and unfriendly looks, and the injudicious if not irritating talk, of many of the English. It may also be remarked that, in the case of the great majority of the Sepoys, the Oude Rajpoots, their childhood and youth had been spent amidst scenes of bloodshed and violence, and associated with the spirit of turbulence and contest with their rulers.

CHAPTER III

THE CAMPAIGN IN THREE STAGES

THE VITAL STRUGGLE

THE war into which the mutiny had thus developed at the end of June 1857, lasted for eighteen months, throughout which the insurgents never appeared to be acting on any concerted plan, or under the guidance of any one ruling spirit.

This conflict of eighteen months may be conveniently divided into three periods—

First, the period of *The Vital Struggle*, in which, during the three months of July, August, and September 1857, the British garrison of India were fighting for existence, unaided by help from England. This desperate conflict ended with their victory in the three contests of the period, viz. the siege of Delhi, the defence of the Lucknow Residency position, and Havelock's advance to its assistance.

In the second period *The Decisive Contest* lasted for six months, from October 1857 to March 1858, during which the reinforcements arrived from England, and the insurgents, who had concentrated in full strength at Lucknow and at Jhansi, were driven out of those positions, and utterly defeated, but not yet crushed.

The third stage was *The Suppression of the Revolt*, during the last nine months of 1858, when the defeated groups of mutineers were being attacked and crushed or pursued, till they eventually dispersed to their homes, the country settled down, and peace was restored.

Each of these periods forms a distinct stage of the campaign, and its story will therefore be divided accordingly. The account of each such stage or period will be arranged under the separate theatres of operations, which coincided closely with what have been already described as the theatres of mutiny.

In the first period, the Delhi theatre was the scene of the essentially vital struggle ; on its issue all depended. It has been shown that, on June 8th, a British force of 3,800 men drove the mutineer force of about 8,000 men within the walls of Delhi ; and that at the end of June, the British, increased by that time to 6,500, were holding and defending the ridge on the north of Delhi against a mutineer army of nearly 30,000 men. The insurgent force there never materially exceeded that strength, but the British continued to get reinforced from the Punjab, from time to time, during the next two months of July and August, partly by English troops and partly by new native levies.

During July the British were practically on the defence, and were kept ceaselessly engaged, either fighting or working—constructing batteries and defensive posts, repelling attacks, or carrying the war into the enemy's ground, and checking their efforts at counter-batteries and at manœuvres to turn their position.

But the enemy's attacks were desultory and isolated, the only one that was driven home being the charge of the 8th Irregular Cavalry into the camp, where it was resolutely met and defeated. With all their preponderance of five to one, they never made a concentrated attack, or attempted a general engagement to defeat and destroy the besieging army, or even to dislodge it from its position. There never seemed throughout to be any recognized leader or guiding spirit, while the Hindoos and Mussulmans were known to be at feud.

By the end of July the English army had lost three commanders in succession—Generals Anson and Barnard by death, and General Reid from ill-health ; and it was now commanded by General Archdale Wilson.

By the middle of August it received a valuable reinforcement from the Punjab in a column commanded by General Nicholson, which raised its strength to 10,000 men, of whom however 1,800 were in hospital ; and, as the battering-train had started from Ferozapore and was likely to arrive before long, the force on the ridge began to take the aggressive ; to press the siege with greater vigour ; and to drive off the enemy from their more advanced positions.

The mutineers soon heard of the approach of the siege-train, and sent off a strong body of troops to intercept it. But Nicholson attacked the party on August 25th, at Nujufgurh, routed them, and so frustrated their design.

At length, on September 6th, the battering-train arrived, and with it the last of the reinforcements that could be available for some time to come, and the strength of the force now stood thus—

	3,300	British troops effective.
	5,400	Native troops.
	2,500	Contingents of loyal chiefs and allies.
Total	11,200	effective men.
Besides	3,000	men in hospital.
Total	14,200	before Delhi.

Steps were now taken at once to breach the walls of Delhi. John Lawrence had apparently been ceaselessly urging on the commanders before Delhi to attack and take it, but this could not be done till the means for breaching its ramparts had been received, and certainly the guns had not come a day too soon. The delay on this point, however, was in no way attributable to the force before Delhi, or its chiefs. Although the guns were now available, it was a most serious problem how they could be used and Delhi battered at once, and further delay averted. The problem, however, had been thought out by Baird Smith and his engineers, and it was solved forthwith. Regular siege approaches were out of the question, and further, it was essential to avoid any movement or sign that would indicate to the enemy the points which were to be attacked. Otherwise they would have time to strengthen those points by retrenchments.

Now the ridge held by the British, opposite the northern face of the city, was not parallel to that face, but, while distant from it at its eastern or river end, inclined nearer to it at its western end. So operations were openly and vigorously carried on at that western end, opposite the Moere bastion, where it seemed natural that the attack should be made ; but other batteries of equal if not greater importance were secretly constructed close to the city walls at the *eastern* end, to breach the Water and Cashmere bastions. The intervening low ground, which was of considerable width, was crossed at night-time, and the batteries were quietly and stealthily constructed behind the cover of deserted garden walls and ruins. There, on the night of the 10th, they were armed with the heavy guns; and on the 11th, the cover in front was thrown down, and the breaching batteries opened fire. Three days' hard pounding made effective breaches without giving the enemy time to retrench them, and next morning the attack was made. In the early dawn of September 14th, the Cashmere Gate was blown in, and by it and by the two breaches (in the Cashmere and Water bastions) which had been made by the battering guns, the British troops stormed the walls of Delhi. Still, from the strength of the mutineer force, it took a week more to drive out that army and capture the city fully.

Thus ended the vital struggle at Delhi, ringing the knell of the revolt. This success at once relieved the strain on the Punjab. The raising of its levies, which heretofore had to be managed with great caution, was now carried on more freely. There was a veritable rousing of the Khalsa in the British interests. At the same time the settlement and pacification of the disturbed districts near Delhi went on apace, and Delhi thenceforward ceased to be a theatre of military operations; being replaced by Lucknow and Oude, to which the defeated army streamed off through Rohilkund, and where it took part in all the fighting during the rest of the campaign.

As soon as Delhi was completely in the hands of the British, such of their troops as could be spared were despatched as a column to clear the Doab (as the country is called lying between the Ganges and the Jumna), and to join the forces operating at Cawnpore and Lucknow. It started on September 24th, and was commanded at first by General Greathead, and afterwards by General Hope Grant. Whilst going down the Doab, it turned aside to Agra, and there, on October 10th, encountered and defeated a body of the Central India mutineers (from the southern group), who had hoped to take it by surprise. After this feat it continued its way to Cawnpore, where it joined Sir Colin Campbell's force, to take part in the Oude operations of the second period of the campaign.

The Oude theatre of operations was the only other theatre besides Delhi in which there were any extensive operations or contests during the first period of the campaign; and although they were equally desperate, they were not of the same vital moment as the contest at Delhi. These operations were in two parts—one, the defence of the Lucknow Residency position, generally known as the Baily Guard; the other the advance of Havelock's force to its aid. These have each a distinct and separate story, till Havelock reached Lucknow; when their operations became united, and ran into the second period of the campaign. This part of the sketch will be very brief, as it is fully dealt with in the detailed narrative.

We left the defence of the Lucknow Residency about to begin, after the disaster of Chinhut. It has been shown in the sketch of the development of the mutiny that, on the morning of that fight at Chinhut, on June 30th, Sir Henry Lawrence was holding two positions in Lucknow; one, the Mutchi Bhown, to command the city and keep it quiet, while the entrenchments were being prepared; the other, the Residency entrenchments, which he had been preparing to withstand an army provided with artillery. The two positions were rather less than a mile apart. During the rest of the day of Chinhut the force continued to hold both the posts, but on the following morning Sir Henry signalled to the garrison of the Mutchi Bhown to evacuate and blow it up at midnight and concentrate at the Residency. This was effected with most unexpected success, the march being wholly unopposed, and all the artillery, except three guns, being brought over.

From July 2nd, therefore, the whole force was collected and closely besieged in the entrenched position. This was an oblong of four faces, of a quarter of a mile each, occupying an area of about thirty-two acres (one-twentieth of a square mile), and situated in the middle of a city some five miles long and two and a half miles wide. Its outline was a continuous enclosure formed partly by buildings and partly by reveted earthwork and artificial obstacles; sufficiently obstructive, so long as it was not breached, to the assault of such an enemy as had to be faced. The garrison was half European and half native. Half the Europeans were disciplined troops, the other half were civilian volunteers. Its strength proved sufficient. There were more guns than could be worked at the same time. There was an ample supply of ammunition. There was no want of excellent water; an abundant store of grain food had been laid in; and a large stock of cattle collected. While cheered by the knowledge that he had thus arranged effectually all that could be arranged beforehand to meet the attack of the enemy, Sir Henry Lawrence was mortally wounded on July 2nd, on the very first morning of the concentrated siege; so falling its first victim.

A few days, which included one sortie, sufficed to elicit important features in the attack, giving grounds for the hope of a successful defence. It became clear, for instance, that the enemy would not face the British soldier on ordinary terms, and also that they would not seriously try to breach the defences with artillery.

The defence, beginning with the fight at Chinhut on June 30th, and ending with Havelock's arrival on September 25th, lasted for some twelve weeks, and was divided into four periods or stages of about three weeks each, by three all-round attacks on July 20th, August 10th, and September 5th.

During the first period the enemy were very busy, but did no real harm, while the defenders settled down into the hope of a successful defence.

At the first attack—on July 20th—the enemy showed their designs and the mode by which they expected to capture the position. They began it by blowing up a mine which was evidently aimed at the Redan battery, but fell far short of its mark and was off the right direction, so that the defences remained intact. The storming parties, finding no breach by which to enter, did not attempt to drive the attack home, but withdrew under a ceaseless but harmless roar of musketry and artillery, which continued for several hours. The defenders suffered only very trifling loss, and were greatly elated by the success and ease of the repulse.

But the mining warfare that was now certain, and which immediately ensued, involved the most deadly peril to the garrison; whose means of labour were small, while those of the enemy were practically unlimited. A simultaneous effort on their part at several points could hardly fail to result in success at some of them; when there would be easy opportunities for the sudden irruptions of large bodies of the enemy, which the small garrison would be wholly unable to meet effectively. Fortunately, however, the besiegers did not adopt these tactics of simultaneous efforts all round the position; so they gave time to our engineers to anticipate them at the weaker points; and for the rest of the siege they continued to make desultory attacks by mining, which, when they came sufficiently near, were all, with one exception, detected by the vigilance of the outposts and foiled by the counter-mines of the engineers. Each of the other two all-round attacks was begun, as before, by the explosion of mines which fell short of the mark; and the storming parties would not really attack when they found there was no breach to make the road easy.

So that the catastrophe, of which there was throughout a ceaseless and imminent danger, never occurred. Meanwhile, however, the strength of the garrison was being steadily reduced by daily losses from the fire of the enemy, and from cholera and illness, and also by the reduction of rations; the position too was being weakened by the crumbling away of the defences under round shot and rain; and the state of danger was increased by the possibility of the desertion of the native troops of the garrison, who had become sceptical as to the approach or advance of any relieving force.

For the closeness of the investment had rendered any communication with the outside world almost impossible, and only three letters had been received; one at an early date stating that the relief would come off in a few days; the others much later, saying that the advance had been found almost impossible at present, and would probably have to wait for reinforcements. So the long-continued delay had led, in the minds of the natives of the garrison, to doubts of the authenticity of those letters and of the statements of the men who had brought them in.

Meanwhile the reply of the garrison to Havelock's letters had a most painful effect, for it stated that they would have no food left after September 10th.

When, therefore, Havelock forced his way in to its rescue

on September 25th, he and Outram and their men expected to find the garrison and inmates of the position dead or dying of sheer inanition; and pushed on accordingly with the desperate efforts and speediness which were suited to the supposed exigencies of the case, but were not really necessary under the actual circumstances.

The army that had been beleaguering the Residency the whole time consisted of some 20,000 disciplined troops, including the whole of the Oude Irregular force, besides the soldiers and retainers of the old dynasty. None of the Rajpoot clansmen joined it till the beginning of September. The Cawnpore mutineer brigade had also joined the besieging force after being defeated by Havelock at Cawnpore, and altogether the army that was collected at Lucknow, investing the Residency and blocking the way against its relief, was not far, if at all, short in numbers of the army that was holding Delhi.

The command of this army was constantly being changed, as also the control and guidance of the operations against the Residency. There were a number of more or less self-constituted authorities, such as the Fyzabad Moulvie, and sundry favourites of the rebel court, which had been formed in the city, with a young son of the deposed king as its nominal head, affecting to act in the name of the Emperor at Delhi.

Of the huge force thus assembled against us at Lucknow, a large proportion, augmented when necessary, used to be kept out on the road to hold Havelock in check; but the chief opposition to him was to be at Lucknow itself, where the necessary obstacles and batteries were in preparation. The weight of the task before him was obvious. To his advance, being the other part of the Oude operations, we now turn.

By the end of June, when Cawnpore had fallen, and the siege of the Lucknow Residency was beginning, a sufficient number of men had reached Allahabad to enable General Havelock to move forward with 1,400 British troops and 500 Sikhs. In the course of a fortnight he defeated the enemy who opposed him in four several engagements, and captured first Cawnpore and then Bithoor, the neighbouring seat of the Nana Sahib. His force of 1,900 men had lost severely in these contests, so that its effective strength now was but small; and at the same time he had only a weak line of communication 600 miles long, to connect him with his base at Calcutta. Still, as that line was being more and more secured by the steady flow of advancing reinforcements, and as his troops were eager and confident, he crossed the Ganges on July 25th, as the first step of a move towards Lucknow, and established a protective depôt on its bank at Mungurwar. He made three separate advances thence towards Lucknow, on July 29th and the 4th and 11th of August respectively; and on each of these occasions fought and defeated the enemy at Busherat Gunge, besides also fighting elsewhere; but was obliged by losses, cholera, and other causes to stay his hand and return to Mungurwar. On the first advance, the special check arose from the receipt of intelligence of mutiny at Dinapore, and the consequent delay in the advance of reinforcements; on the second occasion, it lay in the news of the threatening attitude of the mutineers of the Southern or Central India theatre, who were concentrating from Gwalior and elsewhere on the Jumna opposite Cawnpore; and on the third occasion he had already made up his mind to return to Cawnpore, when he advanced and fought at Busherat Gunge, merely as the proper way of checking the enemy and securing an unmolested retreat across the Ganges. The news from Cawnpore gave serious grounds for anxiety, and it was a matter of paramount necessity to secure its safety, while he had now less than one thousand men to put in line of battle at Busherat Gunge. To face the enormous force collected against him with the strength of only an ordinary battalion, at 600 miles from his base, with his communications interrupted, and to retire successfully to Cawnpore, as he did on August 13th, was a feat that seems to throw into the shade the most brilliant and audacious deeds of the vaunted days of Wellesley and Lake.

The intense sorrow with which Havelock made up his mind to this withdrawal may be easily imagined, but as a military measure it was imperatively necessary. As a political step, it had one singular and unexpected effect. The Talookdars of Oude, who had hitherto remained passively friendly, neither joining in the attack on the

Residency, nor molesting Havelock's advance, now wrote to say that they were obliged to regard the withdrawal of his army as virtually a surrender of the Government of Oude, and that they must now obey and send their followers to support the rebel court at Lucknow. Hence the presence of their retainers was noticed at the attack on the Residency on September 5th, but never before.

General Havelock then recrossed to Cawnpore on August 13th, and the reinforcements he required did not reach him until September 16th, although the British troops had been so accumulating, chiefly about Dinapore, that more than 8,000 infantry were on the line of communications before the end of August. Even on September 16th, the reinforcements that joined Havelock were only two additional regiments; and with them came Sir James Outram, who however chivalrously waived his claims to the command and accompanied the force as a volunteer. Havelock, then, with such troops as could be spared from Cawnpore, again crossed the Ganges into Oude, reached the suburbs of Lucknow on September 23rd, heard there of the capture of Delhi, and on the 25th fought his way in with heavy loss, and relieved the beleaguered garrison of the Residency.

It was a Relief in the sense that the position was so reinforced as to be no longer in danger from any attacks that the army might make, even when reinforced from Delhi; but it was not a Relief in the sense that the enemy were driven away and the families withdrawn to security.

The enemy contested Havelock's entrance fiercely, closed in on his rear, making its junction with the main column a matter of great difficulty, and next day attacked and destroyed a part of the hospital convoy which had been wrongly guided. The extended position occupied by the united forces, the relieving and the relieved, was as closely invested as the original position had been, and though for a week sorties were made daily to clear a way through the enemy, they failed to effect their object.

Now, it had been thought that the food supply of the Residency had been practically exhausted, and at the same time Havelock's force had carried no provisions in with them. So, on finding that they could not make their way out into the open country, the commanders were at first in dismay. But Colonel (afterwards Lord) Napier, the chief of Outram's staff, instituted a proper inquiry and search, which led to the discovery that the supplies, which had been collected and kept in store throughout but somehow ignored, were sufficient to support the whole united garrisons for nearly two months. On this the garrison gave up all thought of withdrawal, and settled down to a steady prolongation of the siege.

In the Eastern theatre of operations, the regiments in the out-stations had mutinied generally during June, but remained in the outlying districts threatening the flank of the road from Calcutta to Allahabad. The only British regiment in those parts was at Dinapore, and there the troops did not mutiny till after the middle of July, when Havelock was beginning his advance towards Lucknow. They were incited to the revolt by Rajah Konwur Singh, of Shahabad, an old Rajpoot chief; and they attacked a post at Arrah in the neighbourhood, which the civil residents of the districts and a detachment of Sikhs had prepared for defence. They defeated, in an ambush, a party of the British regiment from Dinapore which was coming to its relief; but they were kept at bay by the garrison, and were then attacked, defeated, and driven off by a small force under General Eyre. This was all the serious fighting that occurred in the Eastern theatre during the first period of the campaign.

In the Southern theatre, the insurgents seem to have formed into two bodies, one of which drew towards Agra; the other towards Kalpee, on the Jumna, opposite Cawnpore. The Agra party, as has been shown, crossed over to Agra, but were defeated by the column from Delhi. The other party threatened Cawnpore, so as to lead Havelock to recross the Ganges in order to make it secure. When Havelock made his final and successful advance towards Lucknow, he left at Cawnpore a force which was comparatively weak, but would be strengthened by the reinforcements which would be constantly arriving. Tempting though the opportunity must have been, the Gwalior Contingent did not then attack it. They were probably disconcerted by the intelligence of the fall of Delhi.

The only other insurgent troops of any consequence were those of Holkar at Indore; though numbers of petty chiefs, in their mountain strongholds, were in revolt. The Resident at Indore, Colonel Durand, had had to leave it, and made his way first to the friendly State of Bhopal. A column which had been despatched from Bombay towards Indore had halted far south of it, at Aurungabad, in consequence of sinister reports from the Nizam's territory; eventually, however, it advanced in July, was joined by Colonel Durand at Aseergurh, and restored him to his position at Indore on August 2nd. But there had been no serious conflict.

Thus, in the first period of the war, in the months of July, August, and September, Delhi had been stormed, and the strain on the Punjab removed; the Lucknow Residency entrenchments had been successfully defended; and Havelock had forced his way in to its aid, and had reinforced and saved it. All this had been effected without the help of a single additional soldier from England. It had been done by a mere handful of troops in the season of intense heat, and amidst the raging of a virulent epidemic of cholera, followed by the season of the rains and of malarious fever. In all the operations, the success had been largely due to the superior character and resolution of the troops on the British side. In the Delhi operations it was further owing to the support of the Punjab, to the energy of Sir John Lawrence and his staff, and to the genius of John Nicholson and others. At Lucknow it was further owing to the foresight of Sir Henry Lawrence, to the vigilance and constancy of the garrison, and to the success of the Engineers in foiling the efforts of the enemy to breach the defences by mines.

In Havelock's advances it was due to the enthusiastic valour and heroic devotion of his men, and to the combination of skill and prudence with boldness and determination that characterized his own generalship; by which he overcame unprecedented odds, avoiding and averting catastrophes when in the direst straits.

CHAPTER IV

THE DECISIVE CONTEST

THE second stage of the war, when the power of England came into play, lasted for six months, from the beginning of October 1857 to the end of the following March.

For some months the reinforcements from England came pouring into the country, with the China Expeditionary Force as their precursor; and levies of native troops were being raised in the Punjab and elsewhere, till they exceeded the British troops in numbers.

The mutineers collected in strength in the Oude and the Southern theatres of operations. In the Delhi theatre the war was at an end, though at its Rohilkund section the enemy kept the field; and in the Eastern, the mutineers evaded all serious conflict till the close of this second stage; so that this campaign was mainly restricted, during these six months, to Oude and the Southern theatre. The enemy kept concentrating in Lucknow and Jhansi respectively, which accordingly became the decisive battle-grounds of the war. So, during the first five months, the neighbouring districts were cleared of their outlying enemy, and in March, Lucknow and Jhansi were attacked and captured, and the enemy dispersed, to be afterwards pursued and crushed.

The more important of the two struggles lay in Oude, and in October it was only there that any real contest was going on.

Havelock's force and the original garrison were remaining there, invested by the enemy, not at first in any danger of a real attack, but, as has been shown, unable to remove thence through the surrounding thousands of Sepoys the families that had been beleaguered in the Residency. Outram had now assumed the command. A detachment of 500 men of Havelock's force had been left at the Alum Bagh outside the southern suburbs of Lucknow; and the communications were now comparatively frequent and easy, and were supplemented by semaphores erected at the two posts. Outram was made uneasy by the news from Cawnpore, of its being threatened by the Gwalior Contingent from the Southern theatre, much more than by the constant arrival of fugitive mutineers from Delhi. So, feeling secure in his position, and having food enough in store to last for some time to come, he wrote to Cawnpore, deprecating any advance to the assistance of Lucknow till the force at Cawnpore should be strong enough to deal with the Gwalior Contingent, and make its communications secure. The correctness of Outram's estimate of his own position was confirmed by the fact that it was never seriously attacked. Meanwhile, the China force, and the troops that had been collecting below Allahabad, began to find their way to Cawnpore; Hope Grant's column from Delhi also arrived there; and then, in a few days, came Sir Colin Campbell, the new Commander-in-Chief sent out from England.

He was in a dilemma, whether first to deal with the Gwalior Contingent, or to relieve Lucknow. That Contingent, however, kept hanging back; and it might be assumed that reinforcements on their way up from Calcutta would keep continuously arriving and strengthening Cawnpore. Moreover, Sir Colin was inclined to think that Outram, from his chivalrous disposition, was making light of his own difficulties and writing with too great confidence, especially in regard to food. He decided, therefore, as his first step, to advance to the relief of Lucknow with the bulk of his available force. Accordingly, in the middle of November, he reached the post at the Alum Bagh, and forming a depôt there, he moved by a circuitous route to the Residency, reaching and relieving it on the 17th. In doing this he found the contest a very severe one, and was at the same time hampered by having to establish a chain of posts in communication with the Alum Bagh, by which to withdraw the families. With the families withdrawn, the altered circumstances made the retention of the Residency position unsuitable for present purposes, so he evacuated it, and selected instead the Alum Bagh, in which he placed Sir James Outram with a force of 4,000 men to face the rebel army in Oude, and to show abroad that neither Oude nor Lucknow was abandoned by the British. The combined forces that had been holding the Residency position were so reduced as to be unable, on Sir Colin's arrival, to muster 2,000 men.

During Sir Colin's operations at Lucknow, the Gwalior Contingent had crossed the Jumna at Kalpee, made their long-threatened attack on Cawnpore, and were now pressing it hard. Sir Colin's return, however, immediately checked them. First driving them off from the eastern side of the city, and so being enabled to despatch the rescued Lucknow families to Calcutta, he next attacked them in full force, and defeating them thoroughly, drove them in rout back across the Jumna to the Southern theatre of war.

With Cawnpore thus secured in the beginning of December, he began his preparations for a concentrated move on Lucknow. Some delay occurred, owing originally to doubt whether Rohilkund should not first be dealt with, and then to the hesitation of Government respecting the strategy for the concentration on Lucknow; but the eventual decision was that the enemy should be allowed an outlet to the west, that the south of their position should be blocked, and that the attack should be made on its east, supported by flanking movements on the north, along the left bank of the Goomtee.

The enemy throughout made vigorous preparations for the defence. They surmised correctly that the attack would be on the east, where, therefore, they threw up three lines of massive works, but without any flanking defences to the north.

In aid of the projected concentration, and to keep his force secure from attack from the outlying districts, Sir Colin cleared the enemy out of them by sweeping through them with five separate columns. Two cleared the southern districts of Oude; one came down with the siege-train from Agra to Cawnpore and thence to Lucknow; and the fourth, followed by the fifth, the Nepaulese, under Jung Bahadoor, cleared the eastern districts. Meanwhile Outram's force had throughout held the Alum Bagh; and now, early in March, all these columns, besides those troops that had been arriving in isolated detachments, concentrated as one large army, to drive the enemy out of Lucknow.

The attack was scientifically managed, and in seven days placed Lucknow in Sir Colin's hands. It began on March 7th, and the last of the defences was attacked and captured on the 14th. Outram's division started the attack by crossing the Goomtee, which bounded the enemy's works on the north; and advancing westwards it swept the enemy's works by flanking fire, and made them easy to attack from the front. They were then turned and stormed one after the other, and after the 14th nothing was left but street fighting; which quickly drove the enemy into the country by the outlet which had been intentionally left for them on the west. There the most magnificent force of cavalry which had ever been assembled in India was awaiting them to capture their leaders, and to give a telling lesson to the defeated mutineers. But, alas! the commander of that force held it inactive. The chief fruits of the brilliant siege operations were lost. The bulk of the fugitive army, with the Nana Sahib, the Begum, the Moulvie, and all the other leaders of the revolt, streamed out and escaped into the country, taking such routes as they pleased, to rouse the country afresh, to re-form into several smaller armies, and to give an infinity of trouble before they were eventually dispersed or captured or crushed. So ended the operations in Oude, during the second stage of the war.

Next in importance to the operations in Oude, in this stage of the campaign, was the contest in Central India between the Nerbudda and the Jumna. During October, November, and December, it was in two distinct parts: one towards the south, between Indore and the Nerbudda; the other to the north, with its base at Kalpee on the Jumna near Cawnpore.

In the south, Sir Hugh Rose, who had arrived from England towards the end of September, divided his force into two brigades, and took three months to clear that part of the country. In the north, the Gwalior Contingent, under Tantia Topee (who now began to come forward as the ablest leader in the rebel army), kept threatening Cawnpore, with a view to hampering the operations towards Lucknow; and at length attacked it in force at the end of November. Eventually, however, it was defeated and driven back to Kalpee, as has been already described.

From this time, the fortress of Jhansi became the real objective of the campaign in Central India, and the enemy, who heretofore had been only playing at war, now found themselves face to face with British troops under the brilliant leadership of Sir Hugh Rose. The special difficulty he had to overcome was the broken and mountainous nature of the country, covered with ravines and passes—where a handful could check a host,—dotted all over with strongholds, many of which were famous in story, in even recent times.

Sir Hugh's first task was to relieve Saugor, which had been held for the British Government by the 31st N. I. This he effected on February 3rd, after first besieging and storming the fort of Ratghur on the way. He then advanced, and after fighting and defeating the enemy at Baroda, captured on the 13th the fort of Garakota, which had been generally held to be impregnable; thence onward towards Jhansi, forcing and turning a series of passes, and taking such forts as came in his way. So, by the middle of March, six weeks after relieving Saugor, Sir Hugh Rose appeared before Jhansi, though his whole force was not present till the 25th. On that date he opened his batteries against the south face of the fortress. On the 30th, the northern portion of the Central India rebel army approached from Kalpee to attack him and relieve Jhansi. But on April 1st he moved out to meet it on the Betwah, and routed it completely; and then returning, on the 3rd, he stormed and took the fortress. And so ended this stage of the war. This successful result of the struggle for supremacy in Central India, giving the victory and the prize to the British, as had been already done in Oude, sounded the general knell of the rebel cause, though much had still to be done, and that in the hottest season, to subdue and crush the large and scattered bodies of the defeated enemy.

CHAPTER V

THE SUPPRESSION OF THE REVOLT

AT the end of March 1858, the war had been confined to the Oude and the Central India theatres, where Lucknow in the one, and Jhansi in the other, had been stormed and captured, and their defenders driven out and dispersed. With the operations against the various fugitive groups which were then formed, the war entered on its third stage, the suppression of the Revolt.

To deal first with Oude and the adjacent districts. If the Lucknow fugitives had been subjected to a crushing pursuit, and their leaders killed or captured, it is probable, from the analogy of other cases, that there would have been a speedy termination of the campaign. But, as has been shown, the cavalry failed to carry out the part expected from it, and consequently the enemy got off unscathed. This fact became known at once all over the country; fresh bodies of insurgents immediately arose in the neighbouring districts, and became active; and the war was resumed not only with vigour, but over a more widespread area than before. For it now included not only Oude, but Rohilkund to its west in the Delhi theatre, and Azimgurh, and the districts in the Eastern theatre. In Rohilkund, the Rohillas rose under their chief, Khan Bahadur Khan, and joined the fugitive Sepoys; in the east, the mutineers, who had hitherto evaded conflict, were roused by Konwur Singh, the old Talookdar of Shahabad whom Eyre had defeated in August, and began the contest by attacking Azimgurh. And in Oude itself fresh and serious trouble arose in consequence of a grave blunder committed by Lord Canning. After the capture of Lucknow, he issued a proclamation confiscating the property of all those who had joined in hostilities against the Government; and this decree, the Talookdars of Oude found, was held applicable to them. Now they had been absolutely friendly until Havelock recrossed to Cawnpore, and after that the participation of most of them in the war had been more nominal than real. The wholesale ruin with which they were now threatened was felt to be undeserved and intolerable, and drove them to despair; and for the first time, therefore, they rose in full revolt.

Hence, in April, and for some months to come, the stern conflict, which in March had been restricted to Oude, extended to Rohilkund and the eastern districts as well.

Sir Colin's first step, after capturing Lucknow, was to construct there a large and strongly fortified position which effectually dominated the city, and gave a secure basis for the establishment of law and order; and having started this, he proceeded to operate against the several bodies of insurgents that had been collecting at various points.

In Rohilkund, a large body of Sepoys and Rohillas was collected about Bareilly under the leading of Prince Feroze Shah and Khan Bahadur Khan.

In Oude there were three groups: first, in the north-west towards Rohilkund, the Mahomedans kept together under the Fyzabad Moulvie; next, on the north-east were the bulk of the Hindoo Sepoys, under the nominal rule of the Begum and the Nana Sahib; and third, the southern districts were held by the revolted Rajpoot clans, under the general guidance of Rajah Beni Madho, the Bys Chief of Shunkerpore.

And in and about Azimgurh were the mutineers of the eastern districts, with old Konwur Singh as their recognized leader.

For the subjugation of Rohilkund, Sir Colin sent four columns converging on Bareilly; from Lucknow, from Futtehgurh and Budaon on the west, and from Roorkee on the north. On the advance of the force from Lucknow, the Moulvie group on the north-west of Oude retired into Rohilkund, but did not join the other rebel parties. The Lucknow force, under Sir Colin's command, encountered, and after a severe contest defeated, Khan Bahadur Khan at Bareilly. On the same day, the other columns under Jones beat the enemy under Prince Feroze Shah at Moradabad, and then the two forces combining attacked and scattered the Moulvie's army at Shahjehanpur. This was all done in the month of May, after which the province settled down, and gave no more trouble.

To turn to Oude, the north-west group under the Moulvie had moved into Rohilkund, as has been already described, and there been finally defeated at Shahjehanpur; but it had first been attacked and beaten on April 13th, before it left Oude.

The main body of insurgents, to the north-east, were not dealt with till the middle of June, it being very desirable to avoid any needless marching of the British troops in that very hot weather. But in June, that group, under the chief insurgent leaders, moved towards Lucknow as far as Nuwabgunge, where they were attacked and defeated with great slaughter, and with the loss of all their guns, after a severe and determined engagement.

In the south, Beni Madho, who tried in May to hold in force a strong position threatening the road between Lucknow and Cawnpore, was attacked and driven off.

During the rest of that hot summer, detachments of troops kept Western Oude quiet, and a cordon was established round the eastern districts to prevent mischief from the Talookdar's men. And then when the cold weather came in October, a systematic attack was made on the strongholds of the various clans and chiefs, such as Morarmow, Doonden Khera, Shunkerpore, Ameythee, and Rampore Kussia. The clansmen meanwhile were harassing the troops during these movements; leading them a wearisome dance all over those districts, and rarely allowing themselves to be caught and forced to fight. At length, however, all of them who did not submit or were not captured were driven to the east of the Gogra; and then the whole of these remnants of the insurgents in Oude were steadily pressed northwards, till at the close of the year they were attacked on the banks of the Raptee, and driven across it, out of British territory into Nepaul.

The campaign in Behar, in the Eastern theatre, was the first that was actively taken in hand after the capture of Lucknow; for the news of the enemy's attack on Azimgurh arrived just as the siege of Lucknow was coming to an end. Konwur Singh had deferred his movements until Jung Bahadur and Franks' column, from the east, were out of the way and engaged at Lucknow. General Lugard was sent with a strong force to attack him and pacify those districts. But the intrepid old Rajpoot kept up an energetic guerilla war, ever on the move, till he was driven to the Ganges, and there mortally wounded while crossing it. After his death, his followers, including the mutineers of the district, maintained a desultory conflict in the Jugdeespore jungles all through that season of heat and rain. But at length, mainly through the use of mounted infantry, which gave the enemy no rest, no breathing time, they were forced into giving up the struggle before the end of the year, and dispersing to their homes. Thus, by the end of 1858, there was not even the semblance of rebellion left in Upper India.

There remains the contest in the Southern or Central India theatre. After being driven out of Jhansi, the enemy there, under Tantia Topee and the Ranee of Jhansi, first moved up to Kalpee on the Jumna, and again threatened Cawnpore, if not also a junction with the rebels in Oude. But, as before, they were met and defeated, and then turned off westwards, in their own districts, to Gwalior; where they knew they would be joined by the Mahratta soldiery, though Scindia did not lead them. They seized the fort, but then failed to hold it in face of Sir Hugh Rose's troops, who followed them up. There was a hard fight here, their last real stand as an army, in which the Ranee of Jhansi was killed. This occurred in June, and then the bulk of the army dispersed. But Tantia Topee still kept the field with a considerable following. A Pindaree war ensued, in which the several British columns moving against him from several points checked him on every line on which he tried to operate, and held him zigzagging through the jungles of Central India till, early in 1859, he was hemmed in and captured by Major Meade. With this the last embers of the revolt died out.

Thus ended, in complete and unalloyed success for the British, a rebellion and a war in which their chances seemed at first hopeless—so long at any rate as Allahabad was not safe in their hands—and continued to be desperately critical until Delhi was captured. As a fitting close to the story, let us consider some of the most prominent aspects and features of its fluctuations and episodes.

I. The back of the rebellion was broken and our eventual success assured by the end of the first stage of the war, when Delhi had been captured and the Baily Guard (Lucknow) succoured. And the storm had thus been weathered before any help from England had arrived.

II. With our capture of Delhi, all hope of a resuscitation of the Moghul empire collapsed, and the chief leaders and instigators of the revolt had thus early lost their stake and their cause.

III. The rebellion and the war started wisely with the seizure of Delhi, but the failure to concentrate there in greater force was the chief cause of the collapse of the insurgents.

IV. A second and prominent cause was the attitude of the Punjab—passively friendly to the British at first—actively friendly afterwards.

V. The defence of Lucknow aided our capture of Delhi by keeping away from it an army which would otherwise have operated against us there.

VI. The defence and the succour of Lucknow were very materially aided by the passive attitude of the Rajpoot Talookdars and country population of Oude, whose power for mischief was evinced by the part they played in the final stage of the war.

VII. The intensity of the struggle and the gravity of the crisis in the first stage of the war dwarfed all that occurred afterwards, except in respect of the magnitude of the forces that the British Government had in the field; and our success in that first stage was due to the independent action and local efforts of men of genius and exceptional resolution—John Lawrence in the Punjab; John Nicholson and Taylor at Delhi; Henry Lawrence at Lucknow; Brasyer and Neill at Allahabad; and Havelock with his wonderful campaign and its effect on the enemy.

VIII. The forces with which this success was achieved in three months were a mere handful compared with the armies with which at length, after fifteen months, Sir Colin managed to crush the enemy; and yet that enemy was never so strong as in the first stage of the war, for they grew weaker and weaker from losses in men and guns, until in the last stage their ranks received the accession of the Oude Talookdars, in April 1858, after Lord Canning's unfortunate proclamation of confiscation.

IX. The great contests of the war did not lie in the battle-field, except perhaps in Havelock's actions, but in siege operations, as at Delhi, the Baily Guard, Lucknow, and Jhansi; which threw an excessive burden on the Engineer element in the army, and caused the part it played to be exceptionally weighty and important.

X. Our success against the massive fortifications at Delhi, Lucknow, and Jhansi, contrasts with the utter failure of the enemy against the slight entrenchments of the Baily Guard, and teaches what can be effected against overwhelming odds by superior morale, courage, and skill.

XI. The inability of the enemy to storm the Baily Guard entrenchments lay technically in their being foiled, by our successful countermines, in their unceasing efforts to make a practicable breach.

XII. But the greatest of all the military lessons taught us was to be learnt from our difficulties and comparative failure at the outset; from our neglect of the broad rendering of the old Cromwellian adage, "Keep your powder dry."

To turn from the campaign to the revolt that preceded it; the description which has been given of its origin and development points to the circumstances that caused the rising, and tended to shape its course and fluctuations. They seem to teach the greatest lesson of all. To ensure a safe and prosperous rule by the British in India, while aiming as a matter of course at the real good and benefit of the people, we must carefully regard their prejudices and feelings, and scrupulously avoid whatever can tend to cause a common or universal irritation and animosity, or even suspicion, against us. There are points and matters to which they attach an importance which we do not realize, which it is folly for us to ignore, and in which their feelings will override and make them lose sight of all their real interests, and keep them out of sight.

The results of the undue preponderance of the native army—of the absence of any proper strategical occupation of the country—of the want of real military administration—tell their own tale, and need not be dwelt on.

But there are a few minor points in the facts affecting the course of the revolt which may be touched on usefully.

One is the conduct of the Rajpoot Talookdars of Oude. They were most bitter and hostile whilst the Mutiny was brewing, owing to what they held to be a breach of faith. They returned to a friendly attitude under the guidance of Sir Henry Lawrence, were very helpful to English families and fugitives at the outbreak, and held aloof from joining the enemy till Havelock's force withdrew from Oude. They then yielded nominal allegiance to the rebel Durbar, sending their quotas of retainers to the rebel army, but did not personally join in or guide the hostilities. By Lord Canning's proclamation, however, in April 1858, they found their estates confiscated and themselves included among our most virulent enemies; on which they revolted, and led the enormous forces now employed against them such a dance, that it can be readily understood how different matters would have been in the summer of 1857, if they had then acted against us as they did in 1858.

Next, while their chiefs remained friendly or passive, so did their clansmen. When, however, they turned against us, their clansmen went with them. As Lord Canning said, the existence of this feudal feeling—of the devotion of the men to their chiefs—of the sense of allegiance to their natural leaders—was quite unexpected. It practically refuted the statements and teaching of a certain school of administration which had sedulously tried to crush those feelings and relations, and had vainly thought they had succeeded.

A third point is this. By April 1858 the British troops, in the several theatres of operations, formed a gigantic army for India, and were supported by an equally large native army, some 80,000 men from the Punjab alone, besides possessing a splendid force of artillery. The Hindoostanee Sepoys with whom they were in conflict, and who could hardly have approached them in numbers, kept up the struggle, as has been described, without leaders, and eventually without any hope of success. Are we right in continuing to look down on the fighting qualities of these men? We know of their gallantry and devotion in olden days; and never has greater courage, constancy, and fidelity been shown than by the Sepoys who served in the defence of the Lucknow Residency.

May I dwell a little longer on this point? It is not a popular one—and, the Hindoostanee Sepoy is still in disgrace and heavily handicapped in every effort to reassert himself, under the prepossession in favour of Sikhs, Ghoorkas, and Puthans. But I venture to remark that, throughout the Mutiny, while some of the Sepoys were embittered and fought with their whole heart, the bulk of them, who had simply followed, sheep-like, some truculent and self-appointed guide, felt that they were fighting in a bad cause, and against their habitual leaders, of whom they naturally stood in awe. Under such circumstances, their conduct in the field could not draw out their military qualities in a true light; whereas those who remained true to their salt were the real representatives of the valour of their race. With proper management, with their best feelings roused and enlisted, with their old sense of honour cherished and encouraged, they may yet be a valuable support to the British rule of India.

BOOK I

OUDE BEFORE THE SIEGE OF THE RESIDENCY

CHAPTER I

BEFORE THE ANNEXATION

OUDE is a province of which the size can be best described as being much the same as that of Scotland. The maps of India and of Oude show its geographical position and details, but it may be useful to mention some of its prominent features, especially those connected with our narrative.

It lies between the Himalaya mountains of the foreign territory of Nepaul on the north,[1] and the river Ganges on the south. The Rohilkund districts border it on its west, and the Benares districts on its east. The large native fort of Futtehgurh lies on the Ganges opposite to its south-western corner, and the modern European fortress of Allahabad is situated close to its south-eastern angle, at the confluence of the Ganges and the Jumna.

Half-way between its eastern and western frontiers is the capital, Lucknow, on the Goomtee, some forty-five miles from the Ganges; on the right bank of which, at its nearest point of passage, lies Cawnpore.

There is only one other city in the province that need be mentioned—Fyzabad, on the river Gogra, at the eastern frontier. Its importance arises solely from its being the site of two rival shrines—one Mahomedan, the other the Hindoo temple called the Hunnooman Gurhee—which have ever been a chronic source of local feud and conflict, threatening every now and then to develope into fierce and wide-spread religious war.

[1] The general direction of the flow of the rivers is to the south of east, but for brevity's sake I call it easterly, and the other bearings mentioned are in accordance with this basis.

Sometimes called the garden of India, Oude is certainly one of its fairest and richest provinces. Noble groves and woods are studded over its well-watered plains. Its soil is excellent and fertile, and well cultivated, wherever misgovernment has not depopulated the country or led to the growth of thickets and jungles. Only along the northern frontier, where the plains begin to slope gently up to the lower Himalayas, there is a broad belt of natural forest, the haunt of the tiger and the elephant, the choicest of hunting-grounds.

Except where suffering from the results of anarchy, the province was well, even thickly, populated. The ruling race and a large proportion of the city people were Mahomedans of Moghul descent. But the country peasantry and their chiefs were almost universally Rajpoots; a race of fine physique, who formed the nursery of the bulk of the Sepoy army of old. They were the warrior caste of the Hindoo community—divided into clans, and with feudal organization and tendencies—with strong traditional sense of honour, but not naturally ferocious and bloodthirsty like the tribes on our Afghan frontiers. If let alone, they formed an excellent and orderly body of cultivators.

Up to the year 1856 the province had a peculiar appearance in the maps of India, because until then it was still under native rule, and was therefore shown as an uncoloured patch, cut out as it were from the red-tinted expanse of British territory that framed it in on three sides. For during the hundred years of the rise of the British power and its development into the Empire of India, Oude had been allowed to remain under the sway of its native dynasty; while in marked contrast to it, all the surrounding country had been gradually brought under British administration.

The course of events that brought about these results forms a singular story—not the less so from its ending almost suddenly, at the close of the cycle, in 1856, in the suppression of the dynasty and the absorption of the province under British rule.

During the first fifty years, that is, up to the early days of the nineteenth century, while the British were steadily advancing on the path of conquest, and struggling without intermission against their many powerful rivals for supremacy, Oude had passed safely through the storm, and emerged well-nigh unharmed. But its danger had been great at each of the three prominent crises—in the days of Clive, of Warren Hastings, and of Wellesley.

At the Plassey epoch, the Wuzeer or Viceroy, who ruled Oude in the name of the Moghul Emperor, was at first hostile to the English, fought against them, and was defeated. But Clive, instead of exacting the penalty in his power, played, as a matter of policy, the part of a generous victor, and reinstated him as Nuwab or ruler of Oude on terms, ratified by treaty, which attached him thenceforward to the British interest.

Then in the days of Warren Hastings, when the Mahratta armies were at the zenith of their ascendancy and success, and the Rohillas on the western borders of Oude were intriguing for their alliance and assistance, the Oude Nuwab, in danger of destruction from the threatening combination, appealed to the English. Hastings responded to the appeal, supported him in force, kept the Mahrattas in check, crushed the Rohillas, and ended the episode by handing over their province of Rohilkund to the Oude Nuwab, as an addition to the territory already under his sway. This policy confirmed the loyalty, but failed utterly in its second object of increasing the military power, of the court of Oude. For, subsiding into Oriental sloth and disregard of duty, the successive Nuwabs neglected the opportunities and advantages thus offered them, and by folly and misrule lost even such military strength as they had before possessed.

In Lord Wellesley's time, therefore, at the beginning of the present century, when he was contending with Tippoo Sultan in the south, and with the Mahrattas in Central India, and was at the same time threatened with an invasion from the north under the Afghan Zeman Shah, the Oude dynasty passed through a specially acute crisis. For, instead of receiving from it the aid that was to be expected, Wellesley found that the Nuwab was worthless as a military power, had entirely lost control over his troops and subjects, and, in fact, required the assistance of the British for his personal protection and security. So utter was the collapse, so powerless did he feel himself to be, that the Nuwab even proposed to abdicate; though not with any serious intent. So critical, however, was the position of affairs, and so great the irritation of the Government, that the offer was at one time on the verge of acceptance. But the fortune of the dynasty was still in the ascendant. Its shortcomings had not included hostility or disloyalty; so the Nuwab escaped the fate that threatened him, though not scatheless. He was left to reign over his old principality of Oude, but he was shorn of the Rohilkund districts, partly as the price of the aid which had to be given, and partly because, being a frontier province, Rohilkund had to be strongly held; and this, it was clear, could not be done except by the British army.

Thus it was that the Oude dynasty weathered the storms that marked the first half-century of the rise of the British power. But it was not allowed to enter on a new lease of its rule without a fresh treaty, in 1801, which imposed on the Nuwab in emphatic terms the obligation to maintain good government; "to establish," it said, "such a system of administration as should conduce to the prosperity of his subjects, and give security to life and property."

All the surrounding country had been by this time absorbed under British administration—a sufficiently significant warning, it might be supposed, of the necessity of conforming to British policy. And, with this proviso, it seemed now to be fully in the power of the Oude Nuwabs, by simply remaining true to their treaty obligations, to their duty, and to their real interest, to retain in perpetuity, under British protection, the enviable position in which they were now confirmed.

Saadut Ali Khan, the Nuwab of the days of the treaty of 1801, responded to the obligation, and proved an able and vigorous ruler. But his successors were of a different stamp. Brought up in the harem in comparatively peaceful times, they subsided into a life of indolence, ease, and pleasure. They would have nought to do with the troublesome functions of administration. These they handed over, with all the military resources of the State, uncontrolled, into the hands of court favourites, and of the highest bidders for the farming of the revenues. This, with attendant circumstances, as will be described presently, induced a shameful and dangerous state of broadcast misrule and oppression, bloodshed and rapine. For forty years this continued, growing worse and worse. The Government remonstrated again and again. The Nuwabs remained absolutely callous, and never made even a semblance of an effort to interfere, or control and improve the administration. They tacitly ignored not merely the moral duty, but also the treaty obligation involved; till at length the studied violation of the latter, and the resulting danger and wrong to the people, could no longer be tolerated; and Lord Dalhousie, under the orders of the Home Government, suppressed the native ruler in 1856, and annexed the province under British administration.

It is necessary to describe this misrule more fully, and the attendant circumstances, if only on account of its direct effect on the people, and its subsequent influence on their bearing and conduct at the annexation, and in the days of the Mutiny.

The misrule lay, not as Oriental story might lead one to imagine, in any personal ferocity, tyrannical conduct, or violent crime on the part of the Nuwabs themselves, but in the inevitable results of their abstention from the duties of government, and their delegation of its functions and powers—uncontrolled and unchecked—to worthless favourites or unscrupulous bidders for office. These were generally of the ruling Mahomedan race, or astute and wealthy Brahmins; the most powerful of them being the Amils—or collectors of revenue—to whom the revenue had been farmed out, with licence to extort the utmost they could manage, by any means however violent or murderous, without respect to assessments, engagements, or rights of any kind. The Rajpoot population, with whom they had chiefly to deal, were not of a race that would submit tamely to such extortion. They opposed the Amils and their troops by force; and hence rebellion, as this opposition was called, became chronic throughout the province. With the passions of the people thus excited, it was easy for the astute and wily Amils to create animosity between the several clans, and make them turn their swords against each other; so that the whole province became one widespread theatre of partisan warfare and murderous strife, of bloodshed and misery.

This inevitably led to deterioration in the character and tone of the people. A spirit of ferocity and violence was developed, which was not natural to the race; and the traditional Rajpoot sense of honour and of clan and feudal obligations was sometimes greatly blunted, if not absolutely crushed out.

The singular feature of the case, that is of the oppression of the clans by the Amils, is that the numerical strength of the Rajpoots, their physique, and their early training to arms, ought to have enabled and led them to laugh at the efforts of the Amils. But, unfortunately, they were victims to an extreme type of feudal organization which checked combination, leading their chiefs instead to act independently of each other, and to withstand, single-handed, the attacks of the Amils and their troops. They were thus liable to be beaten in detail when, if they had acted together, they must have been victorious by sheer superiority of force. The same tendency was probably the cause of the great states of Rajpootana not having been as successful as the Mahrattas in opposing the Mahomedan armies, during the Moghul and previous epochs.

In the case of Oude, however, the persistence of the Rajpoot race in this system was all the more insane when they knew, on the one hand, that widespread, almost universal, misery was its result; and, on the other, that their constitutional organization provided for such difficulties by grouping the clans into confederacies, where certain chiefs were entitled to summon the rest to join and act in concert against a common foe. All the clans, for instance, to the south of the Gogra were bound to respond to the call of the Rajah of Hussunpore, and those on the north to the summons of the Gonda Rajah.

As it was, however, the custom was for each clan to act independently, to await the visit of the Amil, and to resist his extortions and onslaught single-handed. The chiefs rarely helped each other, but were generally supported by all their retainers and most of their own clansmen capable of bearing arms; and they also from an early date materially strengthened their powers of resistance by the construction of strongholds, walled and fortified villages, surrounded by bamboo thicket fences, and situated in jungles difficult to penetrate. Eventually, there were some 1,600 of these strongholds scattered over the country, belonging generally to the more powerful Talookdars or chiefs, and many of them armed with artillery.

In these they endeavoured to keep the Amils at bay. Where the clans were successful in their resistance, their strength was recognized and they flourished. But if the Amils won in the struggle, the landholders and their men, on being driven out from their strongholds and deprived of their lands, took to the jungles and became robbers and brigands. Their estates and villages were seized by the Amils, whose property they became; the chiefs were themselves ruined, and the peasantry were crushed and generally dispersed; and long stretches of country were frequently depopulated and became desolate wastes.

The cases would seem at first sight to be as bad as they could be when whole clans were destroyed or left the country; when thousands of ploughs—40,000 from one district alone—went over the frontier to Azimgurh and elsewhere; when, as in Nanpara and Toolseepore and other districts, all was waste and desolation; when the natural leaders of the people were lurking in the jungles at the heads of gangs of robbers and dacoits. But it was really worse, and the demoralization was felt to be greater because of a meaner type, when traitors appeared among their number, who by intrigue and court favour obtained means to harry and dispossess their own relations, to be in some instances guilty of parricide, and to use the power of the Amils to crush their countrymen and build up their own fortunes.

Most of these, it may be here observed, such men as the chief of Doondeea Khera, the Mitholee Rajah, and others, came out in their true colours in the Mutiny, and showed themselves, either in a virulent or in a cowardly fashion, hostile to the English, and especially to the helpless fugitives. On the other hand, in contrast to them, and far more numerous, were the nobler men—such Talookdars as the Bys chiefs of Shunkerpore and Morarmow, Hunwunt Singh of Dharoopore, the chief of Amethee, Rajah Roostum

Sah of Dehra, the Bulrampore Rajah, and the like, who maintained their character and position through all the troublous time, were true to their traditional Rajpoot honour whatever their straits, and afterwards played a part in the Mutiny which, when understood, cannot but redound to their credit; and were nearly every one of them actively instrumental in succouring English families in their distress.

Such were the Rajpoots whom the whole power of the Oude court and State had been used to harry and oppress. Of the Amils—who had been the oppressors—most were in the course of time ennobled into rajahs; but no greater mistake could be made than that of placing them in the same category as the old hereditary rajahs of the Rajpoot clans. To the latter there could be no greater insult.

Among the Amils only one family—Brahmins—had risen to real prominence, and chief among them were Durshun Singh, and two of his sons, Rughbeer Singh and Maun Singh. They all three accumulated wealth and property, and were unscrupulous in their mode of acquiring it. But Durshun Singh managed his estates sensibly, and made his people prosperous and contented. Rughbeer Singh, on the other hand, was a ruthless devastator and destroyer. His evil name will never be forgotten in the Gonda and Baraitch districts, which he laid desolate; while Maun Singh was a byword for cunning and shrewdness, and ended, as the story will show, in taking skilful advantage of a critical opportunity to acquire an exceptionally favourable position in the eyes of the Rajpoots and other sections of the Hindoo community.

Such then were the leading features of the misrule that was prevalent in Oude. Let us turn to some of its most important effects.

Although one result of the state of turmoil and strife was to give rise occasionally to flagrant violation of feudal and family obligations, the general effect, paradoxical as it may sound, was to intensify the narrow feudal and clan system, and the feelings it inspired. For it was strongly recognized that the general welfare, and indeed the safety, of the clan, lay in a concentrated organization, in which all were to hold and work together—in which there was an identity of interests throughout all classes—and in which it was of moment that their chief and representative should be a territorial magnate, a man of power and position. With the better clans, the men were devoted to their chief; the chief was the veritable father of the clan: its welfare was his care, and his will was law. It will be seen presently in what a surprising manner this told on the Mutiny.

Another result of the misrule was to create a favourable feeling towards the English. In the contests of the Rajpoots with the Amils, and their quarrels with the Lucknow court and its emissaries, they ever found sympathy and friendly advice and help from the English officers scattered about; and they always knew that the Resident at Lucknow—as the British Minister there was called—was the truest friend they had; ready to interpose, whenever possible, to relieve suffering and secure redress for wrongs.

This feeling moreover was supplemented and strengthened by the fact that in every village there were men who were living on British pensions, and considered themselves identified with British rule, and sharers in its prosperity and renown. At the same time, though the Talookdars were imbued as strongly as their followers with this good-will towards the English personally, they did not feel the same liking towards the policy in force with the British administration. They heard strange rumours of that policy, and of the action of the law courts; of the families of position, and the natural leaders of the people, falling rapidly into decay, and being dispossessed of their estates—partly from the dead set made against them by the doctrinaire school, then in the ascendant, and partly by the intricate working of the law courts, and the chicanery and trickery of the usurer class, who had become all-powerful. The Oude men felt that they would be helpless against such foes; whereas, under the existing *régime*, they might hold their own, though with the chance of much risk and suffering.

Such then were the characteristics and the results of the misrule that had prevailed in Oude for the last century, and that seemed to be on the increase. The weaker clans and landholders had been crushed and ruined, and their positions and estates had been usurped by the Amils, who had become more powerful than ever, and were pressing more strongly against those stouter clans and chiefs who had heretofore kept them at bay.

The Oude Durbar continued provokingly deaf and callous to the remonstrances of the British Government. The Nuwabs believed, in their hearts, that these remonstrances were a mere farce, and that so long as they remained loyal and faithful to British interests, shortcomings in other respects were of no moment.

The position was becoming intolerable; and the British Government could no longer avoid facing the fact that, by its protection and support of the Oude rule, it was sharing in the responsibility for the shameful state of matters in the province. In 1854, therefore, when happily General Outram, who was noted for his generous sympathy with all classes of the native community, with princes as well as with peasants, was the British Resident at Lucknow, he was instructed to investigate the subject and report on it fully. This he accordingly did, and there could be but one tenor to the report. The misrule was so outrageous, so dangerous, so unjust to the people, so flagrant a violation of treaty engagements; it entailed so serious a responsibility on the British Government, by whose protection only it was rendered possible; that it could not be allowed to continue.

The Government of India forwarded Outram's report to her Majesty's Government, and urged the necessity for removing the administration of Oude from the rule of its Nuwabs; suggesting various alternative measures, and dwelling at the same time on the generous treatment which the unswerving loyalty of the dynasty merited at the hands of the British. The decision in England was for absolute annexation, and the orders and detailed instructions reached Lord Dalhousie on January 2nd, 1856.

Meanwhile, during the latter half of 1855, events had been taking place in Oude which confirmed the necessity for the change contemplated, and also affected the state of public feeling. The city of Fyzabad, it has been already shown, was notorious as a centre of religious fanaticism and strife. And now a Moulvie, named Ameer Ali, had started a story that the Hunnooman Gurhee, the great Hindoo temple, had been built on the site of a Mahomedan mosque; having then collected a band of followers, he had attacked the temple, but had been repulsed by the Hindoos who had flocked in to its defence. The story was groundless, and was proved to be so by reference to the archives at Delhi; still the Nuwab by his attitude encouraged the Moulvie; and a religious war would have ensued had not General Outram stepped in and insisted on the maintenance of law and order. The Moulvie, however, continued his threatening attitude towards the temple, and eventually, trusting to the secret support of the Nuwab, advanced to its attack; but was met by troops commanded by English officers, with the result that he was himself killed and his followers dispersed.

This episode destroyed any latent reluctance that there might otherwise have been to remove the Nuwab from the rulership of the province; but it had also two other notable results. One was that the Hindoos of Oude, including the Rajpoot chiefs, knowing the part played in the crisis by the English Resident, became especially well disposed towards the British. The other was that Rajah Maun Singh, hitherto one of the most detested of the Amils, having come forward with his followers to the defence of the Hunnooman Gurhee, and posed as the champion of Hindooism, lost much of his unpopularity, and acquired the respect of the Rajpoots to such a degree as to enable him to act during the Mutiny as the representative and leader of the country community.

Such then was the state of affairs when, on January 2nd, 1856, Lord Dalhousie received the orders from England for the annexation of Oude. The preparation of the detailed instructions and arrangements for carrying those orders into effect, occupied the greater part of the rest of the month. But at length Outram received these instructions, and was directed to depose the Nuwab and assume the administration of the province.

While this was taking place, profound tranquillity appeared to prevail, and public attention was directed chiefly to the coming retirement of Lord Dalhousie; one of the most brilliant of rulers, who had conferred inestimable blessings on the country, but whose iron rule and autocracy had closed the best safety-valves of government, and was leaving behind, hidden and suppressed, a weighty mass of widespread ill-feeling and disaffection.

Before quitting this chapter, which is meant to give a description of the province of Oude, a few further remarks may be made respecting its Rajpoot clans. They were very numerous, some much more powerful than others, some again only septs of others. Their mere names convey no meaning, and have no special interest. The most powerful of them was the Bys clan, who were said to be proof against snake-bites: though of this I never heard any real evidence. They were not of such blue blood as the Buchgotee clan, of which the chief was the Hussunpore Rajah; but, like him, their head, the Rajah of Morarmow, had the privilege and right among Rajpoots of creating rajahs and conferring the Tiluk, or forehead mark of the rank. All rajahs were held to be spurious whose rank had not been derived through some such proper channel as this.

It was a singular circumstance that the Hussunpore Rajah should have retained this right, for he had become Mahomedan. And the story goes that the noted Brahmin Amil Durshun Singh, having on some occasion made him captive, required of him, in vain, that he should confer the Tiluk on him. The Hussunpore Rajah was the supreme head of the confederacy of Oude clans between the Gogra and the Ganges. The Tiloee Rajah (chief of the Kanpooreas) had the seat on his right hand; the Pertabghur Rajah (chief of the Sombunsees) sat on his left; and the Ameythee Rajah (chief of the Bundelgotees) was the standard-bearer.

The tales of the deeds of their men of mark were as numerous, and to the clansmen as exciting, as the tales of the Scottish Borders and Highlands; the most prominent chieftain among them, at that epoch, being Hunwunt Singh, the head of the Biseyn clan. Their ladies, too, were not always in the background. The story runs, that the Amil Maun Singh was besieging Dehra, the fort of the Rajcomars, whose chief, Rustoom Sah, was at that time a boy. His widowed mother, when the garrison could no longer hold out, fastened a bundle of her garments over the gateway by which Maun Singh must enter; and, on evacuating, left an epistle deriding him with the petticoat shelter under which he had effected his entry into the fort! And during the Mutiny, when the chief of Morarmow saved Mowbray Thomson's fugitive party from Cawnpore, the rescue is believed to have been carried through mainly by the influence and energy of his dame, the Thakooranee, as she was called.

CHAPTER II

THE FIRST YEAR AFTER ANNEXATION

On February 4, 1856, General Outram carried out his orders. He announced formally to the Nuwab that Oude and its revenues were to be brought under British administration; while the Nuwab would retain his sovereign rank and title, and sundry privileges and estates, with an annual income of £150,000. The letter from Lord Dalhousie, which he received at the same time, gave the reasons for this decision of the English Government—that the Nuwab had forfeited the position secured to him under the existing treaty by his persistent violation of its most important stipulation, that he should establish and maintain a good government; that his misrule had brought widespread misery on his subjects and become a standing reproach, in which the British Government was involved, owing to its relations with the Nuwab; that this state of matters would not be tolerated any longer, and the forfeiture of his position must therefore be enforced, and the treaty annulled and replaced by a fresh treaty. The loyalty of the Nuwab and his dynasty was recognized, and his status and provision for the future were settled on the terms proposed.

The Nuwab, however, would have nought to say to the treaty. He was the servant of the English Government, while treaties were valid only between equals. But he protested against his deposition inasmuch as he had ever been faithful and loyal, the only obligation he recognized as real and binding. And he would go to the Governor-General, and if need be to the Queen of England, to plead his cause in person.

Three days of grace were given him for consideration, but he remained unyielding, and so General Outram assumed the administration of the province, and issued his proclamation. The Nuwab, true to his attitude, discharged his troops and officials from their allegiance to himself, and enjoined on them implicit obedience and deference to the British rule.

The assumption of the administration by General Outram was effected with perfect tranquillity. This was due, no doubt, in a measure, as regards Lucknow itself, to the bearing and injunctions of the Nuwab; in the country it resulted largely from the prevalent feeling of good-will towards the English; and everywhere it was materially influenced by the terms and tenor of the proclamation, of which a copy, with a separate letter, was sent to every chief and person of position.

Under the proclamation, and the attendant measures which were immediately adopted, careful attention seemed to be paid to the welfare of every class, and to befriending the lot of those who were likely to suffer most from the change. Suitable provision was promised for the collateral members of the Royal Family—consideration and employment for those who had lost office and position. The Nuwab's troops and retainers were to be recruited into the local forces and police, or to be pensioned. All classes were assured of protection and justice, and the full enjoyment of their rights. The land revenue was to be organized on a fair and clear basis, while its first settlement was to be for three years, on a moderate assessment, and to be made direct with those in actual possession, leaving proprietary rights an open question for future decision.

At this juncture, then, there was general satisfaction and contentment, at any rate among the Hindoo community of the province. But the Mussulmans, not only of Oude, but of all Upper India, were embittered and angered by the suppression of one of the few Mahomedan reigning houses which had been left in power; and they now sedulously fostered and propagated the work of sedition, so that the widespread disaffection described in the introductory general sketch presently developed in force.

Outside the province, more than within it, the upper classes were confirmed in their belief in the selfish and greedy turn which was held to characterize British policy. Taking over charge of the administration and introducing a better government, as promised, was all right; but why absorb the revenues of the province, and why degrade a dynasty of which the loyalty was beyond dispute, when such steps were not essential to the mere improvement of the administration?

And so the disaffection of the influential classes was heightened by the annexation of Oude, although the province itself took the change quietly.

But this contentment was not of long duration. At the end of April, Sir James Outram was forced by ill health to resign the rule of the province. While he was there, his conciliatory and generous measures had produced a most beneficial effect; but, even during his time, a tendency had been shown by the revenue officers, in a degree which attracted the attention and drew down the disapproval of the Governor-General, to depart from the terms of the proclamation in respect of the land revenue arrangements; to violate the promises that the assessment should be moderate, and that the settlement should be made direct with the persons in actual possession.

After Sir James Outram's departure, the state of feeling grew rapidly worse. Except in the matter of employing the Nuwab's Sepoys and retainers in the new local regiments and police, there seemed to be an entire cessation and disregard of the beneficent and conciliatory arrangements which had been promised, and in a measure started. As described in Lord Stanley's despatch of October 13, 1858, the members and stipendiaries of the Royal Family were treated with discourtesy, and even reduced to great straits from their allowances being withheld; while the ex-officials and men of influence were studiously kept out of the employment and position which they had been led to expect. All these combined to form the nucleus of a powerful malcontent party. Though thousands of the soldiery had been brought into British service, other thousands had been discharged without the means of subsistence; and, in Oude, to discharge a Sepoy so was to create a bandit.

On the top of this came the General Service Enlistment Act, which, besides its effect on the army, filled with dismay or grave anxiety the Sepoys' homes in Oude, and the hearts of their kinsmen and of the clansmen generally, who had habitually looked to the army as the great field for the employment of their sons, and who now felt that henceforward the British service would be very materially changed, as if from a militia to a General Service Army. So the jungles came to be more and more infested with groups of dacoits or brigands.

Moreover, most serious of all, the irritation among the Rajpoot community, chiefs and peasants alike, grew apace, owing to the increasing violation, already touched on, of the promises respecting the land revenue. Besides the matter of unduly high assessments, the bias shown in deciding on the parties to be dealt with as being in actual possession gave the most serious offence. For the officers usually put forward the villagers themselves, and ignored the Talookdars or chiefs. Now it was a well-known fact, that by whatever process they had obtained the position, the chiefs were usually the parties holding actual possession at the time of annexation, while their followers and the peasantry were virtually only their tenants; and not only was this well known, but it was also universally recognized, that it was owing to this very position and these relations that the Talookdars had acquired that power and station which had cemented the clan organization, and enabled it to resist successfully the oppression of the Durbar Amils and troops. As a natural result, the clansmen were apt to feel that any diminution of the territorial or other wealth of their chief involved a lowering of his status and power, and injured the welfare of the community in general. When, therefore, by the action of the English revenue officers, such rajahs as those of Dharoopore, Amethee, and Dera, such chiefs as Beni Madho and other heads of the great Byswara clan, were mulcted of half their estates, not only were those magnates angered and embittered, but their clansmen sympathized, and joined in the resentment.

Thus it was that after the middle of 1856 the whole of Oude was in a state of bitter disaffection, which the old malcontent party were not slow to foster to the best of their ability; though the Rajpoot community seemed to nourish their own wrongs apart from all others, and to hold aloof from the general sedition.

As the year advanced matters grew worse in Oude as

well as elsewhere. After the close of the Russian war rumours were sedulously spread about of the emasculation of the military strength of England, and the exhaustion of the army and its resources. An exceptionally severe epidemic of cholera had resuscitated an old trick of circulating or rather passing on small bannocks—chupatties they were called—from village to village, as if to speed away the plague. This was regarded as a mystery; and, in the general state of unrest which prevailed, augmented the uneasiness, ending in being held as a signal for preparation for popular commotion.

As the year was about to close, it became known that there would be war with Persia; and the Mahomedan community, already angered by the suppression of the Oude dynasty, became still more exasperated at hostilities with another Mahomedan power.

And then in January 1857, as the fitting close and climax to the rapid succession of events and measures that effected so many breaches in the good faith and trust which formed the foundation of the British power, occurred the cartridge incident, with its startling and exciting effect on the Sepoy army. It was at once seized and used by the disaffected as the most powerful weapon for mischief that had yet come within their grasp. The whole of Upper India was now in a state of agitation and expectancy, and Oude was specially prominent.

A new Moulvie, who has been named sometimes as Ahmed Oolla Shah, and sometimes as Sikundur Shah, openly raised the standard of revolt at Fyzabad, and proclaimed a *jehad* or religious war against the British. At the same time brigandage grew more vigorous, especially where led by a notorious desperado named Fuzl Ali; and matters in this respect came to a crisis when his gang resisted and killed a British officer, named Boileau, who led a party against them.

It was at this juncture, none too soon, that a change was made in the arrangements for the government of Oude, and Sir Henry Lawrence came over from Rajpootana to assume charge of the province.

CHAPTER III

UNDER SIR HENRY LAWRENCE

IN the state of matters that prevailed in March 1857, there could have been no more opportune or fortunate event than the arrival of Sir Henry Lawrence at Lucknow to assume charge of the administration of Oude; for no one could be named who so thoroughly gauged and understood the disaffection that was at work; or who was so competent to deal with it where it was most prominent and threatening, as was the case in Oude.

How he realized the gravity of the crisis was obvious from his conversations whilst on his way from Rajpootana to Lucknow, from the measures he took immediately on arrival, and from his letters to Lord Canning and others. How such a crisis ought to be met he had shown in his writings, and especially in an article penned in 1843, which will be presently noticed. His special fitness to deal with the local irritation was marked by his previous success under equally difficult circumstances in the Punjab, and by the widespread reputation and character which he had thereby gained as a beneficent ruler and a staunch friend of all classes of the people.

On the annexation of the Punjab, he had been placed at the head of its Government, when he had to deal with a fierce, proud, and gallant race, who were smarting under defeat, and embittered by the loss of independence. Holding that the element most essential to sound government was the contentment of the people, he aimed with intense vigour and singleness of purpose at dissipating their resentment, their irritation and distrust, and securing instead their good-will and friendliness. While enforcing with a firm hand the steps necessary for the pacification of the province, the maintenance of law and order, and the satisfaction of the financial and other claims of the State, he adopted a policy of which the essence lay in a scrupulous regard for existing rights, and a liberal and generous revenue administration. Evincing transparently his recognition of the losses and sufferings of the conquered race, in the transition from wild independence to the restraints of a civilized government, and of their claim that that transition should be carried out tenderly, he established, as the method of his administration, a system of thorough accessibility on the part of the local officers, and a cordial and sympathetic bearing. The result sought for was not long delayed. The chiefs and people were soon satisfied that there would be no questioning of rights, no disturbance or spoliation of property, no despotic or aggressive attitude on the part of the Government. He was supported and his policy carried out by an unrivalled body of lieutenants, most of whom he himself selected, trained, and imbued with his own spirit, so that gradually the sense of bitterness and humiliation disappeared from the province. A thorough trust and confidence in their rulers arose among the people. Their intercourse became singularly frank and hearty, and the very best relations were established. This contentment, regard, and good-will constituted the aim and essence of his administrative policy; and, continued as it was after his departure by the school of officers whom he left behind him, it led our bitter enemies of 1849 to side with us in the struggle of 1857.

Moreover, the character and repute which he had thus acquired in the Punjab made his name a household word throughout the land, and, preceding his move to Oude, caused his arrival there to have an immediate effect on the excitement in the province.

His knowledge of the state of public feeling, and his insight into the causes that effected it, were unique; both from his natural sagacity and instincts, and also from the varied opportunities which he had enjoyed and used. These had brought him into close contact with all classes of the country population, and also with the chiefs and people of native States, and of the old feudal races. In the one case he had been impressed with the grave injustice with which the upper classes—who were held to be effete, but were still the natural leaders of the people—were being treated, in the interests, as was assumed, of the peasantry. And, in the other, he had seen the dangerous feeling resulting from the prospect of the possible extinction of the native dynasties by the attitude of Government in minimizing the practice of the adoption of heirs. Adding to these the Mahomedans and other embittered classes, he felt that the grave disaffection of so many large and influential sections of the community tended towards a general combination against the State.

As to the native army, he had long been outspoken about its treatment and want of discipline, its dangerous growth and preponderating strength; and now he was appalled at the animosity roused in it by the General Service Act, and by the blunders of the cartridge business.

He had written of it in 1843, that the true basis of the British power lay in the army being well paid, well disciplined, and thoroughly reliant, from experience, on the good faith, wisdom, and energy of the Government and its leaders. And he had shown the danger that would arise if, quick-sighted as they were, they came to detect any shortcomings in our good faith or spirit, or otherwise to lose confidence in the British.

He had pointed out that constant success had made us careless and blind to the dangers to which we were liable; that it was necessary to be always on our guard as to the sufficiency of our military means, and the efficacy of our military arrangements and organization; and that, above all, timely energy and resolute action would surmount grave and formidable dangers, while want of military spirit or soldierly bearing might lead to catastrophe under even trifling difficulties.

It was under the influence of these convictions and this spirit that Sir Henry Lawrence acted on his arrival at Lucknow; imbued as he was with a profound sense of an impending rising of the troops, and of a possible combination of the whole native community against the State.

He assumed charge of the province about March 20th, took immediate steps, first, for the enforcement of law and order; next, for the reduction of the local discontent and disaffection; and third, for inquiries and preparations to meet the coming crisis.

Brigandage was on the increase, and Fuzl Ali had repulsed and killed the English officer who had tried to capture him. So Sir Henry attacked Fuzl Ali, killed him, and dispersed his followers. The Fyzabad Moulvie was ostentatiously preaching sedition, and proclaiming a *jehad* (religious war). He was therefore forthwith seized and imprisoned.

To deal with the local discontent—the pensions and allowances so long withheld were immediately paid up, and all discourtesy and harshness were peremptorily stopped. Increased employment was given to the old officials and soldiery ; and last, but not least, the wrongs of the chiefs and Talookdars were dealt with. They or their representatives were met in Durbars or at private interviews, at which Sir Henry announced that the terms of the proclamation of February 1856 should be strictly adhered to ; that those at that time in actual possession of estates and property should remain in possession for the three years originally notified ; and that all classes, chiefs as well as peasants, should have justice secured to them, and be protected and assured in the enjoyment of their rights. As Sir Henry's character and antecedents were known throughout the province to be in accord with these avowals, an immediate change resulted. The Rajpoot leaders were not only appeased, but all sense of irritation and anxiety seemed to disappear. The country population settled down into contentment and tranquillity. Brigandage ceased, and the revenues flowed freely and fully into the district treasuries.

Having thus cleared the ground in respect of local difficulties and opposition, he began his preparations for dealing with the impending crisis. He was not yet in military command of the province. Brigadier Handscombe commanded the district, and Brigadier Gray was in special command of the Oude local force. But he procured an improved distribution of the force at Lucknow itself, and having decided in his own mind on the old Sikh fort of Mutchi Bhown as the best local place of refuge in case of an *émeute*, he directed that it should be quietly cleared out, cleaned, and put in repair; dealing with it, however, not as a military work, but as part of the ordinary civil winter repairs. The Mutchi Bhown was a dilapidated building on a high site, and had long been used merely as a storehouse, being no longer thought suitable for any other purpose. Sir Henry examined the city and suburbs and surrounding country in respect of resources and capabilities for defence. He instituted inquiries into the defensive positions in other parts of the province. He summoned in the more intelligent officers from the outlying stations for consultation. He inquired keenly into the character and capacity of the officers of all ranks in the province; being, alas! often told in reply, not of their intelligence, energy, resolution, and influence, but of their carefulness and punctuality in office routine. To get this knowledge at first hand as much as possible, he joined in rackets and at other games, exercised wide hospitality, and gave a large *al fresco* entertainment to the 32nd and other British troops. He saw as much as he could of the native nobles and gentry of Lucknow, and also had long and valuable conversations with various native officers. These conversations fully confirmed his impressions of the unpleasant ideas these men had gradually formed; of their dissatisfaction with their position under the British Government; and of the active disloyalty to which they might be roused.

Though thus profoundly impressed with the certainty of a crisis in the army, and with the probability that it would be supported by a general rising throughout the country, Sir Henry could see, as yet, no sign to indicate the shape or course of action which the disaffection would assume. Hence he could do no more at present for the interests entrusted to him than seek to minimize the local irritation and discontent, prepare for an emergency in an unknown form, and keep up a keen outlook. Needless to say, he was unflagging in his correspondence with the neighbouring authorities and with the Governor-General, urging preparations and improvements in the military positions.

As yet, the ill-feeling in the troops had been shown only by the mutiny of two regiments in Bengal, and by incendiary fires at Umballa, where there was a large camp of exercise. But nothing else overt had occurred anywhere when, on May 1st and 2nd, a local regiment, the 7th Oude Infantry, stationed in one of the suburbs of Lucknow, refused to obey their officers in regard to using their cartridges. Sir Henry next day surrounded the regiment, paraded and disarmed it, and imprisoned, tried, and punished the ringleaders; at the same time promoting and rewarding those who had behaved with prominent loyalty.

Meanwhile the country generally seemed to be fairly

tranquil, and people were moving about the districts and travelling to the hill stations and elsewhere freely, and without serious anxiety. The English community were not yet so much alarmed, as vexed at the unusual feeling that had been evoked, and angry at the blunder that had evoked it. There was no idea prevalent of any real animosity having been aroused, or of any mutiny or revolt against the State being imminent. But at length, on May 11th and 12th, it began to be rumoured that the telegraph was not working, that the postal service was disorganized, and that something unpleasant had occurred up-country. On the 13th and 14th, fairly correct intelligence was received of the outbreak at Meerut and Delhi. By May 14th, Sir Henry knew what had really occurred at Delhi : that the troops in its neighbourhood had broken out in aggressive mutiny, with signs of murderous animosity towards the British ; that they had concentrated on and seized Delhi, and made it the gage of battle with the British Power ; and that further, the Moghul party had there proclaimed the restoration of the old dynasty, and seated the Emperor on the imperial throne. There followed at once a cessation of the Pax Britannica all over the Upper Provinces. The civil administration was disorganized, and to Europeans especially there was no longer safety in travelling or security of life or property. Still, except round the immediate centre at Delhi, there was no sign of the mutiny itself spreading, nor of the rising being joined by any of the native States or chiefs, or any other classes except the predatory castes of the north-west.

Sir Henry's immediate action was to place trusted troops and guns in the Mutchi Bhown, in order to hold it as a place of refuge; and to divide his English force between the cantonments of Murriaon, where the Sepoys were mostly stationed, and the Residency position, where he desired the English families to assemble. The early morning of May 17th saw Sir Henry holding these three positions—the basis of the plans which he had already formed, and was now about to carry out for defence against any contingency that might arise.

CHAPTER IV

LAWRENCE'S POLICY ON THE OUTBREAK

THE long-threatening storm had now burst; confined however to one spot, instead of being widespread, much less universal, as it might have been. But it was unchecked, and had full scope to ravage and devastate as it might list; not a single step had the Government or the military authorities taken to meet it. Not even the chronic and obvious defects in the distribution of the troops and the security of the strongholds had been rectified. Except Fort William (in Calcutta), Agra was the only fortress which was garrisoned by English soldiers. Nowhere had any arrangement been made in the neighbourhood of British troops to have carriage available at hand to facilitate their movement. Yet in the marching season, which had only a few weeks before come to an end, both of these wants could have been remedied without trouble or excitement. It is needless to state more than these simple facts, or to dwell on the blunders or the studied neglect involved. But the result was that all the places of strength—Allahabad, the Cawnpore Magazine, Futtehgurh, Jhansi, and Delhi—were at the mercy of the mutinous army; and the Commander-in-Chief was unable to move forward on Delhi at once, or for many days, even a single regiment efficiently equipped to answer the challenge there given to the British rule.

Thus the outbreak there, although obviously immature, spasmodic, and destructive of any plans for concerted action that there may have been, was allowed to remain so long unopposed that the weakness of the British organization and power became too obvious; and the general mutiny, though deferred for three weeks, was eventually able to burst and spread unchecked in full power.

Nothing is more remarkable than the singular exactitude

with which Sir Henry had forecasted the Delhi catastrophe in his article written in 1843, which has been already alluded to. After commenting on the habitual carelessness of the Government, and its disregard of ordinary military precautions and preparedness, he had shown how possible it consequently was that a hostile party might seize Delhi, and if it was not speedily dealt with, what grave consequences might ensue. "Let this happen," he said, "on June 2nd, and does any sane man doubt that twenty-four hours would swell the hundreds of rebels into thousands, and in a week every ploughshare in the Delhi States would be turned into a sword? And when a sufficient force had been mustered, which would not be effected within a month, should we not then have a more difficult game to play than Clive had at Plassey or Wellington at Assaye? We should then be literally striking for our existence at the most inclement season of the year, with the prestige of our name tarnished." Going on then to suggest that Meerut and Umballa and Agra might say that they had no troops to spare from their own necessities, or that they had no carriage, "should we not then," he said, "have to strike anew for our Indian empire?"

With such convictions and forebodings working on his mind for fourteen years, and doubtless confirmed and intensified by what he saw of the growing disaffection, of the increasing imprudence of Government, and its haughty disregard of precautions, it can be readily imagined what Sir Henry's view of the position was when he heard of the catastrophe at Delhi. He knew that all the needful preparations had been neglected, that consequently the British troops could not move against Delhi for some weeks, and that all that the Government could now do was to summon and collect whatever forces they could manage to spare from elsewhere, and send them on eventually up-country from Calcutta. He knew that the whole of the north-west was in a state of anarchy; but he hoped that his old friends—"his children"—of the Punjab would remain loyal, although he was not without misgivings as to the possible effects of the colder and harder rule of his brother John. He hoped also that the Rajpootana States would keep quiet under the guidance of his brother George. But it is doubtful whether he realized until after another month how the self-assertion of the Moghul party, and the proclamation of the restoration of the Delhi empire, had disconcerted the leaders of the mutiny and of other sections of the revolt, and had upset their plans and unity of action, choking off the Mahratta and Rajpoot States from participation in the rising.

The steps which Sir Henry took at Lucknow immediately on receiving authentic news of the outbreak have been already mentioned. He occupied with all his British and other trustworthy troops the Residency position, the Mutchi Bhown, and the southern end of the cantonments of Murriaon. He had been pondering the matter with the greatest care and utmost anxiety for some weeks past, so as to be ready for the crisis whenever it might arise, and his conclusions and plans, which developed in the seizure of these three posts, will now be briefly stated. I give them on my own authority at first hand. Sir Henry communicated them to me personally on the early morning of May 17th, when he placed me in charge of the defensive arrangements of the Mutchi Bhown; I noted them then and there, and I need not say that they have remained ever since indelibly fixed on my memory.

We must prepare, he said, for defence against a powerful force equipped with artillery, which was almost certain to attack us sooner or later. For the site of this eventual defence he had decided on the Residency position; and he hoped to have its entrenchments sufficiently strong before being attacked in force.

In the meantime we must be ready for local outbreaks, and try to keep the city quiet and under control, as otherwise the needful preparations at the Residency could not be carried out. For this purpose, the Mutchi Bhown was to be made a place of refuge, and so strengthened as to be impregnable against an ordinary *émeute*, and as to dominate and overawe the city.

It was necessary lastly to hold the native troops in check, to separate them from the city, and to keep the country open so as to get in supplies. To this end, he would hold the southern end of the cantonments with British troops.

The work of which the urgency was the most immediately pressing, was that at the Mutchi Bhown. When that had been really brought into the state he desired, then —and not till then—he would breathe more freely, and go ahead fully with his preparations at the Residency. But the Mutchi Bhown, from its small size and dilapidated state, was not to be thought of as a suitable place for permanent defence and shelter, or as capable of standing or being made fit to stand the attack of artillery.

Such were the plans communicated to me confidentially by Sir Henry, and noted at once on May 17th. And there were other aims and ideas by which he was guided—"A resolute and bold attitude must be maintained; the domination of the position at Lucknow must be promptly secured; the safety of the English community must be ensured; the character and position of the ruling race must be maintained at all hazards."

There does not appear to be any authentic record of the reasons for which Sir Henry decided on the Residency as the position for the eventual struggle. But his wisdom in the choice has been impugned, notably by Lord Clyde and by Havelock. Lord Clyde, however, does not seem to have suggested what Sir Henry should have done. Also when he wrote, it was from Lucknow, while he was withdrawing the families, and was specially impressed by the one idea of the difficulty of that operation. Havelock gave his opinion definitely that Lawrence should have moved to Cawnpore; but when he wrote that opinion it was from Cawnpore, before he had realized at the Residency itself what the task and risk of such a movement would have been, with the families that had to be cared for. And it may be well to say a few words on the matter from the recollections of Lawrence's occasional remarks and conversations.

There is nothing on record to show that he had been empowered to quit Lucknow; but, assuming that he had a free hand in the matter, was such a step in the first place *possible?* To move his troops without removing the families was obviously not to be thought of. Putting aside the fact that there was no place at all accessible which afforded greater security than Lucknow itself, to move the families was practically impossible. After the local outbreak it could not have been attempted. If attempted before, it would have precipitated the crisis, and led to a catastrophe worse than the retreat from Cabul.

Supposing, however, that the families could have been removed or have found shelter somewhere and somehow or other, and the British force had been free to move, its retirement from Lucknow would have given the signal for revolt, and have so emboldened the enemy and added to their strength that we should never have succeeded in reaching and crossing the Ganges.

Again, supposing that these impossibilities had been possible, was such a step as retirement from Lucknow advisable? There is no doubt that Sir Henry thought it would have been fatal not only to the British in Oude, but to the British cause in India. The only mode or chance of surmounting the desperate crisis lay, he felt assured, in impressing and discouraging the enemy by showing an undaunted front, and everywhere nailing our colours to the mast.

Hence such a proposal as withdrawal to Cawnpore was never, I believe, even mooted; and Sir Henry resolved to hold on to Oude and its capital, and at the same time to do all that could be done to make the tenure of his position there possible and successful. Practically he found himself limited to the neighbourhood of Lucknow for the site of the position to be held and defended. For in choosing such a site, what were the essentials? Its situation and the features of the ground should make it readily capable of being made defensible against a powerful force equipped with artillery. It must be large enough to contain the families and the garrison, as well as all the live stock and the supplies they would need. It must contain a sufficient number of buildings to shelter the families. It should have an ample water supply and be fairly healthy. Its site should be under protection during the period of preparation, and be fairly accessible to a force advancing to its relief.

A glance at the map[1] of Lucknow is now necessary. As to the suburbs, open as it were to the country; north of the Goomtee there were no sites at all that would answer to any of the requirements; while south of it, Jellahabad, and the

[1] See Maps III. and V.

Alum Bagh, and any others that could be made defensible, were not large enough, did not contain a tithe of the shelter that was necessary, and were distant from proper means of protection.

Then, on coming more into the city, the palaces which were sufficiently large were not only weak against artillery attack except after very heavy preparation ; they were also too large and continuous ; the positions assigned for defence could not have been separated off sufficiently from the rest, and were not provided with suitable sites for batteries and protective works.

On the other hand, with the one drawback that the earthwork portion of the circle of entrenchment would have to be improvised, the Residency site seemed to possess in a fair degree every qualification that was required. It was sufficiently extensive, healthy, and well supplied with water. It had an ample amount of house accommodation and shelter. It commanded the river face and the adjacent ground for half its circle. Nowhere was it commanded by artillery sites, and the higher portions of the buildings in its immediate neighbourhood could be demolished, and so deprived of any command. The features along its trace allowed of good defensive sites and batteries. It was already one of the three posts that were being held in close connection with each other; and lastly, it would be readily accessible to relief by a force advancing through the comparatively open country on the north of the Goomtee.

Whether or not these are accepted as reasonable arguments in support of Sir Henry's selection of the Residency position, and whether or not he had still more cogent reasons for his choice, it does not appear to have ever been definitely stated or argued, or even suggested what other position or alternative measure should have been adopted in preference to it.

The posts that Sir Henry was thus about to hold, his measures respecting them, and the positions and localities that are connected with the defence, will be more easily understood if a descriptive sketch be first given of the city of Lucknow and its prominent features.

As shown in the sketch map, No. III., Lucknow is a city about five and a half miles long and two and a half broad, lying mainly along the southern (or right) bank of the Goomtee, and encircled on its other three sides by a large and deep canal. The western half is a dense city, and so is the southern portion of the eastern half; but its north-eastern quarter consists more of palatial and villa residences, enclosed gardens, and great mausoleums and tombs. An old stone bridge spans the Goomtee at the separating point of the eastern and western halves, and a new iron bridge crosses it about a mile lower down, *i. e.* eastwards. Roads from the two bridges communicate with the cantonments of Murriaon about two miles to the north, and the road southwards to Cawnpore starts from the iron bridge, skirts the Residency position, and crosses the canal at the Char Bagh. The Mutchi Bhown and the Residency position lie close to the river, on its north bank, immediately to the east of the stone bridge and of the iron bridge respectively.

So that the three posts held by Sir Henry were in direct and easy communication with each other; commanded the two great passages of the river; and interposed between the cantonment and the city. The outlines of the Mutchi Bhown and the Residency entrenchments, marked on this map, show what petty spots they formed in that huge and hostile city. But at the Residency Sir Henry hoped to hold additional ground and outposts down to the river's edge and to the iron bridge. And when the relieving force, under Havelock and Outram, arrived, the position was extended eastwards along the river face, and included the whole group of absolutely continuous buildings there, bordering the street, by which they had advanced to the relief.

CHAPTER V

MEASURES BEFORE THE MUTINY AT LUCKNOW

SIR HENRY'S plan, then, on the occurrence of the Meerut and Delhi outbreak, was to hold the Residency position, the cantonments of Murriaon, and the Mutchi Bhown, and to prepare the Residency position for the eventual defence against a powerful force; the key to his plan being to prepare and fortify the Mutchi Bhown so promptly and so strongly that it should dominate and overawe the city; keeping it quiet, and being at the same time available as a temporary place of refuge in case of need.

The prominent feature of the Mutchi Bhown was an old massive-looking pile, of castellated appearance, about a hundred yards square, perched on a natural eminence about thirty feet above the adjacent streets and roads. The platform on which it was built was scarped and supported by stout revetment walls, broken at short intervals into the usual Oriental semi-circular bastions, with the city or western front pierced by a gateway in a double-storied guard-house, strengthened by flanking and other defences. All this was close to the masonry bridge and the river, and commanded the city to the west. Towards the east there were two courtyards at lower levels, lined with small buildings and store-rooms, with a gateway at the east end corresponding with the gateway already mentioned at the western face. There were large and airy arcaded halls along one side of the pile, but the remaining rooms were not suitable for use except by natives or for stores. Though much had been cleared out, the whole place was greatly dilapidated, but its chief defect lay in the passages and communications. These and the doorways were so narrow that carts and guns could not pass through the square pile at all, or get from one end of the position to the other.

All the roofs were flat, and, like the terraces, were lined with parapet walls.

Sir Henry, accompanied by his chief engineer, Major Anderson, gave the detailed as well as the general orders and instructions to bring the position into the state which he desired. The first orders were given on May 17th, and by the 23rd the work had been carried out to his satisfaction. The city and the cantonments had kept quiet, and he breathed more freely.

What had been done was this: the several halls and rooms had been cleared out, cleaned, repaired, and made habitable. One of the buildings had been prepared and fitted up as a powder magazine. The gateways, doors, passages, and stairs had been repaired and improved, and the successive plateaux connected by ramps, for the passage of guns and carts. The walls had been loop-holed, and the parapets heightened and made defensible. Breastworks, platforms for guns, and flanking defences, had been constructed. Six companies of Sikhs and other selected native troops, and one company of the 32nd, besides a complete field battery, were holding the post. Seven eighteen-pounder guns, eight nine-pounders, and eight eight-inch mortars were in position; and some two hundred wall-pieces and small-bore guns (most of them absolutely worthless) had been ransacked out of the old arsenal and ranged along the higher parapets, appearing very conspicuously to threaten the adjacent roads and approaches. Native rumour had it that the Mutchi Bhown was armed with three hundred guns! The Mutchi Bhown fort, as it was now called, had in fact become proof against any attack from the city, and ready to shelter the English families in case of an outbreak, besides having further assumed so powerful and threatening an appearance that the city was overawed, and never once attempted seriously to rise or disturb the peace till the siege began.

During these six days, nothing was done or had occurred at the cantonments, where no works of any kind were even attempted. At the Residency, operations were for the time confined to defining the trace of the position to be held, and erecting a continuous boundary of defence along that trace, by blocking up all the streets and lanes, when they crossed it, except at the points reserved for passage. But the several buildings were also barricaded and loopholed, in readiness for any immediate emergency.

After May 23rd, local security having been obtained through the Mutchi Bhown, the progress of the Residency entrenchments, which were energetically pushed on, became the absorbing centre of interest. Batteries and defensive works were begun; the parapets and breastworks along the outline of the position were steadily enlarged. The system of work adopted was to strengthen the whole position at an equable rate, so as to leave no gaps or unduly weak points in the circle of defence. Meanwhile the buildings and rooms set aside for stores and supplies were being cleared out and filled with the food and other requirements for the impending crisis.

It must be understood that this was not a case in which a theoretically good trace could be adopted, and the works constructed so as to adapt the existing outlines of the position to that trace. For there was no knowing when the position might not be attacked, and the weak gaps in the line of defence, which would necessarily have been left during such adaptations, could not be allowed. The principle adopted was to have a clear line of defence from the outset, weak, of course, at first, but daily gaining in strength, though never so strong and effective as if time had been certainly available to admit of the adoption of a better outline.

At the Mutchi Bhown work was for the time restricted to the storage of supplies, and to the simple improvement of the defences and of the shelter for the garrison. Here too were lodged six men who had been made State prisoners as a further matter of precaution.

At the cantonments nothing special was done, except that the Sikh cavalry were employed in keeping the roads open to the country, from which food and other supplies came pouring in in a most cheering manner.

Meanwhile the districts kept almost everywhere perfectly quiet, as well as the city itself, nor had the mutinies spread at all; but still the challenge of the mutineers at Delhi had not, to all appearances, been taken up by the English army, and Sir Henry well knew what must ensue. Had he not foretold it?

Sir Henry took some further significant steps, in addition to those of the local defences, when after May 23rd, the state of the Mutchi Bhown had relieved him of his more acute anxieties. One of the first was to separate the Sikhs from the other Sepoys. Then, in order to increase the native force on which he could rely, he summoned in from their homes two bodies of pensioners; one of old trained British Sepoys and one of Oude artillery men. Both these companies of auxiliaries gave staunch and loyal assistance throughout the siege. At this and at every stage of his preparations Sir Henry remained firm to his opinion and his policy, of the necessity and the practicability of retaining for the British the loyal support of a sufficiently numerous and valuable section of the native soldiery; to which end it was needful not only to seek out for this active help, but also to avoid the broadcast disarmament which, though strongly urged on him, would have swept away the friendly as well as the hostile Sepoys.

Further, he sent out detachments of troops, chiefly cavalry, into the country to keep it open. One of these detachments, under Captain Weston, was directed to the Mahomedan town of Mulhiabad, which had shown exceptional tendency to disturbance. Another under Captain Gall, with two guns under Lieutenant Ashe, was sent towards Cawnpore. This had been already preceded, in that direction, on May 21st, by a party under Captain Fletcher Hayes. A wing of Harding's regiment of Sikh cavalry was despatched towards Allahabad; while a fifth body of regular cavalry and infantry was sent along the road to Futtehgurh.

While all this was going on, and a bold and vigorous attitude was being maintained, there were daily and ever-increasing rumours of a coming outbreak of the troops at Murriaon, keeping the British force intensely on the alert. At length, on May 30th, a week after the Mutchi Bhown had made the position locally secure, the mutinous Sepoys broke out at evening gun-fire from their lines, and scattered over the cantonments; searching out, gutting, and firing the officers' houses, and sending musket-shots in the direction of the English camp, where the 32nd were drawn up with some artillery ready for action. At the main picket they killed the officer in charge of it, and one of their stray shots killed Brigadier Handscombe.

The loyal men of the 13th N. I. and the 71st N. I. marched from their lines to the English camp and formed up on the flank of the 32nd, while another detachment of the 13th staunchly held the cantonment Government House, occupied by Sir Henry, who had moved over there from the Residency; and he at once took part of his force to the road leading to the city, so blocking it entirely against any attempt of the mutineers to move in that direction. After which Captain Hardinge with his irregular cavalry patrolled the main streets of the cantonment to save officers and disperse the mutineers.

During the night no further conflict occurred, but next morning the mutinous Sepoys, who were seen drawn up in front of their lines, were forthwith attacked. They immediately broke and fled, and were pursued some ten miles into the country. After this the 32nd, with the faithful men of the 13th and 71st N. I. and Hardinge's cavalry, returned to Murriaon; where they remained encamped for the present, so as to maintain the communications with the country, and keep the neighbouring districts quiet. Not without a struggle, however, for the next day a large party of the bad characters of the city endeavoured to cross the river and advance to Murriaon, with the hope of joining and acting in concert with the mutineers. However they were promptly met by the city police, driven back, and dispersed. No movement whatever was made against the Residency or the Mutchi Bhown, and the local regiment at the Dowlut Khana and the Moosa Bagh in the city remained quiet and faithful.

Thus began with Lucknow, on May 30th, the spread of the mutiny over Upper India; after an interval of nearly three weeks of lull since the outbreak at Meerut and Delhi. The only other rising before this had been at the remote station of Nusseerabad, on the western side of India.

CHAPTER VI

THE MUTINIES AT THE OUT-STATIONS

ALMOST simultaneous with the rising at Lucknow were similar risings in or near Oude. On the following day, May 31st, Bareilly and Shahjehanpore mutinied in the adjacent province of Rohilkund on the western border of Oude. Then on June 3rd and the three following days, the stations in the districts on the other side of Oude, that is to its east and south, followed the example—Azimgurh on the 3rd, Benares on the 4th, Jaunpore and Cawnpore on the 5th, and Allahabad on the 6th.

The stations in Oude itself did not break out till stations on both sides of them had risen. The troops at Seetapore, between Lucknow and Rohilkund, mutinied on June 3rd; those at Fyzabad and Durriabad on the 8th; those at Sultanpore and Salone on the 9th, and those at Baraitch and Secrora on the 10th.

The first and, in many respects, the most important and the most singular of the risings at the out-stations was that of Seetapore. The troops there were at first moved towards Lucknow to meet and attack its fugitive mutineers; but as the latter had turned towards the Ganges, the Seetapore party returned to its own station, and then heard of the outbreak at Shahjehanpore. On the 3rd, the regiments there which had in reality been very gravely infected, threw off the mask. One faithful party of the 41st N. I. collected some of their officers and others, and escorted them into Lucknow. But many of the English residents, including ladies and children, were at once shot down; while the rest scattered in flight in several separate parties. One of them, which included Mrs. Dorin, was sheltered and aided into Lucknow by villagers. Another party, led by Sir M. Jackson, and containing some ladies and children, found temporary but grudging shelter with the Rajah of

Mitholee, where some families from elsewhere had already joined. A third party, which also contained two ladies, moved towards Mullapore, and meeting a party of fugitives from Shahjehanpore, turned with them towards Dhowrera, where the chief's family sheltered them for awhile. So that, of the residents of Seetapore, some were shot down by the mutineers; two parties escaped into Lucknow aided, the one by Sepoys, the other by villagers; and two other parties received shelter, though in a half-hearted fashion, from the Talookdars of Mitholee and Dhowrera. It may be added, that more parties from Rohilkund and from the smaller out-stations in the neighbourhood were met and destroyed by the Seetapore mutineers.

The next rising in Oude was at Fyzabad, on June 8th. The Sepoys there, on the approach of the mutineers from Azimgurh and Benares, formally threw off their allegiance; but they did not molest the English residents at all, and indeed helped their officers to escape. The English community separated into two parties. One, which consisted of the civil officers and their families, turned for protection to Rajah Maun Singh, the notorious ex-Amil. He was able to shelter them for awhile in his fort of Shahgunge, but feeling that there was no real security there, he despatched them in boats down the Gogra. After many adventures and escapes, they found protection from various Talookdars, especially those of Birhur and Gopalpore, and eventually reached Dinapore in safety.

The other half of the Fyzabad community, chiefly military officers, formed into three parties. One made for Gopalpore, where they found shelter, and were passed on to Dinapore; another reached Goruckpore in safety; but the third was surrounded by the mutineers from Azimgurh, and destroyed.

Simultaneous with the Fyzabad rising was that at the small station of Durriabad, where, however, a detachment of Sikh cavalry remained loyal, and escorted the residents into Lucknow.

Most of the mutineers from Azimgurh, Jaunpore, and Benares had, as above described, moved on Fyzabad and spread the contagion there; one party of them, however, marched instead towards Sultanpore, on the Goomtee, on the direct road to Lucknow. It was the one out-station, besides Seetapore and Fyzabad, where there were any of the old Bengal troops. The Bengal regiment there was the 15th Irregular Cavalry, a gallant but very bigoted set of Mussulmans, who proved foremost in all the future operations, not only in actual fighting, but in furnishing leaders to the mutineer army. Fisher, their colonel, was an exceptionally popular and energetic officer, but he was at once shot down, though not by his own men. Other officers fell similarly under the fire of the Sepoys, but a few escaped, to find protection and escort into safety from Roostum Sah, the chief of Deyrah. Colonel Fisher had, some days before, sent off the ladies and families to the protection of the Rajah of Ameythee, who loyally sheltered them till he was able to escort them to Allahabad.

On the day after the Sultanpore mutiny, the regiment at Salone, to its south, threw off its allegiance; without, however, committing any atrocities. All the residents of Salone and of Roy Bareilly were protected and eventually escorted into safety by Hunwunt Singh, the brave old Rajah of Dharoopore, and by various chiefs of the great Bys clan.

There remain the risings to the north of Fyzabad, at Baraitch, Gonda, and Secrora, on the 10th and 11th. From all these stations the residents escaped. A few trying to reach Lucknow were met on the Gogra and shot down by the mutineers from Azimgurh. The rest found protection with the Rajah of Bulrampore until they were able to reach Gurruckpore in safety. At Secrora one artillery officer, Lieutenant Bonham, remained behind with his battery endeavouring to keep it loyal. But it was coerced by the other troops; though his men provided him with horses and money, and a party of them escorted him into Lucknow, where they remained with him throughout the siege.

It may be observed that the conduct of the native troops on rising ranged widely—from the atrocities of the Sepoys at Seetapore, and the shooting of their officers at Sultanpore, to assisting and escorting them at Seetapore, Durriabad, Fyzabad, and Secrora.

The villagers on the Gogra were hostile, but elsewhere they seem to have been more or less helpful; a singular circumstance when it is remembered to what turbulence and bloodshed and evil deeds they had long been accustomed.

As to the chiefs, one, the Rajah of Pudnaha, refused all assistance to the fugitives from Baraitch; two, the Rajah of Mitholee and the Dhowrera family, gave but rough and grudging shelter to the English families from Seetapore; while in bright contrast to them stand the Rajahs of Bulrampore, of Birhur, and Gopalpore; Roostum Sah of Deyrah and Hunwunt Singh of Dharoopore; with the chiefs of Amethee and of the Byswara clans; besides many others, who helped into security the fugitives from Gonda and Secrora, from Fyzabad and Sultanpore, from Salone and Roy Bareilly.

Before leaving this subject, it may be noted, that besides the Oude fugitives themselves, refugees from the adjacent provinces found shelter in Oude, one of the most prominent cases being the kindness and protection given by Rajah Hurdeo Buksh to Mr. Edwardes and his friends. Again, the small party that escaped with Captain Mowbray Thomson from the massacre at Cawnpore, were sheltered by the burly old chief of Morarmow, the head of the great Bys clan, after having been first rescued from the clutches of the one malignant Talookdar in that neighbourhood, Baboo Ram Buksh, the detested chief of Doondea Khera.

Nor will it be out of place to point out here, that the two nobles of Oude, who stand prominently marked out in contrast with all the rest in passive or active hostility and misconduct to English fugitives, were the Rajahs of Mitholee and Doondea Khera; and that both of them had been equally in contrast to other Rajpoot chiefs, in former days, in their treachery and disloyalty to their own race. The Mitholee Rajah had swept away his relations, and made interest at the Lucknow court to obtain the succession to the headship and estates of his clan; while Baboo Ram Buksh was at feud with all the other Byswara chiefs from having intrigued with the hostile Amils against them and against the common weal.

Such were the characteristics of the outbreaks in Oude itself. But as the troops that mutinied in the adjacent districts on the east and south took part in the operations of this theatre, the incidents at those stations also may be here described.

The first station to rise was Azimgurh. This step was prompted by the projected removal of a large sum from the Treasury to Benares. The 17th N. I., which garrisoned the station, rose, seized the treasure, and moved off with it towards Oude.

On the next day, June 4th, the Sepoys mutinied at Benares (as fully described in the story of Neill's advance at page 183), and then marched for Fyzabad, being joined by the Jaunpore regiment on the way.

On the following day, June 5th, came the mutiny at Cawnpore. The regiments there made no immediate move agâinst their officers or the residents, but started off for Delhi. The Nana, however, who had heretofore played the *rôle* of a friend to the English, sent his emissaries after them, and enticed them back to attack and destroy the families and the small detachment of British troops; which had now betaken themselves to the hastily got up position that Sir Hugh Wheler had called his entrenchments, but where no adequate preparations had been made for defence, for shelter, or for food.

Then on June 6th, the Allahabad troops mutinied; all except the Sikh regiment that garrisoned the fortress itself. Whilst the regular native infantry were rising and shooting their officers, the Sikhs, held coolly in hand by their Commandant, Captain Brasper, who had singular control over them, kept the fort for the Government till relieved and supported in a few days by the advanced detachments of Neill's party.

One other station must be mentioned, Futtehgurh, a fortress at the south-west corner of Oude on the Ganges. It did not revolt till June 18th, and its small English garrison was not attacked till the 27th.

Now, of all the several regiments that mutinied in or near Oude, those in Rohilkund went to Delhi: some of those from Lucknow and west of it were also thought to have gone to Delhi; but most of them, it is believed, really lingered in Oude, and eventually joined the force that concentrated from the east to besiege Lucknow. The Cawnpore troops remained to besiege Cawnpore, and afterwards to oppose Havelock's advance. They were joined by one regiment from the eastwards, the 17th N. I. from Azimgurh. It had, as above described, mutinied to secure the local treasure, but the mutineers from Benares and Jaunpore, and at Fyzabad, coerced them and made them give up the bulk of their booty. So the 17th, in high dudgeon and greatly embittered, moved off by themselves towards Cawnpore, attacking all fugitive parties that they met on their way.

All the other mutineers of Oude, and from the districts to the east, kept hovering in the eastern districts of Oude, preparing for an eventual concentration and advance on Lucknow.

On looking back a few pages it will be seen that, while the fate of all the other groups that had escaped from the out-stations has been described, two from Seetapore have been left, finding more or less shelter with the Dhowrera family, and in the Mitholee Rajah's country respectively. Their story may be fitly told here, though as regards time, it will be anticipating the course of events.

The party at Dhowrera consisted of eleven persons, of whom three were ladies. They remained there, fairly well sheltered, for two months, when a detachment of troops from the rebel court arrived under the command of Bunda Hussun. The Dhowrera retainers joined this body and marched for Lucknow, taking the party of English refugees with them. Being apprised by friends of their danger, the party of English escaped and fled on the third night. The men gradually found their way into safety through Nepaul, but the three ladies were on an elephant, and in the darkness of the night they got separated from the rest, were pursued, re-taken, and were carried captive into Lucknow; where they met with a cruel death on the day of Havelock's arrival at the suburbs.

The other, the Mitholee party, which included, besides others, Sir Mountstuart Jackson, Captains Orr and Burnes, two ladies and two children, remained in the Mitholee jungles up to October 20th, suffering great privations. The Rajah was all along half-hearted about them, and never attempted to show them any kindness or civility. And when the Lucknow Durbar sent a body of troops to make prisoners of them and carry them off, he put no impediment in their way, though Captain Orr, by the stories he spread of the desperate resistance they would encounter, actually managed to scare them and cause them to return —*re infecta*—to Lucknow. At length, however, an arch-villain named Zuhoor-ool-Hussun appeared on the scene, as an emissary from the Durbar, and persuaded Lonee Singh (the Mitholee Rajah) that the English in India were at their last gasp. So, with the help of three hundred of his retainers, the little band of refugees were made prisoners on October 20th, and carried off to Lucknow, the officers in fetters. There they remained in miserable plight till November 16th, when, on the arrival of Sir Colin Campbell to the relief, the men of the party were taken out and shot. The ladies and children then found concealment and shelter, through the instrumentality chiefly of Darogah Wajid Ali, assisted by Rajah Maun Singh and others, until the following March; when, on Sir Colin's attacking and capturing Lucknow, some of his troops were guided to their place of shelter. Thus their lives were saved after some ten months of deadly peril and unspeakable misery.

CHAPTER VII

LUCKNOW FROM THE MUTINY TO CHINHUT

THE rising at Lucknow, followed as it was by the flight of the regiments that had mutinied, tended to reduce greatly the strain of anxiety in respect of local troubles. The most powerful of the hostile elements on the spot had disappeared. Sir Henry felt that he now had full control of the local situation, and he pushed on apace the work at the entrenchments. The work at the Mutchi Bhown was now only of secondary importance, and lay mainly in the receipt and storage of supplies, and their despatch to the Residency whenever room for them was ready. Meanwhile the roads to the districts remained open, and supplies came in freely. A detachment also of fifty men of the 84th, under Captain O'Brien, arrived on June 2nd from Cawnpore, sent on by General Wheler, as if not wanted there.

In a few days, however, from June 3rd onward, the news began to arrive of the successive mutinies at Seetapore and elsewhere, and of the disastrous fate of Hayes and other officers who, as already described, had been sent out with detachments of troops to keep the country open. And then at length came the intelligence of the siege of the Cawnpore entrenchments.

At Lucknow itself, the rising had been followed on May 31st by an attempt of a body of conspirators in the city to join the mutineers. These had been met, crushed, and dispersed. Many of the prisoners taken in the mutiny, and convicted of murder or of treason, were hanged or otherwise dealt with; after which no further serious disturbance occurred in the city, while the safe arrival of successive parties of refugees from Seetapore, Durriabad, and elsewhere, seemed somewhat to mitigate the gloom that was settling down.

All this work and anxiety, however, told so severely on Sir Henry's health, already much enfeebled, that, under medical orders, he gave over temporary charge of his duties, on June 9th, to a council, with Mr. Gubbins at its head. But only for two days! He then heard that his policy in regard to the retention of native troops was being over-ruled and set aside; so on the 11th he resumed his command, in time to recall many that had been sent away; although not in time to prevent the excitement which the proceedings had created, leading to an outbreak in the military police.

By this date, June 11th, Sir Henry knew that all the troops in the out-stations of Oude had risen; but he had no means of judging as yet what further steps those troops would take; whether they would move on Delhi or attack Lucknow. He had found the Lucknow mutineers neither able nor inclined to face British soldiers; his own force had been strengthened by the return of the company of the 32nd, which he had sent over in the month of May to reinforce Sir Hugh Wheler at Cawnpore, as well as by the additional detachment of fifty men of the 84th, which, as already mentioned, Sir Hugh had sent on to him. For three precious weeks Lawrence had been pushing on the defences and other preparations of the Residency entrenchments, without their being molested. He felt satisfied of the support of an adequate body of native troops, and he was hopeful that his only contest would be with the Sepoys and not with the people of the province, so good had been most of the reports dealing with the conduct of the Talookdars and the villagers. He had therefore arrived at the conclusion that there was no longer any serious danger from the city, or any need for a place of refuge. At the same time he felt that, while the Mutchi Bhown and the cantonment posts must still be retained to keep the city and the roads under control, the preparation of the Residency position for its final purpose must continue to be vigorously pressed on, so as to have it ready to meet the extreme emergency effectively whenever it might arise. It was at this juncture, therefore, when possibly he might soon be too unwell to retain the command, that he definitely announced his military policy to

Brigadier Inglis in his letter of June 11th; a policy, it will be seen, in strict accordance with what he had laid down on May 17th, about the Mutchi Bhown, but now become more precise and emphasized by the development of events.

"I am decidedly of opinion," he said, "that we ought to have only one position, and that though we must hold all three (cantonments and Mutchi Bhown) as long as we can, all arrangements should be made with reference to a sudden concentration at the Residency." The treasure, the food, the mortars, the eighteen-pounder guns, the powder and ammunition—in short, "all the munitions and stores should be got into the Residency, and the nine-pounder field-battery with a few old guns be left to accompany the troops at the last moment. The withdrawal will not be easy at any time, so the less there is left to bring away at the last moment the better."

It has been shown that ever since the Mutchi Bhown was found to be ready on May 23rd, to fulfil its task of overawing the city, the preparations of the Residency entrenchments had been pressed forward as the most essential and urgent work in hand. It has also been explained that those preparations were carried on in an equable manner, so as not to allow of gaps or exceptionally weak points in the defences, and thus the line of defence had been gradually growing in strength. But it was not until towards the middle of June that the projected development of the defences began to be really seen; when the gabions, fascines, sandbags, and other appliances for parapets and gun emplacements, were placed in position, and the batteries and other works assumed shape. These batteries and other details will be more suitably described in dealing with their condition at the beginning of the siege. Here it is sufficient to say that the full time and attention of all the engineer officers and their assistants, with the exception of the one engineer at the Mutchi Bhown, were strenuously devoted to the development of the defences, and the requirements of the Residency entrenchments. These included their fitness to check the attack of such an enemy as the Sepoy was likely to prove; their adaptability for such extension or curtailment as might be found necessary or expedient; and the collection and distribution of impediments—such as palisades, *chevaux de frise*, crows'-feet, and the like, which, on the defences and ditches being completed, were to be fixed or laid down along their front.

The events at Cawnpore and elsewhere were necessarily agitating Sir Henry's mind greatly; but he came unavoidably to the conclusion that assistance to Cawnpore from Lucknow with a huge river lying between, was out of the question. There was a feeble chance that a sufficient force from Allahabad might advance and create a diversion; but, after all, such information as was received of the British troops on their way up, showed them to be in mere petty detachments, of no adequate strength for any real struggle.

And, worst of all, there was no intelligence of any assertion of the English army at Delhi. Realizing as Sir Henry did that it was there that the site of the vital struggle lay, his heart sank with dismay at the blank news from that quarter. On the other hand, there was some comfort in the conviction that the enemy there were not receiving any support from the districts so far south as Oude. The quarter of a million of treasure that was stored in the Residency might turn the fate of the Empire, if it would serve as a bait to the hosts that were still hovering in the province, and keep them back from swelling the hostile ranks at Delhi.

The districts were meanwhile remaining quiet; food was pouring in from the country; the Talookdars were either playing a friendly part or giving no trouble. Supplies were being received from the most unexpected quarters, such as the Mohunts of the Hunnooman Gurhee, and the family of the Bhow Begum.

And then as the Lucknow entrenchments began to develope, as the meagre garrison at Cawnpore contrived to hold the enemy at bay, as the English reinforcements kept creeping on up-country, and as the mutineer regiments kept holding aloof from any real concentration against Lucknow, Sir Henry began to hope that he might have an easier time before him than he had hitherto anticipated.

But a serious misfortune had occurred in the appearance of cholera about June 12th. It gradually spread, and played havoc among English and natives alike, causing the loss of many most valuable lives. Still Sir Henry never relaxed in his vigour in new directions as well as old ones.

About June 18th, some fresh steps for the furthering of the coming defence were taken. At the Redan and other sites, breastworks were enlarged into batteries; officers and men and volunteers were trained to artillery work. The troops and inmates of the Residency were told off to their future posts. The surplus guns and mortars at the Mutchi Bhown were gradually transferred to the Residency. And, in accordance with his suggestions to Brigadier Inglis a week before, arrangements were contemplated and discussed, though they never appear to have taken any practical shape, for holding extended positions, on the first advent of the enemy, and avoiding concentration within the actual entrenchment, so long as the foe could be held at bay.

The development of the Redan Battery, of Innes's post and of the Post-office Battery, all on commanding ground, held out hopes of such power over the river-face as to admit of the occupation of the Captan Bazar, and of the control, in combination with the Mutchi Bhown, of the passage of the iron bridge, especially in the event of the enemy proving half-hearted and wanting in enterprise.

On June 23rd came rumours, which soon proved to be false (although supplemented by letters on the 26th), of the capture of Delhi by a British force; and on that day Sir Henry ordered the construction of two batteries, which had been already lined out, at the Mutchi Bhown, on an elevated site, to command the neighbouring buildings more effectively, as well as the stone bridge and the opposite bank of the river. "The enemy," he said, "were showing such singular backwardness both as to facing the handful of English at Cawnpore, and as to making any move against Lucknow, that he thought it might be worth while, if only it deferred the evil day of *close* investment, to put on every appearance that could be suggested of our determination to make a vigorous and forward defence."

Time he knew to be still all-important, although in fact, at this particular juncture, a week before our actual defence began, there had arisen a certain degree of vigorous re-animation, of recovery so to speak from the gloom produced by the news that had daily been reaching us of disasters. It was obvious that complete success was attending Sir Henry's plans. The defences were close on full development. The very swarms of workmen at the Residency and at the new batteries of the Mutchi Bhown were enlivening and exhilarating. So were the continuous strings of carts and elephants bringing in supplies; so also the stories that were current of the bold defence at Cawnpore; the advance of reinforcements at Allahabad; the friendly attitude of the Talookdars; the rumours of success at Delhi; the halting movements of the enemy, and so forth. Still more so was the sudden discovery, at an old arsenal in the city, of a large store of heavy guns, which were forthwith transferred to the Residency, and placed in position or parked. One of the pieces, an eight-inch howitzer, was handed over to the artillery to be equipped for work in the field. One important feature of the work during the last fortnight was the demolition—down to the lower, but not of the actual lowest stories—of such buildings as skirted the outside of the position. The reason for leaving the lower stories undemolished, but only in ruins, was that they were expected to form a barrier against the impact of any artillery fire that might be aimed low at the defences in order to breach them. It will be seen that this object was fulfilled, but that, on the other hand, the ruins gave the enemy excellent starting ground for their mining operations.

On the 27th came the last piece of good news. Troops were about to push forward from Allahabad, and might reach Cawnpore in eight or ten days. This was immediately communicated through our spies to Sir Hugh Wheler. But, alas! too late. He had come to terms with the Nana—terms of which the meaning and the sequel are but too well known. Of course the intelligence of this surrender at Cawnpore spread like wildfire through the province, and altered the whole aspect of affairs. It at once roused to action the regiments that had been hovering on the north-east beyond Nuwabgunge; and on the 28th and 29th, first of all rumours, and then authentic intelligence, reached Sir Henry of the concentration of the enemy at Nuwabgunge, and of their sending on an advanced force to Chinhut. On the evening of the 29th, the troops in cantonment were drawn in and divided between the Mutchi Bhown and the cantonment. And next morning saw the beginning of the siege in the fight at Chinhut.

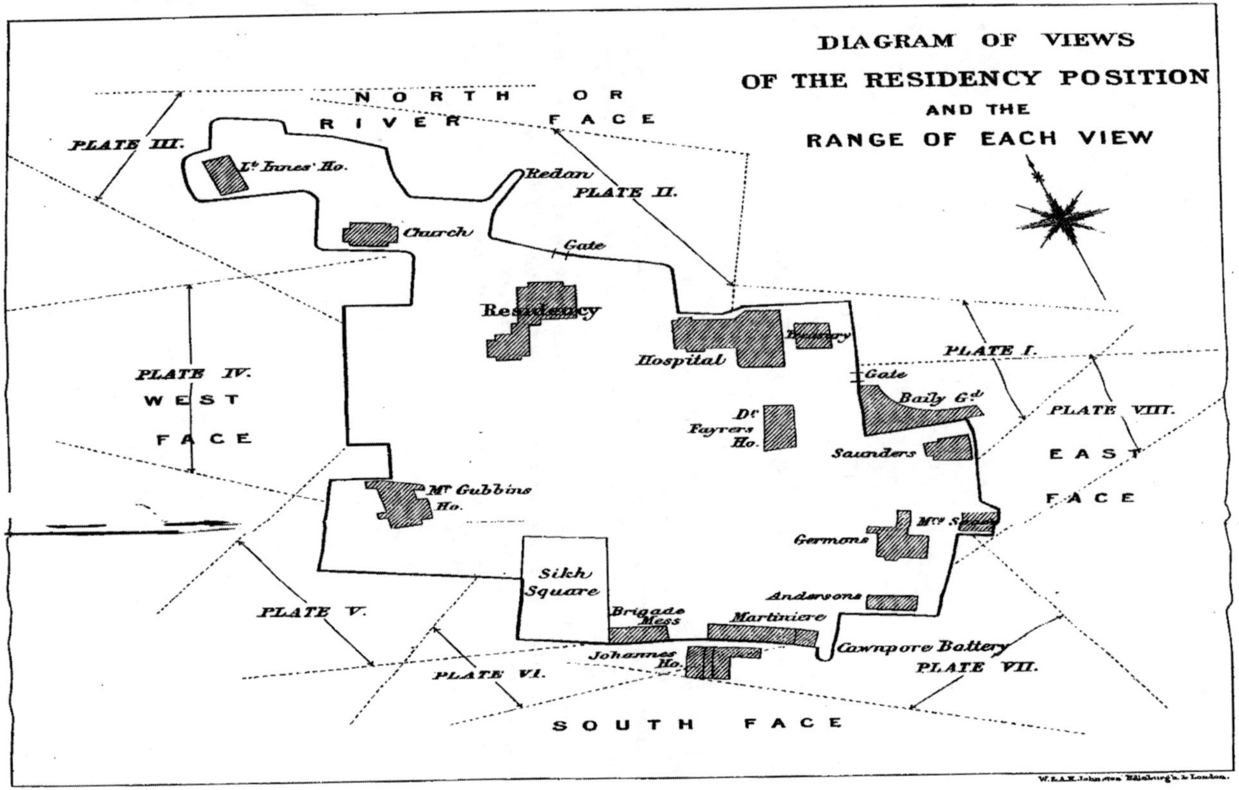

W. & A. K. Johnston Edinburgh & London.

Plate I.

Hospital or East Angle.

[*This is the first of a series of Eight Views of the Lucknow Residency Position, looking into it from the outside. They are meant to be panoramic, circling round from left to right, beginning and ending at the Baily Guard Gate, and each view being connected with the one preceding it and the one that follows it.*

In the Key Sketch which faces each view, the names are entered of the more important buildings and points, and a thick black line shows the boundary separating the besieged from the besiegers.

On the diagram which faces this page is shown the position of the circuit included in each of the eight views.]

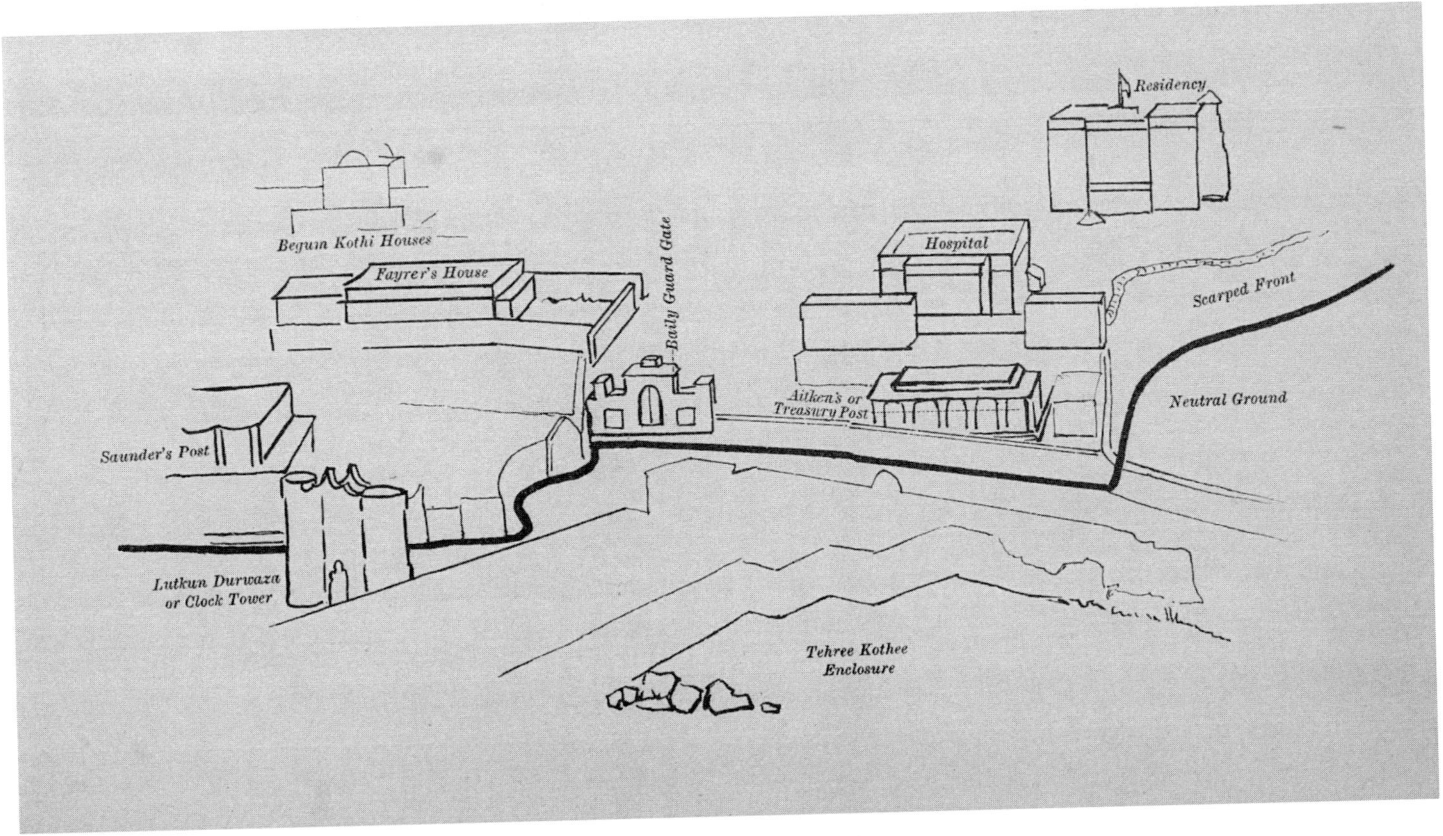
Residency
Begum Kothi Houses
Hospital
Fayrer's House
Baily Guard Gate
Scarped Front
Aitken's or
Treasury Post
Neutral Ground
Saunder's Post
Lutkun Durwaza
or Clock Tower
Tehree Kothee
Enclosure

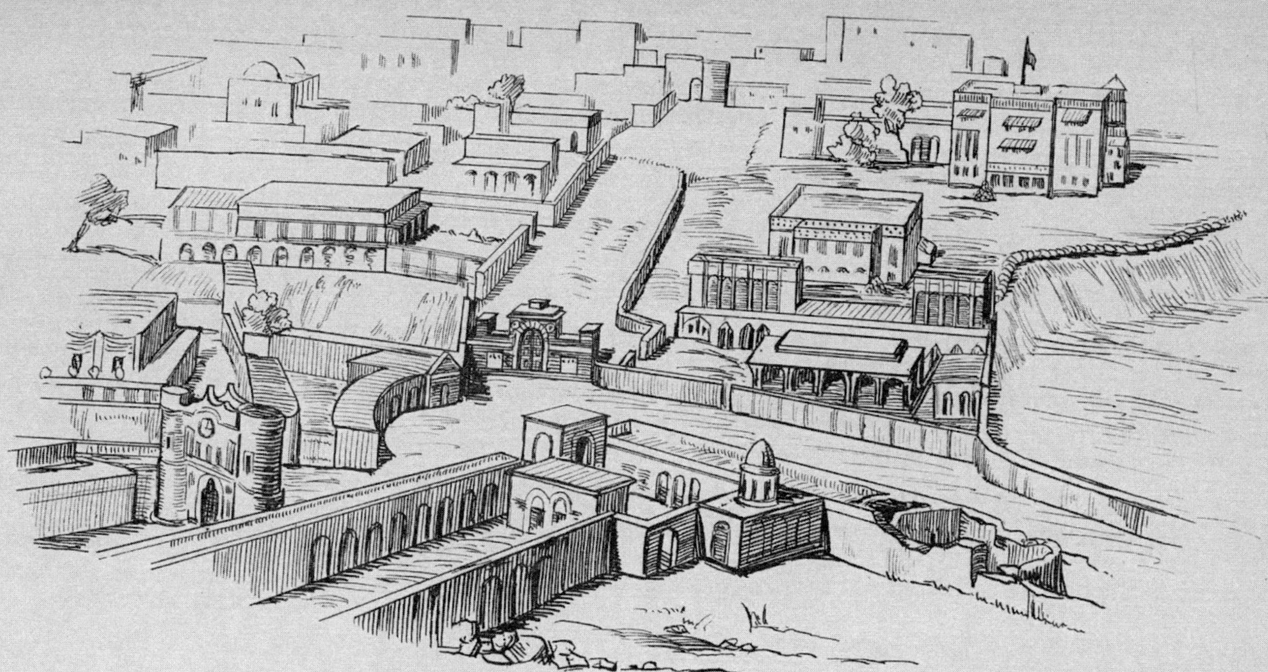

PLATE I.—HOSPITAL OR EAST ANGLE.

NOTE ON PLATE I.

This shows the Eastern Angle, or the north half of the East Front.

The front posts of the position are Saunders' on the left; the Baily Guard Gate; and the Treasury or Aitken's on the Right. Behind Saunders' is Dr Fayrer's; behind the Treasury is the Hospital; behind it again on the right is the Residency.

The Lutkun Durwaza, low on the left, is in one of the streets by which the Relieving Force arrived. The enemy made a battery there, to destroy the Baily Guard Gate, on the 5th September; but our Sepoys at the Treasury Post, after a very short duel, silenced it by a counter battery which they had made.

Saunders' Post was the scene of four successive mining attacks preparatory to the 5th September.

Fayrer's was the only building on this Front in which families were sheltered. It was Outram's Head-quarters, and it was there that Sir Henry Lawrence died.

This and the next Plate show the only scarped and commanding part of the trace of the Entrenchments.

PLATE II.

RIVER OF REDAN FRONT.

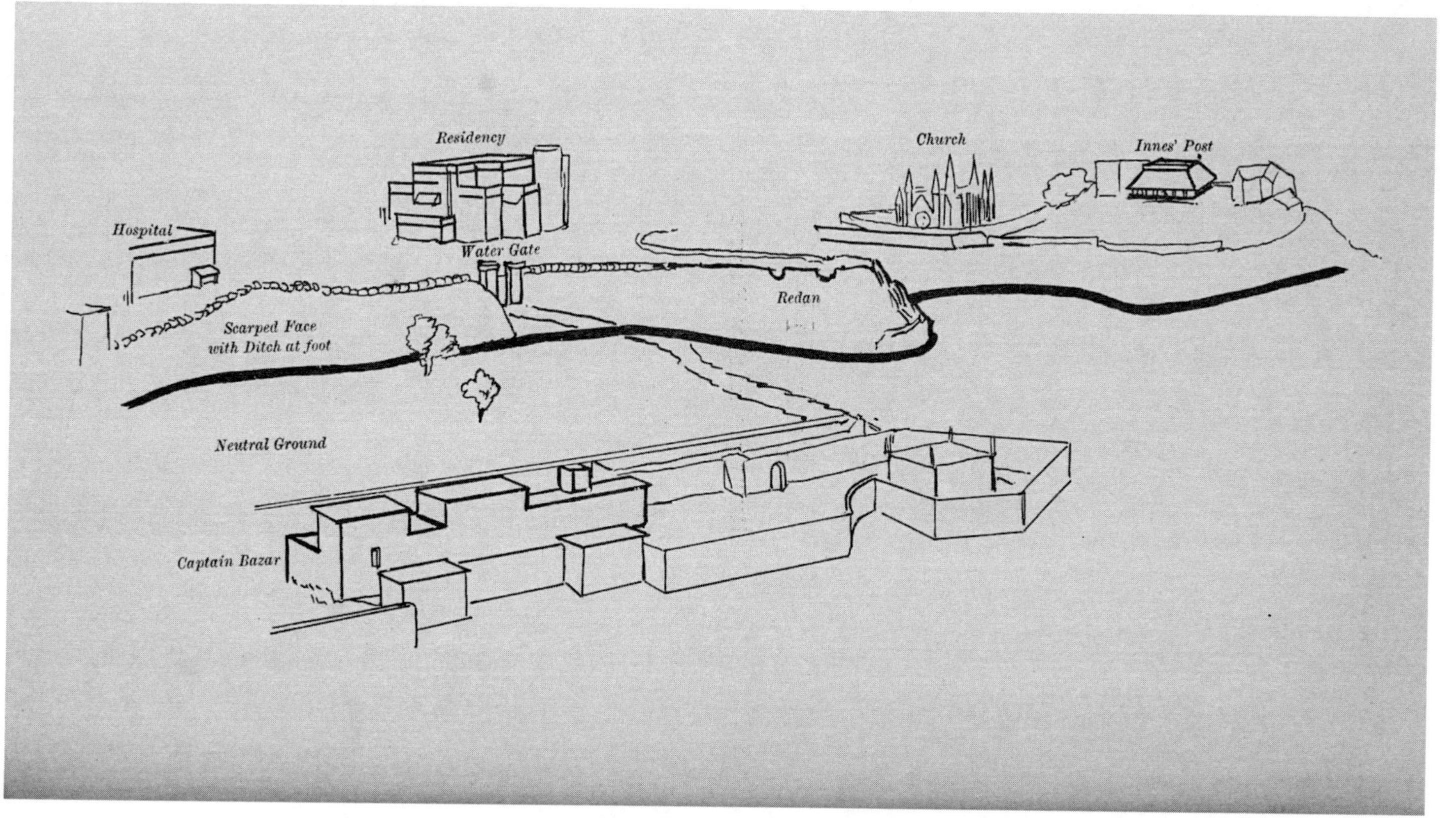
Residency
Church
Innes' Post
Hospital
Water Gate
Redan
Scarped Face
with Ditch at foot
Neutral Ground
Captain Bazar

PLATE II.—RIVER OR REDAN FRONT.

NOTE ON PLATE II.

This shows the North or River or Redan Front, of which the most conspicuous feature is the Redan Battery. At its neck is the Water Gate. On the extreme left is a corner of the Hospital, which was on the right in Plate I. In the foreground is the Captain Gunge or Bazar, from the right end of which the enemy ran two mines, both harmless, to blow up the Redan. The road from the Mutchi Bhown comes in on the right and winds on through the Captain Bazar to the left; at the Mosque, a branch bends up towards the Residency and enters by the Water Gate.

Behind the Water Gate is the Residency.

At the extreme right is Innes' Post, and next it the Church and Cemetery.

The Residency was the only building on this Front in which families were sheltered. It was there that Sir Henry Lawrence received his death wound.

Plate III.

Church or North Angle.

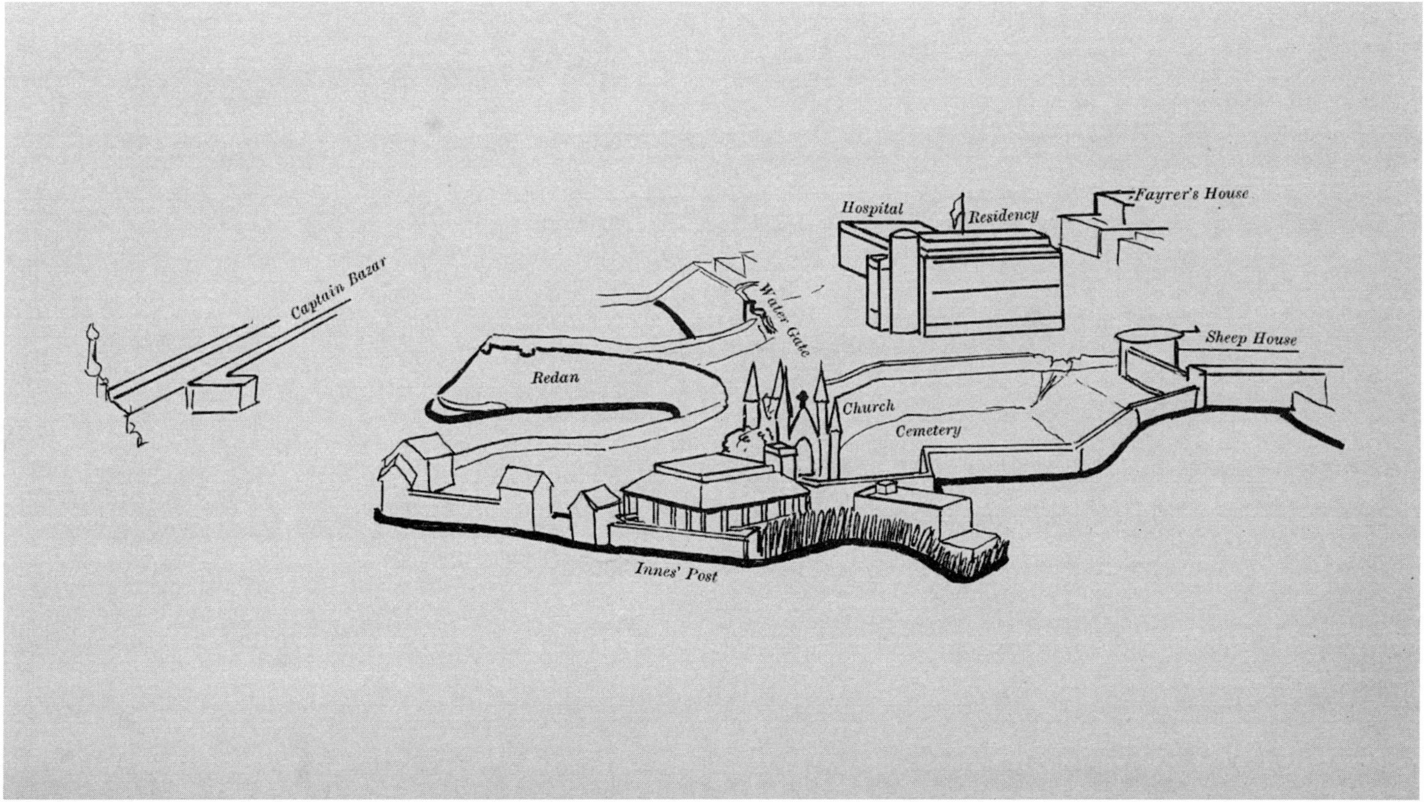
Captain Bazar
Water Gate
Hospital
Residency
Fayrer's House
Sheep House
Redan
Church
Cemetery
Innes' Post

PLATE III.—CHURCH OR NORTH ANGLE.

NOTE ON PLATE III.

This shows the North Angle and the aspect of the Captain Bazar, the Redan, and the Residency from the west. In the immediate front is Innes' Post, and, immediately behind it, the Church and Cemetery. Innes' Post, from its projecting site, was the object of ceaseless fire and constant attacks, especially on the 20th July. It was so exposed that it was not provided with guns. A Battery to aid it, called Evans' Battery, was placed behind the wall in front of the Residency.

On the extreme right is the left end of the Commissariat Buildings of the West Front.

There was no shelter for families at this Angle.

It was from a door in the left wall round Innes' Post that the Sorties used to issue towards the River and the Iron Bridge.

Plate IV.

Commissariat or West Front.

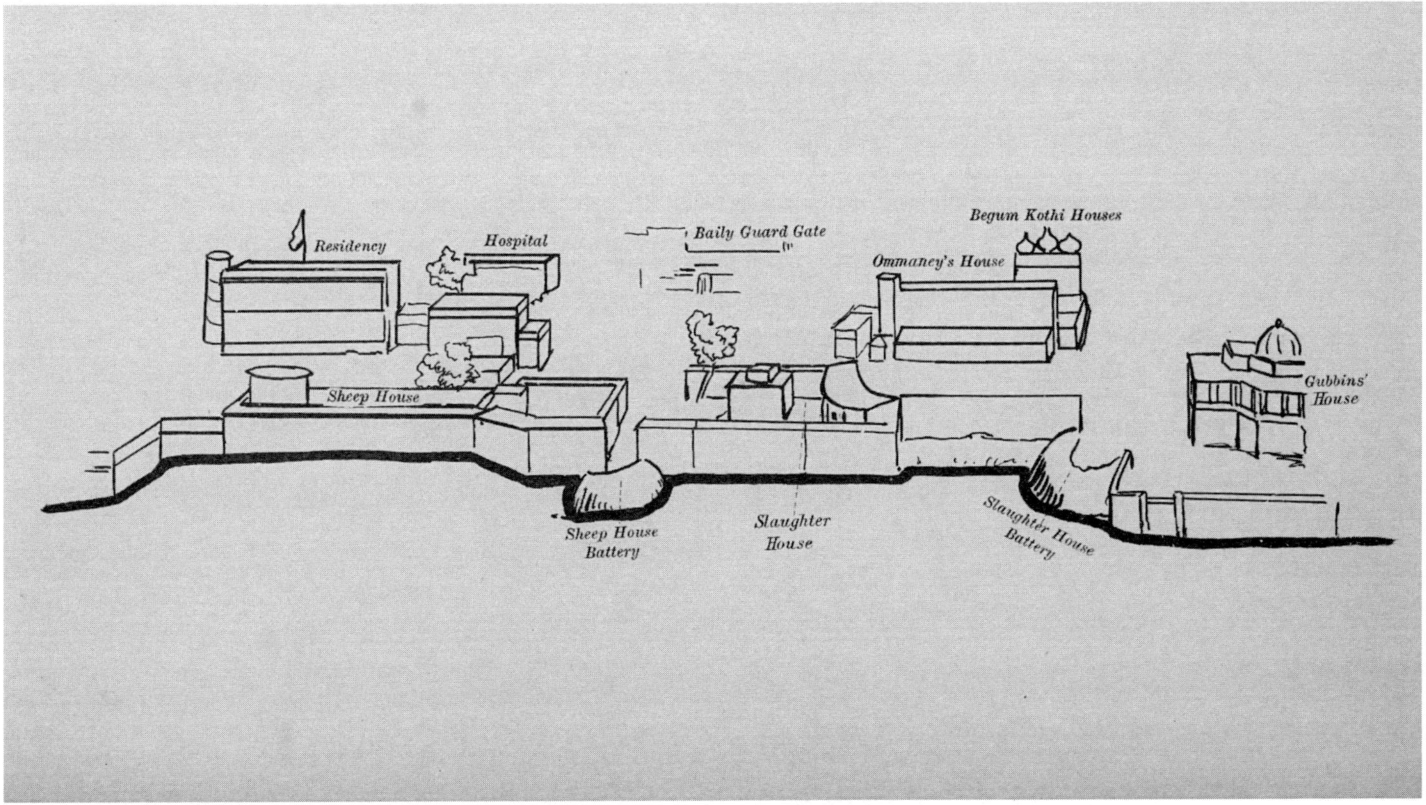
Residency
Hospital
Baily Guard Gate
Begum Kothi Houses
Ommaney's House
Sheep House
Gubbins' House
Sheep House Battery
Slaughter House
Slaughter House Battery

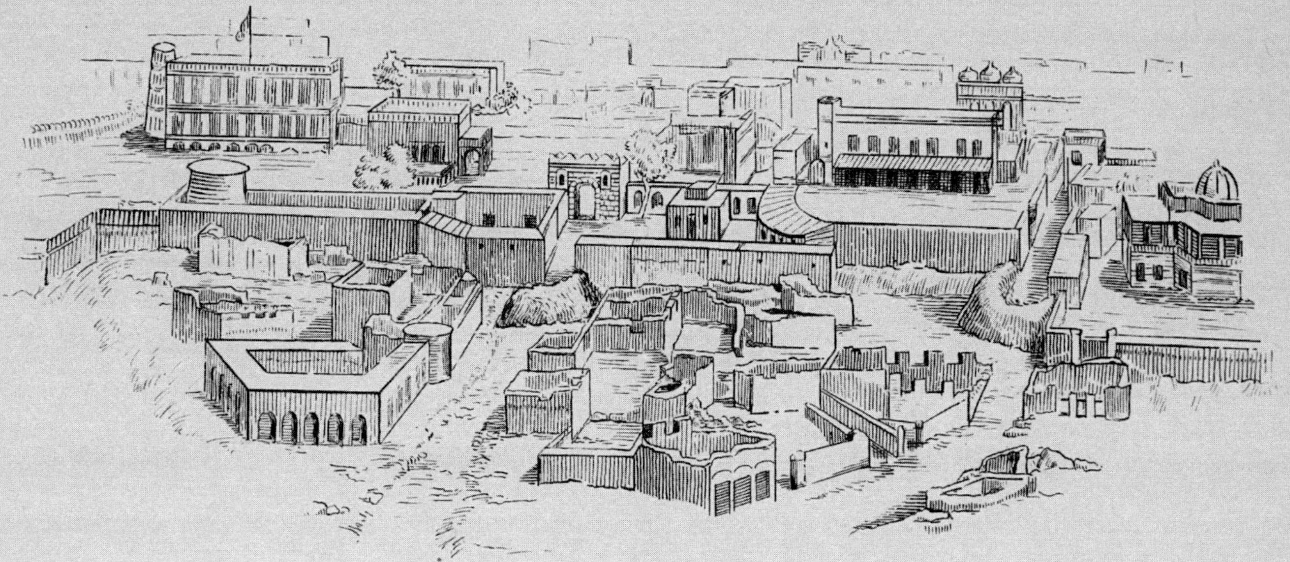

PLATE IV. —COMMISSARIAT OR WEST FRONT.

NOTE ON PLATE IV.

This shows the Commissariat, or West Front. There was never much trouble on this face. The ruins in front sheltered it from Artillery, and prevented any collecting of Troops in mass. Two Batteries at the end of lanes remained unfinished during the first defence. The greater number of the Native Non-combatants of the Garrison were housed in the Commissariat Yards. Behind them are the Residency (of which the two buildings here show clearly) and Ommaney's House. In all of these, families were sheltered. On the extreme right is a corner of Gubbins' House. It was in Ommaney's House that Havelock resided after having been for a few days with Outram in Fayrer's house.

Plate V.

Gubbin's Angle.

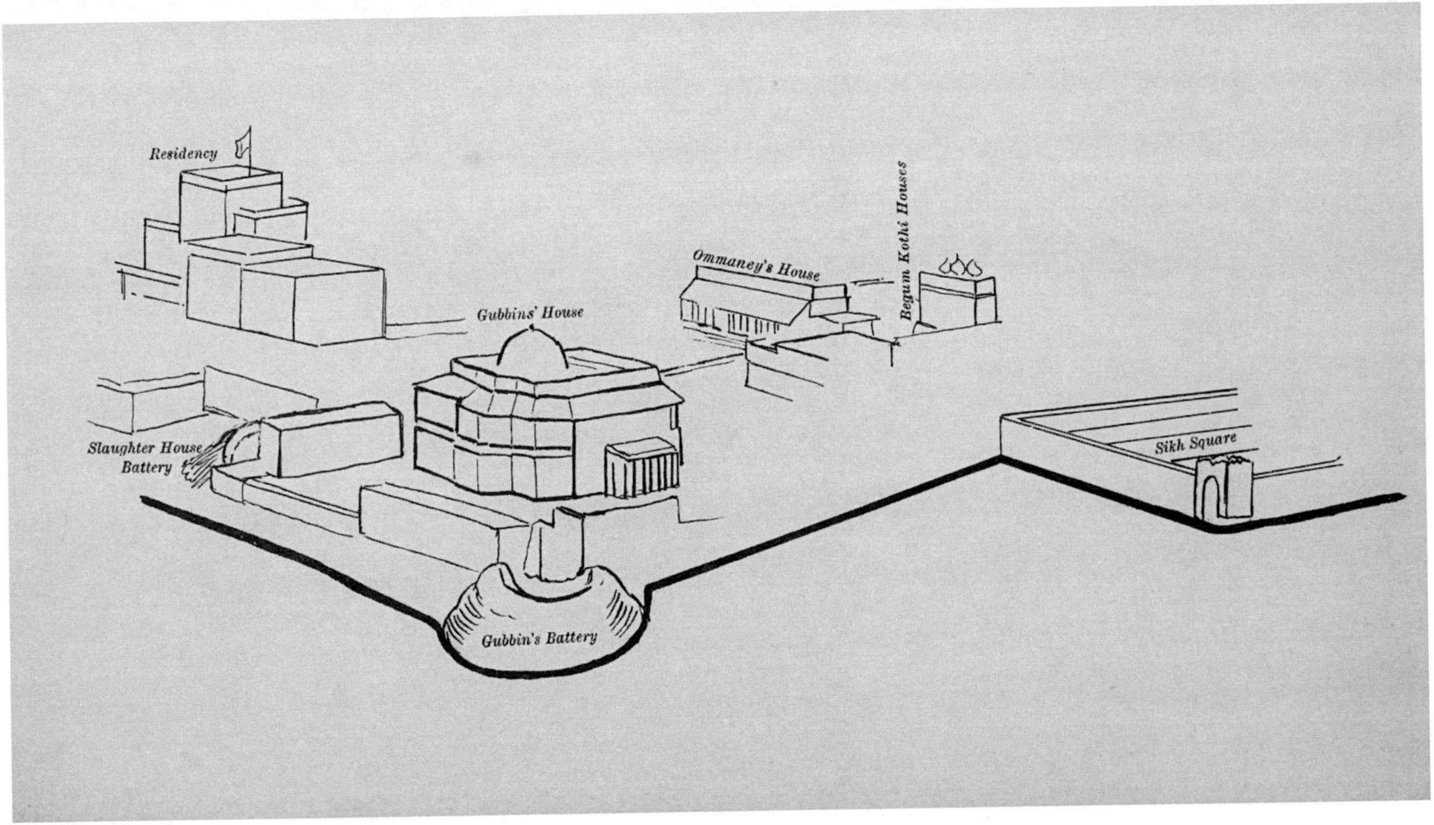
Residency
Ommaney's House
Begum Kothi Houses
Gubbins' House
Slaughter House Battery
Sikh Square
Gubbin's Battery

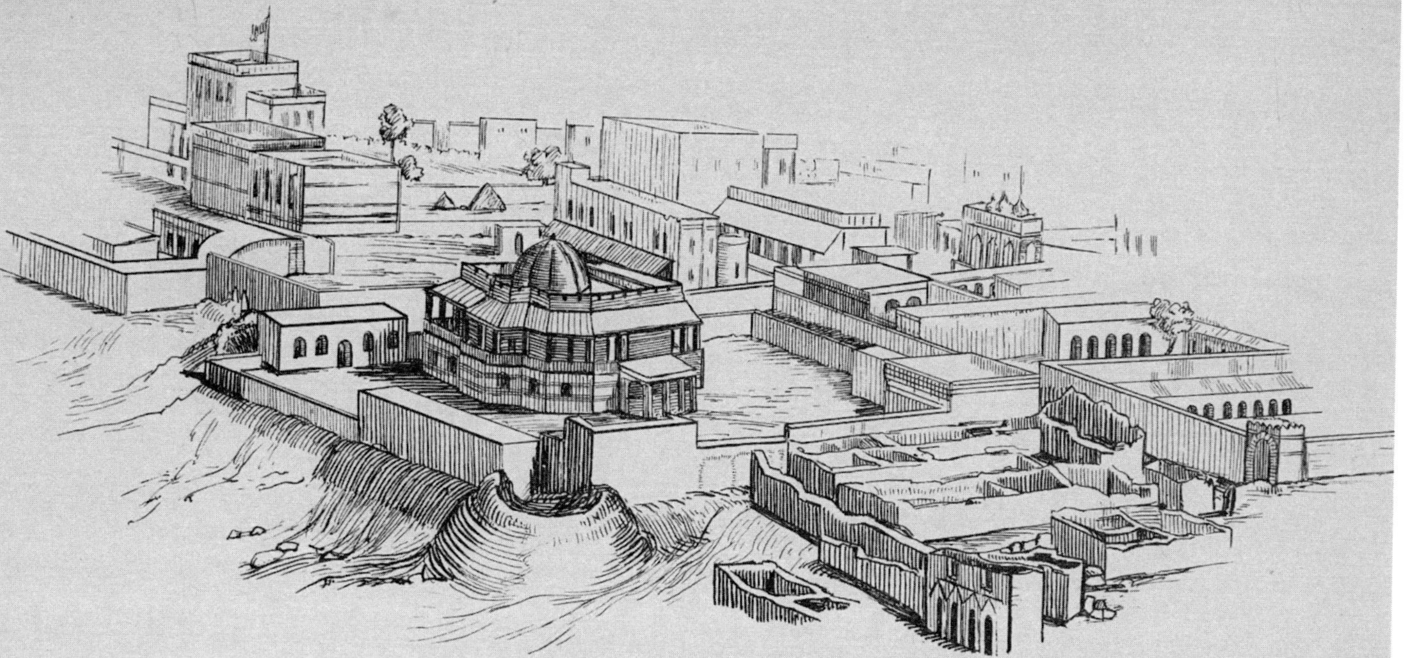

Plate V. —Gubbin's Angle.

NOTE ON PLATE V.

This shows the Western or Gubbins' Angle. Its principal feature is Gubbins' House with its Bastion on its front. The Residency now appears in the extreme left, and on its right are some of the central buildings, including Ommaney's House and the Begum Kothi, in all of which families were sheltered. Towards the right were the Sikh Squares in which the Sikh Cavalry were quartered.

In the foreground is the re-entering piece of ground covered with ruins, from which the enemy tried to attack Gubbins' and the Sikh Square Posts.

Here was one end of the system of Mines, stretching off to the right, by which the enemy tried to breach our defences, and the one breach which they succeeded in making was in the wall at the extreme right.

Gubbins' House was used as the Officers' Hospital, and it was at Gubbins' Bastion that Captain Fulton was killed.

Plate VI.

Brigade Mess Front.

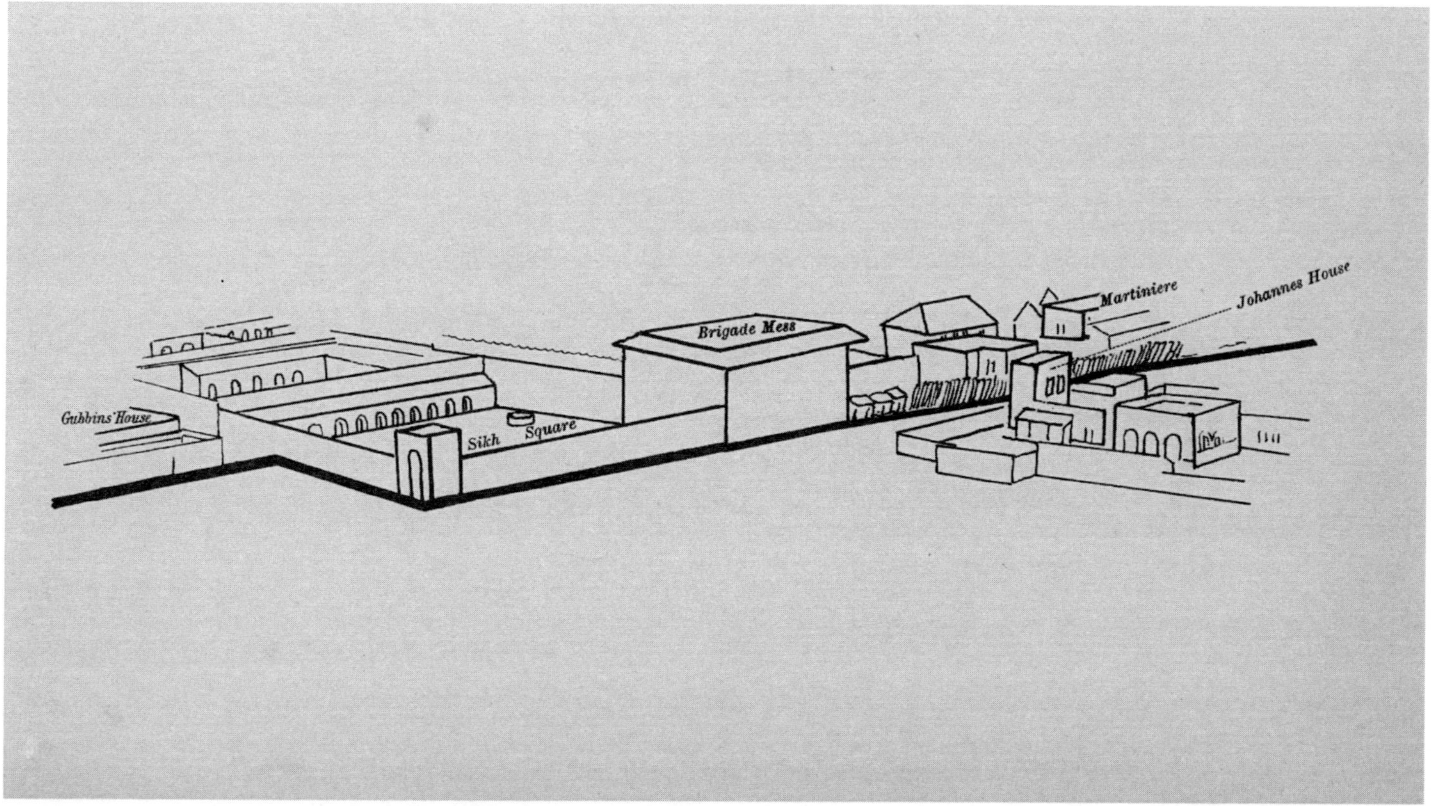
Gubbins' House
Sikh Square
Brigade Mess
Martiniere
Johannes House

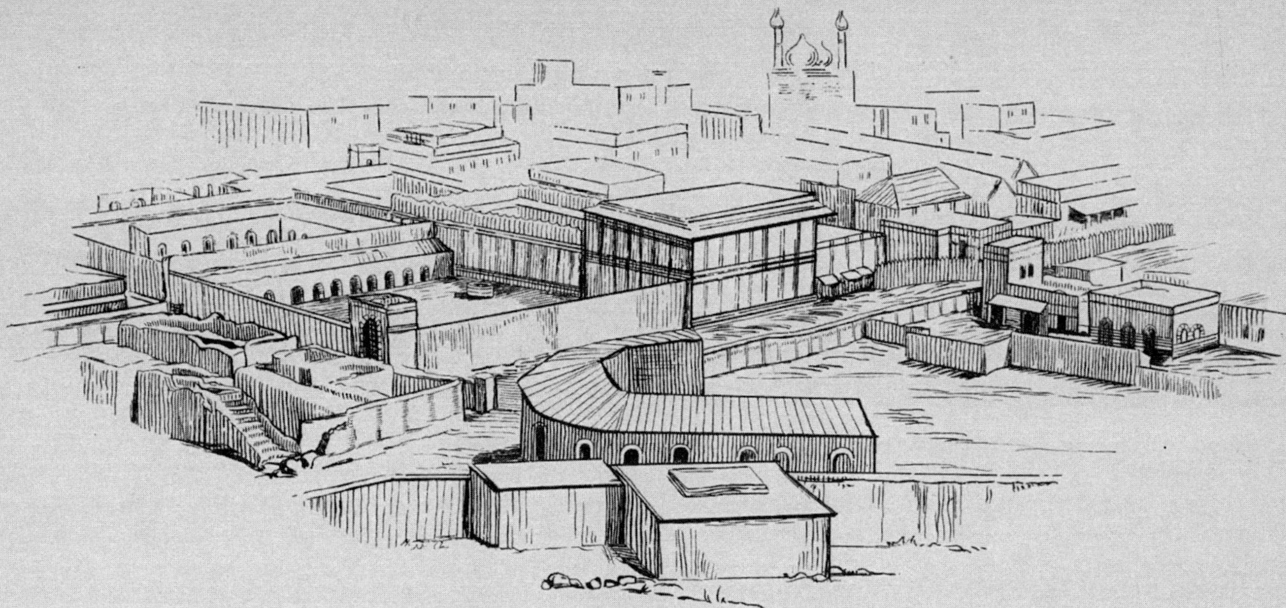

Plate VI. –Brigade Mess Front.

NOTE ON PLATE VI.

This looks up the South Front from its west.

The Sikh Square is now on the left, and the end of the wall where the breach was made shows clearly. From this Sikh Square the narrow street runs along which separated the enemy from our position. Next the Sikh Square is the Brigade Mess and its adjuncts, and then the Martiniere. Between the Brigade Mess and the Martiniere is the lane down which the sharpshooters fired from Johannes' House outside. All these posts on our side were the scene of persistent mining warfare, and on the other hand, we blew up Johannes' House outside by a mine driven below it from the Martiniere.

The Brigade Mess was General Inglis' Head-Quarters. Many families were sheltered in it and the Martiniere and the houses behind them, and the Martiniere school boys were in the Martiniere.

Plate VII.

Cawnpore Battery or South Angle.

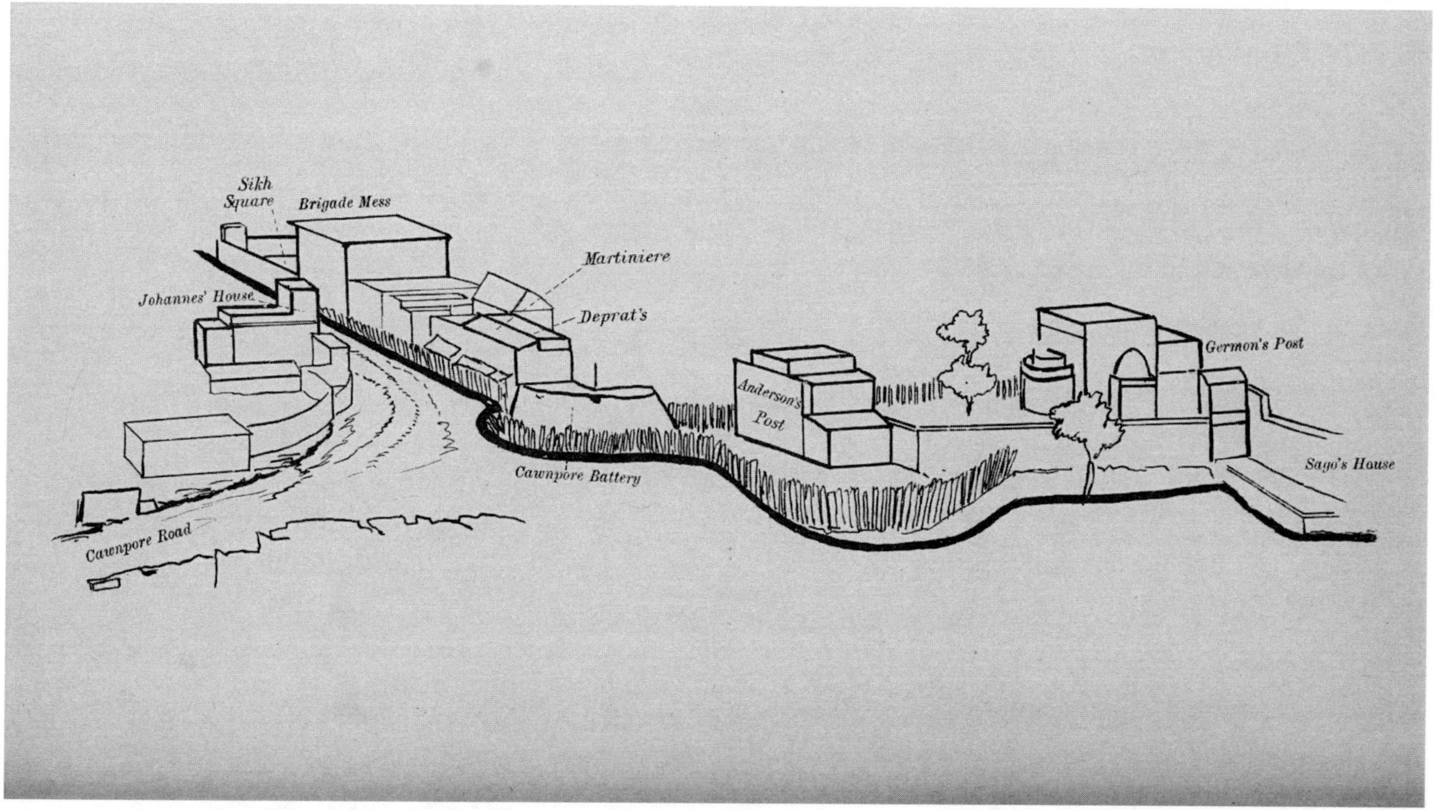
Sikh Square
Brigade Mess
Martiniere
Johannes' House
Deprat's
Germon's Post
Anderson's Post
Sago's House
Cawnpore Battery
Cawnpore Road

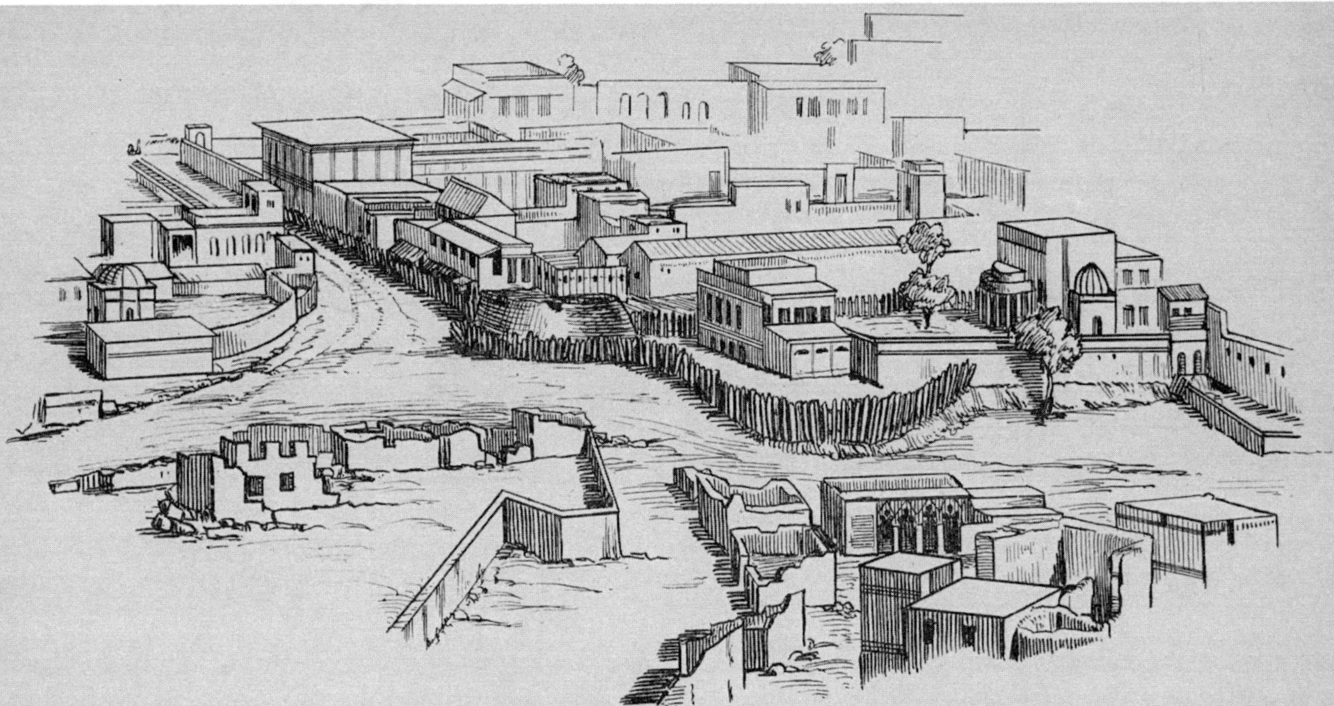

Plate VII.—Cawnpore Battery or South Angle.

NOTE ON PLATE VII.

This is a view of the South Angle, and shows clearly from the eastwards the narrow street of Plate VI., along the south face; with Johannes' House on the enemy's side, and on ours the Brigade Mess, the Martiniere, Deprat's, the Cawnpore Battery, then—circling to the right—Anderson's and Germon's Posts, and the corner of Sago's on the extreme right. These were all the sites of numerous mines and counter-mines.

Johannes' House with its sharpshooters silenced the guns of the Cawnpore Battery for a few days till it was blown up

There were only a few families in the lower stories of the front buildings. The group of buildings near the posts in front of this angle was occupied by the pensioners and the Sepoys other than those of the 13th Native Infantry.

Plate VIII.

Baily Guard Front.

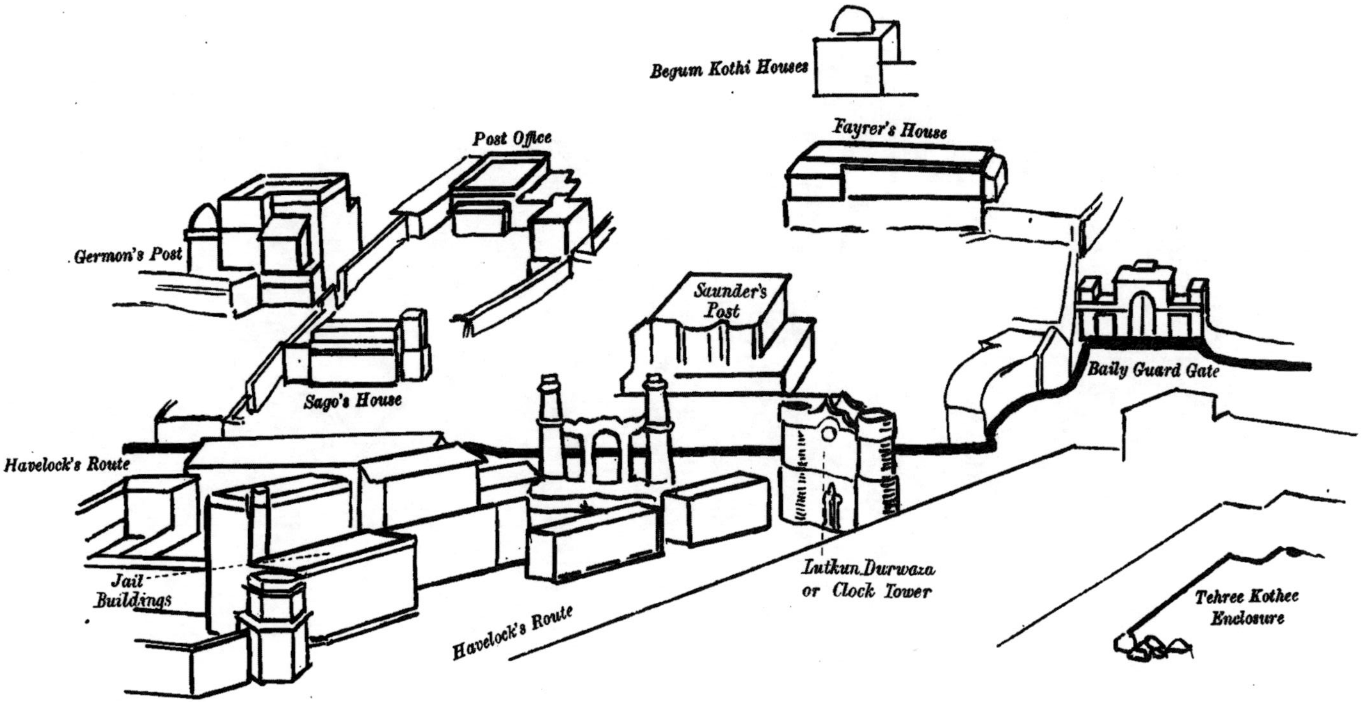

Begum Kothi Houses
Post Office
Fayrer's House
Germon's Post
Saunder's Post
Sago's House
Baily Guard Gate
Havelock's Route
Jail Buildings
Lutkun Durwaza or Clock Tower
Havelock's Route
Tehree Kothee Enclosure

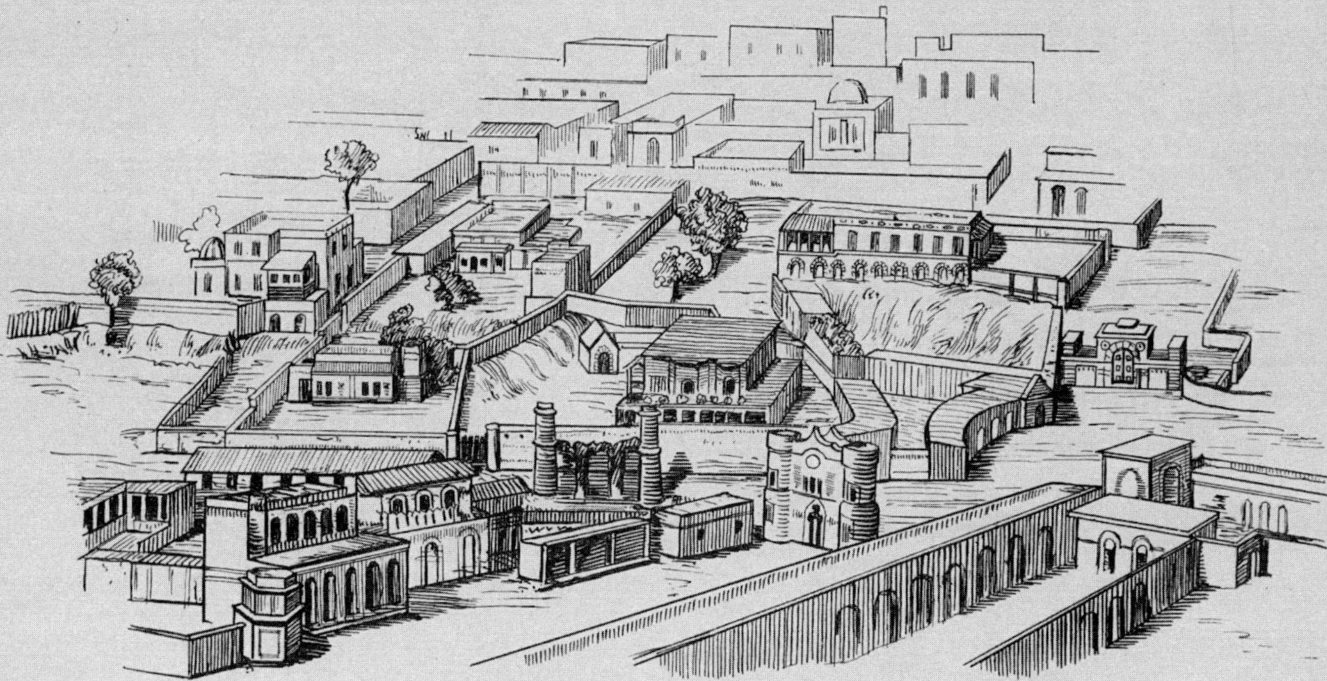

Plate VIII.—Baily Guard Front.

NOTE ON PLATE VIII.

This view of the East Front brings us round to the Baily Guard, which was the central point of the view from which we started.

The two prominent posts in front are, Sago's on the left and Saunders' in the middle; both of them the sites of severe mining contests. At Saunders' ended the continuous system of mines which began at the Sikh Square.

On the left of Sago's, and somewhat behind it, is Germon's, held by the Sikhs of the 13th N.I.

Behind Sago's, on higher ground, is the Post Office, in which was a Battery in a sheltered corner at its outhouses on the right, which swept the front of the Baily Guard Gate.

This view shows the two routes of the Relieving Force.

On this Front there was shelter in the Post Office and Dr Fayrer's, and in the buildings beyond them.

BOOK II

THE FIRST DEFENCE OF THE RESIDENCY

CHAPTER I

CHINHUT AND THE CONCENTRATION

IT has been shown that so long as Cawnpore held out, the mutineer regiments had kept hovering and wavering in the direction of Fyzabad; but that as soon as they heard of Wheler's capitulation, they sent on a detachment to Nuwabgunge, and arranged to concentrate there. This they did on the 29th, their advanced guard moving forward to Chinhut on the same day; and it was on the receipt of the intelligence of this move that Sir Henry withdrew from the cantonment, and ordered a reconnaisance for the morning of June 30th, to feel for and check the enemy's van.

It does not seem to be accurately known what the strength of the enemy's force actually was; but there can be little doubt that it comprised the several regiments belonging to the eastern half of Oude, and those, with the exception of the 17th N. I. from Azimgurh, which had advanced into Oude from Jaunpore and Benares. There were probably—Two regular N. I. regiments; eight Oude local regiments; the 15th Irregulars and detachments of other cavalry; two complete batteries of field artillery; and the contingents of three of the Oude Talookdars—one the Mahomedan chief of Mahomedabad, and the other two petty chiefs near Lucknow itself. Their counsels were divided, and there was no recognized commander; but after much wrangling and differences between the choice of the Mahomedans and of the Hindoos, the command eventually devolved on Burkut Ahmed, an officer of the 15th cavalry. The Talookdars' men, however, held aloof under their own leader, Khan Ali Khan, the lieutenant of the chief of Mahomedabad.

It has been shown that Sir Henry, on the evening of the 29th, hearing of the approach of the enemy, ordered out a force to check their advance. It is quite certain that the information he had received was not definite, while he had not sufficient cavalry to reconnoitre and ascertain correctly the position and strength of the enemy. He believed that they had no real heart for a fight, and he hoped that he would encounter only their advanced guard, and be able to punish them sufficiently to cause their further advance to be slow and cautious. The troops were to stop short under Brigadier Inglis at the Kokrail bridge on the road to Chinhut and Nuwabgunge, and there to rest and get their early meal, while Sir Henry himself and his staff reconnoitred ahead. Major Anderson was not with him, nor had he been told of or consulted about the expedition, which, as every sign indicated, was not expected to be more than an affair between advanced detachments, certainly not a battle with the whole force of the enemy, with the consequences it might involve.

The force, about a third of the whole garrison, with which Sir Henry meant to meet the mutineer vanguard, consisted of three hundred of the 32nd regiment; thirty-six volunteer cavalry; two hundred and thirty native infantry; one hundred and twenty native cavalry; four guns European field artillery; six guns native artillery; and one eight-inch howitzer. This party did not form up at the iron bridge and start for the appointed halting-place, the Kokrail bridge, till long after the hour named; nor did it, when halted, get the food which Sir Henry had ordered to be served out to it. Sir Henry had meanwhile gone forward to reconnoitre, accompanied by some of his staff, but not by Brigadier Inglis, who remained with the troops.

After coming in sight of Chinhut, and seeing no sign of the enemy's advance, Sir Henry at first decided on retiring; but presently he heard that the rebel scouts had fallen back on their supports. Gathering from this that they held back from the contest, and that he still had only the advanced party to deal with, and also learning from Brigadier Inglis (through his aide-de-camp) that the 32nd were ready for the combat, he ordered the force to advance to a point half-way between the Kokrail bridge and Chinhut, where the road, after passing between Ishmailgunge on the left and another village on the right, lay in ground which was impeded and protected against the enemy by a large *jheel* (shallow lake) in its front. Holding these two villages, he trusted to give the enemy a telling lesson, to check their advance, and retard the commencement of the siege, and especially of a close investment.

But, it need hardly be said, his expectations were bitterly disappointed. The enemy were seen almost immediately, advancing and deploying or deployed, and evidently in great force. The native infantry of Sir Henry's column went forward vigorously on the right and seized and held the village assigned to them; but the 32nd, who were similarly to have occupied Ishmailgunge on the left, were exhausted by heat and want of food, and never reached that village. The enemy's skirmishers, instead, anticipated them, seized Ishmailgunge, and receiving the 32nd with an effective fire, stopped their further advance. Avoiding the road, where they were checked by the fire of our eight-inch howitzer, they began circling round our flanks in two bodies, each of them of greatly preponderating strength. On the left, the 32nd had been expected to check any such movement; and the direct result there, as it was the outer flank in respect of the route for retirement, was not of so great moment. On the right our Sikh cavalry should have acted on the enemy's flank movement; instead of which they allowed themselves to be repulsed, and so left our right flank unprotected and our line of retreat in danger. But besides this, the overlapping on both flanks led to a most fatal cross fire on the head of the column; forcing our Sepoys to fall back from their village, causing great loss, and leading to the desertion of Alexander's gunners, and the capture of his two guns; as well as of the eight-inch howitzer, the elephants that drew it having turned restive. The enemy's cavalry then threatened to cut across towards the iron bridge and intercept the retreat of our force, but this attempt was frustrated by the resolute conduct of our handful of volunteer cavalry, and of some detachments on the right flank; as also by the fact that the guns of the Residency commanded that ground, and that the front of the iron bridge was held by Edmonstone's company of the 32nd from the Residency.

The fire of the enemy pressing on caused great loss, but many of our men, it is feared, dropped down from sheer exhaustion, the 32nd on its return being found to have lost 111 men killed, besides four officers, and as many more wounded. One pleasant fact in the midst of so much misery in that retreat was that the natives who occupied the houses along the road helped the exhausted troops with water and milk.

Whilst the fight was going on at Chinhut, the works and operations were being carried on as usual at the Residency and the Mutchi Bhown. Carts were still bringing in supplies, and the defences swarmed with labourers. It was clear that the approach of the Sepoy army was not exciting the ordinary city population. The Mutchi Bhown was, by this time, cleared out of nearly all its supplies and of all the spare guns; but not of the guns at the west end of the position, nor of a large store of powder and small-arms ammunition, for which room had not yet been found or made in the entrenchments. All of a sudden, the work-people disappeared as if by magic, both at the Residency and at the Mutchi Bhown, and in the next few minutes the first fugitives from the fight made their appearance with the announcement of the defeat of the British force.

At both positions the necessary steps were immediately taken to make the gates and entrances secure, and to man the outposts and batteries. By degrees the troops of the Chinhut force rejoined, the city meanwhile keeping quiet. Sir Henry had ordered out Captain Edmonstone's company to hold the iron bridge till the force rejoined, and the guns on the river-face at both posts were now directed on the two bridges to prevent their passage by the enemy. As they had therefore to cross the river lower down, the latter took some hours to come close to the Residency, and they did not get any guns across that day (June 30) at all, nor did they then reach the Mutchi Bhown. They planted their guns on the north side of the river, and sent round-shot and an occasional shell into the Residency buildings; and later in the day their infantry, more or less surrounding the place, fired into the windows, causing a few casualties.

The Mutchi Bhown was hardly molested. The parapet along the near side of the iron bridge had been removed, so that no one could cross it without coming fully under the fire of the Mutchi Bhown. Hnece it was, in fact, late before the victorious Sepoys got access to the city: within which two regiments of the Oude local force were still quartered. These after a few hours rose in mutiny, but escorted their Commandant, Brigadier Gray, and other officers to the Mutchi Bhown.

In the afternoon, efforts were made to signal between the two posts, but the semaphore at the Residency was so damaged by the enemy's fire that it could not be worked successfully.

All that day, the efforts of the defence were directed to making everything as secure as possible, and to repelling the enemy's attempts at close investment.

Fortunately all the supplies, beyond the requirements for three or four days, had been removed from the Mutchi Bhown and stored in the Residency; and, except the guns at the west end and the ammunition (which have been already referred to), nothing had been left in the Mutchi Bhown save some round-shot for the guns and a few shells for the mortars.

During the night of the 30th nothing of moment occurred. Next day musketry fire was poured in from all sides, and shot and shell from the north of the river, but without any serious result. And then the semaphore having been repaired, Sir Henry signalled a message to the Mutchi Bhown, "Retire to-night at twelve. Blow up well." One note had been received during the night, written in Greek characters, asking if the Mutchi Bhown party were able to evacuate, but the answer, which said "Yes," never reached Sir Henry. In fact, it was known that from the previous evening the enemy had swarmed into the ground intervening between the two posts, and cut off all ordinary means of communication.

On the receipt of the message to withdraw, Colonel Palmer of the 48th N. I., who was left the senior officer, summoned all the commanding and departmental officers, and arranged in complete detail for the evacuation. The native artillery drivers had fled during the previous night; so officers had to drive the gun-teams. The State prisoners were to be secured on the artillery wagons, as also the sick and wounded. The guns that were to be left behind were to be spiked at the last moment; and, as the rear-guard left, Lieutenant Thomas, the ordnance officer, was to fire the train that was to explode the magazine.

Meanwhile there was to be absolute silence on the movement, and there was no cessation of the intermittent mortar fire, which, both from the Residency and from the Mutchi Bhown, kept on shelling the ground lying between the two posts. At last at ten o'clock the sentries were strengthened, and the actual preparations began. As midnight approached, the troops were formed on parade, in the lower plattan or court-yard, and every inmate of the Mutchi Bhown was placed in the exact position in the line of march. At twelve o'clock, Lawrence's company of the 32nd, heading the column, marched out of the Eastern gate, the whole column following closely, the rear being brought up by Lieutenant Thomas, who had fired a twenty-minute fuse for the magazine train. The whole force marched on rapidly, expecting every moment to be obstructed and attacked; but it reached and concentrated in the Residency without meeting an enemy or having a single shot fired at it. Then, as the rear-guard got within the gates, a great quake of the earth, a thunderous report, and a brilliant glare announced that the Mutchi Bhown magazine had been successfully exploded.

Thus the first hours of July 2nd saw the whole of the Lucknow force concentrated in the Residency entrenchments, and prepared to hold it to the death; with an ample store of food and of ammunition, with more guns than they could man, and with defences which the results showed to be adequate for their purpose against the enemy investing the position. And so, save for the disastrous episode of Chinhut, Sir Henry's plans had been brought to a successful completion.

The defence thus begun lasted to September 25th, the date of Havelock's and Outram's relief of Lucknow, a period, including the two days of June 30th and July 1st, of eighty-eight days, or nearly three months. It was marked off into four stages of about three weeks each, by the all-round attacks of July 20th, August 10th, and September 5th. The account of the defence will be dealt with under each of these periods separately.

CHAPTER II

DESCRIPTION OF THE ENTRENCHMENTS

THE Residency entrenchments[1] in which the force was now concentrated, lay on the edge of the high bank, from which the ground sloped down, somewhat sharply, to the river Goomtee, on the north. Its shape was approximately a square, with sides about a quarter of a mile long, and enclosing an area of between thirty-two and thirty-six acres. Its longer diagonal was about 700 yards, and the shorter one 450 yards.

For practical purposes, the face which looked on to the Goomtee may be called the North or River front;[2] then circling round with the sun came the East or Baily Guard front;[3] then the South or Cawnpore front;[4] and lastly the West or city front.[5]

Owing to the fall of the ground above-mentioned, the northern half of the position commanded all the adjacent ground, but the southern half was on a level with the neighbouring roads and buildings. The nature of the ground outside the position, as regards facilities for attacking it, varied greatly on each front.

On the North front[6] lay the only clear space where the enemy could be massed in force and sweep up to storm the position, or where they had sites for batteries at effective range to breach the defences, fully exposed to them.

On the other three fronts the intervening buildings and ruins protected the lower defences from being touched by artillery fire, and prevented the movement of large bodies of troops.

On the Northern face[7] the high-road to Cawnpore ran about 100 yards in front of the position, and was lined by

[1] See Map IV. and the Plates. [2] Plates III. and II.
[3] Plates I. and VIII. [4] Plates VII. and VI. [5] Plates V. and IV.
[6] Plates II. and III. [7] Plate II.

walls and shops abutting on them, forming a street called the Captan Bazar; but on reaching the east end of the North front, it turned sharp to the south, and skirted close along the whole of the Baily Guard or Eastern front, till, leaving the site of the entrenchments altogether at the Cawnpore Battery, it wended its way southwards to Cawnpore.

On this, the Eastern front,[1] the road was lined on the off side by the walls of large enclosures, within which were large buildings that could be utilized in various ways for aggressive purposes; though troops for an attack or rush could advance only in columns from comparatively narrow passages.

On the South or Cawnpore front,[2] a narrow street ran close along the boundary walls, and beyond was a mass of ruins or *débris* of buildings which would effectually prevent the movement of troops in any numbers.

On the Western face[3] was a stretch of broken ground some 150 yards wide sloping down to a ravine, across which the enemy never made any serious efforts to advance. Any of the sites beyond it, which might otherwise have answered for artillery, were well within musketry range; effectually stopping their use for that purpose save at one spot.

Such was the nature of the ground and of the positions held by the enemy opposite our several fronts. We turn now to the posts we held along each of these fronts, and it will be convenient to preface this by naming the posts at the four angles or corners, connecting these points.

At the north-west corner,[4] connecting the northern and western fronts, was Innes's post. At the north-east[5] corner was the Hospital post, with the Baily Guard post, in advance, below it; at the south-east corner[6] were the Cawnpore Battery and Anderson's post; and at the south-west corner[7] was Gubbins's post. These were naturally the weakest points in the quadrilateral position.

The North front[8] then lay between Innes's post at its west end, and the Hospital and Baily Guard posts at its east. Innes's post was really on a very advanced site, on a

[1] Plates I. and VIII. [2] Plate VII. [3] Plate IV.
[4] Plate III. [5] Plate I. [6] Plate VII.
[7] Plate V. [8] Plate II.

spur that projected from the Western front, on the alignment of the Northern front. The whole of the Northern front was, as it were, one continuous curtain with the Redan Battery thrown forwards from its centre, and flanking it right and left, while the Residency House lay behind it in support.

It had been hoped that the whole of the ground in its front down to the river would have been held by the garrison, or at any rate have remained neutral. But the disaster of Chinhut had destroyed this chance. The losses there had gravely reduced the strength of the garrison, leaving none available to hold the Captan Bazar, and the exultant enemy had swarmed in on the first evening, seized that street, and completed the investment on that front without opposition.

No post, except the Redan Battery, lay between Innes's and the Hospital posts at the two ends of the front.

We now come to the Eastern front,[1] which was on two tiers, the high level and the low level in front of it. The posts on the high ground,[2] lying between the Hospital post and Anderson's, were Fayrer's, the Post-office, and Germon's, while in front of them were the Baily Guard post, Saunders's, and Sago's. The road to Cawnpore skirted the walls of these front posts, leaving no neutral ground except the width of the road itself. The Post-office position, from its projecting trace, not only provided a strong frontal defence but also enfiladed the face of the Baily Guard post, and in combination with the Redan on the North front, powerfully protected the north-east angle of the position.

The South front[3] had at its two ends, Anderson's and Gubbins's posts; but the whole of the intermediate part of the front was thrown well forward in advance of the extremities, and contained, in a straight curtain, the Cawnpore Battery, Deprat's, the Martinière, the Brigade mess, and the Sikh square posts.

It was on this front that the enemy really lay closest to our position, not being more than thirty or forty feet distant from it along its whole length; but the ground was so entirely covered with ruins, that though they were sheltered, they had no facilities for movement. These ruins protected the foot of the buildings from artillery fire.

[1] Plates VIII. and I. [2] Plate VIII. [3] Plates V., VI., and VII.

In rear of the posts I have named was a second line of posts which supported them, and contained garrisons for their assistance, serving as *retrenchments*, but not like those on the Eastern front, on higher ground.

Lastly, the Western front[1] lay between Gubbins's and Innes's posts, and consisted of three ranges of Residency outhouses, viz. the slaughter-house, the sheep-house, and the servants' quarters, and then the church and cemetery, with Evans's Battery on the high level behind it. This battery flanked the south side of Innes's post, and provided a good frontal defence as well;[2] and Innes's post flanked the whole of this Western front, which, except at that post itself, was never seriously attacked. Two batteries had been started, but had not made much way when the siege began, one at either end of the slaughter-house range.

These then were the several outposts and supporting posts that lay at the angles and along the faces of the four fronts of the position. Their defensive features have now to be described.

Along the whole of the North front,[3] the line of defence, following as it did the edge of the high bank, had been scarped down. The earth obtained thence, and from a small ditch dug along the foot of the scarp, had been used to form a sort of crest of the glacis formed by the sloping ground in front. Ordinary obstacles had been placed along the ditch and the glacis to hamper the rush of the enemy, but they never came into play. The charge, or attack of the enemy, on this front never advanced as far as these obstacles, although it was the only front where there was sufficient open space to admit of a large force being collected for a rush. These were the defences on the outside, so to speak. On the line itself, along the crest of the high bank, and in continuation upwards of the escarp, was a stout, strong, seven-foot-high parapet, reveted with gabions and fascines, topped with sand-bags, and finished with a banquette for musketry.

The Redan Battery flanked the whole of this front with artillery fire, and also, in combination with the guns along the curtain, afforded a powerful frontal defence.

[1] Plate IV. [2] Plate III. [3] Plate II.

Some buildings left on the low ground below were not utilized by the enemy, and were eventually demolished.

Beyond Innes's post, the spur on which it was built projected for a considerable distance into the enemy's ground, and at its end was a small mosque; but neither the ground nor the mosque was used by the enemy. The roof of Innes's post being parapeted, and commanding all the adjacent ground, was the most valuable feature of the defensive arrangements in that direction.

At the eastern end of the Northern front the line of parapet, which was high at the Hospital, descended gradually as it formed the flank of the Treasury or Baily Guard post in the eastern front of the Hospital.

The defences of the Eastern front[1] were quite different from those of the Northern. They did not run along the edge of the high ground that could be scarped, nor, on the other hand, was there any wide spread of ground in front. The whole of this front had as its first line of defence the high boundary-wall of the grounds of the Residency and of the buildings attached to it. Along the northern half of this front, that is along the Treasury or Baily Guard post and Dr. Fayrer's, this wall was lined and strengthened inside by a musketry parapet; along all the southern portion it was merely loopholed, but its trace, except before Saunders's and Sago's posts, gave strong cross-flanking defence. Behind the boundary-walls the front walls of the verandahs of the buildings were continued right and left up to the partition-walls of the grounds; the archways were bricked in, and the whole was loopholed so as to give a second line of frontal fire. Behind the advanced or outposts there were, it will be remembered, the supporting-posts with parapets and loopholes in front, and numerous flanking bends in the walls.

At the north-east angle of the Post-office position[2] was a battery which flanked the whole of the immediate front of the Baily Guard post.

The expectation of the defence on this front was that there could be no strong artillery attack which would not be subdued by musketry, and that without artillery any

[1] Plates I. and VIII. [2] Plate VIII.

attack would have a succession of barricades to capture, which would probably prove beyond its power.

Its weakest point was at the angle where the Eastern and Southern fronts met,[1] at the Cawnpore Battery and Anderson's post, liable as it was to attack by a quarter circle of the enemy's surrounding position.

So the obstacles at this site were made specially strong with palisading, *chevaux-de-frise*, stakes, crows'-feet, and the like, while the parapets and walls of the buildings were pierced by loopholes, and otherwise prepared for all the musketry defence possible.

Along the southern advanced front[2] the position was unique; it was formed by a continuous line of buildings which had been strongly loopholed for frontal musketry defence, its flanking defence being entrusted to the Cawnpore Battery. There was no protection or defence to these buildings against artillery fire beyond musketry range; but the *débris* on the other side of the road which ran close along our outline was expected to shield them from low-aimed breaching fire. They were also lined by a continuous row of small shops, of which no account seems to have been made at first.

As has been mentioned already, one building, Johannes' house, which it had been meant, if not to utilize, then to blow up at the last moment, was not brought into use, but was left at its full height at the beginning of the siege. This was at once found to command and paralyse the Cawnpore Battery. It became the object of sorties, and the cause of much anxiety till it was eventually blown up by our mine. At the west end of the South face there was a re-entering angle of ground covered with the ruins of native houses, which was protected by the cross fire from the Sikh square and Gubbins's front. But all these *débris*, including those in front of the South face, were found to be the most dangerous starting-points and shelters for the enemy's mines.

At the angle of the South and West fronts,[3] the salient of Gubbins's post was one of the weakest points of the position, being inadequately flanked on the west, and was the object of ceaseless attack by the enemy. Otherwise it

[1] Plate VII. [2] Plates VI. and VII. [3] Plate V.

was well defended, being lined by outhouses well parapeted and loopholed. The Western face, between Gubbins's and Innes's posts, consisted of a continuous line of outhouses, which were loopholed and parapeted. There was no real flanking defence; two batteries, which were meant to flank it from near its middle, having only been begun; while the fire from Innes's post was only musketry, though there was frontal artillery fire from Evans's Battery at its neck. But the ground before this face was broken and rugged, sloping down roughly to a ravine which ran along, about 200 yards in its front, towards the river.

The weak feature in the design of the defences was the want of flanking fire except on the Northern front and before the Baily Guard. Elsewhere it was too slight, or actually wanting. As to the artillery of the defence, it may be briefly stated, that there were more guns than could be manned, and that guns were, from the first, placed at every point except one, which seemed to afford a suitable site for a battery for either frontal or flanking fire. That one point was Innes's post. The reason for the omission was that the post was held to be too exposed and dangerous, while the placing of guns there would give the enemy too tempting a reason for a powerful assault. In fact, a gun was placed in position there one night in August and withdrawn the next night.

It may be observed that many of the guns, especially the field-guns, were moved about from time to time. Besides eight mortars at convenient spots, guns were permanently placed in position as follows—

Along the North face, some seven guns, besides three in the Redan. Three in rear of the Baily Guard gate, and one or two in Fayrer's post. Four in the Post-office grounds, two of them to enfilade the front of the Baily Guard post, and two for defence to the east. Three in the Cawnpore Battery. Two at the Sikh square and Gubbins's post. Three, called Evans's Battery, at the high bank overhanging the cemetery, at the neck of the spur leading to Innes's post.

The batteries and gun positions formed during the siege will be described at the proper time. The whole force, English, natives, and volunteer civilians, with the exception of the company of the 84th Foot, which was held in reserve, were distributed permanently, as their garrisons, to the different posts. That reserve of the 84th was lodged in the Residency building, and was only once called out, on the occasion when a breach was made by a mine in the rampart of the Sikh square.

The posts to which only English soldiers were attached were—

The Redan, the Cawnpore Battery, the slaughter-house post.

The following posts were held entirely by Sepoys—

The Hospital post, 71st and 48th N. I.; the Baily Guard Post, 13th N. I.; Germon's post, Sikh Infantry; Sikh square, Sikh Cavalry.

All other posts, supports as well as outposts, were held by a combination of English and native soldiers and volunteers, generally in equal proportions, about thirty to each post.

Such, then, were our several posts, their defences, their artillery, and their garrisons. The buildings that did not form defensive posts will be dealt with later on.

These entrenchments were by no means finished and ready on July 1st; that is, they had not developed into the full strength hoped for ultimately. But the essential principle that had ruled their construction was that they must grow by degrees, as time and circumstances permitted; and the fact must not be forgotten, that during that construction, though there had been no actual stoppage, there had been constant interruptions, interferences, and changes in details, owing to the alarms from the city, the mutiny in the cantonment, the rising of the police, the threatenings from every direction, and the need of safeguarding the families all the time. Further, the work involved was not confined to the defences, but to the storage of supplies, of cattle, and of ammunition, and the housing and the sanitary conservancy arrangements of the families and garrison, Christians, Mahomedans, and Hindoos.

CHAPTER III

ARRANGEMENTS FOR THE DEFENCE

WHEN the morning of July 2nd saw the whole force concentrated in the Residency entrenchments, there was some of the defensive work requiring immediate completion; much confusion still prevailed; and many of the existing arrangements needed prompt rectification, owing to the pressure with which the investment had begun.

It may help to give an insight into that pressure if the distance of the enemy's line of sharpshooters from our walls and parapets be described. These distances were—

Along the North face, the Captan Bazar ...	120 yards
On the Eastern face, opposite the Baily Guard ...	50 yards
On the Eastern face, more to the south ...	25 to 50 yards
Along the Southern face	13 yards
Along the Western face	not close

The total number of souls in the garrison was 3,000, of whom the combatants were 1,720, and the non-combatants 1,280.

The 1,720 combatants included—

British officers (including medical)	133
British N.C.O. and men	671
Christian drummers	51
Volunteers (being all civilians capable of bearing arms)	153
Total Christians	1,008
Native Troops	712
Grand Total	1,720

The 1,280 non-combatants were :—

Christians—Women	240
Children	270
Boys	50
Others	40
Total	600
Natives	680
Grand Total	1,280

The distribution of the combatants among the several posts along the four fronts and in the Residency has been already described.

Many of the English families were sheltered in the lower storeys of the following outposts—Fayrer's, the Post-office, the Martinière, the Brigade mess, and Gubbins's. They were also housed in the lower storeys of the interior buildings, such as the Residency, Ommanney's house, the Begum Kothi, and those in the rear of the Brigade mess. The boys were in the Martinière. The native non-combatants were almost all in the sheds and yards of the outhouses of the Western front. The general hospital was arranged in the lower storey of the large double-storeyed building called by that name, at the north-east angle of the position. This and the minor local hospitals were fully organized, though there was a serious want of chloroform and anæsthetics generally.

Except the Staff and the Engineers, the whole body of the inmates of the position, combatants or non-combatants, were distributed among the several posts; a commandant was appointed to each, and all its garrison and occupants were under his orders, and not allowed to stir from it without his leave. Each commandant was responsible for full knowledge of all the details and arrangements of his post; for its defence if it was an outpost, for a thorough and vigilant watch of all that went on in it and in its front, for prompt report of any dangerous or unusual occurrence, and for taking any immediate action that might be necessary.

Most of the servants had deserted, and consequently the cooking and other household duties for the families devolved frequently on the ladies. The native non-combatants were all assigned specific duties—mostly in connection with the Commissariat department.

Thanks to Sir Henry's forethought, a very large amount of live stock had been collected, and a vast quantity of all essential food supplies had been stored, through the agency and exertions mainly of the Commissariat officer, Captain James, and the district officer, Simon Martin, supplemented by friendly help from Talookdars and others. But, as it had to be stored away at once wherever room for it was found available, doubts, and eventually mistakes, arose as to the amount that had really been collected. This was owing mainly to the fact that Captain James, the Commissariat officer, was wounded in the knee at Chinhut, and thus debarred from that personal supervision and investigation which would otherwise have been a matter of course.

As it was, however, a few officers were told off as assistants to the Commissariat, for the distribution of the food; a scale was fixed (and altered from time to time) of the supply of each class of food—meat, vegetables, bread-stuff, and so on—to every inmate of the position, combatant and non-combatant, man and woman, adult and child, Christian, Mahomedan, and Hindoo. Early every morning the commandant of each post sent to the Commissariat a list of his garrison; and the full authorized supply of food was sent over accordingly for each garrison, which had to make its own arrangements for the cooking and for distribution, to a common mess or to individuals as the case might be.

Thus it happened that throughout the whole course of the siege no one had to search for food, no one felt any actual dearth of food; though all were affected by its poverty and meagreness, and especially by the want of fresh vegetables, and consequently suffered in health.

A few messes, a few individuals, and two or three shopkeepers, had laid in small stocks of wine, beer, spirits, and comforts and supplies of various kinds; but most of them were soon exhausted. The British troops had their regular ration of rum throughout the siege.

It seems almost needless to say that, during the siege, no fresh supplies of any kind were or could be introduced.

A look-out was kept up, as part of the duty, at every post; but a specially important post of observation was established at a high storey of the Residency, whence every movement of the enemy's troops could be seen and reported; and the actual result of this vigilant watch was that every attack and aggressive step of the enemy was anticipated; every attempt, except one, to effect a breach in our defences was foiled and checkmated.

What has been described will, I hope, answer fully the question so frequently asked—How did we get food?

And what has been shown as to the residents of each house and post being strictly confined to it, and not allowed to stir from it, as also respecting the small size of the position, the closeness of the investment, and the fact that every bit of open space was under the converging fire of sharpshooters in the upper storeys of the more distant buildings around us, will answer another question—less frequent but grimly ludicrous—Were we not able to drive about in the evenings?

It has been already mentioned, that most of the servants had deserted, and that ladies had consequently to undertake household duties. They were also valuable as nurses, and for the sewing work required for powder-hose and the like appliances.

Except a very few of the soldiers who had been artizans in their younger days, we had no smith or carpenter except two natives, who proved invaluable.

The British regiment which formed the backbone of the defence, the 32nd, was the Cornwall regiment; and fortunately contained in its ranks a sufficient number of Cornish ex-miners to form the nucleus for the guidance and training of the men of the several posts when the time arrived for taking to mining defence.

The water supply was fortunately very good and abundant, and sanitation had been provided for by the storage and distribution of large quantities of charcoal and lime, over the whole area of the position.

It is impossible to over-estimate the prevision and forethought by which all essential wants had thus been anticipated, in the very midst of the storm of mutiny and alarms and wild anxiety.

Sir Henry, alas! lived barely sufficiently long to see that there was hope that his efforts might end in a successful defence. The concentration was complete by one o'clock on the early morning of July 2nd. He went round, a few hours later in the dawn of that morning, inspecting every post and garrison, and impressing on it what it had to do, and steadying them all to their duty. One shell had already burst in the room in the Residency which he had selected for himself, and now, on returning there after his round, another burst about eight o'clock, wounding him mortally. On the 4th he died, amid the grief of those who felt that they owed their lives to him. Having previously received the assent of the Government, he named Major Banks as his successor in the civil administration, and Brigadier Inglis in the military command, associating with them, to form a council, his chief engineer, Major Anderson.

Major Banks's diary tells of Sir Henry's injunctions for the conduct of the defence: to check and control the firing; to spare and shelter the Europeans; to organize working arrangements for the hours of night; to entrench, to retrench, to traverse the enemy's fire; to enroll all native non-combatants for employment and pay them liberally; to make an inventory of all ammunition and supplies, and watch carefully the daily expenditure; to turn out all horses not needed for military contingencies; to keep up all possible communication with British authorities elsewhere.

These injunctions were of course subsidiary to the one great principle kept in the foreground from the first, never to yield or to show any other than a resolute front and bold heart.

And it may be said, without fear of challenge, that his spirit and example inspired the garrison; though the universal sense prevailed that the ship was now left almost without captain or rudder. So many officers of standing and repute, whose presence had been hoped for, had fallen: Handscombe in the mutiny at Murriaon; Fisher in the mutiny at Sultanpore; and Case at Chinhut. Brigadier Gray had fallen into ill-health. Even Major Anderson—wisest and shrewdest of counsellors—who had served at Ghuznee and in the Afghan War, was suffering from a mortal complaint, which carried him off in another six weeks. And, singular to say, with this abnormal dearth of officers of experience, the one man who had shown marked capacity, coolness, and resolution, who had planned, guided, and carried out the concentration from the Mutchi Bhown, Colonel Palmer, was passed over in absolute silence, and never heard of more either for an adequate command or for Staff duty. It may be safely assumed that had Sir Henry Lawrence survived sufficiently long to learn how Colonel Palmer had played his part in the withdrawal from the Mutchi Bhown and the concentration in the Residency, a position of suitable responsibility would have been allotted to him. But, as has been shown, a few hours of the early morning, spent in hard and anxious work, were all the time that elapsed between the concentration and the hour of Sir Henry's mortal wound.

CHAPTER IV

THE PROCEEDINGS OF THE ENEMY

WHILE the garrison of the Residency was thus settling down to its defence, what were the enemy about?

The regiments that had fought at Chinhut followed up the retreating troops, and gradually crossing the river lower down, reached and surrounded the Residency, and pressing its defenders hard, invested it closely by the night of June 30th. They were accompanied by the three bodies of Talookdars' men who had been present at Chinhut—Khan Ali Khan's from Mohomedabad, and the followers of the chiefs of Ramnugger Dhumeyree and of Mahonah.

After the arrival of the Chinhut force, they were joined by the two local regiments in the west of Lucknow, the military and the city police, and also the Afreedies (Afghans) of the town of Mulhiabad.

It would appear that their success at Chinhut was unexpected—was in fact a surprise to the mutineers, especially in respect of its completeness; for which not only they but the whole of the rebel party and their leaders were quite unprepared. The troops, as has been said, followed on sharp and pressed the investments at once and closely, but they were without guidance, and lost heavily both on June 30th and July 1st. Thence it was that, somewhat sick of fighting, they left their posts on the night of July 1st for a bout of revelry in the city, and so let the Mutchi Bhown garrison march in and concentrate without molestation. Their leaders, instead of commanding them, were engaged in court intrigues, and, beyond assigning the western front of the attack to the Talookdars' men, did not organize the military arrangements till June 7th.

These court intrigues and the organization of the new native Court and Government were matters of considerable moment, for until they were settled, the military operations against the British entrenchments were somewhat chaotic.

At first there were three candidates for the chief power.

I. The Fyzabad Moulvie, Sekunder Shah, also known as Ahmed Oolla Shah.

II. Suleiman Kudr, a relative of the Oude Royal Family.

III. Birjis Kudr, a son of the King of Oude by one of the most energetic of his wives, the Huzrut Mahul, generally known henceforward as the Begum.

The Moulvie had no powerful supporters. The cavalry, including Burkut Ahmed, who had commanded at Chinhut, were in favour of Suleiman Kudr; while the infantry and the old Durbar officials and courtiers seemed to espouse the cause of Birjis Kudr; who was at length, on June 7th, selected and proclaimed Nuwab in the place of his father, now a State prisoner in Calcutta.

Ressaldar Shahabut Deen, of the 15th Cavalry, installed Birjis Kudr on the throne, and proclaimed the conditions of his elevation. All orders from Delhi were to be obeyed implicitly. The army was to select the Prime Minister and the commandants of regiments. The Government was not to interfere with the army in regard to the treatment of the English and of their friends. The pay of the troops was to be doubled.

In full accord with the tone of this farcical arrangement was the selection of the Ministry. The Prime Minister and the Chancellor of the Exchequer were the ex-officials Shurf ood Dowlah and Maharaja Balkishen, who had held those posts under the late Nuwab. The Chief Justice was Mummoo Khan, the Begum's favourite. The War Minister was Rajah Jeylal Singh, a Lucknow courtier; while the men put in command of the troops and the charge of the siege, were not Burkut Ahmed and others who had shown some fitness to lead the troops, but two Lucknow courtiers, Meer Mehndee and Mozuffur Ali, a nephew of the Prime Minister, and Ressaldar Kasim Khan, of the 12th Cavalry. So much the better for the defence! As was certain to result from such ludicrous appointments and such subservience to the troops, the latter threw off all semblance of discipline or obedience to authority.

When on July 7th the new commanders proceeded to

assign the various regiments to the posts surrounding the Residency, the troops would have naught to do with orders or control. They would hold only such posts as they selected for themselves, and placed their artillery where they chose. But the three bodies of Talookdars' men obeyed orders. The posts which the Sepoys avoided were filled by former retainers of the Court, and by men of the aboriginal race, called Pasees, noted as spies and as miners, many of whom were armed with only bows and arrows.

It may be here stated at once, that the siege was marked throughout its whole duration by this want of organization, of discipline, of military spirit, and of courage, and also by the absence of any sign of military knowledge or skill or leadership on the part of the investing force. Some crude devices which they occasionally adopted showed glimpses of ingenuity. But they never, except at the end of the siege, formed a battery, or maintained a continuous fire, or attempted to breach the defences with their artillery. They kept their guns in isolated and sheltered nooks and corners, and fired them at random, hitting mainly the upper parts of the buildings and defences; their shots going in large numbers clear over the entrenchments, and plunging into their own posts beyond. The most effective and mischievous step which they took was to excavate shelter-trenches, from which and from the buildings they occupied they rained a ceaseless fire of bullets into the grounds and buildings; their marksmen systematically making our loopholes and embrasures their special aim. It was to this feature of their attack more than to any other cause that our continuous daily loss of life was due. And it was because they were sheltered in the lower storeys and in the inner courts of the buildings, where bullets could not penetrate, and from which they were ruthlessly prevented from stirring, that the women and children had practically complete immunity from the dangers of the fire of the enemy.

Besides guns more or less worthless, the enemy had two good light field batteries (twelve guns), and also the eight-inch howitzer which they had captured at Chinhut. These they moved about from place to place, and used when the desire seized them. Their store of ammunition for these guns was small, and after a while they had no shells to use for the howitzer except those that, thrown from our own mortars, had failed to burst.

The indiscipline of the enemy has been described. Both before and after the rebel Government was formed, they occupied only such posts as they chose; keeping up, however, a heavy and continuous fire, but doing very little harm in proportion. On the 9th some 300 men made a show of attacking the Baily Guard gate, but were easily repulsed. And then on the 12th and for the next few days they showed signs of occupying and fortifying a position facing Gubbins's at a distance of about 100 yards.

It was to such measures as these that the efforts of the enemy were restricted during the first stage of the siege. They had not as yet been joined by any other regular troops either from the Cawnpore direction, or from those who, after mutinying, had hovered in the western districts of Oude, instead of going either to Cawnpore or to Delhi.

From Delhi they heard that fighting was going on, but from Cawnpore they heard of the successive steps and victories of Havelock's advance; and as he gradually approached Cawnpore, it behoved the besiegers of Lucknow to take more vigorous action. So they resolved on a bold stroke; and set the Pasees, who had joined them in the investment, to construct a mine from the Captan Bazar against the Redan Battery. The Pasees were an aboriginal tribe, skilled in the use of the bow, and expert miners.

At this point we will leave the besieging troops and turn to the British garrison.

CHAPTER V

FIRST STAGE OF THE DEFENCE

To revert to the defence; on Sir Henry Lawrence's death, the important charges, civil and military, were thus held—

Chief Commissioner	Major Banks
His Secretary	Mr. Cooper
Brigadier-General Commanding ...	Brigadier-General Inglis
Head of his General Staff	Captain Wilson
Head of the Commissariat	Captain James
Chief of the Defensive arrangements	Major Anderson
Commanding the 32nd Regiment ...	Major Lowe
In command of the Artillery ...	Captain Simons
Garrison Engineer	Captain Fulton
Commissary of Ordnance	Lieutenant Thomas
Senior Surgeon	Surgeon Scott
Surgeon of the General Hospital ...	Surgeon Boyd
Residency Surgeon	Surgeon Fayrer

The outposts and their supports were at first commanded by the following officers, but changes afterwards occurred in these commands owing to casualties and other causes :—

Innes's post	Lieutenant Loughnan
The North curtain	Colonel Palmer
The Redan Battery	Captain Lawrence
The Hospital post	Lieutenant Langmore
The Baily Guard post	Lieutenant Aitken
Fayrer's post	Captain Weston
Saunders's post	Captain Saunders
Sago's post	Lieutenant Clery
Germon's post	Captain Germon
Post-office	Lieutenant McCabe
Anderson's post	Lieutenant Robert Anderson
Cawnpore Battery and Deprat's post	Relief of Captains
Martinière post	Mr. Schilling
Brigade mess	Colonel Masters
Sikh square	Lieutenant Hardinge
Gubbins's post	Captain Forbes
Outhouses' post	Captain Boileau
Evans's Battery	Captain Evans

Before the siege began some of the officers and men may have had occasional nights off duty, but from the first day of the investment this ceased. No soldier ever had what is called a night in bed; every one slept in his uniform, and with his weapons beside him.

From the first day of the concentrated defence, under the spirit roused by Sir Henry Lawrence, the fiercest energy marked the efforts of the garrison to place the position and the arrangements in order, and to secure the gaps and strengthen the weak points in the defences. The cattle and the horses had, many of them, got loose in the first confusion. These were collected and sheltered. The cattle were then driven over to the sheds which had been prepared for them; a certain number of horses were selected and picketed in the Sikh squares or elsewhere; while the rest were turned out at night and driven off. Most of them, however, straggled back, wandered about close under the parapets, and were shot down, creating a horrible stench for several days. The greater part of the wheat had been stored in the church, and from the first its removal by degrees to the exposed positions was steadily carried on.

The river front, it had been hoped, would for a while at least remain a part of the defence, and consequently a large portion of the powder and ammunition had been stored in pits in the ground there outside the Hospital post; but its removal, though a matter of grave necessity, was not attempted till July 22nd. Close to this magazine some tents had been left standing, and near the tents a large quantity of Bhoosa (fodder for cattle) had been stacked. The enemy managed to set this stack on fire on the night of July 3rd, and a party of officers, under Lieutenant Fletcher, went out and cut down the tents, levelling them, to prevent their getting fired; otherwise terrible disaster might have resulted from their closeness to the magazine.

But of course more important than all else were the defences themselves; and working parties, that took up nearly the whole garrison, were for the first few days kept sedulously employed all night on them, and on the obstructions attached to them.

The weakest points in the trace of the position, in consequence of gaps being left in the work in progress, were at Gubbins's post and at the Cawnpore Battery. Both of these were at once worked at vigorously. At Gubbins's post, not only were the parapets completed, but the groundwork was started of a valuable battery at its salient angle. At the Cawnpore Battery, the line of parapets and obstructions connecting it with Anderson's post to its left and Deprat's shop to its right was finished, and made continuous, leaving the whole circle and trace of defences without a gap of any kind.

More than this, these defences were, throughout the whole line of the position, worked at in respect of repairing, heightening, and strengthening them, and increasing the obstructions and the facilities for free defensive movement, so as to satisfy the requirement, which the engineers had decided to be essential. It was this. The obstructions and impediments must be such that they would of themselves check the rush of an enemy, and keep him at a standstill for the few minutes that would ensure the full fire of the front, both direct and enfilade, coming into play, and the full strength of the local garrison being collected to repel the efforts of the assailants to break through the defences into the entrenchments.

Most of the external obstructions—trenches, palisades, abattis, crows'-feet, *trous de loup*, and the like—had been finished before the investment began; but where they were found to be wanting, they were completed at each post by a few of its garrison in the darkness of night. Then the parapets were raised by sandbags, some of the weaker points were supported by shelter-trenches, loopholes were multiplied, the sites of the gun emplacements were improved and drained, and traverses were erected at the Baily Guard gate, at the Hospital gate, and in the street facing Johannes' house—the start of a system of retrenchments to meet the chance of any successful attempt of the enemy on the first line of defence, and also to protect the passage of the roads behind them.

By the end of a week, that is by the 8th or 9th of July, the improved condition of the defences, the organized vigilance which had been established, the conduct of the enemy, and the increased spirit which the men of the garrison were now showing, combined to confirm the hope of a successful issue to the defence.

The enemy had confined their efforts to a ceaseless but

aimless fire of musketry, and they had shown no serious signs of any intention to use their artillery for breaching the defences, or for any really effective purpose.

On the other hand, two or three instances had occurred of a few bold men at the outposts (notably at the Redan and at Innes's post), stealing out, attacking and inflicting loss on the enemy's pickets, and spiking their guns.

On July 7th there had been an organized sortie. This sortie was made against Johannes' house, which, as has been already mentioned, had been left standing opposite the Martinière post, without its upper storeys having been demolished like those of the other buildings on the same alignment. It had consequently been found to command the Cawnpore Battery, and so it was decided to capture and destroy it. A body of some fifty men charged out from a door in the side wall of the courtyard of the Martinière, broke into the building, and killed its garrison. But before the engineers could arrange the powder-bags for its demolition, the enemy showed in such force that the Brigadier recalled the party, and the object of the sortie was left unaccomplished. This episode, however, brightened up the garrison, as the enemy had suffered severely, and our loss consisted of only three men wounded. Still Johannes' house remained, encouraging the besiegers, and forming a thorn in our side for some time to come.

The rains began on this day in full force, and cooled the air for a day or two, but only for a day or two. Intensely muggy heat then ensued; the constant wet increased the discomfort of the men exposed to it, and cholera and sickness increased. The rain too did considerable damage to the parapets and defences, and made incessant work necessary to keep them in repair. One of its effects was to bring down a wall of the racket court, in which fodder for the cattle had been stored; and it took many days to remedy the mischief thus caused.

Minor attacks and threatenings of the enemy, both by night and day, kept the garrison on the alert. On the 9th, and again on the 12th July, they charged up, about 300 strong, towards the Baily Guard gate, but retired again after a very few minutes. On the 12th they threatened Gubbins's post, and were seen to be preparing emplacements for guns round all the south-eastern angle of the position. On the 14th they began firing a gun for which they had prepared a site opposite the Brigade mess, damaging its upper storey and roof parapets. At this date, too, it was observed from the Redan that an earthwork of some sort, conjectured—and, as it proved, correctly—to be mining, was in progress in the Captan Bazar, near the end adjacent to the mosque that lay immediately below the Redan. The engineer of the post stole out in the dark and listened all over the ground near the apex of the Redan, but heard no sound.

Meanwhile, there was not a word of news from the outer world; a few spies had gone out, but none as yet had come back. And this was the state of matters when the first general attack on the position was made on July 20th.

During the early morning, the officers on duty at the look-out in the Residency had sent in repeated reports of much movement of troops along the surrounding streets and roads; and consequently the several garrisons had been warned to be on the alert, and the whole force was under arms and expecting an attack.

At a quarter past ten it opened simultaneously round the whole position; the signal being the explosion of the mine which had been aimed at the Redan, and of which the signs had been seen, as already described, for several days. But the point at which it was blown up was 140 feet distant from the Redan, which fully accounted for the sounds of its mining not being heard. The length of the gallery up to that point was 160 feet (as found by actual measurement taken by me on September 30), and the starting-point of the mine was 270 feet in a direct line from the apex of the Redan. The direction of the mine was about 20 degrees out of its proper bearing.

This was the longest mine that the enemy ever attempted, and nothing occurred subsequently to indicate that they possessed the skill or the appliances necessary to enable them to carry out a mine which could have reached the Redan from the Captan Bazar, or any other shelter ground in that neighbourhood.

On the signal for the attack being given by this explosion, a furious fire of musketry and artillery was begun all round;

and two large bodies of the enemy charged or rushed forward rapidly as if to storm the position, one at the Redan (where the mine had been exploded), and the other at Innes's post.

The storming party at the Redan found themselves, obviously to their surprise, confronted by the battery whole and sound, instead of in ruins. They were received with a heavy fire from the Curtain as well as the Redan, both of grape and musketry, and, being in a mass, suffered severely. They faced the fire for only a few minutes, and then retired precipitately, never having really approached—much less reached—the obstructions through which they would have had to struggle.

At Innes's post the attack was more prolonged and resolute, and at one time that post seemed to be in danger of being cut off in the rear, as the enemy pressed on towards the neck of the spur near the church. But the further they advanced, the more they were overlapped by the flanking fire from Innes's post on the one side and the western front on the other; and the more telling was the grape, at short range, of Evans's guns. So they, too, after a fairly brave effort, retired precipitately. A few of them, who had gone at the obstructions, got entangled in the abattis, could neither go forward nor withdraw, and were all shot down.

Two comparatively minor assaults were made at the same time at the south-eastern and the south-western angles of the position. At the former, the enemy advanced against the group of three contiguous posts, the Cawnpore Battery, Anderson's, and Germon's. And at the latter, they attacked Gubbins's Bastion.

The charge on the Cawnpore Battery was led by a standard-bearer, who was shot down as he reached the palisades, and none of his supporters ever advanced further. They were effectively checked by the obstructions, and finding themselves under a close and heavy fire, soon retreated as rapidly as they had advanced. Similarly a resolute fire and an unbreached line of defence speedily repulsed the attack at Anderson's and Germon's posts.

The same success attended the defenders of Gubbins's post under Captain Forbes and Mr. Gubbins.

Whilst these several assaults were being delivered, and indeed for some hours after such attempts had ceased, a furious fire of guns and of musketry was maintained over the whole circle of the position; aimed, however, mainly at the crests of the parapets and the upper walls of the buildings. It damaged these considerably, but inflicted singularly slight loss on the garrison. The resulting casualties amounted only to four killed and twelve wounded, most of these occurring in the jubilant carelessness that ensued when the attack was felt to have been defeated, and to be subsiding. During the attack itself the men had behaved well, obeyed orders, kept under cover, and fired only at clear objects. By three o'clock the enemy's fire began to slacken; by four o'clock the attack was at an end; and the garrison was in the highest spirits.

CHAPTER VI

THE SECOND STAGE OF THE DEFENCE

WE left the Lucknow garrison on July 20th, naturally jubilant over their repulse of the first great attack; but this feeling of elation soon gave place to the enhanced anxiety arising from the mining tactics of the enemy coming on the top of the old chronic dangers, and the continued want of all intelligence from the outer world. The usual form of this new anxiety was the dread of being personally hurled into the air; a dread quite reasonable in the occupants of those outposts that formed the outer line in the defences, such as the Brigade mess and the Martinière. Our real danger, however, lay in the practicable breaches that the mines might make suddenly in the defences; through which the enemy, duly prepared for the explosion, could rush forward in overwhelming numbers.

This terrible risk and chance was, of course, specially present before the minds of the engineers; and, under Major Anderson's direction, the following steps were immediately taken to meet it.

I. The commanders of the several outposts told off some of their most intelligent men to listen, at short intervals, for sounds of mining, by laying their ears to the ground, and to report at once if they heard any suspicious sounds.

II. The 32nd, being the Cornwall regiment, fortunately contained a few more or less skilled miners. So Sergeant Day and seven men—Hunter, Abel, Cummerford, Bonatta, Kitchen, Cullimore, and Farran—were selected to guide and instruct the several garrisons in their mining work, and to take part themselves in the more serious and urgent operations.

III. In addition to counter-mines being immediately started wherever the enemy were found to be at work, shafts were at once sunk, and galleries begun at the most dangerous points, in the more exposed posts, such as Deprat's, Anderson's, Sago's, and Saunders's.

IV. The system of retrenchments, already begun, was sedulously continued. These were works in rear of the front entrenchments, and commanding them; and were designed to check any rushes or interruptions the enemy might make after a successful explosion and breach.

At first the situation seemed desperate, as the enemy had unlimited labour at command, especially in the men of the Pasee tribe, known to be expert miners—while the garrison were very much pressed for labour of any kind, much more *skilled* labour—and the line they had to protect was more than a mile in length, half of it being close to sites held by the enemy, who could thence start their mines of attack unseen. Not only were we short of labour, but we were at first almost destitute of entrenching tools; as the labourers had carried most of them off on June 30th, on the news of Chinhut suddenly arriving. But fortunately a search led one night to a valuable supply being found on the roof of Deprat's shop.

These were the measures adopted under Major Anderson's orders to meet the further attacks expected in this new description of warfare; Captain Fulton, aided by Sergeant Day, fixing on the details for the several posts, and the garrison of each post having to carry out whatever work was required there. These measures were initial and precautionary. The enemy's attacks and efforts were, of course, to be met and foiled as they became known.

As it was, they began at once at a few points. The fear was that they might take to mining all round, or at least at a large number of points, far beyond what we could effectually oppose or check.

They continued their starting efforts of July 20th, by six fresh attempts on the 21st, three of them being lodgments at the foot of our defences, and the other three regular mining galleries driven underground from their own position against ours.

The three lodgments were—

No. 1, at the foot of the Redan.

No. 2, in the shops lining the outside of the Martinière.

No. 3, at the foot of the stockade of Gubbins's post, where it approached the Sikh square.

No. 1 was begun by a small party crawling up at night. They were detected in the morning, and forthwith driven off by musketry and grape from the Hospital post, and by grenades from the Redan itself.

No. 2 was attempted by a party of Sepoys, who broke into the shops outside, and began to undermine the wall of the Martinière, the floor of which was higher than the floor level of the shops and the street. But the garrison inside loopholed those walls immediately below the roofs of the shops, and dropped down hand-grenades into them, killing some of the enemy and driving the rest away. One of the loopholes was then enlarged into a hole, through which the garrison broke into the shops, barricaded them effectually, and so included them within the defences of the position, instead of their being merely neutral ground as heretofore.

At Gubbins's post the enemy's effort was made by a comparatively strong party, and was first met by a cross musketry fire; after which the garrison made a sortie and drove the enemy from the position, which they never attempted to re-occupy.

This was the fate of the three attempts to make lodgments for mines.

The three galleries driven by the enemy and detected by sounds and signs were aimed at—

1. The Cawnpore Battery.
2. The Brigade mess.
3. The Sikh square—

all on the South face. They were started from behind walls or *débris* at points distant from thirty to sixty feet from our defences.

At all the three posts that were threatened, shafts were at once sunk, and short galleries driven out to meet the enemy. The work was done by the 32nd for the Cawnpore Battery at Deprat's; by the 71st N. I. at the Brigade mess; and by the Sikh sowars at the Sikh square.

At the two latter posts, the enemy's efforts seemed to cease at once, for some time at least, on hearing our men at work. At the Cawnpore Battery, though there too they stopped very soon, it was from a different cause; for a peculiar incident occurred. The enemy as it turned out were driving their gallery at too high a level—in other words, at too shallow a depth below the surface—so that the ground gave way at some points and showed the site of the mine. On this, Lieutenant Bonham lobbed an eight-inch shell on to it with great precision from a mortar only a few yards off, laid it entirely bare, and so destroyed it.

Thus for a time all these three mines were checked.

A fourth mine had been started by the enemy without attracting our attention, directed against Sago's post on the East face. It was discovered, but not till the 29th, by its roof collapsing like that of the mine against the Cawnpore Battery; only more completely, so as not to require any steps on the part of the defence.

These two galleries—that is, those against Sago's and the Cawnpore Battery—were never proceeded with, or started afresh; but in the case of the other two—those at the Brigade mess and the Sikh square—the enemy began working at them again after a short lull.

Meanwhile, as all these three points that had been threatened on the South face were dangerous, Major Anderson caused our countermines there to be driven well outside our line of defence to a length of at least twenty-four feet.

The Deprat's Cawnpore Battery gallery was thus driven out thirty feet, and protective branches were then driven right and left, so as to intercept any mine the enemy might try to push forward there; the extremities of the branches being charged and kept prepared for explosion in case of the enemy making a wider detour.

The Brigade mess mine was driven out thirty-eight feet, and there halted, the enemy having by that time entirely ceased working.

The Sikh square countermine met with some excitement. On reaching the distance originally ordered, of twenty-four feet, the enemy were again heard at work, and the gallery was turned so as to intercept them, and was there halted. Their miners at length reached our gallery; when Captain Fulton broke down the thin film between the two mines, and drove our opponents out from their own gallery through their shaft from which it had been started. He then laid a charge at their end, and exploding it, destroyed that further part of it. The portion of their gallery in our direction remained uninjured, and this he retained for our own purposes.

In fact, by August 1st all mining contests ceased for a while on both sides; our work for the next few days lying in the continued sinking of shafts, and the starting of galleries at the exposed points, in anticipation of attack. One important fact, specially important to the defence, had been established. The soil was so stiff that the galleries needed no casings or supports of any kind.

During this second stage, then, of the siege, the mining warfare which had been inaugurated may be thus summarized. The enemy had attacked the South face at three points and the East face at one. Two of these attacks had collapsed from the subsidence of their galleries; and of the other two mines, one had been checked and the other captured by our countermines. We had begun a larger number of precautionary mines at the most exposed points; and during the last of the three weeks of this period, no further signs had been seen of any fresh attempts of the enemy; though, as the sequel will show, they were really hard at work. Our opponents' mines were well constructed, but they showed neither skill in managing nor courage in fighting them.

During the whole of this stage there was a lull in ordinary fighting, and in assaults on our posts on the enemy's part; but we made three small sorties—from Gubbins's on the 22nd, and the Redan on July 24th, and from Innes's post on August 8th, chiefly to explore and to drive away lurking parties of the rebels. In the last of these, one of the enemy's guns was spiked; the sorties were not attended with any loss, and they kept up the spirits of the garrison.

The only step taken by the mutineers of sufficient importance to attract attention, was to plant a heavy gun opposite Innes's post, in the street leading southwards from the iron bridge, at a point called Hill's shop, where it could range across the whole Residency position. That gun was thought to have caused more loss of life than all the rest of the enemy's artillery, and it also occasioned many ludicrous and singular incidents. It first opened fire on July 31st; and the harm it did led to a battery being improvised for an eighteen-pounder at Innes's post; the parapet being of earth, filled in between a brick wall on the outside, and a revetment of a double row of piles on the inside. This was made on the night of the 6th. The gun was placed in position in it on the night of the 7th. On the 8th, it entirely silenced the enemy's gun; but General Inglis thought the position a dangerous one, as being a temptation to the enemy, and withdrew the gun the same night, August 8th.

Besides the mining and the construction of this battery, engineer operations of other kinds were ceaselessly going on. Defensive works, new traverses, and retrenchments were erected; the parapets on the north face were heightened, all were being kept in repair and improved—a matter of urgent necessity owing to the damage done by the heavy rains, as well as by the desultory but unceasing fire of the enemy. Lastly, a new magazine was constructed in the underground rooms of a building in the centre of the position, called the Begum Kothi. Hitherto a very large quantity of the powder—240 barrels—had been left [1] in an underground magazine which had been made in the grounds immediately at the foot of the eastern end of the Northern face; and had remained covered by the *débris* of the tents that had been cut down on July 3rd, when the Bhoosa stack caught fire. Now, however, the officers of the garrison were formed into a working party, and on the nights of July 22nd and 23rd, removed the whole of the powder from that old magazine into the new one in the Begum Kothi.

As regards the general state of the garrison, they were losing men daily from sickness, cholera fever, and small-pox, as well as from the continuous rain of desultory fire which the enemy kept up. There was one white-letter day during this stage. There was no death or burial on August 8th.

It may be noted as a singular fact, that each of the four stages of the defence was marked by one death of special importance. During the first stage was the greatest loss of all, Sir Henry Lawrence. In the second stage, Major Banks, who had succeeded him as the head of the Administration, was killed on July 21st by a bullet while examining the enemy's position through a loophole. His death was

[1] *Vide* p. 121.

felt to be a very serious loss, though he had not had time to make his mark on the defence.

There remains to be mentioned the most exciting feature of this stage—the first receipt of intelligence from the outside world. The news, however, told of little more than Havelock's presence at Cawnpore, and his intention to move on towards Lucknow. It was brought by a pensioned Sepoy named Ungud, who had been sent out with messages to our friends, and who now reappeared on July 22nd, two days after the first attack. He entered at Gubbins's post, and was at once taken to Mr. Gubbins, who had been in charge of the Intelligence Department. He brought no letter, but gave full tidings of Havelock's force and victories. Mr. Gubbins sent this information to General Inglis, and asked if he wished to send any letter by Ungud, who was anxious to start back at once. The General replied that he would not write; on which Mr. Gubbins wrote a letter from himself to the Governor-General under cover to General Havelock, giving the particulars of the present situation of the garrison, and sent it off by Ungud. The reason for Ungud's desire to start at once was that the rain was heavy, which gave him the most favourable condition for evading the enemy's watch.

Presently a letter for General Havelock reached Mr. Gubbins from General Inglis; but it was too late; Ungud had started. On the 25th, however, Ungud returned, this time bringing a letter from Colonel Tytler, A.Q.M.G., which ran thus—

"Your letter of the 22nd has reached us. We have two-thirds of our force across the river, and eight guns in position already. The rest will follow immediately. I will send over some news to-night or to-morrow. We have ample force to destroy all who oppose us. Send us a sketch of your position in the city, and any directions for entering it or turning it that may strike you. In five or six days we shall meet. You must threaten the rear of the enemy if they come out, and we will smash them.

"(Signed) B. FRAZER TYTLER.

"P.S.—We have smashed the Nana, who has disappeared, and destroyed his palace, Bithoor. No one knows where his army has dispersed to, but it has disappeared."

Now the letter to which this was a reply had been despatched exactly three days before, in which interval therefore Ungud must have covered about one hundred miles of direct route, besides communicating with Colonel Tytler.

The excitement on receipt of this news was intense. A reply was sent off on the following night, the 26th, to Colonel Tytler, giving a plan of the place, and such information as the General possessed, as well as suggestions for the route to be taken by the relieving force.

It was confidently hoped that that force would appear in a few days. But day after day passed, and nothing was seen or heard of it, till on August 6th another of our spies, Aodhan Singh, the orderly of Brigadier Gray, returned, but without any letter; reporting, however, that Havelock's force had fought two successful engagements on the Lucknow side of the Ganges, but had been obliged to halt at Mungurwar owing to cholera and other causes of loss.

To the garrison generally, this intelligence was very disheartening, though it was obvious that the check was no worse than was to be reasonably expected; whilst all, save a few, were depressed from the constant watching and want of rest, besides suffering from the dread of the enemy's success in their efforts at undermining our position.

This was the state of matters when the second stage of the siege was brought to a close by the second general all-round attack on August 10th. The same signs were seen from our look-out station as on July 20th; so the posts were ready manned when the attack was opened. It began with the explosion of two mines, directed respectively against the Martinière on the South face, and Sago's on the East face; the explosions, which were practically simultaneous, being the signal for the commencement of a vigorous cannonade and musketry fire all round, and for efforts to rush the two posts against which the mines had been directed. But those mines had fallen far short of the mark, though they had damaged the stockading of the Martinière fifteen feet in front; the distance accounting sufficiently for their not having been detected by the defence. The assailants were, as before, foiled and checked by not finding any breach; and being heavily punished by the fire of the defence, retired precipitately and did not renew their efforts.

The attack, however, was not restricted to these two points in the line of defence. Avoiding the north-east angle, at the Hospital post, where they would have had a much longer distance to go over, besides being subjected to flanking fire from the Redan on one side, and from the Post-office Battery on the other, the enemy attempted to storm the other three of the four salients of the position —Innes's post on the north-west, Gubbins's on the south-west, and the Cawnpore Battery and Anderson's post on the south-east. All three parties were accompanied by scaling-ladders, but they were stopped by the obstacles in front, and never passed them; they suffered heavily from the fire while thus checked, and then fled back to their own posts. Only at the Cawnpore Battery a few men penetrated as far as the ditch, and there finding themselves subjected to hand-grenades, speedily followed the example of their comrades. The attack did not last long; but in the evening there was some fresh excitement, owing to a few adventurous Sepoys suddenly appearing inside the outer defences of Saunders's post; where they were promptly shot down.

It was ascertained afterwards that the enemy had lost more heavily on this occasion than on July 20th. Our casualties were seventeen, five being killed, of whom three were English.

Before leaving the story of this second stage of the defence, it may be as well to explain its peculiar feature—the lull in the general fighting, while the mining attack was vigorous and pertinacious. Its cause was this: the bulk of the Sepoys were engaged up to about the 6th in watching and opposing Havelock, the local troops mainly continuing the investment; while the Pasees, not being soldiers, but only workmen, were kept sedulously employed on the mines, working them excellently, but proving failures when it came to fighting.

CHAPTER VII

THIRD STAGE OF THE DEFENCE

THE MINING

AFTER the second great assault the state of the garrison was this—

Besides those who had been killed at Chinhut, we had lost 100 men of the 32nd and 84th since the beginning of the siege; and many officers and faithful Sepoys had also fallen. The women and children were suffering terribly, not merely from losses of life and health, but from the reduction of shelter; for many of the buildings were crumbling away, so that some had to be partly and others altogether abandoned as places of shelter for families. The Residency was nearly uninhabitable, and on the day after the assault, August 11th, a large part of it fell in. Anderson's and Deprat's, the two posts on the flank of the Cawnpore Battery, were nearly in ruins. On the other hand, the garrison had gained confidence in their ability to keep the enemy at bay in their attacks. They had thrown out defensive mines at three important posts on the south face—Deprat's (for the Cawnpore Battery), the Brigade mess, and the Sikh square; shafts had been sunk and galleries started at Saunders's, Sago's, and other posts; and the besiegers were showing no sign of making a simultaneous mining attack all round.

This was the state of matters when the third of the four stages of the siege began. It was the longest of the stages by four or five days, and was marked by its ceaseless series of contests, and by the exciting incidents with which it was crowded. For this reason it will be expedient to devote two chapters to this stage, confining the present chapter to an account of the mining warfare.

The greater part of this mining contest lay in the

enemy's mines of attack and our countermines. Excluding those which developed on September 5th, the closing day of the stage, the besiegers attempted fourteen mines during this stage: seven on the Eastern face, viz. four at Saunders's post and three at Sago's; three at Anderson's at the south-eastern angle; and four on the southern face, viz. two at the Brigade mess and two at the Sikh square. In addition to these were two others which were still in progress when the third attack occurred; viz. one on the West face at the church, and one on the North face towards the Redan. Omitting these two last, the other fourteen were serious efforts to breach the defences, carried out to the best of the enemy's power. They succeeded in one, the west mine at the Sikh square: the one at its east end was neutral in its effects. They were foiled in all the other twelve.

It will be most convenient to describe these several efforts, and the countermines and other means by which they were defeated, post by post, rather than by order of date.

Saunders's post was not known to be threatened till a comparatively late period, August 23rd, when the enemy were heard at work opposite the *left* corner (next the Baily Guard gate), where a shaft had been already sunk, and a gallery started. On the sounds being heard, the gallery was advanced towards the enemy till the 26th, when it was stopped, as by that time all sound of work had ceased. On the 31st, however, five days afterwards, they were again heard; but as if they had started more to the *right*, and were driving from right to left slantwise across the front of the post and of our mine; so our gallery was continued from where it had before stopped, but with a bend in an intercepting direction, till the enemy came close; it was then loaded and fired, the explosion rendering that immediate neighbourhood unfit for further hostile mining. This occurred early on September 1st. But on the same evening, the pick was heard again at a third mine coming direct towards the *middle* of the post, where fortunately we had already as on the left sunk a shaft and started a gallery. We advanced this gallery to a length of twenty feet, and then diverged it to the right, to which the enemy had bent. There, on the afternoon of September 2nd, as we got close, we loaded and fired our mine while the enemy were still at work, again destroying all the ground.

But this did not stop the rebels. We heard them a fourth time, on September 3rd. They were now evidently working from their old gallery, at right angles to it, towards our right, and parallel to our front, skirting the loosened ground. So a third shaft was sunk, this time at the right corner of the post, and a gallery driven outward. By the evening of September 4th, we had driven twenty-two feet, reached brickwork, and pierced through it. We heard the miners driving onwards in our direction, so we halted; and then it appeared shortly that they were not coming quite straight, only very close to us. It then struck our engineer that the enemy on reaching this brickwork would think it was the wall of the post, and would immediately stop work, in order to arrange to load and explode the mine. This proved to be the case. On meeting the wall they ceased working. We picked quietly into the mine, enlarged the opening, and found the gallery full of light at the other end, with one of the miners seated in it. Before he could be shot or captured, one of our party sneezed; the lights were at once put out, and the miner had disappeared. But we had gained possession of the mine; as, however, the enemy commanded its entrance, we exploded it, using a double charge to destroy more of the ground; a safe operation, as it was at a considerable distance from our own line of defence. Thus, on the night of September 4th, ended the fourth attempt of the enemy to breach Saunders's post. It will be seen in the next chapter that this frustrated one of the main designs of the enemy in their plan of attack for the following day, September 5th.

We next come to Sago's post. It will be remembered that one of the features of the attack of August 10th was the springing by the enemy of a mine, directed against this post, but harmless from having fallen short of it. Next evening, August 11th, the enemy returned to work at this mine. The first step taken against this renewed effort was a sortie next morning by twelve men of the 32nd led by Lieut. Clery, who commanded the post. This sortie failed, however, and had to return at once; as it found itself met by a very strong covering party, all ready and on the alert to protect their miners. Our sortie was fortunate in returning without loss. A countermine was immediately begun, or rather a gallery was driven from a start which had been previously prepared. Both the mine and the countermine advanced rapidly towards each other; and on their approaching sufficiently close, Lieut. Hutchinson, who was in charge, loaded the mine and exploded it, while the enemy were still heard at work with the pick.

From this time the enemy avoided further molestation of this post till August 29th, but sounds having been then again heard, a second gallery was started, from its extreme salient; and on September 3rd, a third from its north-east end. Both mines were still in hand when the attack of September 5th took place.

The next post to be dealt with is Anderson's. As it was exposed to the enemy's attack both on its eastern and its southern front, a shaft had been sunk early at its south-eastern corner. The signs and sounds on the eastern front led, on August 13th, after the contest at Sago's was ended, to a gallery being driven from that shaft eastwards; which on the 17th had reached a length of thirty-six feet, and was then halted, for the time, as all hostile sounds had ceased. But on the 23rd, the miners being again heard, though more to the left, a side gallery was driven from the first one, northwards, parallel to the face of the position, starting from a point twenty feet distant from the shaft. On the 27th this too was stopped, and next day a third gallery was driven southwards from the shaft as sounds were heard in that quarter; this was carried on for five days, till further work was not required for the time. At this post, therefore, three galleries had been driven to counteract the enemy's efforts, and had stopped them all without any actual contest.

We come next to the Brigade mess. A countermine had been carried forward by us, before August 10th, from its *left*, to a length of thirty-eight feet, and then stopped and held for listening purposes. On August 20th, the miners were heard at work opposite the *right* of the post. On the 21st, therefore, a gallery from that end was started, which had reached a length of thirty-three feet by the 27th, when it was halted; while the progress of the enemy, who were still driving onwards, was watched. On the 29th they passed the head of our gallery, and then our miners working vigorously to the flank broke into their gallery, seized and held it as far as their shaft, and then loaded and exploded it at that end, destroying the shelter from which it had started.

The rebels, however, seemed to be as determined here as against Saunders's post. For on September 3rd they were heard at work opposite the *middle* of the post, between the two galleries which had been already carried out and were still extant. To meet this new attack, Lieut. Hutchinson drove an intercepting gallery, parallel to the face of the post, from the *left* mine, starting from a point in it thirty feet from the shaft, so as eventually to meet our right mine, and form an underground road which should intercept any approach of the enemy between the two existing galleries. This countermine or listening gallery was still in progress on September 5th.

We now come to the Sikh square, which was the only post in which our opponents succeeded in effecting a breach; a success due to their not having been detected; owing, it was believed, to the noise made by the stamping of the Sikh cavalry horses picketed close at hand.

The Sikh post consisted of three squares, one behind the other, the front facing the south; its right or eastern flank being separated by a narrow lane from Gubbins's post, the front of which, as already described, was thrown further back than the front of the Sikh square. This lane, it may be here mentioned, was swept by a gun which we had placed in position at its inner end.

The enemy had begun two mines from their position before the Sikh square; one directed at our left (the western), the other at our right (the eastern) end of its face. Since the horses were picketed along the eastern side of the square, bordering the lane above-mentioned, it was the eastern mine which was not discovered, and which effected the breach. The western mine had been detected, and on the 16th a gallery had been started, from the west end close to the Brigade mess, to meet it. These two mines, the enemy's and ours, had come quite close to each other, and preparations to load them for explosion were begun simultaneously by the enemy and ourselves on the morning of the 18th. Lieut. Hutchinson had laid his charge, and was tamping when the mutineers began a vigorous musketry fire on the post—evidently an attack—and our Sikh party of miners had barely time to clear out of their gallery and shaft when the enemy sprung both their mines. The one at the east end was effective, and made a large breach thirty feet wide in our line of defence; the other had evidently not been tamped at all, and expended its force along both their own gallery and ours, but chiefly their own; laying in ruins the shelter from which *they* had started.

This explosion was, for the moment, expected to prove, as on July 20th and August 10th, the prelude to an all-round attack. But a few minutes sufficed to show that such was not the case, and that no such attack had been prepared. A rush was made by a small party of the enemy at the breach; but they were at once shot down by our musketry from the Brigade mess, and from the second Sikh square (in the rear), which acted as a retrenchment. Another party made a lodgment at the outhouse at the end of the lane, to loophole the wall so as to fire along the inside of the breach. But our gun (a twenty-four-pounder howitzer) at the inner end of the lane quickly opened upon them and drove them off; another gun was now run down into the Sikh square so as to face the breach; the reserve company (the 84th) appeared to reinforce the post; and all available hands were set to work at both ends of the breach, carrying planks and doors and setting them upright in the opening, each in succession overlapping the preceding one; till eventually the whole thirty feet of breach was barricaded. This barricade was strengthened and finished off by earthwork and sand-bags during the following night.

But in the course of the same afternoon (the 18th) we retaliated on the enemy by making a sortie from Gubbins's post, attacking and taking the shelter from which they had begun their mines, and destroying them all by hasty demolition.

In fact the day which had begun so inauspiciously ended almost gleefully. Three officers and a few men had been blown up by the explosion, but had escaped almost unharmed. Five men, however, were buried in the *débris* of the breach. It may be added that this was the solitary instance when the reserve had to be called out.

During this stage therefore our antagonists had successfully driven and exploded one mine; a second had been exploded without any damage to us; we had checked twelve other mines by our twelve countermines; and had destroyed five of them by our explosions.

As already mentioned, the besiegers had also been at work at two other mines, directed respectively against the Redan and the church, which came to nothing.

It remains to describe the one mining operation in which we took the offensive. This was directed against Johannes' house, the one house which, as has been mentioned, was left close to our position without its upper storey having been demolished. Owing to this, the enemy's marksmen in it were able to play havoc from it in two or three directions, but especially with the Cawnpore Battery, which they practically silenced. It was, therefore, decided to undermine and blow it up; and to me this exciting duty was assigned on August 17th. The mine had to be started from some point in the shops which we had barricaded, abutting on the wall of the Martinière. Johannes' house could not be seen from within these shops, and the first step to be taken was to make a survey and plan of the essential points of the two positions, our own and the enemy's, to admit of a proper design for the operation. The survey was made by climbing on to the roof of the building, crawling along behind the shelter of its parapet wall, and taking (1) the positions of the sites of some shot-holes in that wall, and (2) bearings, through those shot-holes, of the chief points of the edifice to be attacked. I thus ascertained that the building was fifty feet long; and distant forty feet from our wall, and thirty-four feet from where the edge of our shaft must be. The exact proper site for our shaft was also thus fixed. The plan decided on was to drive a gallery out for a length of fifty feet, which would bring us sixteen feet within the face of the building; and then to drive branches right and left, each twelve feet long, which should end at thirteen feet from the side walls. At the ends of these branches were to be short returns, to form the chambers in which the charges should be laid.

This plan was proposed and approved on August 17th, and the shaft was sunk and the mine started the same afternoon. It was kept as secret as possible for obvious reasons; and the 32nd miners were the only men employed on it, with orders to work with as little noise as possible. To make its roof secure, casing was used for that portion of it which passed underneath the ditch and palisade outside the position. On the fifty-foot gallery being finished, two parties were set to work at the two branches. On the evening of the 20th the mine was finished, and it was arranged to fire it early next morning. During the night, the four charges were laid, of one hundred pounds each; and the hose by which they were to be fired was laid along the whole length of the gallery up to the shaft. The tamping was peculiar; the long gallery was not tamped at all, but the junction of the branches at its end was tamped for a length of some ten feet, and their ends at the immediate neighbourhood of the charges were closely tamped and packed.

It was arranged that on the mine being sprung, two sorties should be made right and left of the site of the explosion.

At the earliest dawn of the 21st all was ready; not a sign had ever appeared of the enemy having suspected our design. A brisk fire of musketry was opened from our loopholes and that part of the position generally on Johannes' house, and the houses behind it. The enemy were aroused; they swarmed into Johannes' and the other houses, which were soon seen to be filled with lights; then, when it began to grow sufficiently light, the hose was fired direct—without the usual intervention of a fuse—from the shaft, and in about a minute one shock was felt; the whole of Johannes' house opened outwards, and collapsed like a house of cards. In the midst of the turmoil that ensued the two parties made their sortie, attacked and captured the adjacent houses, and lodging charges in them, destroyed them by hasty demolition.

Thus fell what had been the great thorn in our side; and on its fall, our Cawnpore Battery resumed its proper *rôle* of protecting the south-eastern angle of the position with its adjacent faces. The intensity of this mining contest so strained the powers of the few engineers, that Lieutenant Hay of the 48th N. I., like Lieutenant Tulloch before him, had to be added to their strength, to relieve them of the supervision of the ordinary defences; and most valuable was the aid they afforded.

CHAPTER VIII

THIRD STAGE: GENERAL INCIDENTS

HAVING described the mining operations of this the third stage of the siege, we turn now to the contests and incidents of other kinds.

The sortie that was made from Sago's post on the day after the second general attack has been already dealt with in connection with the mine there. A similar sortie was made on the 13th from Gubbins's post, against the shelter from which the enemy had made their effort at that point, on that second attack, three days before. The mutineers were driven off, but no mine was found, only a deep trench; which, it was afterwards said, had been intended to act as a shelter-trench from musketry and artillery fire. Similar sorties were made into the same position on the 18th and 19th (August), immediately after the enemy had breached the Sikh square; but on these two latter occasions our parties took powder with them, and demolished the shelter that had been left, so as to make it useless for any hostile purposes.

Then two sorties were made on the 21st simultaneously, to the right and left of Johannes' house, immediately on its being blown up. They were led by McCabe and Browne of the 32nd, and have been described in connection with that mine.

Except at Sago's, in connection with the mine there, and at the Sikh square on the occasion of the breach (both of which events have been already described), the enemy entered on no contest with us at close quarters; but they silenced the Cawnpore Battery on August 12th by their fire from Johannes' house, and they constructed batteries opposite the Baily Guard gate and Gubbins's post.

Their action on the Cawnpore Battery led to the removal of one of its guns, and to the reduction of the garrison that occupied it; the men removed from it going into the adjacent posts, Deprat's and Anderson's, though of course remaining on the alert for any possible attack on the battery. The silencing of the Cawnpore Battery was regarded by some as a disgrace. "We" (the besiegers) "were *never* silenced at Mooltan—we silenced *many* of the enemy's batteries" (the besieged) "instead," was the remark of a gallant major. He did not see that the correct inference was the reverse of his conclusion, and that our defence, in which only one battery, instead of many, had been silenced, was entitled to the greater credit. But the answer of the Lucknow garrison to this success of the enemy was the mining and destruction of Johannes' house, and the removal with it of any command on the part of the besiegers over the Cawnpore Battery.

The battery begun by the enemy opposite the Baily Guard gate was at the gateway facing it, called the Lutkun Durwaza. It was for two heavy guns, and was started at the very end of August, simultaneously, and in co-operation with, the mining attack on Saunders's post on the right flank of the Baily Guard gate. The reply to this step was the construction of a counter-battery in the Treasury post, on the left of the gate, by Aitken's Sepoys, who held it; its armament was an eighteen-pounder gun, and a twenty-four-pounder howitzer. The sequel will appear on September 5th.

The enemy's battery opposite Gubbins's was a mischievous one. The first step was to improve the bastion at the salient of the post, but the most important and effective measure was the employment there of an eight-inch mortar, mounted as a howitzer by the ingenuity of Lieutenant Bonham. This arrangement was at once called "the ship," and was taken all over the position, to be used wherever most needed; at Gubbins's it immediately silenced the opposite battery referred to.

The only other effort on the part of the enemy that need be mentioned was an attempt, on August 20th, to burn down the Baily Guard gate. The few men who were engaged in the attempt crawled carefully to the gate, laid their combustibles, and were not detected till they had set the gate on fire; but they were speedily driven off, and the fire was extinguished by our native water-carriers. To prevent any renewal of the attempt, the walls immediately flanking the gate were loop-holed.

The continued rain had meanwhile tended to wear away our defences, which had consequently required incessant work to keep them in due repair. The most prominent mischief it had accomplished was to the buildings; assisted as it was by the artillery fire, which was constantly kept up on them. Such buildings as Anderson's and Deprat's were now practically in ruins, the upper rooms of the Brigade mess had fallen in, and a portion of the Residency itself collapsed on August 11th, burying four men of the 32nd in the ruins.

One other very serious danger that now developed, owing to the heavy rains, was the growth of long grass all over the neutral ground up to the foot of our defences, giving new opportunities to the enemy of stealthy approach. The need of vigilant watch on the part of the sentries was much increased, and explorers had constantly to steal out and search the immediate outskirts of the defences.

As to our losses during this stage, they were heavy among the families. But the officers who were killed or mortally wounded were much fewer than in the previous stages, and one of these, Lieutenant Birch, was shot, through error of course, by our own sentries, while exploring outside. The principal loss in this stage was that of Major Anderson, the Chief Engineer, who succumbed on the 11th to dysentery. His loss was more serious than was generally realized, less as an engineer, invaluable as he had been in that capacity (for Captain Fulton who succeeded him won the admiration and enjoyed the confidence of the whole garrison), than as a wise counsellor of the General in command. Sir Henry Lawrence when dying had urged reliance on his counsel; and it may be safely surmised that, had he lived to be consulted through the remainder of the siege, some grave mistakes that were made (as will be presently shown) would probably have been averted.

The last subject to be dealt with in ordinary course before describing the third great attack, is that of the communications with Havelock; but it is necessary, as a preliminary, to refer to the question of the state of the food supply of the garrison.

The whole of that supply had been collected and stored though not fully arranged before the siege commenced. Two bodies of officers, the Commissariat Department under Captain James, and the District Civilians under Mr. Martin, had been the principal agencies for the purpose. They had been truly indefatigable; and all these supplies had been stored, before the siege began, wherever room could be found or made for them. While this storage was going on, the subordinate officials, doubtless, kept the usual records of the location of the supplies. On the day of Chinhut, however, nearly the whole of this subordinate staff disappeared, and Captain James was grievously wounded in the knee. A staff of officers was appointed to act under him for the control and distribution of the rations; but it seems to be certain that, although it was quite well known where all the stores were, neither he nor they nor anybody knew at this period what *quantity* of food of various kinds, except live stock, was ever actually available; no one seems to have ever been directed to inquire; no stock was taken; no inventory ever existed, so far as records can show, or inquiries have been able to elicit; although there can be no doubt that this was a matter which Sir Henry Lawrence referred to in his dying hours, as one of the most urgent of our necessities. Blame for the omission can hardly attach to Captain James in his wounded state, and certainly not to his newly-appointed and inexperienced staff, whose whole time and attention were required for the supervision and distribution of the rations. But there were plenty of officers available for any such special task as ascertaining and registering the use made of all the available shelter and accommodation, and then measuring up and taking stock of all the food supply stored. This, however, does not appear to have been done, or perhaps even suggested. This subject is here referred to as a preliminary—an important one as it will be seen—to the correspondence with Havelock, to which we will now turn.

It will be remembered, that by the end of the second stage of the siege, on August 10th, the latest intelligence which the garrison had received was of Havelock's actions of July 29th, and his subsequent retirement to Mungurwar. After that, Tytler had, on August 4th, written a letter to Mr. Gubbins; intimating Havelock's intention to advance immediately towards Lucknow, and advising the garrison to be prepared to co-operate on his arrival, even to cutting its way out if need be. But this letter did not reach the Residency till August 15th. Ungud, who brought it, had been for a time a prisoner with the enemy, and had then had to go back to Cawnpore, so that he now brought, not only this letter, but the much later news of Havelock's withdrawal from Oude and return to Cawnpore.

These tidings, of course, caused the deepest anxiety, and the following letter was the reply sent by General Inglis on the following night, the 16th—

"A note from Colonel Tytler to Mr. Gubbins reached last night, dated at Mungurwar, the 4th inst. The latter paragraph, which is as follows—'You must aid us in every way, even to cutting your way out if we can't force our way in,'—has caused me much uneasiness, as it is quite impossible, with my weak and shattered force, that I can leave my defences. You must bear in mind how I am hampered; that I have upwards of one hundred and twenty sick and wounded, and at least two hundred and twenty women and about two hundred and thirty children, and no carriage of any description, besides sacrificing twenty-three lakhs of treasure and about thirty guns of sorts.

"In consequence of the news received, I shall soon put the force on half rations, unless I hear again from you. *Our provisions will last us then till about September 10th.*

"If you hope to save this force, no time must be lost in pushing forward. We are daily being attacked by the enemy, who are within a few yards of our defences. Their mines have already weakened our post, and I have every reason to believe they are carrying on others. Their eighteen-pounders are within one hundred and fifty yards of some of our batteries, and from their position and our inability to form working parties, we cannot reply to them, and consequently the damage done hourly is very great. My strength now in Europeans is three hundred and fifty, and about three hundred natives, and the men are dreadfully harassed; and owing to part of the Residency having been brought down by round shot, many are without shelter. Our native force having been assured, on Colonel Tytler's authority, of your near approach some twenty-five days ago, are naturally losing confidence, and if they leave us, I do not see how the defences are to be manned. Did you receive a letter and plan from me from this man Ungud? Kindly answer this question."

There may be differences of opinion as to whether this picture of the situation was not overdrawn or too highly coloured, and whether an appeal of this sort was necessary or desirable. But there can be no question of the astounding error in the description given of the state of the food supply. Not merely was it here laid down at only a small fraction—about an eighth—of what it really was; but the relieving general received an utterly false idea of the desperate condition, in the matter of starvation and inanition, into which the garrison must sink deeper and deeper after September 10th.

The above was a reply to Tytler's letter of August 4th. For a fortnight no other letter was received from Havelock, though he had written on August 8th to Inglis, mentioning the unavoidable necessity for his return to Cawnpore. This letter never seems to have reached Lucknow. Then on August 29th, a fortnight after the receipt of Tytler's letter, one arrived from Havelock himself, dated from Cawnpore on the 24th, which ran thus—

"I have your letter of the 16th inst. I can only say, do not negotiate, but rather perish sword in hand. Sir Colin Campbell, who came out at a day's notice to command, upon the news arriving of General Anson's death, promises me fresh troops, and you will be my first care. The reinforcements may reach me in from twenty to twenty-five days, and I will prepare everything for a march on Lucknow."

Such then was the position of affairs within the Residency, and such the outlook, when the third general attack was made on it on September 5th.

It began in the same way as on the two former occasions. The enemy sprang two mines, one aimed at Gubbins's, the other at the middle of the Brigade mess; this being the mine which had been checked by the last gallery we drove at that post with the express object of intercepting it. Both mines were far short of their mark, and proved harmless. The enemy had also obviously intended to spring a third mine at Saunders's post—the one we had destroyed during the preceding night. This had clearly been meant to act in concert with the battery they had constructed at the Lutkun Durwaza. So, when the attack began, putting up with the failure of the mine, they opened out from their battery on the Baily Guard gate. The new eighteen-pounder counter-battery, which our Sepoys of the 13th N. I. had made at the Treasury post,[1] was thereupon unmasked, opened out, and at once silenced it. The attack at this quarter forthwith collapsed.

The enemy came on with fair boldness, however, at the Brigade mess and Sikh square, and tried to storm Gubbins's post with some real dash; but they were so steadily and resolutely met and so severely punished that they soon retired, and the whole attack ceased at an early hour. Our loss amounted to three Sepoys killed and one English soldier wounded!

The special feature in this fight was the first appearance among the enemy in any numbers of the Talookdars' retainers, who were evidently placed in front, and lost heavily.

[1] *Vide*, p. 145.

CHAPTER IX

FOURTH STAGE OF THE DEFENCE

AFTER the utter and speedy collapse of their attack of September 5th, the enemy never showed any heart. They never attempted an assault nor a close attack on any single post; but they did not desist from mining, nor from their constant artillery and musketry fire.

In mining, their efforts were now more easily foiled, because there was less ground left available for mining, and at most points we were already at least half prepared to meet them.

On September 9th they were heard at work opposite both the Cawnpore Battery and the Sikh square. At the Cawnpore Battery our countermine for its protection from Deprat's shop had been kept loaded ever since the end of July; and now, on September 9th, when the enemy were judged to have come sufficiently close, its charge was fired and the enemy's gallery destroyed.

At the Sikh square, two galleries were driven out to meet the enemy's approaches. Opposite one they ceased working, but at the other they continued to advance; so on the 11th our mine was loaded, and fired with complete success.

Then on the 10th and 12th there appeared signs of the enemy being at work opposite the following posts; where, consequently, we began and continued defensive galleries up to September 20th.

I. At the middle of the front of the Brigade mess, where we completed an intercepting gallery.

II. At the Cawnpore Battery, along the only firm ground left there.

III. From the Treasury post outward, and then across the front of the Baily Guard gate.

IV. Outward and then across the face of Germon's post.

By these countermines and protective galleries, and from the effects of the mines that had been already exploded, the following stretch of the line of entrenchment was now practically nearly secure against the enemy's mines; viz. from the Treasury post, by the Baily Guard gate, Saunders's post, Sago's, Germon's, Anderson's, the Cawnpore Battery, Deprat's, the Martinière and the Brigade mess, up to the Sikh square.

In fact, the only part of our position then left really assailable by mines was Gubbins's post; for opposite all the rest of the line of the entrenchment, the positions now held by the enemy were too distant to give them, with their crude knowledge and appliances, any chance of success against the experience we had now acquired in the methods for detecting and dealing with their efforts.

During the remaining days of the siege, or at its end, we found the following mines which the enemy had been driving.

I. Towards the church: this was discovered in a sortie, made on the 11th in order to explore and guard against such efforts. It had only been begun; but we destroyed it, and the shelter from which it had been started.

II. A gallery driven by the enemy towards the Baily Guard gate fell in, while it was still a long distance off from our line.

III. A second attempt at mining towards the church was detected and stopped by a sortie on September 21st.

IV. A mine, which we had long felt certain was being directed against the Redan, was found, and blown up by ourselves after September 25th. It had not come so near the Redan as the mine that was sprung on July 20th, and would, in fact, have passed its front or apex at a long distance.

Such then was the mining warfare during the last stage of the siege. The enemy's efforts had become feeble, whereas our defence was now practically assured; a result due partly to our unremitting exertions during the last eight or nine weeks, and partly to the enemy's failures helping to make the ground impracticable for further mining. It was an absolute mistake to suppose, that so long as we held our outposts we were any longer in imminent danger from their mining attacks, or that any mines were discovered from which we ran any serious risk, or, in fact, any risk at all. Still, though the engineers knew this, the garrison did not—and their anxiety about it was undiminished.

The only vigorous steps taken by the enemy during these three weeks lay in the concentration of artillery fire on the Cawnpore Battery and on Gubbins's bastion. Opposite the former they planted guns in two positions, one on its east, the other to the south: while against Gubbins's they established a battery on higher ground, in what was called the Bolund Bagh; doing much damage from it till they were answered by the eight-inch mortars mounted as howitzers, which have been already described as Bonham's ships. They also again tried to place combustibles at the Baily Guard gate, but were detected and shot down.

Still, though they never once made any serious or close attempt at an attack during this last stage, they harassed the garrison greatly by constantly starting furious cannonading and musketry all round, as if preluding an attack. Such alarms, lasting only for half-an-hour or so, occurred nearly every day, and also at night; always making necessary a turn-out of the several garrisons.

On the part of the defenders, there were occasional sorties. Two were made, as already mentioned, to explore for mines in front of the church; and a third was made (on September 6th) from Innes's post, to blow down some small houses which had been left on the low ground just outside the position. Captain Fulton led this sortie. The exit to the low ground was by ladders: and Fulton, having laid his charges, gave the word for the party to retire. He then fired his fuse, but was delayed in return by the party not having retired and cleared off as rapidly as they should. The explosion consequently took place while he was still on the ladder, and he was considerably bruised and contused by the flying *débris*.

There had meanwhile been very heavy rain, which damaged the defences greatly, compelling the garrison to be constantly at work repairing the parapets and embrasures.

Moreover, for reasons which will presently appear, additional work had then to be undertaken in extending the system of retrenchments, *i. e.* of having defensive works in rear of outposts and exposed points; and further, two batteries, of which the sites only had been started, at the heads of lanes in the Commissariat position on the Western face, were now worked at from September 11th.

Besides injuring the parapets and defences, the rains, assisted by the enemy's cannonading, had been more and more injuring the buildings, and reducing our habitable shelter. Two sides of Innes's house were now in ruins; so was one of the walls of the Brigade mess; so were Deprat's, Anderson's, and a part of the Martinière; and the verandah of the Residency had fallen.

Cholera still continued; Captain Mansfield had died from it; scurvy was developing seriously, and the physical strength of the defenders was very sensibly reduced. They had lost in muscle, activity, and vitality. They, that is, the fighting men, had been put on half rations since August 25th, and all others on still smaller rations.

Besides Captain Mansfield, who died of cholera, other officers succumbed to wounds, fever, and other causes—Captain Simons, and Lieutenants Graham, Fullerton, and Cunliffe. But our great loss during this last stage of the siege—our greatest loss, many thought, after Sir Henry Lawrence—was that of Captain Fulton of the Engineers, who was killed by a round shot in Gubbins's bastion. Fulton had succeeded to the Engineer command on Major Anderson's death; but long before that he had, in consequence of the Major's serious ill-health, been in practical charge of the Engineer operations; and had won the confidence of the garrison by his skill, energy, and fertility of resource, besides his exceptional coolness and intrepidity as a soldier. He had realized the great gravity of our position when the enemy exploded their first mine, and had started our defence in mining warfare with almost desperate energy, born of anxiety. Now, before we lost him, he was almost jubilant in the knowledge that we had not lost an inch of ground; that we had stopped every mine of the enemy save one; that we had not only been thoroughly victorious in the mining contest against tremendous odds, but had practically made the position safe against the enemy's further efforts. And with his shrewd and resolute face, and his cheerful bearing, he did more than any other twenty men to keep up the spirits of the garrison. Wherever he appeared, it was the signal to be up and doing.

Besides his other merits, Fulton was a crack shot, and occasionally, especially if the enemy had been worrying any particular post by their sharpshooters, he would get hold of the rifles there and fire severals rounds into the opposite line of loopholes till he had silenced their fire. He sometimes got a friend to guide him in these cases by the use of a telescope or binocular. On one occasion his friend called out, "There are two people at the loophole," on which he fired. And next day there was a report among the Sikhs of the Sikh square, that two men had been killed by one shot at that *morcha*, i. e. *post* of the enemy, one of them being the officer of the 15th Cavalry, who was commanding it.

The enemy were very close round the Sikh square, and conversations, more or less bantering, between the two parties on the opposite sides were of constant occurrence.

By this time, in fact, all was going on well as regards efficiency of defence, except in one respect; and this it was that made further mining attacks possible, causing the necessity for pressing on the retrenchments. I mean the generally growing impression among the natives of the garrison that our position was hopeless; that the story of the approach of a force to our relief was mere moonshine, a falsehood concocted by Ungud to curry favour and get heavy rewards. There was no doubt whatever of the existence of this feeling, and it was impossible to say what shape it might not take. I was told about September 10th by my servant that the tendency was, to hold on till October 1st. And two days afterwards, on September 12, at one of the night-working parties at the new Sheephouse Battery, I had a conversation with the native officer on duty, who told me that the current belief, in which he himself shared, was that all Ungud's stories were untrue, and that there was no British force in our neighbourhood. Fortunately he was startled out of these doubts by some plain facts that I mentioned—the letters Ungud had actually brought in; the handwriting of their writers, which had been recognized; the numbers he had stated of the regiments, and the names of many of the officers; peculiarities in the uniforms, such as the square buttons of the Highlanders, and their bagpipes. All these details, I pointed out, could not be concoctions; Ungud must have seen them, and must have received the letters from some one. I believe that this conversation, including as it did a sketch of what had probably been occurring, had a material effect on the minds of the Sepoys.

These men had, doubtless, expressed their sentiments pretty freely to Ungud. But he had his revenge. On September 25th, there was no more prominent or excited figure than his, watching the advancing troops, dancing and leaping before his hitherto incredulous comrades, jeering and snapping his fingers at them, pointing to the troops in the distance and crying out, "Who is the liar now? Who has been inventing tales, and telling lies about Havelock Sahib, and Tytler Sahib, and Neill Sahib, and Barrow Sahib?"

Had no relief arrived soon, there were, doubtless, many that would have remained with us staunch to the death. There is no braver man than the Rajpoot when his sense of pride and honour are fairly enlisted. Still, many would have disappeared. And with their disappearance, and with our own dwindling numbers, it might have very soon become necessary to draw in our horns, give up some of our outer posts and defences, and hold on to the inner posts, which commanded them and served as retrenchments.

At the same time, it ought to be mentioned that the Sepoys did not stand alone in their distrust of any relief being really imminent. There were officers in the garrison —and they were among the most thoughtful, intelligent, and bravest of all—who, while they, of course, fully believed the information brought by Ungud, did not believe in the possibility of relief. I had casually mentioned the above conversation to one of our very best officers; one of much experience in frontier warfare, and of exceptional intrepidity and vigour. His reply was, "Havelock may come near, but how can he make his way against the large force hemming us in, through the streets or other routes which they are certainly barricading? Also he will probably have other forces to tackle; we hear nothing of Delhi. Ten to one, our small army there has been wiped out, and the enemy may pour down an army from there onto Havelock's, or any other British troops that may be keeping the field here." Such were the thoughts in his mind. We had no knowledge of the support the force on the Delhi ridge was receiving from the Punjab; and without that knowledge he had sound reasons for his views and his anxiety.

Fortunately, however, the siege was now really drawing to its close; to its succour, that is, by the force whom we had been expecting for nearly two months. There were signs daily, in spite of the continuous heavy rain, of movements of troops, especially after September 18th, and of greater activity among the enemy; and, at length on the 22nd, Ungud returned bringing a letter which announced that Havelock's force had again crossed the Ganges into Oude; and there was much rejoicing.

Next forenoon we heard cannonading in the Cawnpore direction, and there was much movement in the more distant streets, but the garrison was not much molested.

On the 24th, the commotion in the streets and the cannonading towards Cawnpore were continued, and in the evening the Cawnpore angle of the position was subjected to heavy fire, though nothing further came of the threat. All that day, however, the garrison remained in a state of much anxiety. If the relieving force had arrived so close on the 23rd, why were there no nearer signs of it on the 24th? Could it have been successfully checked?

Then, during the following night, there were repeated alarms, and the whole garrison practically stood to its arms all night. Then the cannonading was again heard towards Cawnpore, *i. e.* towards the Char Bagh and the Alum Bagh, on the morning of the 25th. Before noon it seemed to cease; then after about an hour, artillery and musketry also were heard, not to the south, but to the east. There could now be no doubt that our friends had worked round the south-eastern quarter of the city, and were approaching us, not through the narrow streets, but across the ground between the Kaiser Bagh and the river, which was comparatively open, though dotted over by detached buildings and walled gardens and enclosures. So the garrison proceeded to aid this advance by shelling its flank from our mortars, continuing this fire till the evening.

Early in the afternoon it was seen that a great exodus of the city people had begun, and that with them Sepoys and troopers were crossing the river and streaming along the road towards cantonments, and also towards Fyzabad. And it was further observed shortly afterwards that the bridge of boats had broken down, as the fugitives, including cavalry, were swimming across the river.

By four o'clock we saw our troops near the Motee Mahul. Then the sound of heavy musketry was suddenly heard; it approached nearer and nearer; and at length the head of the column was seen entering the street that formed the direct approach to the Residency. In a few minutes more the leading men, including Generals Outram and Havelock, were within the entrenchments!

The most imminent danger of the garrison, the danger of a great catastrophe from the successful irruption of overwhelming numbers of the enemy, was at an end. The arrival of Havelock's force may not have been a relief in the technical military sense; but it saved us from certain disaster, as will be shown later.

CHAPTER X

PROMINENT FEATURES OF THE DEFENCE

THE heroic entry of Havelock's and Outram's force, on September 25th, into the Residency entrenchments not only marked the relief of the garrison, but brought its single-handed defence of the position to a successful close. And it is fitting at this stage, before proceeding with the narrative, to touch on what seem to be some of the prominent features and characteristics of that defence.

The first point to be noticed is that, weak and slight as the defences were, their style, combined with the obstacles and impediments which lined their front, was thoroughly effective against the enemy with whom we had to contend. None of our adversaries ever succeeded—and many of them tried, though never in large numbers—to break their way through them. Such adventurous spirits as made the attempt, at the Cawnpore Battery, at Innes's post, and elsewhere, got entangled and caught in them ; and were either destroyed, or so punished by musketry or hand grenades, that they gave up such endeavours ; until the last attack, when the Talookdars' men (Rajwara troops) appeared on the scene. At the same time, it may be remarked that the efficacy of these obstructions, thorough and fortunate as it was at the beginning of the siege, had probably disappeared towards the end of it ; for the continuous rain must have beaten them down or covered them with mud ; especially the abattis and small stakes and crows'-feet.

Next, in consequence of the difficulty they found in surmounting these obstacles, and the certainty of the desperate resistance of the defenders behind the defences, the enemy's efforts were persistently directed to the formation of a practicable breach in them. Never once, from first to last, did they attempt to storm the position, except where they had expected to find an opening made by their mines; and, practically, the essence of the struggle lay in their efforts to make such an opening, and our efforts to prevent it. They attempted from the first to breach—if not by artillery, then by mining.

The third feature of the contest is their utter failure to breach by artillery, and the reason. At first they tried to plant some of the guns at sites near our boundary; but our own artillery fire and our sharpshooting speedily stopped this. On moving back to safer spots, their fire was foiled by their own buildings and enclosures and ruins, which screened from them the foot of our defences, where alone that fire could have had any real effect. In the later days of the siege, they renewed their efforts at sites which they had carefully selected, such as the Lutkun Durwaza, Phillips's garden, and opposite Gubbins's bastion; but they were again defeated, not only by the same fire as at first, but by the new and superior metal then brought against them by Bonham's ingenious adaptation of eight-inch mortars to howitzer work.

One feature in the attack that was most fortunate for us was the absence of vertical fire. The enemy had no mortars; and the carcases and other such missiles with which they occasionally favoured us were hurled from cylindrical chambers dug in the ground.

Another great feature of the contest, the most important of all in my opinion, was the effort to breach our defences by mining. The mining attack always lay with the enemy; with the one exception of our attack on Johannes' house, which requires no additional notice at this point. The enemy's attack, however, may be usefully summarized. It has been described at length in the narrative, and detailed by date and site, and it has been tabulated further on. From this it may be seen that the enemy made thirty-seven distinct and separate attempts to undermine and breach our outer defences; the mass of their attempts being along two fronts, beginning at the Baily Guard gate, and attacking these successive posts—Saunders's, Sago's, Germon's, Anderson's, the Cawnpore Battery, the Martinière, the Brigade mess, the Sikh square, and Gubbins's. Of their thirty-seven attempts, one was successful—that at the Sikh square on August 18th—and thirty-six were failures. Of the thirty-six failures, eleven were due to the enemy's own blundering, and not to our stoppage of them. The other twenty-five were all of them contested by us; and were either checked and stopped before they could injure our defences, or blown up by us and destroyed. This success was due to the vigilance of the outposts in detecting the sounds of mining; and to the genius of Fulton in anticipating the intentions of the enemy, and combating their efforts where detected. The great difficulty on our part arose from the want of labour. The men of the garrisons concerned could dig the shaft or well, and drive out the first few feet of a gallery, but the rest of the work required special labour. But for this want, there would have been no great delay in enveloping the exposed fronts with intercepting galleries, which would have practically averted all serious danger. Towards the end, we were gradually getting more secure; but the garrison did not know or understand this; and the feeling, and indeed the fact throughout, was that at no moment were we secure against the grave chance of a sudden explosion; which might form a practicable breach through which the enemy, fully prepared, could make an irruption in the next five minutes in irresistible numbers. This was the danger that transcended all others, and caused such intense anxiety; and to the way in which it was met and foiled was mainly due the success of the defence.

Another feature of the defence was that the garrison never lost a foot of ground. On the other hand, it extended the neutral ground, driving the enemy farther off at many important points.

Again, there was only one of our batteries that was ever silenced—the Cawnpore Battery—and that was only for nine days, from August 12th to the 21st, when it resumed its duty after the destruction of Johannes' house, which had commanded it. With that single exception our artillery held its own against both the artillery and the sharpshooting of the enemy, becoming strongly in the ascendant after the development of Bonham's ships.

The trace of the position was weak in respect of flanking defences. The North face was well flanked by the Redan; but only half the Eastern front was flanked, viz. by the battery at the corner of the Post-office post. The Western face was to have been flanked by the sheep-house and slaughter-house batteries; but these were only in embryo when the siege began, and Innes's post performed that duty only in part. The Southern face was only slightly, if at all, protected by the Cawnpore Battery, as that was itself so much and so long in difficulties. But I have reason to believe that it had been seriously intended to make a flanking position or outwork of Johannes' house; and that it was this idea which prevented the demolition of the upper storey before the siege began.

It was a marked characteristic of the enemy's sharp-shooting, that its deadliest effect was at our loopholes. An extraordinary proportion of the victims were officers who wished to examine the enemy's position; and after a short time it became recognized as a proper precaution to darken the loophole by a hat or other impediment, thus drawing the enemy's fire, and then to have a good look-out while the enemy was re-loading.

Another prominent feature lay in the sorties. These would have been much more numerous but for the restraint placed on them in accordance with Sir Henry Lawrence's dying injunctions, based on the necessity of averting all needless loss of life. The sorties were of two kinds: (1) those undertaken at outposts without orders from the central authority, and (2) the organized sorties for some specific purpose. The local sorties were made generally by parties of not more than half-a-dozen men. These would creep out through the obstacles, crawl down close to the site of some gun or picket, dash in on it, spike the gun, kill a few of the enemy, create a brief panic, and then return to their own post. In such sorties there was rarely any casualty; and in fact they were generally less in danger from the enemy than from sentries on our own side, who had not received due warning. The larger sorties were generally organized in order to seize and destroy some posts of the enemy; such as Johannes' house, the buildings beyond it, those opposite the Sikh square and Gubbins's, and those outside Innes's post. These were organized from the first on a carefully considered plan. There would be a small storming party, followed by the main body, and supported by the fire from our own position. Usually an Engineer officer and a sergeant dashed out first by themselves, carrying means of explosion. They made straight for the left of some door. If it were open they threw in a grenade. If it were shut they drove in a bayonet or screwed in a gimlet, and suspended on it a bag of gunpowder, which they then exploded, bursting in the door. In either case, on the grenade or the powder being heard to explode, the stormers charged into the building, and were followed by the main party, sometimes charging also into other buildings right or left. Powder-bags specially prepared would be rapidly placed in the houses and exploded, demolishing them more or less. In each such sortie there would generally be two or three casualties; frequently caused, until we learnt better, by the men going not to the left but to the right of a doorway or passage, and so having to expose the whole person on firing into it.

But, in truth, one of the most astonishing features of the defence was the small number of casualties compared with the ceaseless fire, besides actual fighting, to which the garrison was exposed. The most apposite indication of this lies in the case of the 32nd Regiment, which constituted the backbone of the defence. Exclusive of officers, their death casualties at Lucknow up to the arrival of Havelock's force on September 25th were—

Killed at Chinhut	111
Killed outright during the defence	29
Died of wounds or accidents during the defence ...	52
Died from disease	52

And of the twenty-nine killed during the defence, the number who fell in the three all-round attacks of July 20th, August 10th, and September 5th, was only six. This comparative immunity from loss was due to (1) the absence of any command of the enemy over our position except from Johannes' house, so that (2) our parapets and other arrangements successfully sheltered and defiladed the garrison from the enemy's fire; (3) the stern suppression of needless exposure and aimless sorties; and (4) the enforced restriction of the men to the posts to which they belonged, and the stoppage of all unauthorized wandering over the more open and exposed positions.

I have given these figures for the 32nd, both because the only details and nominal lists I have are those of that regiment; and because, forming, as I have said, the backbone of the defence, their figures are typical for the garrison in general.

After the loss of 111 men at Chinhut, their strength at the beginning of the siege (excluding officers as before) was 520, of whom probably 100 were at that time wounded; and during the siege their death casualties were 133 (or about one-fourth), while 154 were wounded.

After losing four of their number at Chinhut, there were twenty-one officers left of the 32nd (besides its two surgeons); of these twenty-one, four were killed or died during the defence, and eight were wounded. One of the two officers of the 84th was wounded. Of other combatant officers, the Staff lost two out of eleven; the Artillery lost five out of nine, besides three others wounded; the Engineers lost two out of five; the officers of the native troops lost twenty out of seventy-two, besides twenty-two being wounded. The non-combatant officers lost eight out of thirty-four, besides nine wounded. Of our Sepoys I do not know the losses, but the casualties of the Hindoostanees of the 13th N. I. amounted, I believe, to more than their whole strength, owing to the number that were wounded more than once.

This is one fact illustrative of the staunch and loyal conduct of our native troops, whose fidelity has become proverbial, and of whom, therefore, I need say nothing more now.

But the subject of our losses brings me to those in our families. At the beginning of the siege there were 240 women and 270 children. Of the 240 women, three were killed and eleven died; of the 270 children, fifty-four died; of the 240 women and 270 children, sixty-nine and sixty-eight respectively belonged to the families of officers of the army or of the Government. Their losses were eight and twenty-three respectively; so that one-third of their children perished. These losses were due to the exposure and hardships, and want of comforts, but not to want of actual food; Sir Henry Lawrence's care had provided against that.

The steady supply and distribution of food and regular rations, so that no one in the entrenchments, at any time, lost life, or suffered from want of sustenance, is one of the most prominent characteristics of the defence.

But the greatest of all, overshadowing all else, was the wisdom of the preparations and the foresight of Sir Henry Lawrence.

MINING TABLE NO. I.

TABULAR STATEMENT OF THE ENEMY'S MINES.

Arranged approximately by date.

General Serial No.	Page.	Post Attacked, and Serial Number in it.		Nature of Attack.	Particulars.
		FIRST ATTACK, JULY 20, 1857.			
1	124	Redan	1	Explosion	Short : harmless.
		SECOND STAGE, JULY 21 TO AUGUST 9			
2	128	Redan	2	Lodgment	Dislodged by artillery and musketry.
3	128	Martinière	1	"	Dislodged by grenades.
4	129	Gubbins's	1	"	Dislodged by sortie.
5	129	Cawnpore Battery	1	Gallery	Collapsed : too shallow.
6	129	Brigade Mess	1	"	Stopped, on hearing our left Brigade Mess mine.
7	129	Sikh Square	1	"	Broken into and destroyed by our countermine.
8	130	Sago's	1	"	Collapsed : too shallow.
		SECOND ATTACK, AUGUST 10.			
9	134	Martinière	2	Explosion	Short : damaged stockade.
10	134	Sago's	2	"	Short : harmless.
		THIRD STAGE, AUGUST 11 TO SEPTEMBER 4.			
11	138	Sago's	3	Gallery	Fought and blown up.
12	139	"	4	"	August 29 : stopped on hearing ours.
13	139	"	5	"	Sept. 1 : stopped on hearing ours.
14	137	Saunders's	1	"	August 23 : stopped on hearing ours.
15	137	"	2	"	August 31 : blown up by our countermine, Sept. 1.
16	137	"	3	"	Sept. 1 : blown up by our countermine, Sept. 2.
17	138	"	4	"	Sept. 3 : blown up by our countermine, Sept. 4.
18	139	Anderson's	1	"	August 13 : stopped on hearing ours.
19	139	"	2	"	August 23 : stopped on hearing ours.

TABLE NO. I. (*Continued*).

General Serial No.	Page.	Post Attacked and Serial Number in it.		Nature of Attack.	Particulars.
20	139	Anderson's	3	Gallery	August 18: stopped on hearing ours.
21	139	Brigade Mess	2	"	August 20: first stopped on hearing ours; then continued, broken into and blown up by us, August 29.
22	140	"	3	"	Sept. 3: first stopped on hearing ours; then
	149			Explosion	Short: harmless in third attack, Sept. 5.
23	140	Sikh Square	2	Gallery	Met our gallery: both galleries destroyed by hasty explosion.
24	141	"	3	Explosion	Successful: simultaneous with 23, on August 16th; made a breach in wall 30 feet long.
	THIRD ATTACK, SEPTEMBER 5.				
25	149	Gubbins's	2	Explosion	Short: harmless.
	149	Brigade Mess	3	"	Short: harmless. (See No. 22.)
	FOURTH STAGE, FROM SEPTEMBER 6 TO SEPTEMBER 25.				
26	151	Cawnpore Battery	2	Gallery	Sept. 9: destroyed by our mine ready since July.
27	151	Sikh Square	4	"	Sept. 9: stopped on hearing ours.
28	151	Sikh Square	5	"	Sept. 9: blown up by our mine.
29	151	Brigade Mess	4	"	Sept. 10: checked by our middle Brigade Mess mine.
30	151	Cawnpore Battery	3	"	Sept. 10: checked by our mine.
31	151	Baily Guard Gate	1	"	Sept. 10: checked by our mine.
32	151	Germon's Post	1	"	Sept. 10: checked by our mine.
33	152	Church	1	"	Sept. 11: destroyed by sortie.
34	152	Church	2	"	Sept. 21: destroyed by sortie.
35	152	Baily Guard Gate	2	"	Collapsed about Sept. 23.
	FOUND AFTER RELIEF OF SEPTEMBER 25.				
36	152	Redan	3		Far short.
37	178	Church	3		Far short.

MINING TABLE NO. II.

TABULAR STATEMENT OF THE ENEMY'S MINES.

Arranged under the posts attacked.

Post Attacked.		Serial No.	Approximate Date.	Nature of Attack.	Particulars and Result.
Redan . .	1	1	July 20	Explosion	Far short.
„	2	2	July 21	Lodgment	At foot, dislodged by fire.
„	3	36	After Relief	Gallery	Far short.
Baily Guard Gate . .	1	31	Sept. 10	„	Checked by countermine.
„ „ .	2	35	Sept. 23	„	Collapsed : too shallow.
Saunders's Post . .	1	14	August 23	„	Checked by countermine.
„ „ .	2	15	August 31	„	Blown up by us, Sept. 1.
„ „ .	3	16	Sept. 1	„	„ „ Sept. 2.
„ „ .	4	17	Sept. 3	„	„ „ Sept. 4.
Sago Garrison .	1	8	July 29	„	Collapsed : too shallow.
„ „ .	2	10	August 10	Explosion	Short : harmless.
„ „ .	3	11	August 11	Gallery	Blown up by us.
„ „ .	4	12	August 29	„	Checked by countermine.
„ „ .	5	13	Sept. 1	„	Checked by countermine.
Germon's Post . .	1	32	Sept. 10	„	Checked by countermine.
Anderson's Post . .	1	18	August 13	„	Checked by countermine.
„ „ .	2	19	August 23	„	Checked by countermine.
„ „ .	3	20	August 28	„	Checked by countermine.
Cawnpore Battery .	1	5	July 25	„	Collapsed, under shell fire.
„ „ .	2	26	Sept. 9	„	Blown up by ours ready since July.
„ „ .	3	30	Sept. 10	„	Checked by our countermine.
Martinière	1	3	July 21	Lodgment	Dislodged by grenades.
„ .	2	9	August 10	Explosion	Short, but damaged stockade.
Brigade Mess . .	1	6	July 25	Gallery	Checked by countermine.
„ „ .	2	21	August 20	„	Checked by countermine, and then blown up by us August 29.
„ „ .	3	22	Sept. 3	Gallery and Explosion	Checked by countermine, then exploded, short, harmless, on Sept. 5.

TABLE NO. II. (*Continued*).

Post Attacked.	Serial No.	Approximate Date.	Nature of Attack.	Particulars and Result.
Brigade Mess . . 4	29	Sept. 10	Gallery and Explosion	Checked by counter-mine.
Sikh Square 1	7	July 25	Gallery	Checked by counter-mine, then blown up.
" " 2	23	August 16	"	Met ours: both destroyed.
" " 3	24	"	Explosion	Successful: made 30 feet breach.
" " 4	27	Sept. 9	Gallery	Checked by counter-mine.
" " 5	28	"	"	Blown up by counter-mine.
Gubbins's . 1	4	July 21	Lodgment	Dislodged by sortie.
" . 2	25	Sept. 5	Explosion	Short: harmless.
Church . 1	33	Sept. 11	Gallery	Destroyed by sortie.
" . 2	34	Sept. 21	"	" " "
" . 3	37	After Relief	"	Short: harmless.

MINING TABLE NO. III.

TABULAR SUMMARY OF MINING ATTACKS.

Attack directed on	Enemy's Mines.								Ours.
		Failures.							
	Successful.	Lodgments dislodged.	Galleries collapsed.	Galleries stopped by hearing ours.	Galleries found after Relief.	Galleries exploded short.	Galleries destroyed by us.	Total.	Successful.
Redan		1			1	1		3	
Baily Guard Gate.			1	1				2	
Saunders's Post .				1			3	4	
Sago Garrison . .			1	2		1	1	5	
Germon's Post . .				1				1	
Anderson's Post .				3				3	
Cawnpore Battery			1	1			1	3	
Martinière . . .		1				1		2	
Brigade Mess . .				2		1	1	4	
Sikh Square . .	1			1		1	2	5	
Gubbins's . . .		1				1		2	
Church					1		2	3	
Johannes' House .									1
Total. . . .	1	3	3	12	2	6	10	37	1
Grand Total.	1				36			37	1

TABLE NO. IV.

MINES GROUPED UNDER THE CHARACTER OF THEIR ATTACK AND OUR DEFENCE.

	TOTAL.
ENEMY'S LODGMENTS TO START GALLERIES.	
1 at Redan, 1 at Martinière, 1 at Gubbins's...	3
ENEMY'S GALLERIES COLLAPSED.	
1 at Baily Guard Gate, 1 at Sago's, 1 at Cawnpore Battery	3
ENEMY'S GALLERIES STOPPED ON HEARING OURS.	
1 at Baily Guard Gate, 1 at Saunders's, 2 at Sago's, 1 at Germon's, 3 at Anderson's, 1 at Cawnpore Battery, 2 at Brigade Mess, 1 at Sikh Square	12
ENEMY'S GALLERIES DISCOVERED AFTER THE RELIEF.	
1 at the Redan, 1 at the Church	2
ENEMY'S MINES EXPLODED SHORT.	
1 at Redan, 1 at Sago's, 1 at Martinière, 1 at Brigade Mess, 1 at Sikh Square, 1 at Gubbins's	6
ENEMY'S MINES DESTROYED BY US.	
3 at Saunders's, 1 at Sago's, 1 at Cawnpore Battery, 1 at Brigade Mess, 2 at Sikh Square, 2 at Church	10
ENEMY'S SUCCESSFUL MINE—AT SIKH SQUARE	1
	37
OUR MINE, SUCCESSFUL—AT JOHANNES' HOUSE	1

CHAPTER XI

MINOR INCIDENTS OF THE DEFENCE

In dealing with Sir Henry Lawrence's policy and measures, for the defence and the preparations for it, I have been guided by my own direct and personal knowledge. The facts on this point are as follows—

On Saturday, May 16th, we were all in a state of grave anxiety, and I for one had no knowledge of Sir Henry's intentions. Early next morning I dressed in uniform for early morning church, and was about to stroll over to the service, when Major Anderson, with whom I was living, asked me to take a drive first with him. He took me to the gate of the Mutchi Bhown, got out of his buggy, desired me to remain in it, and joined a small group inside the court-yard. Presently I was beckoned in, and saw Sir Henry Lawrence, who told me that I was forthwith to take Engineer charge of the Mutchi Bhown. When he began to give me his instructions, I produced my note-book, wrote the instructions down on the spot, and then read them out to him. This was my daily practice throughout that period; with the result that my note-book was very constantly referred to, by Sir Henry, and by Major Anderson and Major Francis, as the authority for the instructions and their date. In the entries for May 17th was the statement of the policy as described (p. 74), respecting the use and purpose of the Mutchi Bhown; the essential need being to construct a properly defensive position at the Residency, and, till this should be completed, to overawe the city and gain time by means of the Mutchi Bhown.

That note-book I retained for many years, till it was lost, with many of my own plans of the campaign, by an accident in 1871. But it had been, meanwhile, the basis for my letters of that period, the fullest of which have now come back to me. The note-book, in those days of intense pressure, carried the weight of orders; and was accepted and used in that light both by Major Francis and Major Anderson; and never, from first to last, was there question, or doubt, or misunderstanding respecting its entries.

Here I desire, while dealing with this point, to pay my tribute of respect and regard for my dear friend, Major Francis, who commanded at the Mutchi Bhown; and to whose support, countenance, and help I owed so much. Imperturbable in temper, of the kindest disposition, resolute and indefatigable, he kept the varied needs of the fort in thorough order; and with his sound knowledge of the Sepoys and his perfect demeanour to them, retained throughout the loyalty of the natives of the garrison. I shall never forget how his orderly, Anokh Singh, told him, on the night of May 30th, that the mutiny in the cantonment was beginning; how Runjeet Singh, the havildar (sergeant) of the pensioners, reported on June 30th that our party at Chinhut was returning defeated; how calmly Francis received the news, and how promptly he proceeded to take the necessary action.

While at the Mutchi Bhown, from May 17th to the night of July 1st, I left it only twice; both times by Sir Henry's orders, to have a look at the defences in progress at the Residency. In one of these visits he took me over the circuit himself, and it was on this occasion that I suggested the inclusion of Johannes' house in our own defences as a flanking work on the South face, similar in principle to the Redan on the North face.

Towards the end of June, when Sir Henry had ordered the construction of the two batteries at the west end of the Mutchi Bhown, and was looking on at the progress of the work, I said to him, with a laugh, "Of course, these batteries will never be used." On this he turned round on me sharply. "What! *you* think we will not be besieged." "Not so, sir," I said, "but when they come near enough to be under our fire, we should have concentrated in the Residency." "Quite right, my boy! Their movements depend upon Cawnpore. A siege there will certainly be, and a long siege; and it will be months before aid can reach us."

While the works were in progress at the Mutchi Bhown and at the Residency, there was no attempt or affectation about keeping them secret. On the contrary, people were allowed (under guidance) to see freely whatever it was advisable for them to see, with the result that the tale was spread broadcast of the powerful position and armament that were being prepared.

Of course, strangers were carefully but easily kept away from whatever was more fictitious than real.

Well-wishers constantly turned up and gave suggestions more or less valuable. It was an old native officer, on leave from a regiment in the Punjab which a relative of mine had commanded, who gave me a hint to remove the nearer parapet of the stone bridge, so that there might be no cover for any one trying to cross over it. It was the same native officer who told me that the athletes were the principal agents for the guidance of the Mutiny; and that as a matter of policy, the best and most popular and influential officers of regiments would, as a rule, be shot when the rest might go unscathed.

It may not be amiss to note some of the minor and lighter features in addition to the graver and more momentous characteristics of the siege; and also some supposed circumstances about which incorrect ideas have been spread, or which did not occur. It has been occasionally alleged in England with emphatic declamation, and with indignation at any denial of it, that the enemy who were investing us did not do so closely and sternly; and that, for instance, the children of the garrison could go outside into the enemy's posts and play with the Sepoys there! Need I say how absolutely ludicrous any such supposition is? Doubtless, the children were made much of by the natives of our own garrison, and only to such a cause as this can the mistaken idea be attributed.

Much of our discomfort and sickness arose from so many refugees from out-stations, as well as the garrison of the Mutchi Bhown, concentrating in the Residency without any spare clothing, and from the difficulty of procuring it, or of washing and changing it when requisite. Many had managed to get their white clothing dyed a dust colour called "khakee." At first I had only two or three changes, and these were *white;* hence, as this would have been fatal when stealing out at night from the Redan or elsewhere in order to explore the ground for sounds of mining or other purposes, I had to change garments with a friend on such occasions, with a grim apology for the possible chance of not being able to return them. Towards the end of the siege my pith helmet was in pieces, merely resting on the top of my head, and it was not till the very end that I could procure another.

I was fortunate enough to retain my servants. The Post-office mess to which I belonged contained twenty-two members at first; and since the others had not kept any of their attendants, my two (father and son) became the cook and table servants for the whole party. Their service was one of no small danger. The boy had to carry everything to the Post-office from the Commissariat yards where the father cooked the meals. One evening the father presented himself looking positively white, and depositing fragments of copper at my feet, gasped out, "My life has escaped!" A shell had burst beside him while he was cleaning his cooking pots, sparing him, but smashing the pots! We generally knew when any shells would thus plunge into our position; as they could only be some of our own, which on being fired from our mortars had failed to burst—a chance for which we were always on the watch.

The only gun of the enemy's which continuously did us serious harm was that at Hill's shop; as it fired straight over the long diagonal of our position, striking either Innes's post, the Residency, Fayrer's, or the Post-office. It seemed to have done most mischief at the Residency. One case there was very singular. The shot caught the end of the punkah fringe, tore down most of it, was checked by it while doing so, and thus getting a circular motion, whirled round a young officer of the 32nd; its eventual impact breaking his leg and causing his death. At the Post-office it played pranks as well as doing serious damage. One of its shots broke the leg of a chair on which a lady was sitting, brought her to the ground, got caught in her dress, and then unrolled itself, out and along the floor, without doing her further harm. Another grazed the forehead, or rather the temples, of a young Engineer as he lay asleep, breaking the skin, and plunging against a treasure-chest beyond, but doing no further harm; and, later, one cut through the pillow on which Montagu Hall of the 1st Fusiliers lay asleep, and then broke the leg of the bed next him.

The strain and exhaustion from the ceaseless work, the tension of anxiety, and the want of sleep, led every now and then to an absolute collapse of some sort or other. With me it twice took the form of sleepy stupor, from which I could not be awakened for a couple of days or more. The first occasion was on July 2nd, after hearing of Sir Henry's mortal wound. Doubtless it resulted from the combination of the shock thereby produced with the reaction on the cessation of the responsibilities of the Mutchi Bhown. The other was, I think, after the blowing up of Johannes' house, when I had remained on watch over the progress of our mine for three days and nights without sleep.

It was this ceaseless exposure and work, and the absolute want of rest, that so wore out the men of the garrison; for there was little to enliven them except an occasional sortie, which would be followed by much jubilation and excited talk. In one of these a specially intrepid soldier of the 32nd was so struck with the gorgeous kincob costume of some native of rank who had fled before him in the Captan Bazar, that he saw, and could talk of, nothing else. Of course there were nicknames and jokes without end, jokes among the officers also.

Scene.—Cawnpore Battery (a comrade arrived from Deprat's shop).

"Well, Bill; anything up?"

"No."

"Jack been here?"

"Yes."

"What did he do?"

"Oh, he looked through this here keek-hole, and then through that there keek-hole."

"And then?"

"He said we must trust to the British bayonet only."

"And then?"

"Why, then he hooked it."

Passing officer to his friend.—"Judicious Hooker!"

But the wearied state of the men sometimes carried them

past the joking stage. One evening, at the Post-office, a man whose turn it was for sentry, utterly worn out, threw down his musket and would have no more of it.

"Put him to bed," was McCabe's order to the sergeant of the guard.

It is impossible to imagine anything more perfect than the management of the men and the example set to them by their officers—McCabe always in spirits; Sam Lawrence, the beau-ideal of manly beauty, always genial and smiling, whether leading a sortie or waiting in quiet expectation of being blown up at the Redan. When, at the explosion there on July 20th, the men made a dart out of the way of the falling shower of earth, "Well, lads, when you are tired of running away, perhaps you'll come back again," was all they heard from their stalwart commander, MacFarlan.

One peculiar feature in our Sepoys, was the sound estimate that they took of the strength and probable result of the enemy's attacks. When Innes's post was attacked, on July 20th, they and the men of the 32nd were on the roof of the house, firing on the column moving up on the left. The 32nd began to think they would get up to the neck of the position and so cut them off; but the Sepoys, understanding what they said, remarked, "No fear of that, they will never get so far."

As an instance of their profound loyalty; when, on the arrival of the relieving force, Aitken took out a few of his men to clear away the enemy's battery at the Lutkun Durwaza, some of the 78th, seeing them suddenly in the turmoil and the dusk, bayoneted two of them, supposing them to be the enemy. "Never mind," said one of them, "it was fated. Victory to the Baily Guard (*Kooch purwa nahin. Kismut hai—Baily Guard ki jye*)."

Whatever excitement there may have been in the other episodes of the struggle, it could never approach the keenness of the mining contests; and the most ludicrous incidents every now and then occurred. I do not think that we ever once hit or captured an enemy's miner in any of the numerous cases in which we seized their galleries; either one of our party sneezed or coughed, or the pistol was wet and missed fire. At Sago's mine, while we were tamping to blow them in, we distracted their attention by starting almost a playful game, the two sides pelting each other with clods over the intervening wall. On one occasion, when we had seized a long gallery of the enemy's, two officers heard the earth falling in behind them. Said one of them, whose merriment was irrepressible, "What fun! they are cutting us off!" Fortunately they escaped; since the earth did not block up the gallery, though much of it fell, and the enemy standing over the spot failed to catch them as they passed back, though they tried to do so.

To describe a good instance of seizing an enemy's gallery, I will here anticipate events and relate my last contest, when I was on the verge of succumbing to the prevalent scurvy. A message had been sent to me to say that something was going on at one of our Chuttur Munzil mines which our miners did not understand; so passing along our intercepting galleries, I came at last to the point nearest the noise they had been hearing. It sounded to me quite close, but very feeble, certainly not like the blows of a pick or shovel. After a while, I formed the idea that the earth was being *scraped*, and planted myself opposite the spot, directing the sergeant to stop at the next bend, and to keep a chain of men, one at each turn, up to our shaft. The noise continued, but only at intervals; at length, on turning round gently, I saw a speck of light on the reverse side of the gallery in which I was squatting; whereupon, feeling sure that that speck came from a light in the enemy's gallery, I moved my eyes about till I found the hole. It was too small for me to see through, but I waited patiently, remaining quite still. Then the scraping began again very cautiously; then it stopped, and I heard whispering; presently more scraping; soon a larger hole was formed, and then I heaved down the film of earth that separated us; but the miners had at once "dowsed the glim," and though I fired shot upon shot after them, there was no reason to suppose that I hit either of them. Of course I followed them up to the shaft from which they had started the gallery, my sergeant speedily joining me. The enemy kept firing down their shaft—a harmless proceeding. A few minutes' work with the pick made a little mound close to the shaft by which we could be protected if the enemy should try to rush the gallery in force, but they did not attempt to do so. Their clamour was uproarious, and then presently skinful after skinful of water was poured down the shaft. They thought we had been loading a charge of powder to blow them up! Our response was shouts of laughter and banter; to which their reply was more firing. In the end we kept the gallery as a listener, so preventing any further attempts of the enemy against us from that house.

For significant instances of the peculiarity of mining warfare and the first impressions it created, I have again to anticipate events. After the first few days of the joint defence, one of the most gallant of our relievers, a man whose enterprise had marked him out even in that band of heroes, had penetrated a mine for the first time; and presently he re-appeared, as if upset. Some concussion had caused the earth to tumble about him and so he returned somewhat quickly. "What did you think?—that the enemy were coming at you?" "I suppose so." "Well," quoth his chief, "no one knows better than you that if you think the enemy are there, you should go at them and not back from them." "Quite so, sir, but I didn't think at all; down below is very different from up above!"

Again, a day or two later, one of the best known men in Upper India, a noted wit and a consummate actor, appeared at the mess dinner, after having been down a mine for the first time. He was carefully prepared with a set expression of dismay and horror, and proceeded to dilate on his experiences till all the novices were in a tremor. When the others proceeded to chaff, he resumed his description, finally offering to put a bottle of brandy at the end of a mine, and to bet 100 rupees that no one who had not before entered a mine would go in and bring the bottle out. The challenge was not taken up! Of course in a few days nearly every one had made the experiment; but it was always felt that the underground contests involved special promptitude, skill, and risks, beyond those of ordinary warfare.

Perhaps I have not made it sufficiently clear, that in these mines and mining contests, the Engineers were left absolutely unfettered, and the Garrison Engineer was free to act without orders. Many a mine against the enemy was exploded, under the exigency of the case, without intimation to the general staff; and not unfrequently our countermines, destructive of the enemy's galleries, caused as much anxiety and perturbation as the enemy's mines of attack. Beyond the Engineer circle, and the officers of the outposts, they were little understood; our constant success seemed to inspire no confidence; the rumoured existence of an enemy's mine invariably caused intense alarm; and the mysterious dread respecting them may be best exemplified by the remark of an otherwise intelligent officer, that nothing would persuade him that the mine in the Captan Bazar, of which he saw merely the mouth, did not pass below the Redan.

In his subsequent despatches, Sir James Outram spoke of six mines having been found, on his arrival, which threatened serious danger to our defences. He certainly never examined or saw those mines personally, or made that statement of his own knowledge. Nor do I know of any authentic source from which he could have received such information. I fear it was on a par with the information sent to Havelock about the food supply. There were plenty of the enemy's mines found and known of at that date, which they had been working at, but which had, so far, been harmless. To ascertain their details, in respect of the danger with which they threatened us, it was necessary to examine or break into them; and neither I, nor any other Engineer who examined and dealt with these mines, found that any of them was approaching a dangerous stage. There was one at the Redan, which I blew up, and a second at the church; two others were known of at the Baily Guard gate, two at Sago's, one at the Cawnpore Battery, three at Anderson's, and one at the Brigade mess; but they were all far short of our boundary, and harmless.

I have mentioned in the course of the narrative that we were at one time in anxiety about mining tools, and that we were fortunate in finding some on the roof of Deprat's shop. It came about in this way. All that part of the defence lay within my beat, and I was mentioning the matter to an officer there, when one of the civilians of the garrison said he had heard that Deprat used to keep a lot of his hardware and other stores on the roof. I immediately desired a ladder to be fetched; but as there was some delay about it, and I knew that there was a staircase *outside*, with a small door opening on to it, fairly screened by its parapet, I crawled up on the roof by that staircase, and found a quantity of most valuable articles, picks, spades, tarpaulins, and the like; on which, causing first a soft floor of straw to be made on the ground inside, to deaden any noise, I gradually threw all these things over, cleared the roof, and then got down by the ladder. No shot was fired at me, nor was I aware of having even been observed by the enemy, though they should have seen me from Johannes' house.

When in actual contact with the enemy, as in sorties, I personally never found them show either determination or malignity. If brought to bay, they fought; but they were much more inclined to avoid close quarters. In the sorties that took place after we were relieved, this came to my notice prominently. In those in which we destroyed the enemy's houses by hasty demolition, the powder charges were laid as we advanced, and blown up as we retired. On retiring, I, as the Engineer, was necessarily the last man, having to fire the mine and overtake the party after they had withdrawn sufficiently far from the site of the explosion; yet I never found the enemy pressing too closely on me, either collectively or singly, or shooting very straight.

For instance: on the morning of September 26th, when I had to guide a party from Innes's post, into the ground that lay river-wards; after scrambling through the long grass into the open, I was absolutely alone, when a large party of the enemy (whom I supposed to be our own men), ran past me, not a couple of yards off, with bayonets fixed, but never attempting to touch me. They continued running for about fifteen or twenty yards; when, on their then turning to the left, I called out to them to turn to the right instead. Then only did one or two of them begin firing at me; on which our party, who had been rather dawdling through the grass, dashed out and charged them. I fired my own revolver in vain. Every barrel snapped! It had got damp during the night work which I had just left.

I know of no occasion in which the enemy resolutely faced one of our sorties in the first defence, except at Sago's mine on August 11th.

They held aloof, in fact, from meeting men who they knew were desperate, while they were themselves, as a rule, acting without any set purpose. In fact they retained throughout the old sense of our superiority, and they trusted for success in the contest to their numerical preponderance.

The men investing the Residency varied greatly. Sometimes they were Sepoys of the regular army, or of the Oude local force; sometimes nujeebs or troops of the dethroned nuwab; and occasionally, as on the West face, they were Talookdars' men, armed with matchlock, sword, and shield. Every now and then Pasees appeared among them, whose weapons were the bow and arrow, reminding one of Dugald Dalgetty. I remember one of our men on being struck by an arrow, tearing it out of his body, and dropping down dead.

BOOK III

HAVELOCK'S CAMPAIGN

CHAPTER I

NEILL'S ADVANCE UP TO ALLAHABAD

OUR narrative, so far, has brought us to the close of the first defence of the Residency on the arrival of Havelock and Outram, and the heroic force which they had led to our relief. During the whole of that defence, but preceded by Neill as pioneer in still earlier days, had Havelock been persistently struggling to advance to the rescue. To that advance our story must now turn.

A glance at any ordinary map of India will show that there are two routes from Calcutta to Cawnpore—one by the Ganges, the other by the trunk road—which meet at Benares, and then go on, side by side, to Allahabad and Cawnpore. Between Calcutta and Benares the route by road is straight and direct, passing through no important city or station; but the river route touches the large city of Patna, with the cantonments of Dinapore beside it, where the 10th was quartered, the only British regiment between Calcutta and Lucknow.

Benares is a large city, the head-quarters of Hindooism, with a native garrison, but with no fortified post; at Allahabad, however, between Benares and Cawnpore, there is a fortress of the European type, which, being situated at the junction of the Ganges and the Jumna, is essentially a strategical position of the very first importance, in fact the key of the Upper Provinces; nevertheless, at the time of the Meerut outbreak it was garrisoned only by native troops, and was absolutely at their mercy.

Hence in the first days of the Mutiny, while the main general object of the Calcutta Government was to send forward troops to protect the country to the utmost, its most urgent military need was to prevent Allahabad from falling into the power of any hostile party, and to secure it instead as the basis and key of our own operations up-country. This was a specific step of incalculable importance to the whole conduct of the war; and it was the primary and immediate objective of the British advance from Calcutta, to be effected, if possible, before any general spread should begin of the Mutiny, which was as yet confined to the Delhi districts.

The story of the advance to Cawnpore naturally, therefore, divides itself into two stages, the first up to Allahabad, the other beyond it.

To proceed with the first stage. When shortly before the middle of May, the Government heard of the Meerut rising, they began immediately to send up-country whatever troops they had to spare, and to follow them up with others as fast as they arrived. At first these troops were forwarded only by the road route (which was the quickest), being conveyed either in horsed vehicles or by the Government bullock train—an organized train of wagons drawn by relays of bullocks, which were picketed at regular stages all along the road. Afterwards they were also despatched on steamers by the river route. Those sent on at first were in detachments. The 84th led the way; then came the Madras Fusiliers on their arrival from Madras; and after them the 64th and 78th on their rejoining from the Persian Expeditionary Force. A detachment of 150 men of the 10th was also sent forward from Dinapore to Benares.

For three precious weeks the native army in these Lower Provinces, as well as elsewhere, delayed in following the example set them at Meerut and Delhi; and during these three weeks there was a constant but thin stream of these detachments of British troops flowing northwards from Calcutta without let or hindrance. As they reached Benares they were sent on to Allahabad; as they reached Allahabad they were sent on to Cawnpore; and even the party of the 84th that reached Cawnpore was sent on by Wheler to Lucknow. So long as the Sepoys refrained from breaking out, so long did the local authorities shut their eyes to the need of securing the fortress of Allahabad—the dominant influence being apparently a chivalrous desire to aid those whose need was thought to be the greatest.

But on June 3rd the spread of the Mutiny, where it could affect this advance, began at Azimgurh, which lay off the road near Benares. The news of it reached Benares next afternoon; by which time, however, fortunately, the detachment of the 10th from Dinapore had arrived, and also a small party of the Madras Fusiliers under Colonel Neill; raising the British force at the station to some 220 men, including half of Olpherts's battery, the other half of which was at Dinapore. Now the native garrison consisted of the 37th N. I., the Loodianah Sikh regiment, and a part of a regiment of Irregular Cavalry. It was thought that the Loodianah regiment would remain staunch; but it contained a large proportion of Hindoostanee Sepoys, which affected its loyalty, or at any rate gave scope for excitement to disaffection. On the receipt of the news of the Azimgurh mutiny, a general parade was, at the instance of Colonel Neill, of the Madras Fusiliers, ordered at Benares for five o'clock that afternoon, with the object of disarming the 37th N. I. But when the time arrived, that regiment, instead of yielding, broke out in mutiny, and began firing at the British line of infantry and artillery. While they were being driven off and dispersed, the cavalry broke out and shot their commandant; which seems to have excited the Sikh regiment. They had remained passive, and had not acted against the 37th N. I.; and now they fired on their officers and wounded them, and proceeded to fire on the British line, and to move as if threatening to charge the artillery. Olpherts, however, having scattered the 37th, now swung his guns round on the Sikhs; and, not caring to allow them to bayonet his gunners, received them with a fierce shower of shot and grape, which checked them thoroughly, and then drove them and the cavalry into precipitate rout; whereby Benares was saved. The infantry following up drove the mutineers out of cantonments, and the British remained masters of the field. This was a matter of the highest moment, not merely from its securing Benares itself as a temporary base, but also from its clearing the way onward, and helping towards the retention of the infinitely more important position at Allahabad.

Neill had now succeeded to the command, and to secure that position was his great aim. Next morning, therefore, he sent off his own men, under Lieutenant Arnold, towards Allahabad to do what he could to seize and hold the fortress; remaining behind himself in order to push the other troops forward to his support, on their arriving, from time to time, by driblets from Calcutta. Neill had already attracted great attention from his exceptionally resolute and vigorous bearing; and here his fierce energy and impetuous action startled and leavened the authorities. After a few days, when he had done all he thought necessary to put arrangements on a sound footing, he finally went on in person on the 9th, taking such additional men as he could with him in horsed vehicles, and reached Allahabad on June 11th.

The garrison there consisted of two regiments—one, the 6th N. I. in the cantonment, the other an irregular regiment of Sikhs under Captain Brasyer in the fortress. On June 6th (five days before) the Sepoy regiment had mutinied, and tried to seize the fort. But the Sikhs, under Brasyer's stern influence, had remained loyal, would not admit the Sepoys, and, supported by a few English volunteers and pensioners, had held the fortress for the State. Next day they were reinforced by Arnold's party; and on the 11th, Neill's arrival secured the position. The day after, the mutineers were attacked and driven across the river into Oude, and British administration was quickly re-established in Allahabad.

This was the first point of primary importance scored in the war, though it never attracted a tithe of the public attention that was due to it. This was owing partly to its having been effected without much fighting, and partly to the more sensational events that were taking place at Delhi, Cawnpore, and Lucknow.

But of the paramount importance of the operation there can be no serious question; nor of the gravity of the crisis. The loss of the fortress was desperately imminent, and, if lost, what the consequences would have been are beyond conjecture. It is enough for practical purposes to point out that by securing it, our virtual base of operations was transferred from Calcutta to an impregnable position 500 miles ahead. It is of interest to note that this turning-point of the war was coincident in date (June 12th) with the decision at Delhi to give up the thought of immediate assault, and to undertake the prolonged siege from the Ridge.

With this all-important success at Allahabad the name of Brasyer must ever be associated; for, on the crisis of June 5th, and until supports arrived, the saving of the fort would have been hopeless except for his personal weight with the Sikh soldiery, and his resolute and undaunted bearing. On the other hand, in the bold and rapid movement of the handful of men that sufficed for the support needed for that purpose, and in the advance generally during that critical period, Neill was the moving spirit, the leading personality, and chief actor.

After June 12th the advance enters on its second stage. For nearly three weeks, even with Neill's fiery and impetuous energy, no further forward movement was found possible. Troops from Calcutta had continued to arrive, but only in driblets, and frequently in entire want of equipment. Thus Maude with his gunners from Ceylon had to improvise a battery from the Allahabad arsenal, get bullocks for its draught, and fit them with harness. Before June 30th Neill had not been able to send on a man to the front. On that day, however, he had succeeded in completing the equipment of a sufficiently strong party, under Major Renaud of his own regiment, for a move towards Cawnpore; and this was his last act in chief command. On that very day, June 30th, his senior officer, Henry Havelock, who had been appointed to the command, arrived to take it over. Warmly appreciating Neill's energy and supporting his views, he at once confirmed his proposal, and sent forward Renaud and his party towards Cawnpore.

One coincidence of dates has already been mentioned. Here is the second. June 30th saw, on the one hand, the defeat of Lawrence at Chinhut and the beginning of the siege of the Lucknow Residency; and, on the other, the start from Allahabad of the pioneer party of Havelock's advance, which was eventually to end in the succour of that garrison.

General Havelock, who thus displaced Neill, for the future, from the leadership of the advance, had, on returning from the Persian Expedition, been appointed to that command, had left Calcutta on June 25th, and, as above shown, joined the front at Allahabad on the 30th. His qualities and career are too widely known to call for more here than a passing tribute of homage; but it will not be out of place to say that, besides the great and pertinent experience he had acquired in serious fighting, such as in Burmah, Afghanistan, and the Punjab, he was unique in those days as a student of his profession, learned in military knowledge, and skilled in the art of war. And he was now about to bring all this experience, knowledge, and skill, to bear on one of the most desperate undertakings ever entrusted to a soldier.

CHAPTER II

ADVANCE TO CAWNPORE

WHEN Havelock, on June 30th, sent forward Renaud's party towards Cawnpore, he had not heard of the surrender of its hapless garrison, and the catastrophe of June 27th. In a few hours, however, messengers and spies arrived telling of it; and the searching inquiry that was at once made destroyed any possible doubts of its truth, or of the new state of affairs that had to be faced.

One result was that the whole of the Cawnpore rebel army was now free to move downwards towards Allahabad and attack Renaud's party, which was advancing in front, isolated, and consisted of only four hundred English and three hundred Sikh troops with a couple of guns, and a few native cavalry. Havelock therefore sent cautioning orders to Renaud, allowing him to continue to advance, but only slowly and warily, instead of expeditiously; and on July 7th he followed on himself with his main force; leaving Neill behind at Allahabad with a sufficient garrison, to organize and complete the arrangements there for the security of future operations.

The force that Havelock thus led out of Allahabad, together with the party under Renaud, amounted to 1,965 men all told, and included Maude's field battery of artillery from Ceylon. Of the 1,965 men, 1,404 were English and 561 were natives. The English consisted of 98 artillery, 20 volunteer cavalry, and 1,286 infantry (Madras Fusiliers, 64th, 78th, and part of the 84th). Of the natives, 18 were gunners, 95 were cavalry, who proved worthless and were disarmed and dismounted after the first flight, and 448 were Sikhs under Brasyer.

A further source of anxiety respecting Renaud's party was that, large as the rebel force at Cawnpore had been at first, there was no knowing to what extent it might not have now been swelled by the mutineers from Azimgurh, Jaunpore, Benares, and Allahabad; or whether these mutineers might not, possibly, be hovering on Renaud's flank and rear instead of pushing forward to Cawnpore.

When Havelock started on July 7th, and in fact all throughout this month, the heat was intense; and he wisely avoided pressing his men for the first couple of days, till they began to get inured to the marching and the heat; but, afterwards moving more rapidly, he overtook Renaud on the night of the 11th, and on the 12th fought the action of Futtehpore.

He had halted four miles short of the town of Futtehpore; and the Cawnpore rebels, who had been marching south to check the British advance, thinking that here they would only have Renaud's party to deal with, came gaily on to the attack with a swarm of cavalry in front. Their force consisted of some 3,500 regulars and a mass of raw levies. On sighting the British it developed its line, with the artillery in the centre, which opened fire. Suddenly it realized that it was in the presence of a much stronger array than it had expected. Maude's guns first replied direct to its artillery, and then took its line in flank at point-blank range; while the British infantry advanced to the front, preceded by skirmishers. In ten minutes the issue was no longer doubtful. It was the first taste the enemy had of the Enfield rifle, and they fled in rout; eleven guns were taken, and Futtehpore was stormed. The victory was thorough, and almost bloodless. Our chief loss lay in twelve men killed by sunstroke.

On the next day there was a halt. On the 14th, the native cavalry which had misbehaved were disarmed and dismounted, and the force again advanced. On the 15th, it fought in succession the two actions of Aong and of Pandoo Nuddee, about twenty-eight and twenty-two miles short of Cawnpore. At both of these sites the enemy had made careful preparations.

At Aong they had entrenched the face of the village, and also held a hamlet in its front; and, on Havelock's approach, they threw forward their cavalry on both his flanks, threatening his rear. Havelock kept together two-thirds of his force to hold the cavalry at bay, and to act as supports where necessary; sending only the remaining third forward in skirmishing order for the actual fight. It was soon over. The Madras Fusiliers stormed the hamlet; the rest of the skirmishers and the artillery attacked the entrenchment, captured it and the village, and drove the enemy out of it pell-mell. Their cavalry had made several fruitless efforts to assail our main column; but being every time badly repulsed, at length fled precipitately to the rear, and the fight was over.

A very sad loss marked this combat. The intrepid Renaud, the leader of the advance, was mortally wounded. Brief, however, was the time for sorrow—short the spell of rest—for Havelock learnt that the enemy was in force in his front, bent on contesting the passage of the Pandoo Nuddee, and prepared to blow up the bridge, if need be. This was to be prevented, whatever the hazard or toil, as the river was in flood, and the destruction of the bridge would amount to a catastrophe, from the serious delay it would certainly involve. So, on again to save the bridge, and secure the passage of the stream!

The enemy had been reinforced by a party of the Nana's followers under his brother Bala Rao, and were sanguine of success. But their position was faulty. They were massed close behind the bridge, which was at the apex of a bend in the ravine; which here formed the course of the stream, the bend being towards the British, while the arms of the ravine lay slantwise along the enemy's flanks. The ravine was lined on the British side with high and steep cliffs, through a passage in which the road led down to the bridge.

There was no halt in the British advance. The skirmishers partly occupied the cliff above the bridge, and partly drew up in the passage leading to it, prepared to charge; while the main force, with the guns, ranged right and left on the cliffs along the arms of the bend, bringing an overwhelming cross-fire to bear on the bridge, and on the enemy massed behind it for its defence. This fire took all the heart out of them. They essayed to blow up the bridge when their mine was not yet ready; Stephenson, with his Madras Fusiliers in the passage leading to the stream, saw the failure, seized the opportunity, dashed over the bridge, captured the guns, and, being rapidly supported by the rest of the force, drove the enemy in precipitate flight towards Cawnpore. And so ended the contests of July 15th.

The success that had thus attended the careful and skilful handling of the troops (the loss *in action* did not exceed thirty killed and wounded) was all-important; for it was well that the men should be eager for combat and full of confidence in their leader, when their spirit and strength and endurance were to be put to the severest test.

On that afternoon, Havelock learnt that the whole of the Cawnpore English community had not been destroyed on June 27th as had been supposed, but that a large party were held captive by the Nana, and might still be saved. So no time was to be lost. They must be rescued at all hazards. There could be no rest till this had been effected, or, at least, every possible effort made towards this end.

In the early moonlight, therefore, of the next morning, July 16th, the force again moved forward some fifteen miles; till they reached a village, Maharajpore, where their rear-guard was to be halted and the baggage massed. The outskirts of Cawnpore, where the enemy were prepared to meet them, were now only about six miles ahead; so after a rest and breakfast, the force advanced about noon to the conflict; which, as will be seen, involved three successive fights.

The rebel force was said to consist of 5,000 regular troops and eight guns, four of which were twenty-four-pounders, besides a mass of irregulars and the Nana's own retainers. But the latter were not present in the first of the three fights.

They were found to be drawn up about half-a-mile behind a point, or fork, where the road to the cantonments branched off from the trunk road along which Havelock was advancing. They were in a curved line, about one and a quarter miles long, crossing and extending beyond both the roads, with both of their flanks and their centre resting on villages. Their cavalry and three of their heavy guns were on their left. Three nine-pounders were on their right. Their other two guns were in the centre. All the guns and the fire of the whole army were arranged to bear on the bifurcation of the roads.

Now the force that Havelock had with him to the front for the fight numbered only 1,100 British and 300 Sikhs; so a direct frontal attack was out of the question; manœuvring was necessary.

Fortunately, at about half-a-mile short of the fork, the ground to the British right (and in front, therefore, of the enemy's left, where his greatest strength lay) was covered by a line of mango groves. Havelock took advantage of these as a screen; and, while placing his cavalry with a force of skirmishers about the fork to attract or distract the enemy's attention, caused his main force to sweep in column to the right, behind and around the mango groves, till it emerged on the enemy's left flank, at right angles to his general alignment (a manœuvre in imitation of the Great Frederick at Leuthen exactly a century before). On gaining the enemy's flank, the column rapidly deployed, and while the enemy was trying to change his formation, swept down his line from its left to its right, taking all his guns and driving him in flight to the rear. At the first, the artillery under Maude took the enemy's position in enfilade, but the contest soon became an infantry battle. The advance was in echelon, the 78th Highlanders leading, then the 64th, the 84th, and the Sikhs, the whole covered by the Madras Fusiliers as skirmishers. The 78th moved down, silently at first, on the heavy battery at the enemy's left flank; and then, when eighty yards short of it, charged it, the men cheering, and pipes playing. That impetuous charge carried them through the enemy's left, rolling up their line close up to their centre; where halting for only a few moments to pull themselves together, the Highlanders again charged onwards, the General himself with them, and captured the centre position and guns; the enemy throughout being bayoneted and driven in precipitate flight to the rear. On reaching the centre, the 78th, utterly spent, were halted, while the 64th, 84th, and Sikhs took up the running, and sweeping on, carried the enemy's position and guns on their right flank; thus in the end routing the enemy from the whole of their position with the loss of all their guns.

While this last portion of the fight was in progress on the enemy's right, a brilliant feat was being performed at the centre, Barrow's volunteer horse (about twenty sabres) charging and cutting up the rear of the enemy, though their cavalry, a whole regiment, was present to cover their flight.

This closed the first, but only the first, of the three fights or phases of the battle of Cawnpore.

For, exhausted though the troops were by the heat, the long march, and then the battle, they had more work cut out for them. The infantry, on re-forming in order, continued its advance, but had to leave the guns behind, as the teams were too spent, for the time, to draw them. After marching about a mile, it was found that the fugitives of the left and centre of the enemy's line had rallied, and were drawn up with a couple of guns in a village to oppose us again. As the wearied British advanced but slowly, they were roused by Havelock's challenge, "Which regiment is going to take that village?" on which they raced for it, two of them driving the enemy out of it, and a third clearing the ground to its right.

Again the enemy fled, and this finished the second fight.

But even now the day's work was not yet at an end; for, as the British force continued its march, it found its front checked by a mass of troops, of which a large proportion were fresh levies of the Nana's, who was now commanding them in person. The situation was somewhat desperate; the men were utterly spent, and they had no artillery with them; while a twenty-four-pounder was playing on their centre, and the enemy's cavalry, which had rallied, had got to the rear and were attacking the wounded. So, while Maude's guns had not yet come up, Havelock ordered the line to advance, although under a heavy fire of grape and musketry; and at length, when they had covered some 1,400 yards, he sent the 64th charging at the twenty-four-pounder. This finished the day's struggle, with its three distinct actions. The enemy lost all heart, and fled in total rout; the victorious army halting for the night on the plain skirting that end of Cawnpore.

This splendid success had, however, failed in one, and that the most prominent, of its objects. On the previous day, the 15th, after hearing of his defeat at the Pandoo Nuddee, and the certain advance of Havelock's column, the Nana had destroyed his captives. The British force did not know, and Havelock did not learn till the small hours of the 17th, that their successive conflicts of the 16th at Cawnpore could no longer save those whom they had been hoping to rescue.

The simple and obvious preparations and precautions that, with the occupation of the Magazine, would have placed the Cawnpore party in a position to hold out for the twenty further days which brought succour, had been neglected. To that fatal error of judgment we owe the ghastliest and the saddest lesson of the Mutiny.

On June 17th, the morning after the battle, the British army entered and occupied Cawnpore; when they learnt and realized the miserable story of the massacre. On that same day, Havelock received Ungud, the one thoroughly successful spy from the Lucknow Residency; heard the story of the death of Henry Lawrence; and at once turned all his thoughts and energies to the passage of the Ganges and an advance to Lucknow.

During the next three days he worked vigorously at constructing an entrenched position on the bank of the Ganges, to enable a small force of three hundred men to hold its own against all comers. He also sent out a reconnoitring force to Bithoor, the Nana's seat a few miles off, which they burnt and destroyed. They found that he himself had fled, and his army had scattered, so escaping further immediate punishment. Then on the 20th, the day of the first attack on Lucknow, Neill rejoined him from Allahabad with a reinforcement of two hundred and twenty-seven men. Yet even with this addition, his effective strength at Cawnpore was less than that with which he had started from Allahabad. This was owing to the heavy losses from the combined results of casualties in action, from the sun, from sickness generally, and specially from cholera; which had now appeared and carried off, besides other victims, his principal Staff officer, Stuart Beatson.

Still the circumstances were wholly altered. Every struggle had issued in success. The men had acquired perfect confidence in themselves and their leader, and were eager for action; while the enemy had lost all heart, finding it a vain task to contend against the British soldier; so that in entering on any conflict, there was the assurance of success on the one side, the conviction of certain defeat impending on the other.

Such was the result which Havelock had achieved by July 20th, when he was preparing to cross the Ganges into Oude, and when the garrison he desired to relieve were repulsing the first general attack on their position.

CHAPTER III

HIS FIRST ADVANCE INTO OUDE

On July 20th, General Havelock had occupied Cawnpore for three days; during which he had been arranging for an efficient entrenchment—some 400 yards by 200, at the debouchure of the canal—for the protection of the station, and also preparing to cross the Ganges and advance on Lucknow. After deducting the garrison, 300 men, needed for the entrenchment, the force he had available for the advance was under 1,500 men, with thirteen field-pieces; the Europeans of the force not amounting to 1,200, all told.

His anxiety was intense, for he knew by this time that the enemy lying between him and Lucknow were in overwhelming numbers, whatever their spirit; that they comprised three separate armies—(1) the force that had from the first been besieging the Residency; (2) the mutineer regiments that had flocked into Oude from the side of Benares and Azimgurh; and (3) the Sepoy troops whom he had defeated on his march from Allahabad. The only regiment that might have been present with this large hostile array, but was missing from it, was the 6th N. I.; which after rising at Allahabad and collecting much plunder, had been driven off by Neill, and had gone away to their own homes; only, it is said, to be robbed and maltreated by the villagers on the way. And besides this force in his front, Havelock was beginning to hear rumours of the approach of mutineer troops from the south of the Jumna; but not as yet of any disturbance below Allahabad. On the other hand, reinforcements were on their way, so, on July 20th, the day of the first attack on the Residency, a start was made of the passage of Havelock's men to the Oude bank of the Ganges. The river was in high flood for a breadth of 1,500 yards, with shoal water for another 1,000; and the passage was effected entirely by the use of ferry-boats, which were either sailed, or rowed, or towed across by a steamer. Guns had been placed in position to cover the passage, but they were never needed. The crossing was never contested or checked. It was managed entirely by Colonel Frazer Tytler and Lieut. Moorsom, taking up eight days, six for the troops and two for the baggage. Each trip involved a passage of six miles, and occupied four hours. As the men landed, they bivouacked about two miles further on, and then gradually concentrated at Mungurwar, a strong and elevated position about six miles from the river. The force was very lightly equipped, carriage or transport being difficult to get. As they gradually cleared out of Cawnpore, Havelock's heart grew lighter in one respect. The men were freed from the temptation to drink with which they had been beset at Cawnpore, and which had threatened to demoralize that heroic band. At Mungurwar there were no liquor-shops, no relics of "Europe stores."

During the eight days of the passage, there had been almost continuous communication with the Residency. As already mentioned, Havelock had seen our emissary, Ungud, on reaching Cawnpore. Ungud had then returned to Lucknow, told its garrison of Havelock's victories, and come back again to Havelock with Mr. Gubbins's letter, but with none from General Inglis. Then he had a second time returned to Lucknow on the 25th with Colonel Tytler's letter, and had now a third time presented himself to Havelock, bringing on this occasion the letter from General Inglis with enclosures from the Engineers, respecting the road or access to the Residency.

Havelock crossed in person to Mungurwar on the 24th. There was an accession of cholera on the 26th. On the 28th all the preparations were finished. Next morning the force advanced, and in the course of the day fought two actions, one at Oonao and the other at Busherut Gunge, respectively four and ten miles ahead.

The peculiar feature of this advance was that it passed along a raised causeway through swampy or marshy ground, which made any extended or flank movement—or in fact any movement except along the causeway—very difficult; while in addition the enemy had prepared both Oonao and Busherut Gunge for defence.

The Oonao position was a double one. In advance was a village that lined the two sides of the road, and was strengthened by walled gardens and enclosures; and in rear was the town of Oonao. Neither position could be turned. Nothing was possible except a straightforward advance.

On approaching the village and finding it held, Havelock attacked it with his skirmishers. Then, before the guns came up, the Madras Fusiliers and the 78th charged the enclosures and the village, fighting from house to house. The 64th, coming up to their support, enabled them to clear out the position and form up on a dry stretch of ground on the Oonao side of the village.

Here, after a brief interval, Havelock joyfully found the enemy playing into his hands, and coming in mass along the causeway to attack him. Our guns were laid to enfilade them as they came on, while the infantry moved more to the flank, some advancing into the swampy ground so as to catch the enemy actually in flank. The Sepoys advanced gaily, until they came sufficiently near, when they halted and opened fire. Then Maude replied with his grape at point-blank range. The enemy suffered heavily, tried to deploy, but failed, and then finding themselves caught on the flank as well as in front, broke and fled precipitately. The British followed up; pursued and captured their artillery, fifteen guns, and the town; and then halted to rest.

After a halt of three hours, and a meal, the force advanced again, marching six miles to Busherut Gunge, of which they found the entrance protected by a battery of four guns and some entrenchments. As the ground here admitted it, Havelock sent the 64th forward on the left flank to turn the town and get at the causeway in rear, while he attacked the town in front. In due time, the frontal assault was made by the 78th and the Madras men, and succeeded; but the enemy on retreating escaped along the causeway, instead of being caught by the 64th as had been hoped.

Still we had won two victories; though at a loss of about a sixth of the force (half of it from cholera and the sun), and with much exhaustion of the ammunition. The prospect, to the General, was very gloomy, almost hopeless. It was obvious to him that his present force was wholly inadequate to win through the difficulties ahead; where the enemy were evidently reserving their strength, and would meet him in positions carefully prepared for defence.

Then, on the following morning, came the disastrous news from Neill (which had reached him by telegraph), that the Sepoys at Dinapore, on his communications south of Benares, had mutinied; and that no further reinforcements were to be counted on for a couple of months! For, not only had those Sepoys mutinied, but the leading chief in that neighbourhood, a very fine old Rajpoot, named Konwur Singh, had risen in rebellion; and, as his influence extended from the river to the trunk road, not only was the safety of the communications threatened, but those districts had thrown off the British rule, and troops that would otherwise have gone on to the front had to be detained for the protection and restoration of order of those districts. Hence it was that the regiments such as the 5th, 37th, and 90th, which Havelock had been counting on for the increased strength necessary for the conflict at Lucknow, were kept back; and he was now warned that they might not be available for a couple of months. This news was crushing—heart-breaking, when added to the cholera that was devastating his force. On July 30th, therefore—a singular sequel to his victories of the preceding day—he made up his mind, not only not to continue his advance towards Lucknow, but instead to retire to his position at Mungurwar. At this stage, however, he had no thought of quitting Oude territory or retiring further to the rear than Mungurwar.

His intention was to remain there as his temporary headquarters, diverting and withdrawing the enemy as much as possible from Lucknow; and thereby to diminish the pressure on its garrison: at the same time taking every possible opportunity of dealing effective blows at the enemy. His reason for selecting Mungurwar as his temporary position was twofold; first, it was fairly close to the river, and in touch with Cawnpore, whither he could send his sick and wounded; and second, the site was high and advantageous for defensive purposes.

It may also be mentioned that no sign whatever had yet appeared during those ten days (nor in fact at any time afterwards) of any Talookdars with their followers joining in the fights or harassing him; but he had heard rumours, though all was quiet to the east, that there was an inclination towards some turbulent gatherings at Roya, on the western or left flank, where the Nana was said to be sheltered.

Such was the state of matters, and such were Havelock's intentions when on July 31st he retired to Mungurwar. This narrative is meant to be mainly one of military operations; still it is reasonable to dwell for a moment on the bitterness which the brave old General must have suffered when he turned his back on Lucknow; on his sense of the censure and outcry which the step would raise against him; on his sympathy for the almost irrepressible mortification and anguish of his gallant troops at the thought of retreat; and on his noble and resolute firmness to do the right thing, in spite of all such obstacles.

On retiring to Mungurwar, he wrote of it to Neill, and caused a telegram to be sent to the Commander-in-Chief in Calcutta, saying that without another 1,000 men and a battery he could not possibly move on Lucknow.

And now harassed as he was to the extreme of endurance, he was to be further worried by Neill's bearing at Cawnpore. Incidents had occurred previously, pointing to Neill's readiness to criticize and condemn Havelock's action; and he now wrote to Havelock condemning his retrograde movement in terms which may be justly described as unprecedented and unmeasured from a subordinate to the General in command. Havelock's reply was brief, peremptory, and conclusive; but the incident, of course, altered permanently the relations between the two men.

Neill was now sending Havelock intelligence of the approach of the 42nd N. I., a mutineer regiment from Saugor, and of the threatened gatherings on the banks of the Jumna. But he also sent him over a few reinforcements, a company of the 84th, Olpherts's half battery, two heavy guns, and two field howitzers.

On the 31st, Havelock had been able to put only 850 men in line, after providing for his guards and such other requirements, out of a total strength of 1,350 men. Four days later, *i.e.* on August 4th, he still had only 1,400 men, all told, including his Sikhs; with whom, having heard of the Sepoys again collecting at Busherut Gunge, he marched against them there a second time, in pursuance of his plan to deal them effective blows whenever an opportunity occurred.

He adopted the same plan of action as before, sending the 78th, the Sikhs, and Maude's Battery to make the turning movement. The enemy saw it, would not face it, and fled before it could be completed, though not without losing some 300 men; while our loss was but two men killed and twenty-three wounded. Seventy-five men, however, went down with cholera and fever. Havelock was thereby confirmed in the hopelessness of an advance with his present force, and under present circumstances; so he here consulted his three principal Staff officers on the matter, and found that they all agreed with him, excepting only his ardent and intrepid son, who would hardly be convinced.

One peculiar feature in this second fight at Busherut Gunge was the presence among the enemy of some Talookdars' men. But, as their chiefs had not joined, it is thought that they belonged to these districts, and had been coerced by the Sepoys, and forced to accompany them to the scene of action. If this was not the case, the men were probably those of Doondiakhera from the east, and Nirput Singh's from the west.

On August 5th, the day after the fight, Havelock had not 900 men present to put in line, yet he now received still more pressing intelligence of the approach of the enemy to Cawnpore. So he returned again to Mungurwar, to be ready to recross if necessary; though not yet proposing to give up his hold on Oude territory.

If this date be compared with the events already described at Lucknow, it may be gathered that, after their second defeat at Busherut Gunge, the rebels were still aware of Havelock's weakness and difficulties, and of the extent to which Cawnpore must engage his attention; and that consequently the bulk of the Sepoy force that had been fighting him returned to Lucknow, helping to press on vigorously the measures which culminated in the second general attack of August 10th.

At Mungurwar during those next few days, the letters received from Neill became more and more anxious, describing his straits as likely to be desperate, with 4,000 men and numerous artillery threatening him close at hand. So Havelock having first written on August 6th to the Commander-in-Chief, intimating his intention to hold on to Oude, now wrote on the 9th saying that he would probably have to return to Cawnpore.

On August 4th, the day preceding the second march to Busherut Gunge, Colonel Tytler had written the following letter to General Inglis—

> "We march to-morrow morning for Lucknow, having been reinforced—we shall push on as speedily as possible—we hope to reach you in four days at furthest. You must aid us in every way, even to cutting your way out if we can't force our way in. We are only a small force."

This letter, however, did not reach General Inglis till the 15th; after, as will be seen, Havelock had evacuated Oude.

But now on the 8th—four days after Tytler wrote the above letter—Havelock wrote to Inglis stating—

> "Imperious circumstances compel me to recross the Ganges. When further defence becomes impossible, do not negotiate or capitulate—cut your way out to Cawnpore. Blow up your fortifications, trenches, etc. by constructing surcharged mines under them and leaving slow matches burning."

But there seems to be no record or trace of this letter having ever reached its destination.

It is to be remembered that meanwhile the last news Havelock had of the garrison was by Inglis's letter of July 26th, now a fortnight old. In fact there was singular delay (felicitous delay, it may be held) in the interchange of receipt of grave intelligence between Havelock and Inglis.

He remained at Mungurwar till the 11th, two days after reporting to the Commander-in-Chief his probable return to Cawnpore. For the last three or four days he had been preparing for his re-passage of the Ganges; his actual movements, when the time for it arrived, having of course to be guided by the attitude and position of the enemy. And on August 10th (the day of the second general attack on

Lucknow), Havelock learnt that the force of the enemy at Busherut Gunge was sufficiently strong to require to be defeated and driven to the rear, before he could safely attempt the crossing of the river. He therefore determined on that day, the 10th, to attack the enemy at Busherut Gunge on the morrow, and then to turn back to Cawnpore.

August 10th then saw—

At Lucknow, the repulse of the second general attack.

With Havelock; his preparation for his last fight in Oude for the present, as a preliminary to his return to Cawnpore.

At Cawnpore; Neill seriously threatened by the Nana's followers and the mutineers from Saugor, and by the Gwalior Contingent at a somewhat greater distance.

At Furruckabad, on the west; the Nuwab with some 12,000 men threatening the flank.

South of Allahabad; reinforcements checked in their advance; being detained by the disturbed state of the country consequent on the Dinapore mutiny, and Konwur Singh's rebellion, although these mutineers had been defeated and Arrah relieved a week before by Major Vincent Eyre.

As to Oude itself, the strength and composition of the enemy's forces has been already described, and there is no reason to suppose that they had changed. The court were engaged with Durbar intrigues and with endeavours to get hold of English fugitives, rather than with military arrangements; *and the mass of Talookdars were still holding aloof and keeping in touch with the authorities at Benares.*

From Delhi, and up-country generally, there was no authentic intelligence; and the information received by the natives was probably neither fuller nor more authentic than ours. It was known that the British force was still facing Delhi, but that all Central India was disturbed, and that the people at Agra considered themselves in peril.

CHAPTER IV

HIS WITHDRAWAL TO CAWNPORE

WE left Havelock on August 10th at Mungurwar, preparing for an immediate return to Cawnpore consequent on the threatening aspect of affairs there, the stoppage of reinforcements, and the absolute impossibility, with his present force, of his affording any aid to the Lucknow garrison.

For his re-passage of the Ganges, as speedy a mode of transit as possible was essential, owing to the probability that the enemy would press on him during his withdrawal; and in view of this, his Staff and Engineers—Colonel Tytler with Lieutenant Moorsom, and Captain Crommelin with Lieutenant Watson—had been taking advantage of the gradual lowering of the flooded water to improve the means of transit. The plan adopted was to confine the ferry portion to the main channel, 750 yards wide; to span three minor channels by bridges of boats; and to construct a causeway of planking and timber, overlaid with grass and earth, along the remaining 1,300 yards, all more or less inundated, of the whole stretch of a mile and a quarter, which lay between the high banks on the two sides of the river.

By the 11th these arrangements had been carried out; Havelock had sent all his sick and wounded, his stores and baggage, across to Cawnpore; and was left with only his fighting force in light marching order, free for rapid movement. In the evening he advanced to Oonao, and next morning, the 12th, he moved forward for his third fight at Busherut Gunge. The enemy were entrenched. Havelock first used the heavy guns, by which he had been recently strengthened, to pound their position; and then, with the same manœuvre as formerly, sent the Madras Fusiliers to turn their flank, and the 78th to charge them in front. The enemy were soon routed, and fled in disorder with a loss of some 200 killed and wounded; after which Havelock took his force back to Mungurwar the same evening, preparatory to recrossing to Cawnpore next morning.

Let us pause for a moment and consider Havelock's situation and attitude on August 12th. He was 640 miles from his base, and confronted by an enemy 30,000 strong, with at least forty guns, intervening between him and the Lucknow garrison, in ground which he knew they had been preparing for defence. His own force was now reduced by casualties and disease to only 900 men, including Sikhs, available to place in line of battle.

It was with such means as these that, relying on the support of the promised reinforcements, he had dared to advance so far in the hope of rescuing Lucknow. Is there in the annals of our history of which we are so proud—in the wars of Clive, of Wellesley, of Lake, or of any other of our famous leaders—any record of odds so overwhelming, so undauntedly and brilliantly faced?

And now his reinforcements were stopped, his communications with his base below Allahabad were intercepted; various hostile forces, amounting to fully 20,000 men, were hovering on his flanks and on his rear within striking distance of Cawnpore; and rumours were rife of the active hostility of the whole fighting population of Oude under its Talookdars, who had hitherto remained quiescent.

Still, in this desperate plight, he stood calm and resolute, with his judgment clear and unclouded. Regardless of aught save his duty and his discharge of his trust, he crushed the bitter disappointment and anguish that were gnawing at his heart, and turned his back on the goal for which he had been striving, to start on one of the most dangerous of operations—a retreat across a huge river with a powerful enemy close on his heels.

It may not be amiss to add a word of thankfulness that his letter of the 8th had not reached the Residency, and that he did not at this most trying crisis receive any such thrilling appeal as Inglis penned to him four days afterwards.

On the evening then of August 12th, Havelock was back

at Mungurwar. Next day he stood on the bank of the Ganges. His force marched along the new causeway and the bridges of boats, and then, at eight o'clock, began the passage by ferry. By two o'clock all, excepting the rear-guard, had crossed into Cawnpore. That rear-guard broke up the bridges, and bringing with them the boats and the gear of the bridges, overtook their comrades safely by the evening. The blow last struck at Busherut Gunge had effectively stopped any close pursuit.

Thus it was that, with rare skill and care, Havelock carried out one of the most difficult and dangerous of field operations, and placed his whole force, without loss, in the Cawnpore position. It was not till four days later that the enemy were found to have followed up in strength, and to be occupying the opposite bank of the river.

But before he had started on his return to Cawnpore, the insurgent leaders had already begun to adopt fresh tactics, of which he was not aware till some days later, probably not till the 20th. With their overwhelming superiority in numbers, they were now wisely taking advantage of it to employ large detachments in operating on his flanks and communications, instead of, as heretofore, only in his front.

Moreover, now that he had retired from Oude, that step produced a political result which probably had never crossed his imagination. Hitherto all the Talookdars, with trifling exceptions, had remained passive; now, however, there arose a general consensus that they must regard Havelock's return to Cawnpore as an evacuation of the province, and a surrender of its rule to the Lucknow Durbar; and from this time the Talookdars, as the Benares authorities heard from some of them direct, were constrained to send contingents of their clansmen to take part in the operations at Lucknow.

As yet Havelock had not communicated more to Calcutta than a brief announcement of his return to Cawnpore. He had on the 9th, as already mentioned, written of his intention to make that move. His letter had shortly given the reason for it; viz. his inability, with his diminished numbers, to make head against 30,000 men and forty guns, and the demand for his presence at Cawnpore consequent on the critical state of matters there. Nor did he write more at length on reaching Cawnpore. He was weighted with matters of intense gravity, more than sufficient to occupy his full time and attention; nor did he yet know that Outram had been appointed, on the 5th, to the command which superseded him and would check the independence of his operations. Also he was specially preparing, whilst giving his force a couple of days' rest, to attack the enemy at Bithoor; where they were said to be 4000 strong, and entrenched. It was expedient to dispose of them before the other bodies of troops that were threatening him could combine with them and make the task more difficult. This party at Bithoor was said to be made up of three groups; half of them were the Nana's retainers; another detachment comprised some of the regiments that had been all along opposing him, and had now crossed back from Oude to operate against Cawnpore; and the third were the 42nd N. I. and other mutineers from Saugor, who had been repulsed from the fort there by the loyal 31st N. I.

Havelock's whole force at Cawnpore consisted of Brasyer's Sikhs and some 1,400 British soldiers, of whom about 350 were already disabled by wounds or sickness, while cholera was raging at a rate that would leave no fighting men available in another six weeks.

Such were the circumstances under which Havelock moved out on August 16th to attack Bithoor. Having a great superiority in artillery, he began by cannonading the entrenchment for a while, and then sent his infantry to storm it. The enemy fought as they had never fought before; especially the 42nd N. I., who came forward from their position, charging and crossing bayonets with the Madras Fusiliers. They were of course repulsed, leaving sixty men dead on the ground; and the British following up drove the enemy out of Bithoor, and thoroughly routed them with the loss of 250 men and their guns. Our casualties were seventy, twelve of them being from sunstroke.

Next day Havelock returned to Cawnpore, where he learned two things. First, the rumour which there had been of the Oude troops proposing to act on his communications with Allahabad was proving true; and the situation was growing critical, as they were apparently massing at Dalamow, and preparing to cross over to Futtehpore, the scene of Havelock's first battle. So the steamer that had been waiting at Cawnpore was despatched down the river with 120 men and three guns, under Captain Gordon of the 6th N. I., to do whatever was possible to stop the passage.

The other thing he heard of was the appointment of his old friend and commander in Persia, General Outram, to supersede him. He did not learn this by letter, but by seeing it in the *Calcutta Gazette.*

Severe as the blow must have been, he accepted it loyally, and set about such preparations as were necessary, knowing that his independence was now checked, and he must await orders, except for emergencies.

Then, on August 19th, he wrote two letters to the Commander-in-Chief, not yet knowing that that post had been taken over the day before from Sir Patrick Grant by Sir Colin Campbell.

In one of these letters he gave a full statement of the situation in Oude and at Cawnpore, and of the reasons for his return to Cawnpore. He showed how his force would have been a mere skeleton on reaching only the outskirts of Lucknow; how the issue must have been its annihilation, the loss of Cawnpore, and the abandonment of all that part of the country to the enemy; and he added that if he had prolonged his operations in Oude, there would have been a danger of Neill being overpowered and Cawnpore lost. Reinforcements were indispensable.

In the other letter he told of the expedition to Dalamow.

By next day, August 20th, he had received and answered Inglis's letter of August 16th, as already described. He was also relieved in a measure by the success of Gordon's expedition, which had had some skirmishing with the enemy on the bank of the river, but had effected its object by capturing and removing all the boats in that neighbourhood; thus precluding the possibility of any passage of the river by the rebels in force.

He heard too of the steamer having been fired at from forts on the Oude side of the Ganges; which, as it had not occurred before, confirmed the rumours of a change of attitude on the part of the Talookdars.

Intelligence had also arrived of Major Eyre's defeat of Rajah Konwur Singh at his fort of Jugdeespore, and the consequent improvement in the aspect of affairs in the disturbed districts there. Havelock was therefore now in hopes that some of the seven battalions which he knew to be present to the south of Allahabad would soon be arriving to reinforce him.

Hence it was with feelings little short of dismay that he now learnt that Outram was proposing to stop the advance of these troops to the front, and to divert them instead to a separate movement, under his own leading, on Lucknow; starting from Jaunpore, and marching through Oude between the rivers Sye and Goomtee; part of this scheme being that Havelock should advance again as before into Oude, and co-operate with him on his nearing Lucknow.

On examining dates, Havelock saw at once that Outram must be entirely in the dark as to the situation at Cawnpore, and that he was at that time, August 20th, steaming up the Ganges and practically inaccessible. So he forthwith telegraphed to the Chief, information and particulars which he felt certain would ensure the despatch to Cawnpore of the reinforcements of which the stoppage had been thus threatened.

His first telegram was on the 20th, briefly intimating that he was now threatened by the Gwalior Contingent with its twenty or thirty guns, and soliciting reinforcements.

To this he received a reply from Sir Colin, and telegraphed back to show him matters fully and clearly. But the communication being by telegraph and not by letter, has, from the curtness of its wording, been misconstrued. His message was to this effect. He was threatened by three forces; the Gwalior Contingent from Kalpee; a body of 12,000 men at Furrackabad; and the Oude troops opposite Futtehpore, who might at any moment become 20,000. Prompt reinforcements were needed to avert what seemed otherwise an unavoidable alternative—the withdrawal from Cawnpore to Allahabad. He requested reply by return of telegraph.

This has been construed as an inclination and a proposal to withdraw. The real case was precisely the reverse. He had no intention whatever of withdrawal. On the contrary, he was determined that the crisis should be averted which was threatening to bring about either the retreat or the annihilation of his force. He knew as a certainty that, with a man like Sir Colin Campbell, the exposition of the situation would lead to his being reinforced. And, as a fact, he was promptly promised reinforcements; whereupon he wrote on the 24th to Inglis the letter which, as already mentioned, reached him on the 29th; expressing the hope that reinforcements would reach him about September 18th, and enable him to advance again to the relief.

Havelock had been perfectly correct in his conviction that Outram was ignorant of his real situation. Sir James had been wrongly informed that the cause of Havelock's failure to reach Lucknow was the destruction of the bridge over the Sye, and his inability to force its passage against the swarms of the enemy. So when intelligence reached him of the actual circumstances and of Sir Colin's views, he at once abandoned the scheme he had been devising, and ordered the 5th and 90th regiments forward towards Cawnpore, telegraphing and writing to Havelock of it, and intimating at the same time his intention to leave to him the command of the advance to Lucknow.

Thus happily ended this phase of anxiety. Meanwhile, Outram's proposals had not been the real cause of the delay that had occurred. He had not halted such troops as were most to the front. He had meant that they should cross over and join his march higher up; the troops he had proposed to take with himself *viâ* Jaunpore were lower down. There were altogether at that time between Allahabad and Calcutta, the following regiments:—the 5th, 10th, 29th, 35th, 37th, 53rd, and 90th, besides drafts for the 64th, 78th, and 84th, and these were all being kept in those lower districts instead of being sent on to the front; not from any orders of the Chief, but from the want of any local authority recognized as in command; which led to their being detained by the interference of local officers, diverted from their proper course, and so frittered away broadcast. Thus, while Havelock's force could barely muster 1,100 men, some 6,000 men, who might have been on their way to the front, to the real seat of operations, were kept pottering in those lower districts south of Benares.

Meanwhile, although he was losing men, Havelock was not molested seriously by the enemy; his successive blows and victories had evidently disheartened them, making them loth to attack him; and he kept on doing all he could to prepare for the next advance.

Outram reached Allahabad on September 1st. On the 3rd and 4th, the 5th Fusiliers and the 90th Light Infantry also arrived there, and were at once sent on without halting.

Such was the state of matters with the British advance on September 5th, the day of the third general attack on the Residency, the close of the third stage of its siege.

Meanwhile, there was no special news from Delhi; nor in Oude was there any important change, beyond what has been already mentioned—the submission of the Talookdars to the rebel government, and their supporting it with their contingents.

CHAPTER V

HIS FINAL ADVANCE TO LUCKNOW

BEFORE Havelock started on his final advance into Oude, Sir James Outram reappeared on the scene. He has already played a prominent part in our story; chiefly, however, as a civil administrator carrying out the annexation of Oude. Now, however, he comes forward as a soldier and a general; a noble exemplar of high-minded and generous bearing, worthy of the Bayard of India, towards an old friend and comrade whose career of exceptional distinction might otherwise have been checked. Outram had shown his capacity as a commander in the recent campaign in Persia; but he had been less noted as a general in important operations, than as a brilliant and daring soldier in partisan warfare; with the eye and instincts of a sportsman, full of resource, enterprise, and boldness verging on rashness. How these qualities came into play will be seen presently.

After September 5th, Havelock's chief anxieties and efforts were in respect of the preparations for an immediate advance towards Lucknow on the arrival of the reinforcements. The state of the river was at that date at its very worst for any arrangements for its passage; since the floods were at that stage of subsidence when the inundations were not yet getting cleared; while shoals were forming which impeded the use of the steamer and of ferries, without being themselves fit for bridging or for causeways. Hence he was in constant correspondence with Outram on the matter, and about September 10th it had been very nearly decided that Outram, with most of the reinforcements, should cross into Oude about a day's march lower down, where he would be less likely to meet with opposition; and should then advance along the bank to attack and clear off the enemy opposite Cawnpore and at Mungurwar, Havelock crossing and joining him during the operation.

However, the reports during the next few days of the state of the river, and of the enemy's position, showed so much improvement as to lead to this scheme being abandoned.

By some singular coincidence, the threatening of the enemy's musters towards Kalpee, and at Furrackabad, which had been so serious about August 20th, seemed to subside almost suddenly a fortnight afterwards, when the reinforcements began to move upwards from Allahabad to Cawnpore. And as a matter of fact Havelock remained there practically unmolested till he finally left it for Lucknow. Only on the Oude side did the enemy show any activity, and seem inclined to give trouble.

Havelock's Engineers were meanwhile steadily at work preparing, from such timber-yards as they could find, the appliances and gear for any boat-bridges which might be wanted; and at the same time a close watch was kept up, it seems needless to say, on the movements and proceedings of the Sepoys on the opposite bank. But they never, after all, threw up on it any batteries or works of any moment, though they held it for a length of some four miles in considerable force.

Further down the river, however, the Oude troops were more aggressive. On September 9th, a party of 400 men, intended to be only the advanced guard of a larger force, crossed over to the right bank with four guns, with the intention of raising the country between Futtehpore and Allahabad. Vincent Eyre was thereupon sent against them with a detachment of 5th Fusiliers and others of the reinforcements. After marching forty miles, he caught them on the early morning of the 11th, drove them into their boats, and preventing the boats by his fire from being unloosed, destroyed the whole party. A small number of loyal men of the 12th Irregular Cavalry, who were with him under Lieut. W. T. Johnson, then went in pursuit of another detachment of which they heard, but which escaped before they could be reached. After this lesson, the enemy did not repeat the attempt. This little party of the 12th had been detached under their bright and gallant young adjutant, Charles Havelock; and while their comrades were murdering their Commandant, Holmes, they had remained staunch, and kept down the Azimgurh and Cawnpore districts.

On September 15th, Outram joined Havelock at Cawnpore with the first half of the reinforcements. Next day the rest of them arrived, and Outram issued his famous order waiving his rank and position, and handing over to Havelock the command of the relief operations.

No one can contest the noble and chivalrous feeling that prompted the act; but the actual position and the dilemma that resulted must be recognized. Outram's object was to ensure to Havelock the honour and credit and renown of the relief; but at the same time to do his utmost to aid him, and if need be to sway him into adopting his own plans, thus fulfilling his own trust. Hence he never really gave Havelock a free hand; while the keenness, persistency, and masterfulness with which from the first he pressed his own views and plans showed that, though giving over the nominal command, he expected his advice to be implicitly followed, and so to exercise the real guidance of the operations. Under the unique circumstances of the case, it was practically as impossible for Havelock to contend against this, as it was repugnant to his regard for Outram to question his views. The result was that, throughout the ensuing advance, much was done nominally under Havelock's orders which was not in accordance with his judgment and inclination, but for which the responsibility remained with him.

Now that he was maturing his arrangements for the relief, Havelock was, as a matter of necessity, greatly guided by Inglis's letters describing the state of affairs in the entrenchments. The letter of August 16th, already cited, had threatened that provisions would give out by September 10th; and a second letter had reached Havelock early in September, in reply to his note of August 24th mentioning the prospect of reinforcements. In this second letter, which was dated September 1st, Inglis said—

"In consequence of your letter, I have reduced the rations, and with this arrangement, and our great diminution in numbers from casualties, I trust to be able to hold out from the 20th to the 25th inst. Some stores we have been out of for the last fifteen days, and many others will be expended before the above date. I must be frank, and tell you that my force is daily diminishing from the enemy's musketry fire, and our defences grow weaker daily. Should the enemy make any determined efforts to storm this place, I shall find it difficult to repulse them, owing to my paucity in numbers, and the weak and harassed state of my force."

This, the last letter Havelock received before crossing the river, led him to the unavoidable conclusion that by September 25th the food supply would be wholly exhausted, and the garrison reduced to a state of desperate weakness, almost to inanition, from prolonged starvation. Hence his plans included the provision (1) of forty days' rations to be thrown or brought into the entrenchments for the benefit of the garrison, and (2) of transport for the withdrawal of the families by detachments.

It may be added here, though it deals with a somewhat later matter, that on September 19th, when he again stood on the soil of Oude, he was greeted by a third letter from Inglis dated the 16th, three days before, in which the situation is thus described—

"The enemy have continued to persevere unceasingly in their efforts against this position, and the firing has never ceased either day or night. On the 5th, they made a very determined attack after exploding two mines, and almost succeeded in getting into one of our batteries. . . . We have been long on reduced rations, so I hope to be able to get on pretty well until the 1st proximo. If you have not relieved us by that time, we shall have no meat left. . . . I am most anxious to hear of your advance, to reassure the native soldiers."

The only change in the state of affairs which this indicated to Havelock, was that the food was being made to last a little longer by the lowering of the rations, and that consequently the strength and vitality of the troops must have been terribly reduced; while the enemy, on the other hand, seemed to be bolder in their assaults.

So his view of the desperate straits of the garrison remained pretty much as before; gloomier, if possible, from an impression of the besiegers showing signs of increased vigour and boldness, both in their attacks and in their mining. Hence, with all his outward calmness, he was intensely anxious and nervous respecting the security of the garrison, and was bent on joining them on the earliest day he could. At the same time, he bore in mind that the straightest route is not always the shortest, and that massive buildings and barricaded streets, if well held, might block the way against the bravest troops. Hence, feeling convinced that he would have to face an enemy that had never yet shown their real strength, but had wisely reserved it for contest in ground of their own selection and preparation, he meant, on reaching Lucknow, to avoid any entry into it; and instead to march through open country, approaching the Residency by the north bank of the Goomtee and the iron bridge, after circling the city and crossing the river to the east. And, in accordance with this purpose, he arranged to convey with him the means of bridging the Goomtee.

Outram, on the other hand, of a more sanguine temperament, had heard stories, native reports, of the success of our mine against Johannes' house, and of the consequent elation and improved spirits of the garrison; and he believed that their straits were not at all so desperate as Havelock supposed. He held that the success of the impending advance would drive off the enemy, would open the country, attract food and carriage, and lead to a restoration of some sort of government.

Such seem to have been the views and plans, somewhat divergent, of these two noble-hearted and heroic leaders; both of them thoroughly single-minded, and having but one, and that the same, object in view.

It has been already described how the idea had been for a while entertained, but afterwards dropped, of Outram crossing the Ganges a day's march below Cawnpore. Havelock had prepared all the arrangements for crossing the whole force over on the morning of the 17th by boats aided by steamers. But Outram, on his arrival at Cawnpore, negatived this plan; and bridging operations were begun, which were only now becoming practicable. As it was, a deep channel 700 yards wide had to be bridged up to an island which had been formed in the course of the subsidence of the floods; and between this and the high bank beyond lay a stretch of ground about equally wide, and more or less swampy. Havelock proposed to occupy this island with a strong detachment to cover the construction of the bridge; Outram, however, thought that the detached troops would certainly suffer from the swampy nature of the ground, and that they might effect the same object by placing heavy guns so as to command the island, and the ground beyond, from the Cawnpore bank. As the bridge progressed, however, it was attacked, and a party of Brasyer's men had first to be sent over to hold the island; and next day they had to be supported by some British troops and four guns. On the night of the 18th, however, the bridge was finished, and on the 19th the force crossed over to the Oude side of the river.

The reinforcements that Outram had brought with him were about 1,450 men.

Havelock now left behind him at Cawnpore only a very small force, as there were no present signs of any enemy threatening it, while reinforcements of infantry, artillery, sailors, and Madras Sepoys were advancing upwards from Benares and Allahabad.

The Division with which he advanced towards Lucknow was thus composed—

Artillery	1 heavy and 2 light Batteries 282 British				Total 282
Cavalry	109	" Volunteers and	59	Natives ...	" 168
Infantry	2388	"	341	Sikhs ...	" 2729
Total	2779	"	400	Natives ...	" 3179

The artillery consisted of Eyre's heavy battery and Maude's and Olpherts's field batteries, all under the command of Colonel Cooper. Olpherts had managed by great exertions to convert the draft of his battery from bullocks to horses, and to pick up and train men to drive them—an invaluable increase to the efficiency of the column.

The cavalry consisted of English Volunteers and of loyal men of the 12th Irregular Cavalry, commanded by Captain Barrow.

The infantry were in two brigades—

Right brigade under Colonel Neill, composed of 5th Fusiliers; 64th Regiment (detachment); 84th Regiment, and 1st Madras Fusiliers.

Left brigade, under Colonel Hamilton—78th Highlanders; 90th Light Infantry, and Brasyer's Sikhs.

On the 19th this force, all, save the heavy guns and the rear-guard, crossed to the left bank of the Ganges and took up a position there, driving the enemy off to Mungurwar, after a merely nominal resistance. On the 20th, the rear-guard and Eyre's guns joined the column, and all was prepared for the start for Lucknow. On the morning of the 21st, the force began its march in heavy rain. Its first move was, of course, against the enemy at Mungurwar. It is not certain what the troops were that held that position; but it is known that part of them were the Native Infantry that had been at Cawnpore, the 1st, the 53rd, and 56th. The 2nd Cavalry that had been at Cawnpore was the only part of that mutineer brigade which did not cross into Oude.

On nearing Mungurwar, Havelock sent part of his force to the left to turn the enemy's right, and after cannonading their position, advanced to attack their front. On this they broke and retreated, their retreat turning into a flight, which was continued, with only occasional halts and checks, on through Oonao and Busherut Gunge. Our cavalry, which had been leading the turning movement, kept up a steady pursuit, playing havoc with the fugitives all through the pelting rain, and capturing their guns, and the colours of the 1st Native Infantry.

The impetuous Outram, here thoroughly in his element, was ever in the fore-front, and twice owed his life to the younger Havelock, to whom his father had entrusted the watch over the General's safety. By the evening, the force was collected about the Serai on the Lucknow side of Busherut Gunge; where it bivouacked for the night. The next day's march was absolutely unopposed, and brought the force across the Sye; the bridge over which at Bunnee, instead of being destroyed as Outram had been told six weeks before, had not even now been tampered with. On halting, the force heard the guns in Lucknow, and fired a royal salute, in hopes of its proving a signal to their friends; but the distance was sixteen miles, and the signal, being against the wind, was not heard.

Next morning, however, September 23rd, Havelock advanced, and his guns were heard at the Residency before the day was over. For the first ten miles there was no opposition; but as they came in sight of the Alum Bagh, a large enclosure on the road about four miles short of the Residency, they saw the enemy, about 12,000 strong, drawn up to block the way; with their left resting on the Alum Bagh, and their right protected by a swamp. The battle here was to be the first part of the contest for the actual entry into Lucknow, and the junction with the Residency.

It will be expedient at this stage to study the map of Lucknow. It will be seen that on the south it is girt and enclosed by a canal, which is large and deep, and is crossed by the road from Cawnpore at the Char Bagh. The Char Bagh is two miles from the Residency, the road between them passing through dense city. Nowhere else on the south is there any tolerable passage of the canal. The Alum Bagh is two miles short of the Char Bagh on the road from Cawnpore, and is an obligatory point to hold, whatever the route selected for access to the Residency. The battle for its possession was now to come off.

Havelock again adopted his turning manœuvre. Neill's brigade was halted on the road with the heavy guns, to pound the enemy and the Alum Bagh in front, while the left brigade with Olpherts's battery moved along the swampy ground on the left till it overlapped the enemy's line, then turning to attack it on the flank and roll it up. At the same time the first brigade made their advance. The combined attack in front and flank routed the right and centre of the enemy, but their left held the Alum Bagh; and this was at length charged and stormed by the 5th Fusiliers, who on entering found that the 78th, one of the flanking brigade, had almost simultaneously forced their way in through the main entrance of the enclosure. In ten minutes not one of the defenders was left within its walls, and the pursuit of the routed force was taken up by our handful of cavalry and Olpherts's guns, and continued nearly up to a building called the Yellow House, close to the Char Bagh bridge. All this fighting had been done under heavy rain. And now, as the cavalry halted and turned back from their pursuit, there came the brightest augury of success. A messenger brought up a letter to Outram, on opening which, he rapidly sent its message down the line of troops. They heard and received it with ringing cheers, for it brought the news of the storm and capture of Delhi, nine days before. A joyous ending to an exciting day!

CHAPTER VI

THE SUCCOUR OF THE RESIDENCY

HAVELOCK'S force then, having driven the enemy out of the Alum Bagh on September 23rd, halted there the next day in order partly to prepare it for retention as a defensive post in rear of the advance, and partly to mature the plans for the final move.

There was a choice of four routes [1]—

No. 1. First to the Char Bagh Bridge, over the canal, on the main road, and thence straight on by that road direct to the Residency. This was the *direct* route.

No. 2. To the Char Bagh Bridge, as in No. 1; and after forcing it, to turn to the right, circle round the city on the *inside* of the canal till reaching open ground; then to turn to the left, and advance to the Residency by the plain between the Kaiser Bagh, and other palaces, and the river. This was the *Inside Canal* route.

No. 3. Avoiding the road altogether, to strike from the Alum Bagh at once to the east (or right), and circle *outside* the canal till reaching the Dilkoosha; then turn to the left, and crossing the canal by the bridge there, take thence the same course as in No. 2. This I call the *Outside Canal* route.

No. 4. The same route as No. 3 up to the Dilkoosha; after reaching which to continue the advance to the *river*, bridge it, cross to the other side, and then turning to the left, march westward, seize the iron bridge and the Badshah Bagh facing the Residency on the other side of the river, and so relieve it. This was the *Trans-Goomtee* route.

Havelock was still desirous of adopting No. 4, which would avoid street-fighting; but Outram held that the route should be changed, as the ground had become too

[1] See Map V.

swampy after the recent heavy rain to admit of the movement of artillery and carriage; and also that the news of Delhi would lessen the opposition, and make the advance easier. He thought route No. 2 the preferable one, as beyond the Char Bagh Bridge he did not expect any serious fighting. To this course, then, Havelock gave his consent, though with reluctance; as he believed that all could go on by No. 4 except perhaps the heavy guns. It was arranged that, on the force advancing, Major MacIntyre should remain behind in command of the Alum Bagh, with a garrison of 300 men, in charge of the sick and wounded, the baggage, and the reserve of food and ammunition.

The force started on September 25th at half-past eight, after breakfasting; Neill's Brigade leading, headed by Maude's Battery and some of the 5th Fusiliers. The first opposition met with was from some guns placed at the building called the Yellow House, which were soon silenced by Maude's Battery; and then the column advanced, but all the time under fire, to a bend in the road, where it turned for a straight run of 200 yards to the bridge; while on the right were the enclosed gardens from which the bridge received its name, and still further to its right some rising ground, which flanked and commanded the bridge. Outram guided a party of the 5th to this rising ground, while the skirmishers of the Madras Fusiliers under Arnold lined the canal bank to the left of the road, the rest of the regiment remaining under the cover of the garden wall.

It was found that the bridge was blocked at the Lucknow end by a battery of six guns, including a twenty-four-pounder, with a breastwork in its front; while behind it was a cluster of high buildings, loopholed, and held with musketry.

Two of Maude's guns were brought up to the bend of the road, and opened fire on the battery and the buildings. The enemy replied, and soon swept down the gunners. As our skirmishers were making no impression, and matters were looking too critical to wait for Outram's flank movement to develope, Neill was directed to carry the bridge, and ordered his men to form up. But before they could do this, Arnold anticipated them, dashing forward with his skirmishers over the bridge, accompanied by Colonel Tytler and Captain Havelock. The whole of this party, except Havelock and Corporal Jacques (who was afterwards killed), were swept down by the hurricane of fire from the battery and from the loopholed buildings; but before the battery could reload and fire a second round, the Madras Fusiliers, who had followed and charged over the bridge, cleared the breastwork, stormed the battery, and won the passage of the Char Bagh canal.

The loopholed buildings that supported the battery were then stormed and held; and the road was clear for the rest of the column.

Meanwhile, a body of the enemy, with a couple of guns which had been driven off from the Yellow House, had retired eastward instead of over the Char Bagh Bridge; and re-forming in some enclosures, where they were well sheltered, had opened fire, from their guns in the road which they covered, on the flank and rear of the second or left Brigade (Hamilton's). The rebel position was strong; but the 90th charged it and captured the guns; which Olpherts, who with Colonel Napier had accompanied the charge, carried off in triumph, horsed by some of his own battery.

The 78th Highlanders were now told off to hold the bridge and the rear till everything had passed; while the main column itself, with Outram and Havelock at their head, turned to the right, and advanced along the road which skirted the canal till it reached the Begum's palace, near the bridge by which the road from the Dilkoosha enters the city. This palace was a strong building, and might threaten the flank of the march. So its entrance was blown open in order to make it indefensible, and the column then passed on, heading forward towards the river so as to get into the more open ground; and on reaching the Secundra Bagh, turned sharp to the left, bearing straight on the Residency.

Up till now the column had not met with any serious opposition since leaving the Char Bagh. The reason was obvious—the enemy had not thought of the British column adopting any other than the direct route; nor was it till late in the day that they realized the circuitous line that it was taking, and collected in force to oppose it.

In fact Havelock found the Secundra Bagh, the Shah Nujeef, and the Motee Mahul quite empty; such fire as opened on him was from the left on his attaining the Motee Mahul, and also from the Badshah Bagh on the other side of the river. The fire from the left was mainly from a battery at the eastern corner of the Kaiser Bagh, but partly also from musketry from the 32nd mess-house.

At the Motee Mahul the column was halted; partly to rest it and let it recover its formation, partly to enable the rear to join it safely, and partly to give the chiefs an opportunity to discuss the final step.

The Residency was now only 1,100 yards off, the Chutter Munzil group of palaces blocking the way along the river for a length of about 800 yards; its nearest enclosure, a garden, being about 300 yards distant, while the intervening ground was occupied by only a few empty buildings. The road to the Residency began with a street on the left of this enclosed garden, running between it and the Hirun Khana (or deer yard); thence by a sheltered space to a gate known thereafter as Neill's Gate; where it turned to the right, and aimed for the Residency.

At the Motee Mahul, the generals resolved to leave a strong rear-guard there, to make with the main force for Neill's Gate, and there decide on the further line of route. As the rear took some time to come up, the force remained halted at the Motee Mahul till late in the afternoon, and as even then there was still no sign of the 78th, a party was told off to return and meet and guide them on. Presently, however, the regiment was seen marching along the road in front of the palaces on the left flank. So the force emerged from the Motee Mahul; Lieutenant Moorsom being sent forward to reconnoitre the palaces, and ascertain whether they were held by the enemy. On emerging, the force was assailed with a very heavy fire of artillery and musketry from the Kaiser Bagh on the left, but not from the Chutter Munzil buildings, which Moorsom had been sent to reconnoitre; and they continued to be under fire till they reached the space between the buildings or enclosures at Neill's Gate, where they found themselves comparatively sheltered, and remained halted for a short time. Meanwhile, as had been decided, the Motee Mahul was not evacuated. The wounded and baggage and heavy guns were left in it under the charge of Colonel Campbell of the 90th with one hundred men.

While halted at the space which may be called Neill's enclosure, the generals were anxiously awaiting Moorsom's return, for if the palaces were found unoccupied, the route through them up to the very ramparts of the Residency would be safe. Otherwise the route must be by the streets, which, it was now clear, the enemy were prepared to defend, though they would hardly have had time to prepare any barricades or material obstructions. This short length of street fighting was unavoidable. There had been none heretofore—all the previous loss had been at that brilliant feat, the forcing of the Char Bagh Bridge.

While halted at Neill's enclosure, the force was joined by the 78th Highlanders, who had been left behind at the Char Bagh Bridge to hold it till all had passed on. They had been having their own share in the fighting, to which we will now turn. So long as the main column was still within hail, the 78th were at first unmolested at the Char Bagh; and they employed the interval in throwing into the canals the guns which they had just captured, as there was no means available for their transport. But, after a very short respite, the enemy came down the Cawnpore road again on them in force, and a combat ensued, of which the 78th stood the whole brunt for some hours. The contest was one of musketry for most of the time, but at the end the Highlanders charged and stormed a temple which formed the enemy's strongest post. On this the Sepoys brought up three field-pieces, and continued the fight for another hour. While this was going on, all the rear, with the companies of the 90th that formed its guard, had come up and passed on; so the task allotted to the 78th was over. They therefore charged the enemy afresh, drove them back, and, capturing the guns, ran them back to the canal, hurled them in like those taken at the bridge itself; and then started on their march to overtake the main column.

This last hour of fighting, however, had given the rear-guard such a start that the 78th never recovered touch with it, and hence, on reaching the bridge where the open ground began, instead of going onwards to the Secundra Bagh as the rest had done, they turned sharp to the left, following the road—at first a street called the Huzrutgunge, which skirted the face of the Kaiser Bagh and led to Neill's Gate—and thence onwards towards the Residency. Up till now they too had had no serious fighting during the march; but as they neared the Kaiser Bagh they heard the firing to the front and right. Then, while seeing the main column emerging from the Motee Mahul, they came on the flank of an enemy's battery at the Kaiser Bagh, stormed it, and then passed onwards, edging somewhat to the right towards the street which the main column had just entered. Thus was its junction effected; and not only so, but this regiment became the head of the column which now comprised the whole force, excepting the men left in the Alum Bagh and the Motee Mahul. Brasyer's Sikhs were immediately behind the 78th.

While they were thus being drawn up in position for a rapid advance, a discussion on the route to be taken was going on between the two generals. They had been anxiously awaiting Moorsom's return from his reconnaissance, and Outram, impatient at the delay, had gone himself to reconnoitre, but had come back not able to find any opening or means of entrance into the Chutter Munzil, though not attacked from it. As it was now getting dusk, Havelock wished to move on at once and take his chance through the streets, through which his course would after all be now less than half a mile. He was strengthened in this view by hearing from Olpherts (who being asked had expressed himself warmly in favour of an immediate advance) that he would have no difficulty in placing one of his guns in position on the other side of the gateway, firing down the street towards the Kaiser Bagh, and so protecting the rear of the march. Outram, however, urged a further halt (by which, as his written statement shows, he meant only a *short* halt), while seeing with Moorsom whether there was not really a practicable route through the Chutter Munzil. But Havelock, as his official report states, thought he meant a halt *for the night*, and to this he demurred. Any sign of the force being effectively checked and foiled in its efforts to reach the Residency might, he felt, affect the natives of the garrison so as to lead to fatal results. It was essential, therefore, he said, that troops should be thrown into the Residency at once; otherwise it was possible that the worst might happen to the garrison. But while he himself led the head of the column by the open streets, Outram, he pointed out, might remain where they were standing, and bring on the rest of the column by any better way he might discover.

Outram, however, though he had given over the command, would not surrender the post of honour; and so waiving further discussion he placed himself at the head of the column, crying, "Let us on then in God's name." On this Olpherts moved his gun out through Neill's Gateway into position, and then—the Highlanders leading, with Brasyer's Sikhs immediately behind them—the force also emerged with Outram and Havelock at the head and started on its zigzag route to the Residency. First it turned to the right for a few yards till it reached the Khas Bazar; when it turned to the left, and found itself under a hot fire sweeping down the long narrow street. Before reaching the Khas Bazar it had been under fire only from the rear; but this was a very telling fire, though answered by Olpherts's gun. Tytler, the Quartermaster-General, was at once dangerously wounded, and a few minutes afterwards Neill was shot dead.

On turning up the Khas Bazar, and finding themselves attacked from the front, the 78th charged up the street and overshot the point at which they should have turned towards the Residency. Outram, however, quickly halted the leading companies, and ordering them to draw back, took off the centre companies as the new head of the column, followed by the rear companies and by Brasyer's Sikhs, straight down the road; till they debouched on the Residency position, opposite Saunders's post, and there found their way in, first through an embrasure at Aitken's post, and then through the Baily Guard gate itself. And thus did Havelock and Outram, and the heroic column which they had been leading, effect amidst ecstatic cheers and shouts that junction with the garrison for which there had been so long and fierce a struggle.

Almost immediately after Outram had guided the centre

companies of the 78th over the direct road to the Residency, Moorsom, who had been unable to find any route through the Chutter Munzil, overtook the column, and guided the rest of it and the guns by another street; which ran behind, but close and parallel to Outram's route, till it crossed the Pyne Bagh, and went straight down on the Baily Guard through the Clock Tower; where the enemy slewed their guns round and gave them a parting shot.

Although the loss sustained by Havelock's force is to be deplored, it was trifling in proportion to the difficulties to be overcome, and the strength of the opposing army. A desperate feat cannot be accomplished without loss; nor had there been, as alleged by some, any confusion or bungling. That the rear-guard (the 78th) lost touch of the main column, and joined it by a shorter route, involved no demerit, and entailed no difficulty nor loss.

Without any regard whatever to what was still to follow, what had still to be done, and what was not done, this junction on the evening of September 25th, though it may not have been a relief of the Lucknow Residency in the technical military sense, was a relief of the garrison in all essentials from a common-sense point of view. It was a succour in the direst straits. It was a rescue from a situation of the most imminent peril. It was a relief from the most harrowing and agonizing dread of the ever-impending chance of a breach in the defences, without a moment's warning, through which the enemy, all ready prepared, might rush in overwhelming numbers which nothing could withstand. Further, when the imminent accession of the Sepoys from Delhi is remembered, as well as the sceptical feeling that existed in the minds of Sepoys in the entrenchments, there can be little doubt that Havelock's arrival saved the garrison of Lucknow from the fate of Gordon at Khartoum.

BOOK IV

THE SECOND DEFENCE OF THE RESIDENCY

CHAPTER I

EFFORTS TO WITHDRAW THE GARRISON

THE 25th of September, when Havelock and Outram entered and succoured the Baily Guard, marked also the close of the first stage of the war in Oude; for it proclaimed in favour of the British garrison the issue of the contest for the Residency entrenchments; which had constituted the gage of battle in Oude, as Delhi had done in the Upper Provinces. These two great operations, the capture of Delhi and the succour of Lucknow, were both of them effected without aid from England, and about the same date.

From this turning-point, when Havelock's great task had been accomplished, and the rescuers and the rescued had joined hands, our story will deal with the operations of the combined force, of which Outram now assumed the command.

His first task was to pull that force together; for though the junction had been effected, the relieving force had itself become somewhat dispersed and scattered, owing to the nature of the struggle of that day. The enemy had not been, as always heretofore, driven back, defeated, and dispersed in rout. Our troops had on this occasion been obliged, in order to effect their special and immediate object, to charge *through* the enemy in a column, leaving the rear-guard behind at the Motee Mahul. Moreover, the column itself, while its head had reached the Residency, was lengthened out and advancing but slowly with its guns and wounded, checked and impeded by the trenches and other obstacles on its route.

The most impervious and effective of these obstacles was the battery with which the enemy had blocked up the Lutkur Durwaza, facing the Baily Guard gate. But Aitken, who commanded at that post, on seeing the relievers approaching, promptly led out a party of his men, Sepoys of the 13th N. I., with entrenching tools; and proceeded to demolish and clear away the earthwork of that battery. Having accomplished this, he broke into and seized the adjacent posts right and left—the jail buildings on the one side and the Tehree Kothee enclosure on the other. This position, the Tehree Kothee, had hitherto been held in force; now, however, only a few of the enemy were found in it, and they were taken prisoners without a shot being fired. During the greater part of the night, the troops, the wounded, and the guns that had been checked by the obstacles and so delayed on the road, were being guided into the Residency and into the Tehree Kothee enclosure just seized. Hence, by the morning, part of the relieving force were inside the entrenchments, part were in the grounds of the Tehree Kothee, and part were still in the street from the Pyne Bagh, while the rear-guard were half-a-mile behind in the Motee Mahul.

As I have said, Outram's first task was to collect these several parties and to hold a compact position. The rear-guard, in the Motee Mahul, with the hospital and the heavy guns, was found to have practically lost touch with the rest of the force; and 250 men of the 5th Fusiliers and a detachment of Brasyer's Sikhs were sent back on the morning of the 26th to reinforce and help them in.

But the fire from the Kaiser Bagh was found to be too strong to admit of the rear-guard convoy being moved out. Accordingly the reinforcing party seized and occupied the gardens and buildings lying adjacent to the Motee Mahul, between it and the Chutter Munzil Palace, the advanced garden of which was also partially held by the 90th Regiment.

While this was being done, Outram proceeded to carry out his second object, the occupation in one direction at any rate of an extended and compact position. He specially desired to hold the whole river-face from the iron bridge to the Chutter Munzil; and to start this extension, a party of

150 men of the 32nd under Major Lowe, made a sortie from Innes's post down to the river. They encountered a considerable body of the enemy, and swept them off to the left up to the iron bridge; but they failed to get beyond the buildings at the near side of the bridge, or to seize and hold the end of the bridge itself. The rest of Major Lowe's party swept on to the right to the Tehree Kothee, which they entered, and then joined hands with Aitken's detachment, which, as before described, had made a lodgment there during the night. In the course of this clearance of the river-face, an eighteen-pounder and several light guns were captured. Later in the day these two parties, with others that joined them, felt their way on through the rest of the Tehree Kothee, and then penetrated into the Furhut Buksh Palace and enclosure; which thus, by the evening, came fully into our hands, leaving only the Chutter Munzil buildings and gardens between the position held by our main force, and the posts held by our rear-guard with its reinforcements. But these Chutter Munzil buildings were, it was known, occupied by the enemy, though their strength was uncertain. On the river-face they had kept quiet, though they had blocked all the outlets there. The advance eastwards from the Residency had not penetrated beyond the Furhut Buksh, and all efforts to enter it from other directions had failed or ended in disaster. No member of the old garrison was familiar with the ground, which was known to be a veritable labyrinth; and by a very sad mistake a party of the wounded had, during the day, been guided into what proved to be almost a *cul-de-sac;* and had become exposed to a murderous fire, from which few of them escaped.

It had also been planned early in the day to continue the extension of the position along the southern face of the Residency, but this was postponed owing to the need, now become obvious, of concentrating all efforts on the extricating of the rear-guard from the Motee Mahul, and bringing it into our own position.

This task was entrusted to Colonel Napier, afterwards Lord Napier of Magdala, who henceforward plays a leading part in our story. He had accompanied Outram as his chief of the Staff, but, from Outram's surrender of his command, had until now been serving as a volunteer. The party he led out consisted of 100 men of the 78th, with a few additional officers. Guided by Cavanagh, afterwards distinguished by his feat of carrying plans and despatches to Sir Colin Campbell through the beleaguering host, they debouched from the Furhut Buksh on to the narrow bank along the river, and advanced by it; skirting the Chutter Munzil and the minor posts held by the 5th Fusiliers, till they joined the rear-guard in the Motee Mahul.

The position was under a strong fire from the direction of the Kaiser Bagh; and one at least of the heavy guns, which had been planted at an opening in the face of the Motee Mahul to answer that fire, had got into difficulties. Three of the senior officers of artillery were killed, but Olpherts, who had accompanied Napier's party, succeeded in extricating the last of the guns, and then, warned by the weight of the enemy's fire, urged Napier to withdraw at once during the darkness of night, while he would be unseen, instead of waiting for the early dawn as at first intended. Accordingly the hospital, the reserve ammunition, and all that could be transported by camels or doolies, were brought into the Furhut Buksh by the route which Napier's party had taken. The rear-guard itself with the heavy guns, which required a wider road than the narrow bank, were brought into that part of the advanced gardens of the Chutter Munzil which the 90th were already holding. But hardly had this been effected when an opening was found, or made, into the adjacent Chutter Munzil enclosure, which was then attacked from both sides. It was strongly held; but the attack was impetuous, the enemy were annihilated, and a continuous position along the river-face was thus secured during the dark hours of the night of September 26th.

The force being thus collected, Havelock took command of the new portion of the position; which was generically known as the Chutter Munzil, and consisted of the group of buildings and enclosures extending from the Tehree Kothee through the Furhut Buksh to the Chutter Munzil Palace and its advanced garden. Napier was, for a time, appointed to aid him in widening and strengthening it for contest, if need be, in the Kaiser Bagh direction. Meanwhile Inglis remained in command of his old entrenchments;

and Outram set himself (from the morning of the 27th) to his task of opening out from this combined or extended position, and getting into touch and communication with the city. As yet he had been greatly disappointed at the fierce opposition he had encountered on reaching the city, and the stubbornness of the enemy in clinging on to their fighting behind walls.

And now on September 27th the first sortie was ordered, in view of seizing the posts the enemy held opposite our south-eastern front from the jail to the Cawnpore road. But this sortie was not successful; that is, it did not extend our position, nor secure any result of importance. The experience gained by the old garrison of the effective way of managing these sorties had been set aside; the troops having, after their first irruption into the enemy's position, dashed forward without guidance, went off the proper track; and, though they stormed batteries, took guns, and killed many of the enemy, were unable to retain their ground, and eventually returned into the entrenchments.

The necessity of careful preparation and definite schemes of operations was so obvious that the whole of the next day, the 28th, was spent in organizing the sorties for the 29th.

These sorties of September 29th did not touch the site of the sortie of the 27th. They were in three columns, two of which operated on the South front from the neighbourhood of the Brigade mess, and the third from Innes's post on the north-west towards the iron bridge.

The two from the Brigade mess cleared the whole of that front; taking, blowing up, and destroying such houses and batteries as had been attacking that face of the position, including those that had done so much mischief to Gubbins's bastion. The breadth of the range thus cleared was about 300 yards, and the results were invaluable to that front of the position for the rest of the siege.

But the most really important of the three sorties was that from Innes's post. Outram was intensely anxious to secure the iron bridge, as the most likely means of opening communications with well-wishers in the city. The sortie, however, never reached the iron bridge nor occupied the houses leading on to it. It only got as far as Hill's shop, near it, where it captured and destroyed the gun which had played such havoc during the first siege by its fire over the long diagonal of the entrenchments.

The force employed in these sorties of the 29th was 700 men, and the loss in killed and missing was three officers and fifteen men. The failure, however, to get the iron bridge was a bitter disappointment to Outram; not only for the reasons which have been stated, but also from his rapidly increasing anxiety about the food supplies. He resolved on one more effort to open out his communications, and summoned up Napier from the Chutter Munzil to organize and carry it out.

Next day, September 30th, while the preparations for it were being made, he caused the various mines of the enemy which had been found to be examined and destroyed; and in the evening he ordered out the cavalry to endeavour to make their way through the enemy to Alum Bagh. But they found the investment so close and strong that all their efforts failed, and they had to return to the entrenchments.

Next day, October 1st, the final sortie began. Its real object was to secure possession of the Cawnpore road to a sufficient distance to admit of troops forcing their way to the Char Bagh, with several other and ulterior objects in view. But during October 1st and 2nd no direct sign was shown of this intention, the operations having apparently the same object as before, the widening out of the position. The enemy's attention was first of all distracted, in the dawning hours of October 1st, by the commencement of a battery (a mere feint) indicative of an attack on the Kaiser Bagh, in the east, from the Pyne Bagh; and then in the middle of the day the real sortie charged out, taking the route that should have been adopted on the 27th. Its objective was to capture Phillips's house and garden, with its battery, which faced our Cawnpore battery on the south and flanked the Cawnpore road. The party worked close up to the garden, occupied the houses commanding it, and loopholed the walls so as to obtain the requisite fire on the desirable points. The sortie of the 29th had already cleared the flank on the other side of the Cawnpore road; and accordingly next morning a detachment was sent over there; Phillips's garden was attacked by infantry on both flanks, and by the artillery in the entrenchments in front; and was then stormed and taken with a loss of only two men killed. All the guns in the garden were destroyed, and the house itself was blown up. Positions having been thus secured on both sides of the Cawnpore road, the additional preparations were carried out on October 2nd, to make them serve as a base for operating along the road. Accordingly on the 3rd the sortie turned down it, attacking, seizing, and securing house after house on both sides, and by its own artillery fire preventing any obstruction by the enemy's guns. This advance was continued till the evening of the 4th; when a bend of the road was reached which seemed favourable for still further progress.

Now, however, the operation was suddenly stopped, no fresh advance was made, and the evening of October 4th marked an entire change in the apparent aspect of affairs and in Outram's plans. For it had now been ascertained—but only now—that the ideas about the exhaustion of the food supply had been all along incorrect, and founded on some entire misconceptions; and that there was no reason for any present grave anxiety about it.

It will be remembered that Havelock had forced his way through all obstacles into the Residency in what might be thought a desperate if not reckless manner, under the belief, founded on Inglis's letters, that the food of the garrison must be exhausted and its inmates starving. On reaching the Residency it had at once become obvious that their plight was not really so severe, and that rations, howbeit meagre, were forthcoming for every one. Still, the conviction remained in the minds of the generals that they "were coming to their last biscuit"; hence Outram's intense anxiety, and his persistent and desperate efforts to open communications with the city and the country. But this belief, or idea, was confined to the generals and a few of their most trusted Staff. When, however, Napier joined Outram from the Chutter Munzil on October 1st, he had become sceptical on the subject, and now, as chief of the Staff, personally inspected the several stores. He had expected to have a search, but he found that no search was necessary. The

Commissariat officers in charge of the supplies knew where all the stock was, and pointed it out. Instead of its being exhausted, there was an ample supply for all for some time to come; the mist on the subject was thus cleared off at once, on proper inquiry being instituted. Those officers had never known or surmised the false impression that had been conveyed to Havelock and Outram, nor had they ever given or been asked for any returns on which it might have been based.

I do not know how the misconception arose, or how it was ever explained; but it would appear that Sir Henry's dying orders, to have an inventory taken of the supplies, were not carried out; and that those officers in charge were never called on to measure up their stock, or to report specifically how it stood at any time—the only process for arriving at a trustworthy or responsible estimate. All the supplies, I need hardly remark, had been laid in before the siege began. For six weeks they had kept pouring into the Residency through the agency of Captain James, the local Commissary-General, and of Simon Martin, the civil officer in charge of the Lucknow district; as well as in the form of gifts from well-wishers from various quarters. James and Martin had been indefatigable beyond all praise, and the test of their ability and energy lay in the broad fact of the huge actual accumulation which they made—so huge that it left a surplus after supporting the combined garrisons till November 20th. While they were collecting these supplies their storage and its records lay in the hands of the native subordinates; but on the day of Chinhut all these natives fled; with them the lists disappeared; while Captain James was laid up, incapable of moving, throughout the defence, from a very severe wound received at Chinhut. Hence when once the siege began, a few officers, wholly new to the work, had to be appointed to the direct charge of the supplies and their distribution as rations; the only guidance or supervision that James could or did give them being by way of advice and instruction in those particular duties; while he reserved to himself the general control, though really disabled for such responsible work, or for any personal watch of the state of the stock in hand. Possibly it was thought that others could make an equally good estimate; and the only explanation I can suggest of the misleading announcement to Havelock in August is, that perhaps General Inglis meant to allude only to his supply of *meat*, in which case his estimate was a just one; or that the information or inspection by which he was guided had overlooked, or not been aware of, some of the large storages in which the grain supply was kept. There were at least four, one of which, a large swimming-bath, had hitherto remained untouched.

Now, however, the inquiry made elicited the fact that there was an ample supply for immediate wants, although it took a few days to measure and calculate what the actual quantities were, and a few days more to decide on the reduced rations that should be issued, and to estimate the duration of the supply.

This discovery, then—or rather the knowledge resulting from this inquiry—altered, as I have said, the whole aspect of affairs, and caused an entire change in Outram's plans. It altered the aspect of affairs, because there existed no longer any immediate, or even early, necessity to procure fresh supplies, and the danger of starvation was distant instead of acute. It affected Outram's plans, because their primary cause and aim was in connection with this danger, the removal or reduction of which enabled him to draw in from the somewhat desperate schemes he had meant to adopt in order to meet it.

Outram at once stopped making further efforts to seize the Cawnpore road, or otherwise open out his communications. The struggle and difficulty with which the bend of the road had been reached showed him that any advantage we might gain by a further advance would not compensate for the losses which it would certainly involve; and accordingly, two days later, on October 6th, the sortie drew back into the eventual position, the 78th being left to occupy the new post which had been formed on the site outside the old entrenchment which the sortie had first captured. This post was henceforward known as Lockhart's, from the name of its commandant.

The successive changes which Outram had to make in his plans, consequent on the difficulty in opening out his communications, and the pertinacity of the enemy, are matters of importance.

When advancing to the relief, he had hoped to come into touch at once with the city, and perhaps to establish a sort of provisional Government in British interests; at any rate to throw supplies into the garrison, strengthen it with part of his own force, and withdraw the rest of it, taking with him the sick and wounded, and the 470 women and children whom the garrison had been protecting.

Then his letters of September 30th and October 2nd show that he had already abandoned the idea of withdrawing the families, and proposed to fight his way out with the bulk of his troops to the Alum Bagh, leaving the 90th behind with the old garrison to strengthen it and continue the defence.

After finding on October 4th that there was a sufficient supply of food for present wants, he wrote that he would hold on to the position with his whole force; and began 'a long and sustained correspondence with the Commander-in-Chief and others, respecting the proper measures for the advance of fresh troops to the relief of Lucknow.

Meanwhile the new or extended portion of the position at the Chutter Munzil had been getting expanded and consolidated, as will be more suitably described in the next chapter.

But whilst all this had been going on at the Residency, the force that had been left isolated in the rear at the Alum Bagh had been in a critical position, though it had escaped serious attack to a wonderful degree. It consisted of 280 Europeans, a few Sikhs, and four guns, and had charge of some 130 sick and wounded, the baggage, a quantity of cattle, and some 4,000 camp-followers (natives). Supplies and reinforcements were daily expected from Cawnpore, but they did not come till October 7th, when a convoy arrived with a party of 250 men and two guns. No attack had been made on the position, but the enemy's cavalry had kept hovering round and cutting up any of the camp-followers whom they found straggling about. With the supports thus received, and the defensive works they had constructed, the force at the Alum Bagh felt fairly secure at the time that Outram settled down for a prolonged defence of his position.

Meanwhile the enemy were being greatly reinforced in

numbers. At first—that is, on September 24th and 25th —a large proportion of the Sepoys had cleared out of Lucknow, so that in the first few days after Outram's arrival the hostile force seemed to consist more of the old Durbar retainers and Talookdars' men than of Sepoys. On the other hand, at the end of September those Sepoys who had fled, returned, and the fugitive troops from Delhi also began to swarm in; so that practically the army which was now beleaguering the British position was a very powerful one; containing moreover a new element of great importance, in the experienced troops who had been in daily conflict with the British force on the Delhi ridge. Lastly, the Talookdaree troops were under the sway of the ablest and most unscrupulous and false of the Oude Amils —the Brahmin Rajah Maun Singh; who was playing a double game, trying in insidious correspondence to assume with Outram the *rôle* of a secret friend, while aiming all the time at supreme influence with the rebel force.

We can now estimate properly the true importance of the succour of Lucknow, and of the dangers which it averted. There was no longer any immediate danger from mining; and fear of starvation was groundless. On the other hand, the danger of the natives of the garrison deserting was very serious; and serious also the consequent risk of our outposts being captured, owing to the weakening of the garrison, as well as from the fresh mining which would then have ensued. Yet although neither the relievers nor the garrison were then aware of it, the Relief was in fact but just in time to save us from another positively overwhelming danger, far more serious than these. For just at this time, the ranks of the enemy were swelled by large bodies of veteran troops pouring in from the mutineer forces which had been besieging Delhi; men who could fight. A very few days later, they would have intercepted Havelock's attempts at a junction, as they did thwart Outram's at a withdrawal; but for our reinforcements, they would certainly have captured our outposts and overwhelmed the garrison. This was the imminent peril that Havelock's Relief averted; and by averting it, he saved the Residency and the lives of the garrison.

CHAPTER II

THE BLOCKADE

THE preceding chapter dealt with Outram's efforts to open out his communications with the city and the country, and to extricate the families of the old garrison; and related the circumstances that, on October 4th, brought about his decision to cease from those efforts, reverting instead to a pure defence in an extended position. Annoying and humiliating as the change of plan and attitude may have been, right glad he was, it can hardly be doubted, that he was able to adopt it; and it will not be out of place to quote here extracts from the successive letters which he wrote, showing the gradual fluctuations in his views from the sanguine and impulsive ideas that were seething in his fertile brain before he reached Cawnpore; dominating the operations of the advance to the relief in September, until he had to recognize the futility of his efforts and of his schemes, and the practical superiority and success of the enemy.

September 7th.—"Our present object is merely to withdraw the garrison after forming a provisional government of influential inhabitants to maintain the city on behalf of the British Government until we can conveniently re-occupy it."

September 17th.—"The moral effect of abandoning Lucknow will be very serious, as turning against us the many well-disposed chiefs in Oude and Rohilkund who are now watching the turn of affairs, and would regard the loss of Lucknow as the forerunner of the extinction of our rule. Such a blow to our prestige may extend its influence to Nepaul, and will be felt all over India."

September 30th.—"It was evident that there could be no possible hope of carrying off the sick, wounded, and women and children (amounting to not less than 1,500 souls). Want of carriage alone rendered the transport through five miles of disputed suburb an impossibility.

"There remained but two alternatives, one to reinforce the Lucknow garrison with three hundred men, and leaving everything behind to retire immediately with the remains of the infantry upon the Alum Bagh, thereby leaving the garrison in a worse state than we found it . . . while it would have been impossible for any smaller force than the remainder of our troops, diminished by these three hundred men, to have any hope of making good their way back, and that not without very serious loss. I therefore adopted the second alternative, as the only mode of offering reasonable hope of securing the safety of this force, by retaining sufficient strength to enforce supplies of provisions, should they not be open to us voluntarily, and to maintain ourselves even on reduced rations until reinforcements advance to our relief."

October 2nd.—"Insurgents are too strong to admit of withdrawing from the garrison. Sick, wounded, women and children amount to upwards of 1,000. The force will retire, therefore, after making arrangements for the safety of the garrison by strengthening it with all but four of our guns, and leaving the 90th regiment. . . . The remainder of our force will make its way back to Cawnpore."

October 6th.—"I have been obliged to abandon the intention of withdrawing any portion of this force for the present, the obstacles to communicating between the Residency and Alum Bagh being too formidable. . . ."

Outram, then, having resolved to continue on the defensive in an extended position, it has now to be shown what that extended position was; how it was obtained and secured; and how, after that, it was held and defended. His decision was made on October 4th, but the full position was not secured until the 8th. The portion that was effected by the sortie which was in progress on the 4th, was not defined and occupied till the 6th, nor was it brought permanently into the boundary alignment till a few days later.

The position into which Outram withdrew on October 6th consisted of (1) the old Residency entrenchments extended down to the river; (2) the Chutter Munzil extension, from the Tehree Kothee through the Furhut Buksh to the

Chutter Munzil and its advanced gardens; and (3) the new post, outside the junction of those two positions, now held by the 78th under Lockhart, which had just been secured on the termination of the efforts described in the last chapter. It will be best understood by examining the map.[1] (1) The Residency entrenchments need no explanation or description, nor does (2) the addition to them of the ground on the river-face acquired on the day after the arrival of the Relief. No other addition was made to it; but the *neutral* ground on its southern face had been much expanded by the sortie of September 29th. (3) The new post held by the 78th was absolutely new, and its preparation for defence forms a special episode which will be told presently. It filled up a gap between the southern face of the Residency and the jail buildings of the extended position. The continuous extended position (2) along the river-face, had been secured on September 27th, when it last appeared in our story, but at that time it consisted only of the buildings and enclosures which bordered the river-face; whereas now, that is by October 6th, it had been widened out southwards up to the streets by which Moorsom had guided the relieving force into the Residency.

The operations by which this had been effected have now to be described. The Tehree Kothee, the jail buildings, and the Furhut Buksh had been very promptly secured and assigned for occupation to the regiments that were to hold them. But the contest at the Chutter Munzil and the buildings and gardens on its outer boundary was severe and prolonged. The advanced garden was first secured, not without a series of efforts. The attack on the outer Chutter Munzil buildings was carried on step by step from September 27th to the first days of October, the houses at the junction of the Cheenee Bazar and the Khas Bazar being captured on September 30th. In these operations the 90th were on the left, or the advanced garden side; Brasyer's Sikhs were on the right, and held eventually the projecting position bordering the Pyne Bagh; while the 5th Fusiliers were in the middle.

While this was being done, a good communication was made from end to end of the position, by which the heavy

[1] Map IV.

guns that had been parked in the advanced garden on the morning of September 27th, were conveyed into the Residency entrenchments.

As soon as the boundary that we meant to hold was reached, the enemy began to have recourse to their old subterranean warfare. Being comparatively experts, they at first had the advantage over the new garrison, of which the commanding Engineer, Captain Crommelin, had unfortunately been seriously disabled by a wound. On October 3rd and 5th, they blew up mines directed at the wall of the advanced garden. The first one failed, being short of its mark; the second was successful, and made a large breach, which a column of the enemy then essayed to storm; but they were forthwith repulsed with heavy loss, and fled precipitately under the fire of the 90th. They then made a second breach by burning down one of the gates of the garden. These breaches and the commanding fire from the adjacent buildings called the Hirun Khana, led to the construction of trenches in the garden to serve both for shelter and for communications.

Then on the 6th, the day on which the sortie of the 1st was drawn in, the enemy blew up our picket at the junction of the Cheenee Bazar and the Khas Bazar, and penetrated in considerable numbers into the building; but were soon driven out again, with a loss of some 450 men. They continued, however, to hold a mosque which threatened that post, and, in fact, attacked it on the 8th, when they were repulsed with loss; after which we worked into a vault underneath the mosque, and blowing up a portion of it, barricaded and secured the rest, gaining a clear command of the two bazars or streets.

With this, the consolidation of the new position was practically effected; and with Lockhart's post at the same time added to the old entrenchments, as already described, the defence of the extended position, as a whole, was now practically begun. These operations had caused a loss of fifty men killed to the relieving force (in addition to the 196 killed previously since leaving Cawnpore), and of nineteen men to the 32nd (of the old garrison).

During the defence of the extended and consolidated position—the second defence, as I venture to call it—that position was as closely invested as before along a large part of its circuit, but not everywhere. On the whole river-face the enemy were cleared off, and were entirely on the opposite bank; and on that part of the old Residency entrenchments which was continued as part of the boundary of the second position, (viz. the South and West faces from the Cawnpore Battery, round by Gubbins's, to Innes's post,) the rebels now kept more at a distance. The neutral ground had been greatly widened out, partly by the results of the sortie of September 29th, and partly by the mining operations of the first defence.

During this second defence, the old position was never seriously, if at all, attacked, even by mines; and the defensive operations were confined to repairing and strengthening or sometimes extending the defences. The Cawnpore Battery was almost entirely reconstructed. The sheep-house and the slaughter-house batteries were completed; and the mound that stretched out from Innes's post was secured by a series of zigzag trenches, which also gave an effective command over the end of the iron bridge.

In (3) the new post—Lockhart's—held by the 78th Highlanders, the contest was one of mines; which, on our side, were constructed by the men of that regiment under the guidance of Lieutenants Hutchinson and Tulloch. The enemy began their underground work at once, opposite our left corner, while the garrison were strenuously engaged in barricading and strengthening the post; exploding their mine while the 78th were still at their first shaft, but with only slight damage to the post, as it was ten feet short of the outer enclosure. From that time up to about the 20th, this warfare at Lockhart's post was incessant. Our galleries aggregated a length of 500 feet. Every effort of the enemy was defeated; and two of their galleries were captured and held by us as listening galleries. One of them was very long, and its capture, which was attended by some amusing episodes, was followed by other entertaining but fruitless attempts of the enemy to find its course or alignment from above ground, in order to break into it.

In the Chutter Munzil position also the contest was now practically confined to mining warfare of the most persistent kind. The enemy made sixteen fresh efforts besides those made up to October 8th; but now they were always defeated; seven of their mines being destroyed, and seven others captured and held by us for our own purposes; besides which, we also attacked three and destroyed two of the enemy's posts with our own galleries. It will be seen on comparing the figures, that the number of attacks by the rebels was not so numerous as during the first siege; but the amount of mining involved was much greater and much more arduous. In the first defence, a great many more mines were exploded, and by this means much ground was made impracticable for further adjacent mining. But in the new position, the whole front became protected, not so much by the explosion of mines, as by being covered by intercepting and other galleries, aggregating nearly 1,100 yards in length. Moreover, as the soil was looser, the actual construction of the galleries was much more laborious, by reason of its involving the use of supports and casings, which were never needed in the first siege.

Added to this; after their successive defeats, the enemy's miners had become very wary, and had taken to digging with the trowel instead of with the pickaxe, which prevented their being heard till they were quite close.

Further, many of the listening and attacking galleries were very long, and the ventilating arrangements were necessarily crude, making the work specially irksome and difficult, owing to the foulness of the air.

Such was the nature of the warfare from October 8th—almost entirely mining—for about a month; when preparations were started for measures to assist or act in concert with the second relieving force, whose advance and approach were then becoming imminent.

Meanwhile, in spite of the closeness of the investment, the practical safety of the garrison had become and continued undoubted, and the shelter of its inmates was much more secure than of old. All anxiety as to any successful attack or irruption of the enemy was at an end; and there was a material relaxation of the former strictness about leaving one's own garrison or residence. There was altogether a great reduction of discomfort, as there was now a large number of natives—camp-followers of Havelock's force—available for general service. To the old garrison the relief was very material and sensible.

During the six weeks which this second defence lasted after the last sortie was drawn in on October 6th, the dangers and loss of life from conflict with the enemy and from their fire was very greatly diminished, as well as the discomfort which has been already dealt with. The only exact information I have is respecting the 32nd Regiment, of which the losses in *killed* (exclusive of those who died from accidents and wounds) stand thus—

July 2,	to September 25	29
September 26,	to October 6	9
October 7,	to November 16	0

During this period also, the work devolving on the generals was comparatively slight. The outpost officers and garrisons were holding their posts, and, with the aid and guidance of the Engineers, were countermining the enemy or blowing up their posts; but Outram personally was keeping up an energetic correspondence with the outer world, as has been described. Of course the whole garrison was suffering from the poverty of rations, and the troops were longing to be again at open combat with the enemy.

Throughout this month the detachment at the Alum Bagh under Major MacIntyre continued to hold its own successfully. As already mentioned, it had been strengthened on October 7th, by 250 men and two guns from Cawnpore; and on the 25th, 500 more arrived with a convoy, thus making the force secure and able to extend its foraging expeditions. After this, detachments of 100 men went backwards and forwards on various escort and other duties from time to time. The enemy tried to place guns in position at various points, but they were all silenced by the battery which Major MacIntyre had constructed; and the garrison practically met with no losses.

Meantime the communications were much more open and easy than before, so that the garrison at Lucknow was being constantly cheered by the news which arrived almost daily of the approach of strong reinforcements. About the 10th, intelligence came of the advance from Delhi of Greathed's column (afterwards Hope Grant's), of which the ultimate destination was Lucknow; and it was at one time thought that it had come as near as Futtehgurh on the

8th. This idea, however, was incorrect, as the column had turned aside to Agra instead of coming on direct. There were reports also of the advance of various regiments up-country towards Cawnpore from the China Expeditionary Force.

Though the communications between General Outram and the outer world were so much more frequent than during the first defence, there was no real increase in private letters. I was the fortunate recipient of one letter; and I never heard of any other letter reaching any one. Mine was brought by a soldier of the 78th, who, seeing it at the Post-office at Cawnpore, had brought it away with him in the hope of delivering it to the addressee. In this he succeeded, meeting me in the lane between the Post-office and Fayrer's, and showing me the tiny document, without knowing at first that he was giving it to the proper person.

Up to the middle of October there was no intelligence received of any threatening of Cawnpore by the Gwalior Contingent or other troops from the south of the Jumna; but the defeated Sepoys from Delhi had been reaching Lucknow, and had also been disturbing the country in other directions, such as at Bithoor. The gathering there, in which the Nana Sahib was present, was attacked and dispersed on the 18th.

Outram sent to the Alum Bagh two letters of advice and suggestions for the officer who might arrive in command of the relieving force—one on the 14th, the other on October 30th, in addition to what he had written to Cawnpore on the 28th. Their value to Sir Colin will be seen presently.

Outram's views and anxieties and his communications to the outer world were necessarily coloured by his ideas of the state of the food supply. The rations were slightly reduced from time to time at short intervals; and, bearing this in mind, extracts from his letters in order of date will best show the progressive aspect of this question. The dates on which he wrote, and the prospects on these dates, were as follows, in October—

On the 7th.—"We have grain and gram, bullocks and horses, on which we may subsist a month."

On the 9th.—"Our grain alone and gun bullocks may possibly be eked out for a month, and but little else for twenty days."

On the 11th.—"Our grain, allowing it to be all good, will last only till November 6; our meat not so long."

On the 16th.—"Our atta and bullocks will last only till November 18."

On the 20th.—"Our food, upon a very reduced ration, may possibly last till November 20."

On the 28th.—"We can manage to screw on till near the end of November on further reduced rations."

It is to be remembered that in all such rough statements of the probable duration of supplies, there was a liability to vagueness as to the kind of supplies referred to—whether, for instance, it did or did not include gram or meat, or might possibly refer to meat only; if it included meat, whether it included horse-meat as part of it; and whether the grain food included gram, which is customarily food for horses only, and not for man.

It may be said at once that no discovery or find of any store of food, which was thought to be unknown before, was ever made after October 2nd. All the supplies that then existed were measured up, and the stock estimated and recorded. By the end of the siege the beef was exhausted, its last issue in rations being made on the very last day of the defence. The supply of wheat had been so husbanded by the quiet and almost imperceptible reduction of rations, that, when the garrison marched out, it took with it the supplies needed to at least the end of the month, as estimated by Outram at the end of October.

While thus keeping his friends at Cawnpore, the Commander-in-Chief, and others, as correctly informed as he could of the prospects of the garrison, he also sent out from time to time advice and instructions for such forces as might be advancing to his relief. He wrote three such letters on the 11th, 13th, and 14th; and then again, in great detail, at the end of the month. In those first letters he showed that he expected at least two regiments, the 23rd and 93rd, almost immediately from Calcutta; he urged the commander of the columns from Delhi, whom he assumed to be the probable relieving General, to move on with all speed to the Alum Bagh, and there concentrate for his final effort; believing that his presence there as the pioneer of the advancing flood of troops would break up the hostile force in Lucknow; and in the third of these letters, that of October 14th, he advised the route eventually taken by Sir Colin, with some deviations in the details.

It was not till near the end of the month that he heard of Cawnpore being threatened by the neighbourhood of the Gwalior Contingent, and the advice he then sent out to Cawnpore on October 28th was—"It is so obviously to the advantage of the State that the Gwalior rebels should be first effectually destroyed, that our relief should be a secondary consideration. I trust, therefore, that Brigadier Wilson" (in command at Cawnpore) "will furnish Colonel Grant" (commanding the Delhi column) "with every possible aid to effect that object before sending him here." It was in this letter that he mentioned that we could manage to screw on, as regards food, till near the end of November.

His letters of the 30th and 31st contained complete detailed advice for the route,[1] the sites of batteries for the relieving column; a system of signals to show its arrival at the different positions on the route; and information of the steps the garrison would take on receiving those signals.

It is legitimately open to question whether Outram was right in advising this route (No. 3) so strongly as the only one to be thought of. One reason against it was that, as customary with natives, the enemy would certainly expect that since the first relief had come by the route between the palaces and the river, the second relief would also advance by it; they would accordingly prepare the posts along that route for defence; and there would be heavy and serious obstruction, though not as serious as in actual street fighting. Another reason was that Havelock had been strongly in favour of route No. 4, and had not adopted it in the first relief only on account of the validity of the special objection to it at that particular date; viz. the swampy condition of the ground after a continuance of heavy rain, which prevented the movement of the heavy

[1] Route No. 3, see p. 218.

guns. With the absence of this special and temporary objection, there were strong reasons in favour of route No. 4. It would probably be unexpected by the enemy, and therefore unprepared. It was certainly much more open ground, and much freer from obstructions or strong positions for the enemy to hold. The Badshah Bagh, the only large enclosure on the route, would not be a place of strength to the enemy, while it would be a valuable place of shelter for the families on their withdrawal; and with the command that had now been gained of the iron bridge from Innes's post, there would be no difficulty in the relieving force getting possession of it. Such are my reasons for thinking that Outram might have suggested route No. 4 as well as No. 3. As it was, Sir Colin followed Outram's plan, with some modifications, and arrived on the plain before the Kaiser Bagh on November 16th.

The operations by which Outram proposed to aid the relief, and which, at any rate, would be in concert with its advance if it adopted the route he advised, were: to blow up the most mischievous buildings in the close proximity of the advanced garden; to throw down the garden-wall, after forming heavy gun-batteries inside the enclosure, so as to command and sweep the ground by which the relief must advance, thus clearing it of the enemy; and to batter whatever adjacent buildings they might hold in force. So from about the end of October, two batteries for the heavy guns were under construction in the advanced garden, while mines were driven out into the buildings called the Steam-Engine and the Hirun Khana; the latter ending in three branches, one of which required to be very long, about three hundred feet from the shaft to its extreme point.

The orders given required that these preparations should be completed on November 12th; but they were not put into use till the 16th; with the result that much of the powder that formed the charge had got damp and failed to operate with the proper effect; also the mine that was directed against the Engine-house was stopped by an open trench. Still the mine at the Hirun Khana blew up a breach by which the building was entered and captured, and held. The front wall of the advanced garden was sufficiently thrown over to admit of the guns afterwards levelling it properly; and the two batteries opened out with due effect on the neighbouring palaces and buildings occupied by the enemy, enabling the minor ones intervening between the garden and the Motee Mahul to be attacked and seized. Next day the fire and movements of the garrison co-operated with the relieving force. The Motee Mahul was captured, and our generals with their staff ran the gauntlet of the enemy's fire to the Koorsheyd Munzil, where they were received by Sir Colin, and the relief and junction were effected. For the operations of this junction, Outram had been unable to muster 2,000 bayonets!

Next day, November 18th, the fiat went forth that the Residency was to be abandoned. With what bitterness this was heard by the old garrison may be readily imagined; the position they had so long and so resolutely held was to be given up—the British flag, the emblem of their assertion of their country's supremacy and honour, was to be hauled down. One more meed of gratitude than they probably knew of they owed now to the noble Havelock. His last official act was to urge on Sir Colin, with definite proposals, the retention of the old position, and other arrangements in its support; and in these proposals he is believed to have been supported by Outram. But it was not to be. The subject is dealt with in the next chapter in connection with the relief, and need not be further touched on here.

Next day, the 19th, began the exodus of the families; they left the advanced gardens by twos and threes in the course of the day, revelling in the fresh air and the fresh food. Their course was along a lane, which had been screened off so as to conceal all movements till they reached the Secundra Bagh; and there they halted till dark, when they went forward in a column to the Dil Koosha. On the 22nd the garrison evacuated the Residency, and the whole force concentrated in the Dil Koosha. Two days afterwards they moved on to the Alum Bagh, and with this the tale of the defence may be said to end.

The families accompanied Sir Colin in safety to Cawnpore, and were then sent down, in December, to Allahabad and Calcutta. But at the Alum Bagh, on November 24th, at the close of the defence, a fit and touching date, Henry Havelock calmly breathed his last—worn out by hardship and illness; a true, heroic, stern, God-fearing old warrior, happy in the knowledge that his deeds had stirred to the depths the hearts of his Queen and his country, and rejoicing in the thought that those for whose succour he had struggled so long and so gloriously, were at length safe under the protection of Sir Colin's army.

CHAPTER III

RELIEF BY SIR COLIN CAMPBELL

THE last chapter brought our story up to the close of the defence under Outram, and the relief of the beleaguered garrison by Sir Colin's force. The advance and measures for that relief have now to be described. Heretofore all operations had been conducted by the Generals in local command; now, however, the Commander-in-Chief was appearing personally on the scene; affecting the mode and course of the contest—in this relief to begin with—by his own views of the military and political situation, and his own knowledge and experience of war.

That experience was large and varied. He had fought throughout the Peninsular War, beginning with Moore's retreat to Corunna. He had served in China, and then in India during the Punjab Campaign; and afterwards in command against the hill tribes at Peshawur. Finally he had earned great distinction with the Highland Brigade in the Crimea. He enjoyed the highest repute as a good soldier and a sound commander; but he had never had an opportunity of showing his capacity as a General in charge of great operations; much less in such a crisis as that with which he had now to deal. And though full of energy and vigour, he had now reached the ripe age of sixty-five years.

The time of his arrival in India was in the gloomiest days of the struggle. It was in the middle of August, and the outlook then seemed almost hopeless. Delhi had not yet been captured. The Punjab was expected to turn against us at any moment. The Lucknow garrison was apparently in the most desperate straits. Havelock had withdrawn back to Cawnpore. Mutiny and insurrection had broken out in the Lower Provinces, and they were so disturbed that the troops were being detained there which had been meant to assist in the operations above Allahabad. Moreover, all Central India had risen against the British, so that the task which Sir Colin appeared to have before him *at that stage* was the re-conquest of the whole Bengal Presidency at least.

But by the end of October, when he undertook the direct command of operations, a great change had come over the scene—Delhi had been captured; the Punjab was secure, and had begun to assist the British actively with fresh levies; the Delhi district, the centre of the great struggle, had been cleared of the rebel army. The Lucknow garrison had been succoured, and though both they and their relievers were as fully beleaguered as ever, the enemy that was now investing them seemed powerless to attack them, though it now virtually consisted of the whole mutineer array of Upper India. British troops had come south from Delhi to Cawnpore; other troops had already gone north from Calcutta to Cawnpore. One half of the China Expeditionary Force were well on their way up-country; the other half had started, and the pioneer regiments of the great reinforcing army from England had already arrived. The storm had been weathered—the tide of British supports were sweeping up rapidly. Still Sir Colin seemed weighed down with a sense of the gravity of the situation, as if it were as great as ever. Had he grounds for this? How did the present situation really compare with the past?

The numerical strength of the enemy was somewhat less than it had been, by reason of their losses, while they had not as yet received any material accession to their strength, and their army that at Delhi had been behind massive defences was now in the field or in the open city of Lucknow.

Our force of some 2,500 men that had before been in the open at Cawnpore was now helping to hold in security, until relieved, the positions at the Alum Bagh and in Lucknow. And the spirit of the enemy at Lucknow could be gauged by their never venturing to attack the weak Alum Bagh post seriously.

Delhi had been taken by 3,300 British soldiers, aided by 8,000 native troops and allies; 2,500 men had been able to penetrate through the enemy into the Lucknow Residency.

Whereas Sir Colin had now at his disposal 5,000 men free for movement on Lucknow; 2,000 men in Lucknow; 1,000 men at Cawnpore; the second half of the China Force on its way to Cawnpore; several battalions of reinforcements from England already arrived and moving upwards; the Punjab now actively siding with us, and raising and sending down fresh troops towards Oude.

All this surely implied a momentous improvement in the state of matters to be dealt with by the Chief, both as to the difficulties to be overcome and his means of meeting them.

But his grave view of the situation, notwithstanding, is shown by his writings. His letters said, "I have made up my mind not to hazard an attack which would compromise my small force. . . . Sir James Outram is in great straits. . . . My object—to extricate the garrison from Lucknow—I will do, if it can be accomplished with the ordinary military risks; but there are larger interests pending than even that great object, and I must watch over the safety of the small body of troops with which I begin this undertaking."

Such were Sir Colin's recorded thoughts, estimates, and anxieties as to his situation and his resources at the end of October, though the incomparably more slender means by which an incomparably graver crisis had been quite recently met and overcome seem sufficiently obvious.

In this spirit of caution he entered on the command and guidance of the relief.

The column, which now came under his leadership in November 1857, and effected the relief of Outram's garrison, was made up of two bodies of men: one, the column which had been despatched south from Delhi, the other the gradual collection of reinforcements from the Calcutta direction.

The column from Delhi, which left it about September 24th, consisted of 1,800 infantry, 600 cavalry, and sixteen guns. The infantry were 500 of the 8th and 75th Regiments, and the rest the 2nd and 4th Punjab Infantry. The cavalry were the 9th Lancers and three squadrons of Hodson's Horse. The artillery were a field battery, and two batteries of Horse Artillery, each short of one gun. At first the force was under the command of Colonel

Greathed, and moved down the Doab (*i.e.* the Mesopotamia, or "land between the rivers" Ganges and Jumna) in pursuit of the fugitive mutineers from Delhi. After overtaking and defeating them at Bolundghuhur, on September 28th, and again at Malagurh and at Allygurh, it moved to the right to Agra, whither it had been urgently summoned. There, on October 10th, it had an unexpected battle with the Indore Brigade of the Central India mutineer army, which it routed and punished in a crushing manner, capturing thirteen guns. The column then turned towards Cawnpore, and was overtaken shortly by Colonel Hope Grant, who assumed its command; and after another combat at Kanouj, it reached Cawnpore on October 26th.

The reinforcements which came up from the Calcutta direction consisted partly of the troops which had been detained below Benares while Havelock was still at Cawnpore, and partly of the new arrivals of the China Expeditionary Force. Some of these reinforcements had already been sent on to the Alum Bagh, as has been mentioned; and Hope Grant found that the troops which Brigadier Wilson could transfer to him at Cawnpore, added to his own column and to the Alum Bagh garrison, would bring up his force to nearly 3,800 men. So he crossed the Ganges on October 30th, and marched towards Lucknow. A further reinforcement of 1,200 men was expected; and Sir Colin meant to push on himself and join them at Allahabad, as soon as he could take on two additional regiments thence to Cawnpore. Till he could do so, his own presence was required at Calcutta more than elsewhere.

The new troops that Hope Grant took on with him from Cawnpore, were the 93rd Highlanders and a wing of the 53rd, with detachments for the regiments already at the front. After crossing the Ganges, he pushed on with the intention of reaching the Alum Bagh speedily; but he now received orders from Sir Colin, which led him to halt and await his arrival at Buntheera beyond the Sye river. Its bridge at Bunnee had been by this time broken down, but the stream was now easily fordable.

At Buntheera, Sir Colin Campbell joined him on November 9th. He had left Calcutta on October 27th, reaching Cawnpore on November 3rd; and having heard from

Outram that he could hold out till near the end of the month, he halted there a few days to organize the arrangements for the security of Cawnpore and his communications. The danger that threatened was from the Gwalior Contingent, a compact and well-disciplined force of some 5,000 men with a powerful artillery; increased to 10,000 men by the Nana Sahib's followers, and the rebels who had joined them when they were hovering on the south of the Jumna near Kalpee. This body of men had never been far from that neighbourhood, that is from within a short distance of Cawnpore, since Havelock returned there in August; and I have no authentic knowledge of the reason that prevented their advancing on Cawnpore, when Havelock and Outram left it after the middle of September. To hold Cawnpore against this array, Sir Colin left 500 British soldiers and 550 Madras troops as the permanent garrison of the entrenchment there, under General Windham; whom he also directed to forward on to Lucknow the additional reinforcements that were likely to arrive from day to day, unless he should find it necessary to detain them at Cawnpore for its defence. It is somewhat unfortunate that he did not require Windham to increase his force up to some specified strength before forwarding on reinforcements, for it was known that the Gwalior Contingents were really showing signs of advancing, and that they were a compact, united, and well-trained force with a powerful artillery. This action was a departure from the cautious procedure which he had laid down for adoption.

Sir Colin then joined Hope Grant at Buntheera on November 9th, halted there a couple of days, and concentrated his force at the Alum Bagh on the 12th; having a smart action with a body of the enemy on the way, and afterwards taking possession of the old fort of Jellalabad.

At the Alum Bagh, he settled in detail his plan of operations for the relief. He had decided on it, in a general way, before leaving Calcutta, and now he had before him the proposals which Outram had sent out on October 30th; besides the maps and papers brought out still later from the Residency by Mr. Cavanagh, who had penetrated through the investing army in disguise. And he now definitely decided (in opposition to the urgent advice of his chief engineer, who was in favour of Route No. 4) to adopt Route No. 3; slightly deviating however from the exact line proposed by Outram near the Secundra Bagh.

This route[1] was, in its general course, what has throughout this narrative been called No. 3; and although it entirely avoided all street fighting—even the small length which Havelock had from Neill's Gate to the Residency—it had to pass the series of strong posts by which Havelock had advanced, and which, though not then held by the enemy, were sure to be occupied by them on this occasion. On the other hand, Route No. 4 was free from all the objections which seemed to prey on Sir Colin's mind. It was along absolutely open ground. The Badshah Bagh would have been no obstacle, and would have been useful; and the sole objection to the route at the time of Havelock's advance did not exist now. Further, Sir Colin had with him a very powerful heavy artillery, which, with room to handle it, could have mastered any flanking or other artillery the enemy might oppose to him; and also a very smart body of Engineers with effective equipment. As it was, he lost much of this advantage from the cramped space in which he had to manœuvre.

The force now collected under Sir Colin, including (I believe) the reinforcements that arrived on November 14th, was probably rather more than the 5,000 men which Hope Grant had expected. Of these, 400 men were to remain at the Alum Bagh as its garrison; of the rest, 3,800 were infantry in three brigades, and comprised the 93rd, the 23rd, and the 8th, besides a wing of the 53rd, and detachments of the 82nd and other regiments, as well as the 2nd and 4th Punjab Infantry. The cavalry were the same as had been with Hope Grant, with the addition of two squadrons of the Military Train. The artillery was very strong, and included—eight heavy guns of Peel's Naval Brigade, one heavy battery of Royal Artillery, two and a half field batteries, two Horse Artillery batteries, and a mortar battery; and there were four companies of Sappers and Pioneers.

On the 13th, Sir Colin reconnoitred in force to his front

[1] See Map V.

and his left, in order to deceive the enemy; and then, on the morning of the 14th, moved off to the right, circling round to the Dil Koosha. On reaching the Dil Koosha, the contest began. At this spot itself the resistance was short; for finding their flank threatened, the enemy abandoned the Dil Koosha and retreated to the Martinière. Then the Martinière also was attacked and taken; and these two posts, the Dil Koosha and the Martinière, were held as defensive positions, round which the troops bivouacked that night. In the evening, the rebels from the west of the canal brought a fire to bear on these positions; but they were held in check by the 93rd along the canal, and were then attacked on their own ground and routed by the 53rd and the 4th Punjabees. During the afternoon a semaphore was erected on the Martinière and signals exchanged with Outram according to the preconcerted code. The rear-guard were engaged with the enemy during all the 14th, and the 15th was spent in concentrating the troops and arranging for the struggle of the following day. After setting aside a force of all arms, containing the 8th regiment and half of the cavalry, with five guns, to hold the Dil Koosha and the rear, the column left available for the operations towards the Residency was 4,200 strong.

Altogether this array was very much stronger than any that had before met the enemy in Oude; but this enemy, it is to be remembered, now included the bulk of the mutineer army from Delhi in addition to the Oude mutineer force that had all along occupied Lucknow and the neighbouring districts.

Outram's proposals were that the force should cross the canal by or near the bridge on the alignment of the Huzrutgunge road, attack the old infantry barracks and the Begum's Palace, and then turn to the right for the Secundra Bagh. But Sir Colin, in reconnoitring on the 15th, came to the conclusion that this route was held in great strength by the enemy. He resolved therefore to cross the canal further north near the river, and advance thence by the more open ground along the river-bank towards the Motee Mahul, where he expected Outram to sortie and meet him.

To mislead the enemy, he repeated his tactics of the 13th; and from the evening of the 15th he maintained a fire on the Begum's Palace, and in that direction generally, as if that was to be his route of attack.

On the morning of the 16th the force crossed the canal close to its debouchure into the Goomtee, and then advanced along the bank of the river; finding itself, however, cramped up in narrow roads between gardens and buildings till it emerged into more open ground close to the Secundra Bagh, an enclosure 150 yards square, with massive walls bastioned at the angles. The enemy in it had not expected the attack in this direction, and having closed up all the gateways on the opposite side, were caught as in a trap. They had no guns, but their walls were stout, and, owing to the nearness of the enclosures round it, the attacking artillery were subjected to a very telling fire. Blunt's battery of horse artillery lost a third of its men, but Travers's two heavy guns at length effected a breach in a corner of the enclosure. The attack was ordered; the 93rd Highlanders and the 4th Punjabees raced for the breach and entered it together; and the defenders, upwards of 2,000 men, a compact brigade of three complete regiments, were absolutely annihilated. Thus was the first important post held by the enemy stormed and secured—a post which formed practically the key to the passage of the canal on the right—no advance in the meantime being made on the left, only the bridge there being strongly held, as on the 15th.

In the afternoon the advance on the right was continued from the Secundra Bagh, the next objects of attack being two posts called the Kuddum Kussool and the Shah Nujeef. The former was captured by the Punjabees. But the latter, which had massive walls forty feet high, withstood all efforts to breach it the whole afternoon, and its fire kept playing havoc in Peel's Naval Brigade and Middleton's Battery, which had been brought close up under its walls. At length, however, by a happy chance, the 93rd, who explored round the building, found a small opening in its rear wall; whereupon an entrance was effected and the position captured.

No further movement was made that day, either to the front or to the left flank, which was still exposed to the fire from the (former) barracks (of the 32nd), from the

Begum's Palace, and from other positions along the Huzrutgunge road; only a strong body of infantry bivouacked between these barracks and the Secundra Bagh.

But in Outram's position, as has been already shown, the programme which had been arranged, for co-operation with Sir Colin, was carried out on the 16th; the front wall of the advanced garden was thrown down, the mines nearest the adjacent buildings were blown up, leading to their being forthwith captured and occupied; and the batteries in the advanced garden opened out on the more distant buildings.

The Motee Mahul was the only position which, on the night of the 16th, was left intervening between the relieving force and Outram's advanced posts. It was, however, strongly supported and protected by the old 32nd mess-house, of which the proper name was the Koorsheyd Munzil; and the two had to be attacked and captured together.

Next day, the 17th, Sir Colin's earlier operations were towards the left flank, in order to secure the whole of the open space; and so the old 32nd barracks and Banks's house were attacked, captured, and occupied. After that the Koorsheyd Munzil, which was a strong position, and surrounded by a broad, deep ditch, was first subjected for many hours to the fire of Peel's ship guns. At three o'clock it was captured, along with a strong little post close to it called the Tara Kothee or Observatory. Then a simultaneous move was made from the Koorsheyd Munzil on the one side, and Outram's position on the other, against the Motee Mahul, which was speedily occupied; and the junction of the besieged with their relievers was effected. These operations had been attended with the loss, in killed and wounded, of 45 officers and 496 men. Outram had not been able to muster 2,000 bayonets.

And then, on the following day, the old garrison heard that the position which they had so long and so resolutely held, was to be abandoned.

Opposition to the measure was futile. The Chief had made up his mind, whether rightly or wrongly I do not propose to argue; though I hope to be excused for suggesting that, in questions of military operations throughout this struggle, their political aspect, that is their effect on the spirit of the enemy, was a point of nearly as great moment as their purely military or strategical bearing. And the enemy would now certainly think and feel, and proclaim that they had, at length, so mastered the British as to have driven them into evacuating and surrendering the recognized seat of their rule and power. However, on the 18th the fiat went forth; on the 19th the families moved out by twos and threes, in the daytime, along a lane which had been screened off from the enemy's fire, to the Secundra Bagh; and then at night, in a continuous stream, to the Dil Koosha.

By the 22nd *everything*, the treasure, the food, and all the guns that had not been destroyed, had been removed out of the Residency without the enemy's knowledge; their attention having throughout been turned to the ceaseless artillery fire which was being poured on them; on that night, the garrison evacuated the position they had held for six months, and the army concentrated on the Dil Koosha, and then on the Alum Bagh and its outlying posts, without any molestation from the enemy during the movement. There it halted from the 24th to the 27th. During this time Sir Colin was preparing partly for the move towards Cawnpore, and partly for the further measure on which he had resolved—the occupation in force of the Alum Bagh, as a position from which to keep the city of Lucknow in check, and proclaim that Oude was not evacuated, nor Lucknow finally surrendered. Outram was to remain in this position with a division of about 4,000 men, while the rest of the army, with its rear thus protected, moved on to Cawnpore.

Thus was the old Residency position relieved, its garrison withdrawn, and the new position or force at the Alum Bagh, under Outram, substituted for it.

BOOK V

CAPTURE OF THE CITY OF LUCKNOW

CHAPTER I

PRELIMINARY OPERATIONS ON THE GANGES

SIR COLIN'S first measure after relieving and evacuating the Residency was, as already stated, to place Outram in the Alum Bagh position, as it was thenceforward called, to keep Lucknow in check. He left with him for this purpose about 4,500 men; 500 of whom, however, were to be detached to the Bunnee Bridge; the 4,500, of whom 3,400 were English, consisting of 340 artillery, 370 cavalry, and the rest infantry.

The apex or front of the position was the Alum Bagh enclosure (about two miles from the Char Bagh), from which it bent or curved back right and left, so as to form a sort of semicircle, with a radius of about two miles. Outram disliked the position on account of its being so close to the canal and the city that the enemy could attack him freely at their own convenience, while he would be unable to pursue and punish them properly after repulsing them. But Sir Colin adhered to the site, as its significance was obvious and must tell on the people of the province, especially with Outram in command.

Having settled him there, Sir Colin's next step was to return to Cawnpore; partly in order to take the Lucknow families there and send them down thence to Allahabad and Calcutta, partly to deal with the Gwalior Contingent, which had been so long threatening Cawnpore, and thus begin to clear the ground for his subsequent operations.

On November 27th, therefore, he started from the Alum Bagh; and next morning, on advancing from Bunnee, he became aware that the Gwalior Contingent had forestalled him and attacked Windham at Cawnpore. Accordingly, taking the cavalry and horse artillery with him, and leaving the rest of the force to follow on with the convoy, he pressed forward to Cawnpore in great anxiety about the bridge. But he found it safe, crossed over, and joined Windham; and having discussed the situation and settled on the immediate arrangements, he recrossed in the evening back to his camp, three miles on the north of the river, where his force and the convoy had just begun to arrive.

Windham was indeed being hardly pressed, and to describe the situation properly the tale must go back to the time of Sir Colin's advance towards Lucknow.

It has been shown that the Gwalior Contingent, a compact and well-disciplined body, amounting with other troops to some 10,000 men, with a strong force of artillery, about 38 guns, had been long hovering on the south of the Jumna. They had now come under the guidance of an able leader, Tantia Topee, who had resolved to make a dash at Cawnpore when it was left sufficiently weak and unsupported, and thus break in on the British line of communications. He waited patiently till Sir Colin and all the available troops were moving into Oude. Then he concentrated at Kalpee, and leaving 3,000 men there with 20 guns as his rear-guard for the time, he crossed the Jumna on the 9th (the day on which Sir Colin joined Hope Grant), with the rest of his force—7,000 men and 18 guns; and then, when Sir Colin was fully committed to the struggle at Lucknow, he moved forward to the north, forming a chain of posts across the Doab as he advanced, and reaching the Ganges at Sheorajpore some twenty miles above Cawnpore. There he came into touch with the rebels in Oude, and was joined by some 4,000 of the Nana's followers, and apparently by other troops as well. Windham heard of all this, and was perplexed by the orders which he had received; but this is a point into which I do not propose to enter. He had been loyally forwarding on to Sir Colin most of the reinforcements that had been arriving, and on the very day on which he felt constrained to make a movement to check the advance of the Gwalior army, he had sent out a small force to the Bunnee Bridge in support of Sir Colin.

Windham had occupied a position on November 17th, on the western boundary of Cawnpore, to cover it in the direction of the enemy's probable advance; but they were nearer him on the south than on the north, so he moved his outlying force on the 24th southward to a passage of the Ganges canal, about eight miles from Cawnpore; where, on the 26th, he encountered and defeated the enemy's right column, about 3,000 strong, capturing three guns.

By this time the Gwalior force had been joined by most of the men and guns which had been left at Kalpee; and while they thus first attracted Windham's attention on their right, their real movement in force was on their left along the bank of the Ganges, their aim being the bridge across that river near the entrenchment.

Windham's force, on defeating the enemy's right wing on the 26th, pursued them a short distance; and then, after returning to the scene of action, continued its retirement still further up to its original camp in front of the city. During this movement the defeated enemy, and especially their cavalry, turned back from their flight and followed Windham up closely. Still he hoped that the punishment he had inflicted would delay the enemy's closer attack. But during the night of the 26th the centre and left of the rebel force advanced on Cawnpore on its northern or Ganges side, as their leader had planned; and at noon on the 27th Windham found himself attacked along his whole front. The enemy had an overwhelming superiority in artillery, which they used to the utmost; keeping their infantry in cover, and driving the British back by their converging artillery fire. By night they had forced Windham back step by step to a line of posts only a quarter of a mile from his small entrenchment.

Next day, the 28th, Windham had arranged his force of 1,700 men thus: right wing under Carthew on the Ganges, left wing under Walpole on the canal, himself with the centre in support, and the 64th in reserve in the entrenchment.

The enemy persistently attacked all day, but their chief efforts were against Carthew; their great object, as already shown, being the bridge over the Ganges. Carthew's force was quite inadequate, and he had only two guns; so that by the evening he was forced back into the entrenchments, and with him the 64th, which had gone forward to his support. The enemy were now in dangerous proximity to the bridge, while Walpole had also fallen back on the entrenchment. Such was the situation when Sir Colin arrived.

Early on the following morning, the 29th, he lined the bank of the river with Peel's naval guns. Their fire and that from the guns in the entrenchment gradually mastered the enemy's fire from the ground near the river, which they had seized on the previous evening, and then the rebels retired, setting the buildings alight. On this Sir Colin's force and the convoy began crossing over from Oude; and this passage did not end till the evening of the 30th, when the troops and the families were encamped on the plain on the Allahabad side of the canal, comparatively secure from molestation.

The arrival of the leading troops of Sir Colin's force the Cavalry, Horse Artillery, and Hope's Brigade, had at once placed the contest on a more assured footing.

From the 1st to the 5th there was some desultory fighting, but after the families had been despatched towards Allahabad on the evening of the 3rd, Sir Colin matured his plans on the two following days.

An important feature in the topography of Cawnpore and of the contest was the Ganges canal; a wide and deep artificial stream, which flowed down the district in a course more or less parallel to the Ganges, till, on nearing Cawnpore, it was only about four and a half miles from the river. Here it curved round in a quarter circle of that radius, debouching into the river at the entrenchment. It ran through the city near its lower (or south-east) end, cutting off a part of it called the General Gunge. Except in the immediate neighbourhood of the entrenchment, the enemy held all the ground between the canal and the river; while the British held the entrenchment, and the plain to the south-east of the canal.

Sir Colin's plan was to separate the enemy inside the city and on the river face from those outside the city on the Kalpee side, *i.e.* between the city and the canal; to hold the former in check while he attacked and defeated the latter; and then to turn on the former and possibly capture that force.

Windham occupied the entrenchment with a sufficient reserve; the rest of the force—5,000 infantry, 600 cavalry, and 36 guns—were employed for the action, and were drawn up under cover on the eastern or Allahabad side of the canal, facing it; all the enemy, except on the right flank, being on the other side. The Infantry Brigades, from the right (nearest the entrenchment) to the left, were Greathed's, Walpole's, Hope's, and Inglis's. The plan was this: Windham was to start the battle by opening artillery fire from the entrenchment against the city, so as to draw the enemy's attention in that direction. Greathed's Brigade was to attack and occupy the General Gunge (the small part of the city that lay on the Allahabad side of the canal), hold the canal there, and prevent any attempt of the enemy to cross it. Walpole's Brigade was to dash across the canal, and advance skirting the southern face of the city, masking all its points of egress, and preventing the enemy inside the city from joining the enemy outside; while Hope's and Inglis's Brigades, with the cavalry, were to cross the canal to the left, and then sweep onward driving the enemy there before them.

Windham began his cannonade about nine o'clock. Greathed carried out his part of the programme about eleven, and kept up a continuous fire from the position he had gained on the enemy in the city. Then Walpole charged across the canal, and, aided by the Artillery fire massed on the left, advanced and hemmed in the city, blocking its gates. Hope's and Inglis's Brigades following, with their movements screened by the dust of the cavalry, attacked the enemy on their side of the canal, drove them across, stormed the bridge (one of Peel's ship guns leading), and advanced rapidly, driving back the enemy (their right wing) along the whole open space between the city and the canal, which had here curved so as to become parallel to the city and the river. The advance became a continuous charge, especially when our men came in sight of the rebel camp. When they reached it, they had captured all the guns of the enemy, whose right wing was in full flight towards Kalpee. So Sir Colin, sending the Cavalry and Horse Artillery under Hope Grant in pursuit, ordered General Mansfield, his chief of the Staff, to turn to the right and advance towards the river; so as to attack the enemy's centre and left, cut off their retreat, and thus drive them into the river and destroy them. That body of the enemy under the fire from Windham's guns, and from Greathed's and Walpole's Brigades, seeing how their right wing was faring, had begun to withdraw from the city and retire along the Bithoor road. Here they should have been met and attacked by Mansfield at a position called the Soobahdar's Tank; but, by some blundering, he failed to intercept their line of retreat, and so they streamed off towards Bithoor almost unscathed and unmolested. After such a complete victory over the right wing, it was a severe blow to Sir Colin that so large a body of the enemy should have thus escaped. However, on the 8th (after a complete day's rest) he sent off Hope Grant with a picked force in pursuit of them towards Sheorajpore. By the evening he came up with them just as they were attempting to cross the river, and defeated and routed them utterly, taking all their guns, and inflicting very heavy loss.

The number of guns thus taken on the 6th and the 8th was thirty-two, and the total British loss was ninety-two killed and wounded. The success was complete. The enemy disappeared from the scene, never again to appear there. Sir Colin's communications were safe, and he was free to set about his further operations there.

These further operations were practically unconnected with Oude, and will, therefore, only be lightly touched on. His present aim was to clear the districts lying westward between the Ganges and the Jumna, and this he effected by the use of three columns. One moved under Walpole from Cawnpore on December 18th, first towards Kalpee, and then up the left bank of the Jumna to Mynpoorie and Bewur. Practically it did not encounter any enemy. The second column came southwards from Delhi under Seaton. It left on December 9th, about 2,000 strong, gained two victories on the road, and joined Walpole at Bewur on January 3rd. The third column, under Sir Colin's personal command, marched against Futtehgurh and Furruckabad on the Ganges opposite the boundary of Rohilkund and Oude. It left Cawnpore on December 24th; when nearing Futtehgurh it encountered the enemy (troops of the Nuwab of Furruckabad) at the Kalee Nuddee, and routed them completely, driving them across the Ganges into Rohilkund. Next day, January 3rd, Sir Colin seized the fortress of Futtehgurh, where he was joined by Seaton and Walpole; which made the troops now with him amount to 10,000 men.

By this time other troops were gradually coming up-country, and fresh levies were being raised and trained in the Punjab; so that Sir Colin could rely on soon having a very large army at his command, both for overawing and reducing the various districts into submission, and also for carrying out any special enterprises. What his first enterprise should be was the point now in question. He was for clearing Rohilkund, and had addressed Lord Canning to that effect on December 22nd. To this the Governor-General had replied at great length on the 29th, showing that, in his opinion, Oude should be first dealt with and Lucknow taken. This decision he now confirmed in his letters of January 7th and 8th, after considering Sir Colin's arguments.

From this date Sir Colin's task was the concentration of troops for the attack and capture of Lucknow. His anxiety was still excessive; though nothing else, nothing that he dwelt on, approached to one quarter of the risk that he imposed on Outram, in requiring him to hold on at the Alum Bagh with 4,000 men, when he knew from authentic sources that 95,000 hostile troops were concentrated in Lucknow, by whom he might be attacked at any moment, as also perhaps by the Talookdars of Oude.

The forces that Sir Colin hoped to have at his disposal were—

I. Those that were already with him on the Doab.

II. The additional troops still due from Calcutta.

III. The siege-train from Agra and the troops with it.

IV. A column from the Punjab promised him by Sir John Lawrence, which should advance from Roorkee through Rohilkund.

V. Outram's force at the Alum Bagh.

VI. A division under General Franks which was holding the eastern frontier of Oude.

VII. A Nepaulese army under Jung Bahadur which was also approaching from the east.

For some time there was discussion and correspondence respecting the mode and direction of the attack. Before this, when Sir Colin's plans had been to clear Rohilkund first of all, it had been urged that the troops should then converge on Lucknow, and that the enemy should be hemmed in; and Napier had included an attack on its west in his scheme. But now that Rohilkund was to be left in the enemy's possession, it was decided that, instead of attacking Lucknow on the west, there should be an outlet left on that side, by which they might try to escape, to be then caught by the cavalry in the open; while the south face should be blocked, the north be taken in flank and turned, and the direct attack be made from the east.

All this time the enemy in the city were being carefully watched, and Outram knew fully of their proceedings; including the construction of massive lines of defence against the British attack, which they expected from the eastward. All their former leaders, mentioned in the early days of the first defence, were still ruling and holding court. They had been collecting all the troops they could. There were more than 30,000 mutineers of our old regiments, and 60,000 of the old Oude troops or Nujeebs, besides the Rajwara contingents—that is Talookdars' retainers—whom they had summoned in from throughout the province.

Meanwhile, these Talookdars, though they had sent their contingents to Lucknow by the Durbar's orders, ever since Havelock had recrossed to Cawnpore in August, had not, any more than before, taken personally any active part or shown hostility against us.

It will be remembered how, after being previously hostile to us up to March 1857, they had been pacified, and became friendly, under Sir Henry Lawrence's control; how they had helped us with provisions for storage against the siege; how they had protected the residents of out-stations and assisted them into security; what names there were among them that should be held in honour by our countrymen for their kindly aid—as Hurdeo Buksh, Morarmow and other Byswara chiefs, Hunwunt Singh of Dharoopore, Rustoom Sah of Dehra, and rajahs such as those of Amethee and

Bulrampore. It has been shown how they had remained absolutely passive until Havelock had recrossed to Cawnpore; and that they had then been obliged to acknowledge the rule of the rebel Durbar, and to send contingents of their followers to the army at Lucknow, but had not themselves joined personally against us.

Yet the friendliness which all this really indicated had never been recognized, still less taken advantage of. They were still remaining passive; though their contingents were at Lucknow, and had fought well against us when they had been required to fight; better, it was said, than the regular Sepoys. But they were either under no special command, or under the command of the Brahmin Maun Singh, the craftiest of Amils, one of the most detested of the oppressors of the Rajpoot Talookdars and peasantry. This was not pleasant either to these contingents or to the chiefs. Unassisted and unguided, they were practically powerless; and they, and the province generally, were dominated and terrorized by the huge Sepoy army at Lucknow.

Still the power of these Talookdars was really very great, as was proved by the trouble they afterwards gave us when they really turned against us; and, considering the friendliness that they had evinced, it is reasonable to suggest that skilful negotiations through well-selected agents might have ranged those men and their clans on our side.

As it was, they were ever reckoned in the weight against us. The tendency was to treat them, without thought, as enemies. Hunwunt Singh's fort of Kalakunkur was fired at from our river steamer; and it was seldom that they were spoken of save as unmitigated scoundrels and ruffians. Anyhow the Rajpoot chiefs were not enlisted in our favour. And hence the Lucknow rebel Government were able to distribute these Talookdaree troops among such commanders as they chose to elect—to the Moulvie, to Maun Singh, to Mahomed Hoossein, to Mehndee Hussun, and the like.

At this stage, when Sir Colin is preparing his combinations for penetrating into Oude and attacking Lucknow in force, let us turn to the defence of the new position at the Alum Bagh, which Outram had been required to undertake, with 4,000 men, against all the efforts of the enemy, more than 90,000 strong, only two miles off.

CHAPTER II

PRELIMINARY OPERATIONS IN OUDE

OUTRAM had been left at the Alum Bagh on November 27th with a force, including 500 detached to the Bunnee Bridge, of about 4,400 men, of whom 1,000 were natives. The object with which this force was thus left in the immediate neighbourhood of Lucknow was, in Outram's own words, to retain a military footing in Oude, to maintain the honour of the British arms, and to represent the authority of the British Government in the province. Sir Colin considered it desirable, both on political and strategic grounds, that the position should be in close proximity to Lucknow. It was within a mile and a half of its suburbs, and its advanced post was within gunshot range of the outworks of the city; which swarmed with the concentrated strength of the rebel force of the Upper Provinces, amounting, according to a careful estimate prepared in January, to 95,000 men, exclusive of the Rajwara troops actually present.

The Alum Bagh enclosure, fortified, as he had directed while in the Residency, was the post that formed the chief defence of Outram's right front, which was nearest the enemy. The old and tumble-down fort of Jellalabad protected his right flank; extemporized field-works guarded his left front and left. His force was encamped in the open across the Cawnpore road, with defensive works thrown up on the alignments between those posts.

As has been already noted, Outram objected to the position, and proposed to be allowed to move more to the rear. This was in the early days of the defence during December, when Sir Colin's views were that Lucknow should not be attacked till the very last, till Rohilkund and all the neighbouring districts had been conquered and cleared—not, in short, for another ten or twelve months.

Outram held that the close proximity to Lucknow was

objectionable for these reasons—the enemy were able to attack and worry him whenever they chose without his having a chance of retaliating, and pursuing and punishing them in return. His position was cramped and liable to surprise, and consequently required a stronger force to hold it securely, and also to maintain his more lengthened communication with Cawnpore. Further, to remain in the vicinity of Lucknow without making any effort to take it was liable, in his opinion, to be interpreted as a declaration of weakness. He held that, so long as he remained on the soil of Oude, a position nearer Cawnpore was preferable for these military reasons, without being open to any objection on political grounds; for it was immaterial what particular spot he occupied as a proof that we were not deserting Oude, while it would be futile to attempt to move troops about or re-establish any civil Government so long as we were not in possession of the capital.

But Sir Colin slighted his objections; and after he had defeated the Gwalior Contingent, went so far as to propose that the 4,000 men at the Alum Bagh should be reduced by 600 infantry, half of the cavalry, and Olpherts's Battery. But Outram's strong remonstrance prevented this being carried out. Still this proposal is an instance of the singular contrast between Sir Colin's estimate of the difficulties Outram had to face, and of those that had to be met by himself and others elsewhere. For nowhere else was there, during all these months, any hostile force, or group of forces, of which the strength was not insignificant compared to the rebel army, of which the focus was at Lucknow, and which might attack Outram any day in full force. What, for instance, compared to it was the Rohilkund gathering, to meet which Sir Colin had collected 10,000 men at Futtehgurh?

For three months Outram occupied this position. During that period the enemy attacked him, and he defeated them, on six separate occasions—December 22nd, January 12th, 16th, February 15th, 21st, 25th. For dealing beyond his lines with such attacks he had only about 2,000 men available, with one horsed battery; for of his full complement of 4,000, 600 had to garrison the Alum Bagh and Jellalabad posts, 400 were absent on convoy, and 1,000 were absorbed by brigade and camp requirements or were in hospital.

The first attack on him was on December 22nd, when he had been left nearly a month without serious molestation. The enemy at Lucknow had, at first, been cowed by the handling and losses at Sir Colin's hands; but they had gradually recovered their spirits on hearing of the occasional successes, duly magnified, of the rebel troops at Cawnpore, and their impunity elsewhere; and also from the accession to their strength of the troops that had escaped over into Oude after December 8th. The rebels had succeeded thoroughly in establishing a blockade of the Alum Bagh as regards supplies, and nothing was to be obtained except from Cawnpore under convoy escort. At length, on December 20th and 21st, Outram was informed by his spies that the enemy meant to circle round his right flank and intercept his communications; and that they numbered 4,000 infantry and 400 cavalry, with four guns. So he moved out against them on the early morning of the 22nd with some 1,200 infantry, 200 cavalry, and six guns. Attacking their rear about a mile from the canal, he at once defeated it, inflicting considerable loss, and capturing four guns; when their main body, fearing to have their retreat intercepted, withdrew by a wide detour to the Dil Koosha. This was a cheering success, and gave good augury for the future.

The second attack was made three weeks afterwards, on January 12th, with the object of enveloping his position and assailing him all round; and the foe therefore came out in force, some 30,000 men. One of their commanders, Mausoob Ali, had been threatening the convoys between Alum Bagh and Cawnpore, and Outram had therefore been obliged (as was probably the enemy's intention) to detach a large escort, and weaken his own position more than usual. So, when the attack came off, after providing for the several posts and pickets, he had available for movements in the field only some 1,500 infantry and Olpherts's battery, with the Military Train as cavalry in support.

The enemy first attacked on the left, and were allowed to come sufficiently near; when they were met by such a fire from the guns in position that they fled precipitately, while Olpherts's guns and the cavalry drove off those who had been trying to get at their left rear. While this was going on the enemy attacked the right in great force, chiefly infantry. But the right brigade turned their flank and drove them northwards, bringing them under the fire of the Alum Bagh post guns. They made fresh efforts, however, both on the left and the right, but were again repulsed; and after a fifth effort at the Alum Bagh post, where they were heavily punished by both artillery and rifle fire, they withdrew, disappearing about four o'clock into the shelter of their own works. Our loss was trifling.

A third attack, similar to that of the 12th, was made four days later. The enemy were in fewer numbers, but they advanced more boldly, and were therefore more heavily punished. Again our loss was insignificant—one man killed and seven wounded.

After a skirmish on February 15th, in which the Moulvie was wounded, they made a vigorous attack on the left and centre of the position, and eventually on the Alum Bagh post; keeping up their fire till late in the evening, though they lost considerably, chiefly from our artillery fire. This I call the fourth attack.

By this time the enemy appear to have obtained better knowledge of the ground around Outram's position, and to have taken advantage of the surrounding groves and other cover to construct trenches, and to arrange for means of collecting in force; which of course enabled them to make much more sudden and heavy attacks than when they had first to traverse the outlying ground beyond.

So, on February 21st, they made their fifth attack, the signs by this time growing strong and clear that they would not have many more such opportunities; as the British advance was beginning, both from the east and from Cawnpore. The attack this time was in front and on both flanks, with efforts to turn the rear. The frontal attacks were, as heretofore, steadily met and repulsed by artillery and rifle fire; while the turning movements were encountered on the Jellalabad side by the Volunteers and Native Cavalry, and on the left by the Military Train. It was estimated that the enemy's loss was heavier than on any of the previous attacks.

Up to now the reinforcement that had from time to time joined Outram, had amounted to 2,400 men, less the 75th regiment, which had returned. And now there arrived, as the pioneers of the army for the siege of Lucknow, the 1st Bengal Fusiliers, Hodson's Horse, two squadrons of Hussars, and Remington's troop of Horse Artillery. It was when Outram had received these additions to his force that the enemy made their last attack on him on February 25th. This time they were in great strength. The trenches in front were held in great force. There were large masses of infantry and cavalry, with several guns on the left, and on the right there were thirty regiments of infantry, one thousand cavalry, and eight guns.

The attack on the left was soon repulsed; that on the right was shrewdly dealt with under Outram's personal guidance. A strong body of cavalry was sent out from the right rear to sweep round and get on the enemy's rear. Another force of cavalry moved forward on the right front, flanked by infantry, to intercept the mutineer column from the canal; and then the main force advanced against that column and began driving it back. The enemy now saw the danger on their flanks and rear, and began a rapid retreat; but too late, for our two turning bodies of cavalry came down on their flanks, the Military Train charged into their rear, and there was a great rout. The city reports laid their loss at from 400 to 500 men.

Such was the last of the attacks. The thought inevitably arises, that the enemy's conduct in connection with the Alum Bagh, whether before Sir Colin's relief or during the following January and February, cannot be held to have evinced the skill and prowess demanding huge forces and elaborate precautions to deal with them. Battalions were now required by the Chief instead of companies; whereas the enemy themselves seem to have been affected less by numbers than by energy in action, and by boldness and promptitude in attack.

I now turn to the other forces concentrating for the siege. Besides Outram's, I mentioned six columns or groups—two from the eastward, three with Sir Colin, and one from Roorkee. This last column did not after all join for the fray at this period. The districts in its own neighbourhood were held to be in too unsettled a state; but possibly a part of the troops meant for that column may have come round by Agra instead with the siege-train, which started thence for Cawnpore on January 22nd. This siege-train convoy, the force he had with him at the Kalee Nuddee, and the additional troops streaming up from Calcutta, were the three columns which were quoted as being with Sir Colin; and they moved into Oude by degrees from Cawnpore, as the time for action approached, without any conflicts.

The columns that were to penetrate Oude from the Benares districts were two: one under General Franks; the other a body of Nepaulese troops under the famed Jung Bahadur.

General Franks's field force consisted of three British regiments, the 10th, 20th, and 97th, six battalions of Nepaulese under their General, Pulwan Singh, two field batteries, and some other guns, but only some thirty or forty cavalry. He had been keeping clear the districts on the eastern frontier of Oude, and had had some small affairs latterly at Nusrutpore and Soraon; but at length he was ordered to enter Oude by the Sultanpore road on February 19th. The enemy that had been waiting near the borders of Oude to confront him were under the ex-Amil, Mehndee Hussun, with about 10,000 men; while another body of 8,000 men, under his Lieutenant Bunda Hussun, were in advance at Chanda, nearer the frontier. Except some 2,500 disciplined Sepoys, these men were all Rajwara troops, chiefly matchlockmen, with no heart for the contest while under the leading of Mahomedan court officials. Their artillery was very miscellaneous, and drawn by bullocks.

Franks encountered the Chanda force early on the 19th, defeated them easily, and then advanced and changed front to the left, from which direction he heard that Mehndee Hussun was advancing. Him also, when he appeared on his flank in the dusk of the evening, he defeated with the same ease, and then bivouacked for the night. The want of cavalry prevented full or even a fair advantage being taken of this success. But practically there had been no serious conflict or struggle at all on this the first day of the advance.

Two marches ahead, however, there was a difficult ravine to be forced at a pass guarded by the Fort of Budayan. This was susceptible of defence, and might occasion serious loss; so Franks tricked the enemy. Making arrangements openly as if for a halt half way, he instead marched the whole distance in one day, and crossed the ravine, reaching and seizing the fort just in time to anticipate the enemy's force. Holding the fort securely, he brought up the rest of his force, and the rear-guard, and halted his men during all the 22nd to rest and refresh them for the next day's impending battle at Sultanpore; hoping also that those bodies of cavalry which he knew were pressing on from the rear to join him, might arrive in time to be used in the combat. These were the Lahore Light Horse, Vivian's Puthan cavalry, and Aikman's Jullundur Levy; but, as will be seen, they were just a few hours too late for the fray.

The Sultanpore action was skilfully managed. The whole force of the enemy, re-assembled from the recent fights and joined by fresh arrivals from Lucknow, were now under the command of Guffoor Beg, an artillery general of the late Government. The road by which Franks was to advance crossed a nullah or ravine on the confines of Sultanpore. It was deep and easy of defence where crossed by the road. It was *very* deep, and broken into a series of ravines a mile more to our right as it neared the Goomtee; but to the left it was much narrower and shallower, whilst it was lined by groves of trees at intervals throughout. Franks adopted the same manœuvre as Havelock had done at the battle of Cawnpore. He halted part of his force before reaching the ravine, and sent forward some skirmishers and his horsemen to its bank to raise a dust, conceal his movements, and distract and draw the fire of the enemy. Then he took a strong force with a large party of picked skirmishers round by the left, and crossing the ravine where it was shallow and where they were screened by the groves, he turned to the right, and moved down on the flank of the enemy drawn up in line defending the ravine. As he emerged from the groves he deployed his line, but sent his skirmishers well ahead at the enemy to do the fighting. Struggle there was none. Under the fire from the front and flank and rear, flight began at once, commencing with a horsed battery which had been on their extreme right. Soon the plain was covered with fugitives, flying either towards Lucknow or towards the river. The slaughter from our artillery and rifle fire was nothing to what it would have been had our cavalry arrived. But as it was, Franks utterly dispersed the enemy and took thirty-four guns; as many, he laughingly boasted, as had been taken at the siege of Moultan.

His whole loss in the three actions he had fought was only two killed and sixteen wounded. The secret of this lay in the formation of his fighting force being not in line but in open skirmishing order.

The road was now clear, and he was joined in a few hours by the much-longed-for cavalry, of whom a party were forthwith sent in pursuit. And now Franks received orders to advance to Selimpore, a march short of Lucknow, by the "29th inst."—a curious slip, as it was the month of February, and there would be no 29th inst. This he easily did without further fighting, and then, on being summoned forward, he joined the army near the Dil Koosha on March 4th, having on the way attacked and captured the guns in the fortified village of Dhorwara.

This successful march, if the enemy's forces are properly considered in detail, as well as their leaders and the resistance they made, points to some significant conclusions. It is quite certain that the bulk of the enemy consisted of matchlockmen, Rajwara or Talookdaree troops, and that they did not fight well; in fact hardly fought at all, except when forced to stand at bay. Moreover, during the whole of this period, not one of their leaders was of their own race, Hindoo Rajpoots; they were all Mahomedans and ex-officials of the Lucknow court—such as Mehndu Hussun, Bunda Hussun, Guffoor Beg, Fuzl Azim, Mahomed Hoosseyn, and so forth. In fact, the conduct of the Rajwara men under these circumstances—very different from what it was on other occasions when led by their own chiefs—seems to point irresistibly to the conclusion that their chiefs held aloof from these hostilities, and that the men were in their hearts with their chiefs, and joined grudgingly in the fighting.

But this march of General Franks, besides being important in itself, was valuable from its clearing the way for Jung Bahadur's army following in its rear.

Jung Bahadur had, early in the winter months, sent down

in advance various bodies of Nepaulese, which had been of material help in clearing the Goruckpore and Azimgurh districts, and had latterly detached six battalions to form part of Franks's force. He had followed himself, with additional troops, at the end of December, and now crossed the Ganges into Oude on February 25th with some 9,000 men. He first attacked and captured the fort of Ambarpore, and then marched forward steadily to Lucknow, his progress being undisturbed by the enemy, of whom Franks had cleared the road. But he did not reach the camp at Lucknow and take part in the operations there till March 11th, four days after the siege had begun in full vigour.

Practically, when the troops that Sir Colin had sent forward from Cawnpore to the Alum Bagh had collected there by the end of February, and Franks had joined on March 4th, they, with Outram's force which had been holding the Alum Bagh, began operations on March 5th.

CHAPTER III

THE SIEGE AND CAPTURE OF THE CITY

THE city of Lucknow,[1] which the enemy now held in force, and which Sir Colin was about to attack, had been prepared strongly for defence according to the enemy's lights. Putting aside the idea of any attack from the westward of the Cawnpore road, they had protected the city along the canal face from the Char Bagh eastwards round to the Goomtee; and also for a mile or so, as a flanking defence, to the west of the Char Bagh. Along that part of the canal to the east which was bordered by dense city—that is up to Banks's house—the defences were a line of parapet with occasional batteries, and barricades at the outlets of roads and streets; but from Banks's house to the river there was a line of massive earthwork ramparts, with bastions and batteries at close intervals. This was their first or outer line of defence.

The portion between Banks's house and the river was almost a straight line, with only a slight curve outwards towards the Dil Koosha. Behind that line, it will be remembered, lay the broad plain narrowing to the west, by which both Havelock and Sir Colin had advanced to the relief of the Residency; a plain bordered on the north by the Goomtee, and on the south by the long street beginning with the Huzrutgunge at the Begum's house, and then skirting a series of palatial buildings ending with the Kaiser Bagh. Over this plain were dotted the several enclosures and buildings that had given so much trouble to the relieving forces—such as the Barracks, the Secundra Bagh, the Shah Nujeef, the mess-house or Koorsheyd Manzil, the Motee Mahul, and others.

The second line of defensive ramparts which the enemy had constructed started from the Emambarah, one of the

[1] See Map V.

palatial buildings above referred to, connecting it with the mess-house, and then went on to the Motee Mahul and the river.

The third line, at right angles to the other two, merely covered, at a close distance, the entire front of the Kaiser Bagh.

They had not constructed any defences on the north side of the Goomtee, but had contented themselves with occupying it with a considerable body of troops, chiefly cavalry.

The numbers of the enemy were believed to be much the same as had been there during Outram's occupation of the Alum Bagh position; but all the Sepoy troops had been called in from the outlying districts, and the Rajwara troops had been withdrawn and sent there to take their place. The enemy had, as I have said, made up their minds that Sir Colin would attack them on the eastern portion of the canal; and Sir Colin proposed, while gratifying them so far, to attack that position not only on its front but also on its flank, from the north. His dispositions and arrangements were these—

His force on March 2nd was about 19,000 men and 120 guns. Franks's column was due in a couple of days, and Jung Bahadur's a week later; and these two would bring the total strength up to 31,000 men and 164 guns.

At first his force was in three divisions—

Outram's at the Alum Bagh; behind it, echeloned on the Cawnpore road, *Lugard's;* and then *Walpole's*, with which was the siege-train. The cavalry were under Hope Grant and Brigadier Campbell. Sir Colin re-arranged this. He proposed to place under Outram part of his own division, and all Walpole's division, with Hope Grant's cavalry; and to leave the rest of Outram's division as a brigade under Franklin at the Alum Bagh. The new disposition he arrived at was to send Outram's force, thus organized, across to the north side of the Goomtee; to place Lugard's division opposite the Dil Koosha portion of the canal; to leave Hodson's Horse as a connecting link between it and the Alum Bagh; and to give to Brigadier Campbell and his cavalry the task of holding the ground to the west of the Char Bagh and Alum Bagh. Franks's column, on arrival, was to form up, at first in support, and afterwards on the left, of Lugard; and Jung Bahadur was to come into line on the left of Franks, so filling up the gap to the Alum Bagh.

Sir Colin began operations on March 2nd, by moving out from the rear of the Alum Bagh position to the right, and circling by a wide detour round Jellalabad towards the Dil Koosha. The force he took was Hope Grant's cavalry, a strong body of artillery, and Lugard's division. It drove in the enemy's outlying pickets and advanced to the Dil Koosha plateau; which was found to be under very powerful and accurate fire from the enemy's batteries, along the front line of defence, especially at the passage of the canal by the Dil Koosha road. He therefore moved the column somewhat to the rear, to be more secure from the fire, but seized the two posts of the Dil Koosha Palace, and the Mahomed Bagh; where, in order to reply effectually to the enemy's guns, he proceeded to construct two powerful counter-batteries. These opened fire next day, and silenced the enemy's guns, causing them to be withdrawn. On the 4th, Walpole's division, with the rest of the siege-train, moved over from the Alum Bagh, and all encamped on the Dil Koosha position, where, at dusk, Franks's column also marched in and joined.

That same evening, two bridges were begun from the Dil Koosha position across the Goomtee, on a stretch of that erratic river, that ran eastwards, near the village of Beebiapore. By next morning, the 5th, one of them was finished; a strong picket was then thrown across, and a defensive bridge-head begun at once. On the night of the 5th the bridges and the necessary arrangements were completed, and the whole of Outram's force had crossed over by daybreak. Until that force had advanced sufficiently in its turning movement, that is until the 9th, Sir Colin's troops at the Dil Koosha remained inactive, not even attacking the Martinière, which continued to worry them with its fire; but Franks's column moved up and replaced Walpole's division on Lugard's left.

Outram's column, after crossing the Goomtee, moved in a northerly direction towards Chinhut, and on striking the Fyzabad road, turned to the left. On reaching Ishmaelgunge (the actual site of the battle of June 30th, with which the siege of the Residency began), a body of the enemy's cavalry were seen in the front, and our cavalry were sent at them. The enemy fled and were followed up, and the pursuit brought our cavalry into broken ground close to the enemy's infantry posts. This necessarily checked them and caused some loss, especially to the leading regiment, the Queen's Bays, whose Major, Percy Smyth, was killed. There was a spice of romance about this charge of the Bays; for it was the first occasion on which that regiment had ever been in action, and the men were eager to be the first to get it its baptism of fire. They had been at Nusrutpore with Franks, but no real fighting occurred on that occasion. After the enemy had been driven off, the column encamped for the night at Ishmaelgunge.

Here Outram was still considerably short of the distance he had to advance in order to turn the enemy's first line of defences; while they were holding, to protect its flank and rear, a small post called the Chukkur Kothi (race-stand) on his left front near the river; which had to be taken to admit of his turning operations being properly effected.

Outram's camp halted at Ishmaelgunge during the 7th and 8th. On the morning of the 7th he was attacked in force, but defeated and drove off the enemy; and the rest of the time was spent in clearing the ground and advancing his pickets, which entailed constant skirmishing. On the evening of the 8th he received his heavy siege-guns (twenty-two), and sent back to Sir Colin one of his Horse Artillery Batteries, and the 9th Lancers. At the same time he began, and during the night completed, two powerful batteries; one on his extreme left for his principal objective, *i.e.* to enfilade the enemy's line of defence, and take the Martinière in rear; the other to batter the Chukkur Kothi, and assist his own advance up the left bank of the Goomtee.

Next morning, the 9th, the ball opened, the enfilade fire began, and Outram attacked and captured the Chukkur Kothi; he personally leading half his force in a frontal attack, while Walpole with the other half worked round to its flank and rear.

It was taken with but slight loss, and then the whole

combined column advanced up the left bank of the river till it seized and held the Badshah Bagh; and was able, from the position it occupied, to sweep the flank and rear of such of the enemy on the other side as might try to hold both the first and the second line of the defences, up to the Kaiser Bagh Palace itself. Meanwhile, his battery on his extreme left which had, since the morning, been enfilading the enemy's first line of defences, had driven the occupants from its northern end; and a gallant feat was now performed by Butler of the 1st Fusiliers, who swam the Goomtee, climbed the enemy's parapet, and there signalled to Adrian Hope, who was leading Sir Colin's attack, to show that these works had been evacuated by the enemy.

The time had now come for Sir Colin, after about five days of inaction, to make a move and deliver his frontal attack; of which the aim was to storm the enemy's line of defence, and then to capture the great row of palaces along the Huzrutgunge, and the posts between them and the river. The troops he used for this purpose were Lugard's division and Franks's, which had stepped into the line before held by Walpole's. At first Lugard led, and Franks was in support.

The first move was against the Martinière, which was in advance of the first line of defence. Sir Colin had opened a very heavy fire on it from the Dil Koosha early that morning, the 9th, but waited, before making his advance, for the signal agreed on to show the capture by Outram of the Chukkur Kothi—the hoisting of the British flag on its roof. At two o'clock the signal was seen, and Hope's Brigade, supported by the rest of Lugard's division, immediately advanced and captured the Martinière without any real contest; the enemy flying at once, mostly across the river. Hope's Brigade continued the advance towards the right front, saw Butler's signaling, crossed over the enemy's earthworks at the river end, and then, turning to the left, swept down to the other end, near Banks's house; the rest of the attacking force crossing the line of entrenchments about its centre. They halted for the night about the positions near the Dil Koosha road bridge, and thus closed the operations of the 9th March.

On the 10th Sir Colin attacked on the left and captured

Banks's house, and the first of the houses and enclosures in the long line of palatial buildings along the Huzrutgunge, thus securing the basis of his further advance on that line. Outram, on the north of the Goomtee, was attacked by the enemy, whom he defeated and drove off as usual; and then, while using his cavalry to patrol and clear the ground to his west and north, constructed gun and mortar batteries against the posts which lay in the line of Sir Colin's attack, thus fully and effectually carrying out his *rôle* of flanking and furthering the main advance and struggle under Sir Colin.

On the 11th marked and important progress was made. Batteries had been constructed and guns placed in position at Banks's house; and in the morning they opened a powerful fire on the Begum's Palace, the first of the strong positions along the Huzrutgunge. While this was going on, Lugard advanced on the right against the detached posts, seizing, without opposition, first the Secundra Bagh, and then the Kuddum Russool and the Shah Nujeef, the scenes of the conflict of November 16th. The latter were specially important posts, from their close proximity to the enemy's second line of defences; and their seizure was due to the enterprise of two engineers, Medley and Lang, who, reconnoitring for themselves, found them empty, caused supports to come forward and secure them, and then threw up defences and works against the next forward movement.

By the afternoon the batteries at Banks's house had breached the Begum's Palace, and it was accordingly stormed, Hope's Brigade leading. The contest was severe, as the enemy were more resolute than usual, while the position consisted of several strong buildings and enclosures which were held in force, bravely defended, and had to be attacked one after the other. The 93rd Highlanders and the 4th Punjabees working together as if one regiment, gained on the enemy inch by inch; and when at last they had expelled them, there were 600 Sepoys' corpses left within the walls. This struggle was marked by the death of the famed Hodson, an ideal leader of cavalry, whose services, whatever his faults, real or alleged, had been simply invaluable throughout the war.

Whilst Sir Colin's troops had thus been gaining ground on the south of the Goomtee, Outram had been operating up the left bank. He advanced up to the road running from the iron bridge to the cantonment, in two columns; the left under Colonel Pratt skirting the river, the right under Walpole proceeding by the Fyzabad road, with the cavalry under Hope Grant sweeping the flank up to the cantonment; the two columns being connected by a line of skirmishers, which, as well as the left column itself, met with considerable opposition. On reaching the iron bridge steps were taken to seize and secure its northern end, in the course of which that most able officer, Lieutenant Moorsom of the Quartermaster-General's department, was killed, to the general regret, and Outram's special loss.

The right column with the cavalry then continued the advance, reconnoitring through the crowded suburb up to the stone bridge, surprising on its way the camp of the 15th Cavalry and the Sandeela Contingent; but as the defences and posts at the stone bridge were found to be very strong, the column returned to the iron bridge, and later on back to camp, leaving the necessary posts and pickets held in force.

On the 11th, then, the Begum's Palace had been secured, also the Secundra Bagh and the Shah Nujeef, and Outram had advanced and was holding as far as the iron bridge. The artillery and mortar fire on the line of palaces and other buildings and positions was duly maintained; and a special episode of this day was the arrival of Jung Bahadur's army, which next day duly took up its position opposite the canal between Banks's house and the Char Bagh, as had been arranged.

During the 12th and 13th the actual progress was not much marked outwardly. The engineers were steadily forcing their way through the several palaces, such as Jaffir Ali's and Jarour ood Dowlah's up to the Emambarah, the troops occupying and securing them as they were seized.

Meanwhile Outram was halting, his orders not warranting his further advance. On the 12th, however, Jung Bahadur had formed up on the line assigned him, and on the 13th he had been requested to cross the canal on his front and work through the city on the left of Lugard's advance through the palaces. Now on the 14th the lead of that advance was transferred from Lugard's to Franks's division.

By that morning, the 14th, the situation was this: Sir Colin's main column had penetrated and sapped through the palaces up to the Emambarah, and had made a breach in its walls; on its left the Nepaulese were working through the ordinary city; on its right he held the position in front of the enemy's second line of defences. On the other side of the river Outram had turned that second line of defences and seized his end of the iron bridge. On that day he asked leave to force the iron bridge, and operate against the enemy's posts behind their second line, but he was prohibited by an order *not to do so if it would cause his losing a single man.* The bridge was blocked by a battery and held in force by the enemy; so he had to remain passive.

Not so Franks at the range of palaces. The breach having been made in the wall of the Emambarah, Sir Colin gave the order for the storming of that position. The attack was made by the 10th Foot and Brasyer's Sikhs, the stormers being two companies of the former and sixty men of the latter. After a sharp struggle they made good their entrance and drove back the enemy, who, once they saw the lodgment made in force, fled precipitately, leaving the Emambarah in the hands of the English. In their flight they emerged through its great gateway, and turning to the left, streamed down the street towards the Kaiser Bagh, with some of our stormers following in close chase.

But General Franks had sent on his Adjutant-General, the younger Havelock, with the attacking party to guide its movements. And he led the 90th and others of that party, not in pursuit of the fugitives, but by a line parallel and close to their route into the next palace; which was separated by only one other building from the Kaiser Bagh, and from which he found he could command the three nearest bastions of the third line of entrenchments running along in the immediate front of the Kaiser Bagh. Bringing a musketry fire to bear on these bastions, he drove the enemy off and forced them to quit the guns—one of them an eight-inch howitzer—and he also led them to see that their second line of defences was taken in rear at this end, after it had already been turned by Outram's operations at its river end, and was practically no longer tenable. So some of them at once began to desert those works and to take shelter in the buildings and enclosures which still lay between the ground we were holding and the Kaiser Bagh. Brasyer, however, seeing the chance, led his men by a bastion which had been evacuated into that intervening position, and being followed up by supports, cleared it entirely of the enemy.

This was the limit of the programme for the day, but circumstances sometimes destroy the value and the real practicability of such limits in military operations, especially in dealing with the Asiatic. Once get them on the run, and it is as dangerous and mischievous to halt in the advance as it is advantageous to press it on. So young Havelock called up the 10th to support Brasyer, and they followed up the enemy into the Cheenee Bazar; that part of the prolongation of the Huzrutgunge which skirted the Kaiser Bagh (or rather the tomb of Saadut Ali on its front), and lay inside the third line of defences. This movement consequently turned that third line of the enemy's defences, and supported those of our stormers who, after taking the Emambarah, had followed close on the heels of the flying enemy.

Now, at this juncture, the enemy who had been posted in the middle of their *second* line of defence, and had been holding the Tara Kotee and the mess-house (the Koorshid Munzil), began to find, as those on their right had already done, that their position had been turned, and that they were in danger of being cut off from their line of retreat. So they began pouring down towards the Cheenee Bazar and the Kaiser Bagh, some 5,000 or 6,000 in number; and if they had forced their way, would have been a very awkward foe for the handful of our troops who had penetrated into the Cheenee Bazar. Again young Havelock came to the rescue. He guided the Sikhs near him to the bastions in the enemy's *third* line, seized them, turned their guns on the tide of the enemy rushing over from the posts in the *second* line, and checked and drove them off; forcing their flight in the direction of the Chuttur Munzil buildings.

Then the main column of attack followed up and secured the posts which had thus been seized. After them speedily came up the supports, led by Franks accompanied by Napier. Thereupon the rest of the division was summoned up; our troops who were holding the Secundra Bagh and other posts in front of the enemy's second line were told that that line was clear; and they forthwith advanced and captured the Motee Mahul, the mess-house, and the other intervening posts.

Franks at the same time sent forward his own column into the courtyard of Saadut Ali's mosque; where they stormed the enclosures and gardens of the Kaiser Bagh itself, and cleared it of its defenders, so capturing and securing the very heart of the enemy's position.

Numerous had been the rumours of the desperate measures and arrangements that the enemy had adopted for the defence of the Kaiser Bagh; and Sir Colin was much discomposed and disturbed on hearing of its sudden capture and occupation, fearing that there would be great explosions of mines and the like. He is believed to have even sent orders to evacuate it, and to have received from Franks in reply the English, or rather the Irish, equivalent of the famous "J'y suis, j'y reste." But thus it was that on March 14th, Franks's column in the one day captured the whole of the enemy's positions from the Begum's house, whence it started, to their last real stronghold, the Kaiser Bagh; considerably anticipating Sir Colin's programme, and at the same time enabling the second line of the defences to be carried, and the posts beyond them occupied.

On March 15th little was done; no special progress was made at the palaces, except in the way of clearing, securing, and strengthening; but Walpole's division was required to watch very closely the river face at and between the two bridges. Also the two cavalry brigades—Hope Grant's from near the iron bridge, and Campbell's from the west of the Alum Bagh—were directed respectively to pursue the fugitive Sepoys along the Seetapore and Sandeela roads, by which they were assumed to have fled.

On the 16th there were three important events. First—Outram was directed to re-cross the Goomtee to its right bank and join in the operations there. Second—a great mass of the enemy, taking advantage of the gap or unprotected space on the north of the Goomtee—caused by this movement of Outram's, combined with the absence of the cavalry on the Seetapore road—forced their way across the stone bridge; and then turning to the right, circled round the rear of Walpole's division, and escaped unmolested by the Fyzabad road into the open country, there to re-assemble and continue the war. Third—the enemy endeavoured to retaliate, and interrupt our communications with Cawnpore, by an extensive attack in force on Franklin, at the Alum Bagh, which was for the time unsupported by Campbell's cavalry. Each of these three episodes needs some more detailed account. Outram crossed the Goomtee near the Secundra Bagh by a temporary bridge; he left Walpole's division to watch the iron and the stone bridge, took with him Douglas's Brigade, and was joined on crossing by the 20th and Brasyer's Sikhs. He advanced to the Kaiser Bagh, and then turned to the right and pushed on to the Residency. Capturing it at once, his force followed on the heels of the enemy, taking in reverse the guns and posts along the right bank of the river. Supported by the fire of the heavy guns, which he left at the Residency to play on the Mutchi Bhown, he stormed it with the 1st Fusiliers and Brasyer's Sikhs; and then, still pushing on, he turned the stone bridge and captured the great Emambarah near it. With this he ended his operations on the 16th.

The enemy had been flying before him all day, and after reaching the stone bridge, some crossed by it and engaged Walpole's division so as to occupy and divert its attention, whilst the rest of the fugitives crossed the river in the best way they could higher up, and, as noted above, escaped round the flank and rear of that division.

The movement of the enemy against the Alum Bagh was in great force, their infantry threatening its front, and their artillery and cavalry its left. But they were met with such vigour by Franklin's cavalry (Military Train and 7th Hussars) and artillery (under Eyre and Olpherts) that they were repulsed, and retired without Stisted's infantry having been at all seriously engaged.

Meanwhile Jung Bahadur, with his Nepaulese, had been

clearing the city between the palaces and the canal, though his progress had not yet reached so far as the road from the Residency to the Char Bagh.

Thus closed the proceedings of March 16th, after which the operations lay simply in forcing the enemy westwards through and out of the city.

On the 17th and 18th Outram's advance took him past the Hooseynee Mosque and the Dowlut Khana up to Shuruf ood Dowlah's house, and near Ali Nukkee Khan's; while Jung Bahadur had also worked along on the left. It was now known that a considerable force of the enemy, consisting of its most resolute troops, meant to make a final stand at the Moosa Bagh, on the extreme west of the city; and it was believed that they were animated by the presence of the Begum, the young Nuwab, the Moulvie, and all the other leaders of the rebel party except the Nana. So Sir Colin arranged for an effective finishing stroke. Outram was to attack the position, aided by flanking fire from the north of the Goomtee, while Hope Grant's cavalry on the right (to the north of the Goomtee) and Campbell's on the left should catch the enemy as they were driven out. Outram carried out his part of the programme thoroughly; capturing the position and clearing it of the enemy, who fled in large masses along the road where Brigadier Campbell was to have caught them. Campbell, however, failed, and the enemy escaped with but slight loss.

Lucknow had been taken, but the foe had not been crushed nor even punished, and they were free to re-assemble elsewhere in their thousands and tens of thousands.

So Sir Colin lost nearly the whole of the hoped-for fruits of his capture of Lucknow, and he had to thank himself for it; first from his checking Outram on the 14th; then from his misguided pursuits of the 15th; and finally from failing to ensure proper leading for his splendid force of cavalry, at the most opportune and critical moment of the war.

Thus ended the second stage of the war in Oude. The British loss in the capture was 127 killed and about 600 wounded.

BOOK VI

SUPPRESSION OF THE REVOLT

CHAPTER I

THE HOT-WEATHER CAMPAIGN

OUR narrative left the siege of the city of Lucknow brought to a successful close on March 19th, by its complete capture and the expulsion of the rebel troops, after a struggle of less than a fortnight. After so signal a proof of the power and prowess of the British, and with no marked rallying point left to the enemy, it was reasonable to expect that they would offer but little further resistance, and gradually disperse to their homes. Instead of this, however, hostilities at once broke out afresh, and over a much wider area than before; being no longer confined in their real force to the province of Oude, but being spread, with equal if not greater virulence, over the adjoining province of Rohilkund on the west, and the Azimgurh districts on the east. Moreover, the hostility in Oude itself was both enormously increased and specially characterized by the active accession of the whole country population, the Rajwara troops, the followers of the Talookdars of Oude, with whom the contest assumed the aspect of a genuine guerilla war, of which no signs had ever hitherto appeared. The causes of this increase of virulent hostility and the accession to it of the country population were quite unmistakable. They were two: first, Sir Colin's failure to prevent or even check the escape of the rebel troops and their leaders, or to pursue them effectively when driven out of Lucknow; and second, the issue by Lord Canning of his Confiscation Proclamation.[1]

The unimpeded retreat of the rebel army in the two

[1] See Appendix XIII.

detachments of March 16th and 19th, and the escape of the whole of their leaders, naturally emboldened them and led to their gathering afresh in new groups in Oude itself, mainly in its north-west and north-east; while the weakness which it seemed to indicate in the British, caused the Rohillas to rise in Rohilkund under Khan Bahadur Khan and Prince Feroze Shah; besides inciting old Konwur Singh of Shahabad to raise commotion afresh in the Azimgurh direction; so that Sir Colin had to despatch troops and organize operations at once in those two almost fresh theatres of war. This was especially disappointing and vexatious, because it would involve a hot-weather campaign, with all the exposure and the mischief that would follow to the young and unacclimatized troops fresh out from England, while the new levies that were being raised in the Punjab and the north-west were not yet fit to relieve them to any material degree.

The cause of the outburst of hostility on the Oude country population was, as I have said, the proclamation issued on March 20th by Lord Canning; generally known as the Confiscation Proclamation. It was a singular act on Lord Canning's part, because he seemed to stand almost alone as its author, and alone in his insistence on it. He was strenuously opposed by Outram, who prophesied of it precisely what happened. It was condemned by every authority and every class in India. It raised a storm of surprise and indignation in England, and caused the severest crisis in the fate of the English Ministry. Its policy was defended with his utmost ability by Lord Canning; but however just and sound theoretically, results showed that it was practically a blunder, and led to the very wide-spread increase which has been mentioned in the hostility of the country. All the chiefs, except some half-dozen men of no importance, were declared to have been guilty of rebellion and of waging war against the Queen, and to have consequently forfeited all their proprietary rights. Some hair-splitting conditions and offers that were mentioned at the same time were neither cared for nor believed. The chiefs realized that their position was desperate, and they rose *en masse* in active rebellion; which they certainly had not done before.

Outram raised very strong and well-argued objections to the Proclamation, but even these were far short of the facts that might have been urged against it. He virtually admitted that the Talookdars had rebelled, but pleaded that it was natural that they should do so, and that they should be treated as honourable enemies. Yet this story will have been told in vain if it has not shown that the mass of these Talookdars had, since Sir Henry Lawrence's arrival, and owing to his line of action, refrained from a hostile bearing; to as great a degree as could be expected, or as was possible, under the despotic native rule and powerful army that dominated the situation at Lucknow and throughout the province. It is only necessary to recall how they had aided the fugitive residents of out-stations at the outbreak; how they had helped Sir Henry Lawrence with supplies; how with three exceptions they had held aloof from joining the rebel army, either personally or through their retainers; how they continued this loyalty till Havelock evacuated Oude territory and returned to Cawnpore; how even then they sent to the rebel camp only such contingents as were demanded, and personally remained passive; and how, throughout the rest of the campaign, they had abstained from any harassing of the British troops—in marked contrast with their conduct after this Proclamation was issued.

This much, however, can almost certainly be said in excuse for Lord Canning, that he was ignorant and mistaken on these points; that in point of fact very few persons did know of them at the time; and that more general knowledge of them did not spread, nor reach the highest quarters till a later date.

But the Proclamation had a still deeper and more widespread effect than on the Talookdars alone. It was viewed as a declaration of the British Government that, on becoming sufficiently powerful, there was no despotic action which it would not take if it so willed; and as confirming the truth of all the worst charges which the malcontents had been in the habit of making, respecting the intentions and aims of the British.

The enemy in Oude now consisted of four actively hostile parties—

1. The mutineer Sepoys.

2. The resuscitated forces of the Nuwab—the Begum's troops as they may be conveniently called.
3. The Mahomedan followers of the Fyzabad Moulvie.
4. The Talookdars and their retainers and clansmen.

The numbers of the parties 1 and 2 had now diminished considerably. They had taken the leading part in all the military operations heretofore, had been now thoroughly defeated, and were somewhat sick of the struggle. But the Moulvie's force was becoming a more prominent factor in the struggle, and was acting as a focus of Mahomedan hostility; while the Rajwara men under their chiefs, all over the province, had started their old style of guerilla warfare; which lay, not in aggressive and combined movements against the common foe, but in stopping and cutting off supplies, checking and harassing the movements of the troops and emissaries and officers of Government, making and threatening local attacks, frustrating every effort to introduce civil administration, and encouraging marauders and brigandage.

The Talookdaree gatherings and warfare were mainly in Byswara and the south-east of Oude; but the three other parties collected in two groups; one on the north-west of Oude towards the Rohilkund border, under the leading of the Moulvie; the other on the north-east, consisting of all the *four* classes of rebels, and forming themselves into four separate bodies, though keeping together without any one recognized chief; a large number of persons exercising more or less influence and command over the several sections, such as the Begum, Mummoo Khan, Jeylall Singh, the Nana's brother, various officers of the Sepoy troops, and the like.

These three gatherings came to a head not simultaneously but at different and successive periods—the north-west first, then the Talookdars in Byswara in May, and afterwards the north-east gathering in June. Before dealing with these hostile bodies, Sir Colin arranged for securing proper command of Lucknow itself, by starting the construction of a large fortified position on the south bank of the Goomtee facing the stone bridge, called the Mutchi Bhown fort. It was about half a mile each way, and included within its enceinte the old Mutchi Bhown citadel at one angle, and the Great Emambarah and other large edifices at other points; and was bordered by a large clear esplanade on its landward faces which had involved a sweeping demolition of the denser part of the heart of the city.

Also the old Residency position was now surrounded with ramparts on a more correct trace, and formed a separate detached fort.

While these were in progress, and before dealing with the threatening gatherings in Oude, Sir Colin sent off troops to Azimgurh and to Rohilkund.

The column directed against Rohilkund was commanded by Walpole, and was to sweep up the left bank of the Ganges to clear and settle those districts. The part it played was important, and requires description. Walpole left Lucknow on April 7th, and in a fortnight reached Rhodamow, near which was the jungle fort of Roya, held by a Talookdar named Nirput Singh. He was not a man of any power or following, but his father, Jussa Singh, though he had not risen against the English in Oude, had been a staunch friend of the Nana, had joined him at Bithoor, and had been killed in one of his combats with Havelock. The son had followed in his father's footsteps, and had given a home and shelter in Roya to the Nana when driven out of Bithoor.

Nirput Singh was now holding out in Roya, and had to be attacked. The fort was small, not, like some others, many miles in circumference. Its strength lay in its thick mud walls and deep ditch surrounded by an impervious thicket of bamboo jungle; which, however, as was the case with all such forts, was not equally strong all round, but had some faces weaker than others, and also gaps here and there by which access was easy. Putting aside the more powerful modes of attack, in which artillery and mortars come into play, the recognized and well-known mode of capturing these places without serious loss was to discover the weak points and gaps and then force an entrance.

Now General Walpole would not adopt any such plan. He had a splendid little force, the Highland Brigade (42nd, 79th, and 93rd), the 4th Punjabees (old comrades of the 93rd), the 9th Lancers, and a Punjab cavalry regiment, with two batteries of Horse Artillery and some heavy guns and mortars. But he would not take advantage of the opportunities such a body of troops gave him. He did not reconnoitre. He did not listen to the information tendered him. He simply sent his Highland regiments forward to pierce through and storm the defences at the strongest points. The result was a heavy loss in men and officers, especially in the death of that ideal soldier, Adrian Hope; and a positive repulse, inasmuch as the British force was withdrawn from the attack. Nirput Singh evacuated the fort during the night.

Walpole proceeded on with his force after this into Rohilkund, and he no longer takes part in the warfare in Oude. But this episode of Roya had a most serious effect. Its fame, as a matter of course, spread with exaggerations throughout the province, and emboldened the Talookdars.

Sir Colin presently proceeded to conduct and control the operations in Rohilkund in person, and Hope Grant was left in command in Oude to meet and suppress whatever efforts the enemy might make. It was, doubtless, hoped at first that the enemy would be gradually scattered and dispersed; but it soon became evident that this could not be effected in this hot season, and that the organized and thorough crushing out of the rebellion must be deferred to the cold weather; present efforts being confined to the attack and dispersion of important gatherings.

The first movement against such gatherings was made on April 11th, when a force under Hope Grant marched by the Seetapore road against the party of Mahomedan rebels, who, under the leading of the Moulvie, formed what I have called the North-west group. They were really in touch with the insurgents in Rohilkund, but at present were in the Mahona direction, at Baree, some twenty-five miles from Lucknow. Grant's column was about 3,000 strong, with some eighteen guns, and contained British and native troops of all arms. As they neared Baree, the Moulvie tried to turn their flank and get at the baggage; but the flanking movement was detected and defeated, chiefly by the charge of the 7th Hussars. After this the Moulvie's men would not bide the British attack, but evacuated the village which they had occupied as their stronghold, and then withdrew in retreat and disappeared. This force apparently retired to Rohilkund; to form part of the gathering with which Sir Colin had to deal in that province, and which does not concern our story.

From Baree, Hope Grant turned to the right to Mahomedabad and the Gogra, hoping to catch the Begum at Ramnugger or Bithoolee. But she had fled on his approach, and so his immediate task was to co-operate with Jung Bahadur's army which had started on its return to Nepaul.

It was about this period that Maun Singh, the Brahmin Talookdar and ex-Amil, who had hitherto tried to play a double game, and to stand well with both the British and the rebels, now openly tendered his allegiance to the Government and held his fort of Shahgunge in their interests. The enemy soon appeared before his fort and besieged it, and there he remained till relieved in June.

But to return to Hope Grant's movements. The gathering on the north-west having been cleared off for the present, he returned to Lucknow. He did not, however, rest there, but led a force to disperse a party of the enemy that had collected on the south and were threatening, from the east, the Ganges end of the Lucknow and Cawnpore road. This was the beginning of the Byswara gathering; but it was not the same body that assembled afterwards under the leading of Beni Madho. It consisted chiefly of the followers of another Byswara chief, Baboo Ram Buksh of Doondea Khera, who had been an avowed malcontent from the outset, though he had not joined in the siege of the Residency. This expedition lasted about a fortnight. On May 1st, Hope Grant reached Poorwa, and then took the fort of Punchingaon. On the 10th he appeared before Ram Buksh's fort of Doondea Khera. This was very large and very formidable, but he found it evacuated. Two days later he found the enemy drawn up for contest at Sirsee, and there attacked and defeated them thoroughly, dispersing them, killing one of their leaders, Amruthun Singh, and taking their guns.

On the 25th the gathering under Beni Madho developed. He was by repute the best soldier, the most influential chief, and the most popular leader of the Byswara clans;

and now, large though his gathering was, he avoided any serious engagement, at once adopting the ubiquitous tactics of genuine guerilla warfare—skirmishes and surprises—ceaselessly harassing and then eluding the British troops; which he could easily do, as his followers (of whom he is said to have had over 80,000, chiefly matchlockmen), scattered over the district, knew every inch of the ground. Hope Grant was not long in seeing that against such an enemy as this our troops must remain comparatively passive and on the defence during the summer heats and rains. So leaving others to deal, for the present, with the enemy in Byswara, Hope Grant started early in June to attack the hostile force of the north-east. Here he was able to be of much more use, for this body of the enemy had now gathered to a head, and like the mutineer army before the siege of the Residency, had advanced from the Fyzabad direction and concentrated at Nuwabgunge, eighteen miles from Lucknow. This group, as has been already described, was made up of four different parties, each under a separate leader; and was without much cohesion in the parties or unanimity and concert in the chiefs. There were Sepoys of the regular army, troops of the old court of Oude, Talookdaree troops, and such of the Mahomedans as had not followed the fortunes of the Moulvie into Rohilkund. These four groups kept more or less apart, instead of acting in unison under one acknowledged leader. Hope Grant had a strong division, two British and one Punjab Infantry regiment, three batteries of artillery, some six squadrons of British cavalry, and 900 native cavalry. He marched against the enemy at night, turned the right of their position, and took them by surprise in the morning. They fought well, especially the Talookdaree troops, who routed Hodson's Horse; but after three hours of hard combat had to fall back, leaving 600 dead on the field. This victory dispersed the enemy, and had also the effect of checking and turning back the additional hostile bodies that were in motion to concentrate on Nuwabgunge. The defeated enemy had fled in different directions—to Gonda, to Fyzabad, to Sultanpore, and so on. Hope Grant followed towards Fyzabad, and at the same time sent a column towards Sultanpore. On his approach to Fyzabad the enemy who were besieging Rajah Maun Singh in his fort of Shahgunge close by dispersed and disappeared; and Maun Singh being thus relieved, Hope Grant had then to turn to the right to support the force at Sultanpore. Here occurred the last real combat in the heat of that summer. The enemy were in considerable strength, 14,000 men with fifteen guns, but the difficulty to be overcome was the passage of the Goomtee, which had to be crossed, as they were on its right bank. This operation occupied from August 25th to 27th, but at last it was effected, and the battle came off on the evening of the 28th. The enemy were the assailant, but they were checked in their attack, then driven back, and finally put to flight, leaving Sultanpore in Hope Grant's possession.

During the next six weeks the operations were desultory and isolated; being directed chiefly to clearing and strengthening the posts we had already seized and meant to use as the starting-point for the cold-weather movements.

The enemy in Oude now consisted mainly of the Talookdaree troops; followers of such chiefs and leaders as Beni Madho, the Rajah of Ameythee, Hunwunt Singh, and the like. Sir Colin determined to reserve his real attack on them till the winter, and meanwhile, to save his men as much as possible from further exposure during the trying heat and malarious rainy season. The mutineer Sepoys who had belonged to the two northern gatherings had now in great part disappeared and dispersed. Their cause was gone, and they had to make the best of their plight.

But the Mussulman fanatics, and the adherents of the Oude Durbar, and of the Nana, were still in force. Moreover, the whole country population of the province was in dogged rebellion, and had to be subdued; and Sir Colin was planning to effect this during the coming winter.

CHAPTER II

FINAL WINTER CAMPAIGN

SIR COLIN, then, had determined that, during the coming cold weather, the Province of Oude should be thoroughly subjugated. The general outline of his scheme was this. Oude was bordered on the west by Rohilkund, and on the east by the Azimgurh districts, which had been already reduced to submission, and were held in force by our troops. The Gogra, running through the province somewhat parallel to the Ganges, divided it into two parts, the southward part being itself subdivided into two by the line of road that ran from Cawnpore to Lucknow and onwards. Each of these three parts was to form a separate theatre of operations. The two to the south of the Gogra were to be attacked first, and simultaneously; and the enemy in them that were not crushed were to be driven into the district north of the Gogra, which would thus form the final seat of operations.

In the two theatres south of the Gogra, Sir Colin had three lines of troops with which to operate. On the west was the Rohilkund line; on the east was the Azimgurh line; and in the middle was the Cawnpore and Lucknow line, with Lucknow as the great centre of all. The troops in the two outer lines were to advance inwards, beginning at their southern ends, and so gradually edge the enemy off to the north, and then drive them across the Gogra. The middle line at the south end was held by Evelegh, who was to operate to the east or west according to the exigencies of the occasion.

Now the region north of the Gogra, lying between it and the Nepaulese Himalayas, into which the enemy were to be driven, is a triangle; with its apex at the west and its base at the east, where the space is wide and the mountains are distant from the river. As the mountains run westwards, they incline towards the river, till at length they meet it at its debouchure, forming the apex of the triangle. Sir Colin's plan, in this final part of the war, was to guard the Gogra strongly so as to prevent any slipping back of the enemy into the southern districts; and then, having formed a line, so to speak, at the base of the triangle on the east, to sweep upwards through the narrowing districts, forcing back the enemy before him till they should be dislodged, or captured, or driven into Nepaul.

Further, in the eastern of the two southern parts, Sir Colin had to deal with a crowd of large jungle forts, and with the clansmen of the district; he therefore determined to hem these in and coerce them locally as much as possible. So the lines from Lucknow round by the Gogra to Fyzabad, and along the Goomtee were very strongly held; and, in attacking any fort, he designed to concentrate on and around it, so as to make escape almost hopeless, and lead, if possible, to its surrender without fighting. Afterwards, as he drove the enemy before him, and captured their towns and positions, he proposed to occupy them with police, and so re-establish civil administration.

In October the operations began; and first of all in the western district south of the Gogra. For here the ball was opened, not by the British but by the rebels. The enemy collected in force, 12,000 men with twelve guns, and marched on our post at Sandeela in the heart of that district, on October 3rd. On the 6th, its garrison, which had shut itself up in the fort, was relieved by a small party under Major Maynard, which forced the enemy off for some four miles; and then, on the 8th, Brigadier Barker with a strong brigade arrived from Lucknow. Barker, after a fierce fight in which he lost eighty-two men killed and wounded, defeated the enemy thoroughly; and a few days afterwards he turned the tables, attacking and taking their fort of Birwah.

Meanwhile our movement inward into that part of Oude from the Rohilkund side began on the 18th. Under the orders of General Seaton, who kept watch over Rohilkund itself, two columns penetrated Oude; one under Colonel Hall from Furruckabad at the south end, towards Roya and Sandeela; the other under Brigadier Troup from Shahjehanpore, further north, towards Seetapore.

While Hall advanced from the west, Evelegh cleared the ground along the Ganges from the south end of the middle line up to Sandeela. Then Barker, co-operating with Hall, captured Roya on October 28th; and thus the south part of that western theatre was cleared of the enemy, and held by our own police; while the Ganges became free for navigation.

Brigadier Troup, on the north, when desiring to move from Shahjehanpore on Seetapore, found that he had first to deal with the Rohilla chief, Khan Ali Khan; and began by defeating him and driving him across the Gogra. Having thus gained the clear command of that frontier, at the extreme west of Oude, he then crossed the boundary into Oude, and took the fort of Mithoolee.

In the next month, November, Brigadier Barker advanced *northwards* from Sandeela, clearing the country right and left, and at the end of the month secured Khyrabad and Biswah; leaving, however, a gap on the Lucknow side, though nearing Troup on the other flank. To co-operate with him, Brigadier Troup, after capturing Mithoolee, also moved northwards in advance of his left, driving the enemy before him to Aligunge, near the Gogra, across which most of them were forced after a sharp action on the 17th. Then he turned to his right and marched along the right bank of the Gogra, and reaching Biswah on December 2nd, effected his junction with Barker.

At this time Evelegh, in the middle line, had been directed to operate on the north-west of Lucknow, to fill up the gap between Lucknow and the site of Barker's operations. In doing this he took the fort of Oomeria, on December 2nd.

So that now all that western district had been subdued, and all its rebel troops, with one exception, driven across the Gogra by Barker's forward and Troup's flank movement. That exception was that Prince Feroze Shah, when being hemmed in on the Gogra near Biswah, escaped past and between our troops with some 1,500 men, and doubling back south by Sandeela to the Ganges, crossed it and then the Jumna, and finally joined the Central India rebel army; so disappearing from the scene in Oude.

Thus was the western district cleared and subdued by the beginning of December; and I now turn to the contemporary operations in the eastern district. These were conducted under the personal guidance of Sir Colin Campbell.

Before they were begun, our troops held in force the line from Sultanpore *viâ* Pertabgurh to Allahabad; and also from Sultanpore north to Fyzabad; but, since it was essential to prevent any opportunity for the enemy to escape eastwards across the Sultanpore-Fyzabad line into the Azimgurh districts, Sir Colin began his operations by strengthening the Sultanpore position, and detaching Hope Grant to his eastward flank to co-operate with a column which he directed to advance under Colonel Kelly from Azimgurh into Oude. This Colonel Kelly did, driving the enemy before him, and securing Akbarpore and then Tanda; near which he halted on October 30th, to watch and guard that flank during the ensuing operations.

The flank within which he wished to hem in the enemy being thus provided for, Sir Colin's first step in his direct operations westwards was to send forward a brigade under Wetherall towards Rampore Kussia, the stronghold of the Khanpooria clan, and there to co-operate with Hope Grant in capturing it. But Wetherall did not wait for that co-operation, and finding the weak point of the fort in an almost impregnable triple circle of defences, attacked and stormed it on November 3rd, with a loss of eighty men.

Continuing westwards, the next point to be attacked was Ameythee, a very strongly fortified position belonging to its powerful chief, the Rajah Lal Madho Singh, who had been conspicuously friendly at the outbreak, and instrumental in aiding English families and escorting them into security. To operate against this fort three columns concentrated on it—on its east, Pinckney's (Sir Colin with it) from Pertabgurh; on its south, Wetherall's from Rampore Kussia; and on its north-west, Hope Grant's. While thus concentrating, Sir Colin summoned the Rajah to surrender, which he did eventually on November 10th; not, however, till he had seen, from the strength of the attack by which he was menaced, that resistance was hopeless. But though he surrendered personally, most of the garrison, some 4,000 men, of whom 1,500 were Sepoys, had evacuated the fort and escaped during the night.

The next move, still westwards of course, was against Shunkerpore, the stronghold of its chief, Beni Madho. The three columns that had taken Ameythee were to concentrate on it on its north, east, and south; while Evelegh's brigade from Poorwa on the Lucknow-Cawnpore line was to advance on it from the west. But the latter was delayed by the resistance he met with on the way. As with Ameythee, so Sir Colin summoned Beni Madho to surrender. The fort was a huge one, some eight miles in circumference, but its defences were incomplete and full of gaps; and Beni Madho, who was a soldier of ability, knew he could not hold it. He replied accordingly that he would evacuate the fort, but would not surrender personally, holding himself a subject of the Nuwab of Oude, and not of the British Government. So he and his followers, said to be 15,000 men, with several guns, marched out of the fort on the night of the 15th, taking their route to the west towards Doondea Khera. On their way, however, they were met by Evelegh on the 17th, and defeated with the loss of three guns, though their escape westwards was not averted.

On becoming, next morning, aware of Beni Madho's flight, Sir Colin sent off (1) Wetherall's brigade, now Taylor's, towards Fyzabad, to prevent his circling round to the east, and to keep that line secure; and (2) Hope Grant to Roy Bareilly and Jugdespore, to its north, to get into more immediate contact with Beni Madho, if he should be trying to escape in that direction. After leaving a detachment to destroy the fort, Sir Colin himself followed on to Roy Bareilly with Pinckney's Brigade to effect a junction with Evelegh. On the 19th, he heard of the successful combat of the 17th, and gathered that Beni Madho had been effectually kept to the south between Doondea Khera and the Ganges. To hem him in, he continued his march westwards parallel to the Ganges, up to Buchraon, between Doondea Khera and the river. There he turned, on the 21st, to his left, and bore down on Beni Madho on the morning of the 24th. He found the opposing force drawn up in line of battle, with its back to the river, and its front protected by a jungle of thorny scrub, which had been filled with skirmishers. Sir Colin advanced against Beni Madho in line; infantry in the centre, cavalry on the flanks, guns between the infantry and cavalry, and the whole preceded by skirmishers. These last forced the opposing skirmishers back through the jungle; and on the latter emerging from it defeated, the enemy's entire line broke and fled along the banks of the river, without ours having to come into action at all. Beni Madho escaped along the river-bank; then turned and fled north; and eluding the several columns that met but only checked his progress, he crossed first the Goomtee and then the Gogra.

Meanwhile the troops that had been all along left on the Lucknow-Fyzabad line had tackled and defeated all the local gatherings, and gradually driven them all to the north of the Gogra; including the Begum, Mummoo Khan, Nirput Singh, the Nana and the rebels that followed them. Thus by the end of the month, the eastern district of Oude south of the Gogra had been cleared of the enemy, and police posts and civil administration established; while the precisely similar measures, already described, were being carried out in the western district.

And now the last part of the programme, the finale, the subjugation or expulsion of the enemy in the triangular tract on the left of the Gogra, had to be carried out. A necessary preliminary to this end was the construction of a bridge at Fyzabad, the point on which the line that had to sweep up the district must turn. This had been effected by the strenuous exertions of Lothian Nicholson R.E., with the support of the Fyzabad garrison, against the persistent fire and opposition of the enemy on the opposite bank. These were under the command partly of the ex-Amil Mehndee Hussun, and partly of the Gonda Rajah; who, as shown in the description of the province, was the recognized head of the federation of the whole of the Rajpoot clans on the left of the Gogra. The arrival of Taylor's Brigade (from Shunkerpore), and afterwards of Hope Grant's column, enabled action to begin at once. And so on November 25th, Hope Grant had crossed the bridge, had attacked and routed the Gonda Rajah's and Mehndee Hussun's following, and had thus secured the means for starting the required movements and operations.

Here Hope Grant remained till about December 6th, clearing the line across the districts to the hills as well as he could, capturing Bunkussia and other forts belonging to the Gonda Rajah and other chiefs, and awaiting the arrival of a column from Goruckpore under Rowcroft which was to take part in the final operations.

After defeating Beni Madho, Sir Colin had returned to Lucknow; and now on December 5th he started thence with a very strong column, an infantry division, a cavalry brigade, and some fourteen guns, en route to Fyzabad *viâ* Nuwabgunge Barabankee. But on reaching this latter point, he heard that the enemy under Beni Madho were encamped at (another) Nuwabgunge, on the other side of the Gogra, close at hand, at its passage at Byram Ghaut; and were holding the fort of Bithoorlee, and threatening to recross the river southwards. So Sir Colin halted to protect that passage, and sent orders to Hope Grant to advance (up the left bank of the Gogra) to Secrora, which lay on the east, close to Bithoorlee. This movement led to the enemy's evacuation of the position they were occupying; and accordingly leaving a sufficient force to hold the Byram Ghaut and construct a bridge there, Sir Colin proceeded with the rest of his column to Fyzabad.

On the 14th the active operations began. Sir Colin's column advanced from Fyzabad to Secrora; Rowcroft's column, which had come up on the right, was directed northward across the Raptee, and then turned to the left to Toolseepore, whither also Hope Grant was detached to co-operate with him; while Evelegh's brigade followed in the rear, as a reserve, and to stop any doubling back of the enemy.

Rowcroft on the right then advanced against Toolseepore, captured it, and was there joined by Hope Grant, whose cavalry prevented the enemy doubling back. From this point they instead drove them steadily forward towards Bhinga, till at length, in the first days of January, the insurgents were forced across the frontier and took refuge in Nepaul, leaving all their guns in Hope Grant's possession.

Meanwhile the main column under Sir Colin had advanced from Secrora on December 15th against Baraitch, where the Begum and the Nana were, with the troops that still adhered to them. It reached Baraitch, which the enemy evacuated on its approach, retreating towards Nanpara and Pudnaha. From Baraitch a force had to be detached under Colonel Christie to move close up the left bank of the Gogra, to aid our posts on the other bank in preventing its re-passage by the enemy with whom it had a smart action on December 23rd. Sir Colin was somewhat delayed in his advance from Baraitch, partly from having to wait till Hope Grant came sufficiently forward on his flank, and partly to enable the police arrangements to be properly organized; on the 23rd, however, he made his advance towards Nanpara. On arriving there he found it deserted; but the enemy were said to be at Burgidia, a short distance ahead, and he moved on it on the 26th. Finding them drawn up for action, he formed up his troops on their front, and then suddenly moving on their left, he attacked them on that flank; on which they fled precipitately, abandoning their guns. Next day, December 27th, the force advanced on the neighbouring fort of Musjidia, which was shelled for three hours, and was then found to be abandoned. These forts were all in a corner or neck of the triangle in which the space between the river and the mountains was of the narrowest.

During the 28th and 29th, the enemy were being pressed up further and further towards the hills into the narrow space where the Raptee debouches from the mountains and reaches the plains; till it became known that they were massed at a spot called Bankee, and meant to make a last stand there. Their position was at the edge of forest ground; Sir Colin moved his force forward during the night, attacking them in the early morning with his horse artillery and cavalry, and then with skirmishers. The enemy never made any attempt at a resolute stand, but kept retiring before the skirmishers, who with the guns and cavalry advanced following them up. At length they were forced back from the jungle into more open ground with the Raptee behind them. Thereupon the 7th Hussars and 1st Punjab Cavalry charged them, driving them headlong into and across the Raptee. With this episode in the last day of December 1858 ended the long-sustained war in Oude, and with the birth of 1859, peace was restored to the land.

No one will be inclined to dispute the thoroughness of Lord Clyde's work in this final winter campaign, and his subjugation of Oude. But the strength of the forces now at his disposal was enormous; and the consequent facilities for carrying his work into effect made the task easy. Not only had he then some 80,000 English troops under his command, but by this time the Punjab levies alone are said to have rivalled them in numbers; and no ordinary local gathering was attacked without the force employed being as large as that which had undertaken the siege of Delhi or the succour of Lucknow. There was no such skill or hardihood, no such generalship involved, no such dread inspired in the enemy, as had enabled Havelock to confront the armies of Oude, and to face the dangers by which he was surrounded, with less than 1000 men available for line of battle.

In this last campaign also the contest was chiefly with the Talookdars and their followers; and the trouble they now gave, and the hostility they showed, may be fairly gauged by the force we had to use against them. Comparing this with the fact that Havelock was never harassed by them at all, it seems to be certain beyond all dispute that they at the earlier period held positively aloof from all hostility; and that the allegations on which they were adjudicated rebels, and deprived of their property by the Confiscation Decree, were virtually groundless. Keenly must Lord Clyde have felt the blunder involved, and the blindness of the Government to the consequences that were to result from it.

As a fitting conclusion to this narrative, I venture to contrast the beginning and the ending of the struggle in Oude.

In the one case, Henry Lawrence's thorough knowledge, sound instincts, and statesmanlike action minimized local animosity; while his wise precautions, resolute attitude, and bold measures enabled him to prepare the Residency position for an effective defence by a mere handful of men, and to hold back the rebel army of Oude from joining at Delhi, or from operating outside the province.

In the other case, Lord Canning roused the whole province, gratuitously and needlessly, into desperate hostility; while the escape of the rebels and their leaders from Lucknow, under the blundering management of the cavalry, led to a fourfold expansion of the theatre of war; and in order to cope with the situation thus produced, tens of thousands of troops were employed, under Sir Colin's method, where before tens of hundreds would have been expected to achieve the required success.

APPENDICES

APPENDIX I

THE MISGOVERNMENT OF OUDE BEFORE ITS ANNEXATION

EXTRACTS FROM OFFICIAL CORRESPONDENCE

COLONEL SLEEMAN. *June* 21, 1849.

THERE are at this time in Oude 246 forts or strongholds, mounted with 476 pieces of cannon, all held by landholders of the first class, chiefly Rajpoots; not one of these landholders now feels it safe to entrust himself within the camp or cantonments of an officer of the Government. . . . These estates are well cultivated, often in spite of all the best efforts of the contractors and collectors to prevent it, in order to reduce them to obedience. It is not at all uncommon for the landholders to have the land ploughed and the seed drilled in at night by stealth when beleaguered by the king's troops; and this accounts for the land being so much better cultivated than those of other native States in the midst of disorders that would soon make them waste in any other country or state of society.

Maun Singh and Rughbeer Singh have large forces with artillery fighting every day for the possession of the lands which they get by fraud and violence.

GENERAL OUTRAM TO GOVERNMENT OF INDIA. *February* 6, 1855.

Paragraph 2. In the district of Nanpara, the warfare which has continued for three years past, has of late assumed a more serious aspect in consequence of the determined resistance to the king's troops of the partisans of the late Rajah's young son, the rightful heir, who has been dispossessed by the young widow with the aid of the Amil, and the support of the Oude troops.

Nanpara, one of the richest districts in Oude, and yielding the late Rajah £30,000 yearly, is reduced to such a state that it does not now yield anything at all. The whole of the villages are deserted and in ruins.

The rebel son of the Tootseepore Rajah has lately joined the Nanpara malcontents. He quarrelled with and wished to dispossess his father. He, in November last, collected a force of about 2,000 men, attacked the king's troops at Toolseepore, took the king's guns, plundered the treasury, and since then, having united his forces to the rebels of Nanpara, he is devastating the country far and wide.

GENERAL OUTRAM TO GOVERNMENT OF INDIA. *March* 15, 1855.

98. In the same proportion as the landholders are compelled to maintain armed followers to repel over-exactions on the part of the Durbar, are they driven to over-tax their ryots to supply those retainers.

MINUTE BY GOVERNOR-GENERAL. *June* 18, 1855.

10. The revenues are collected without system, by force of arms; the Amils are left to plunder uncontrolled; the ryots have no security from oppression, nor redress for injustice.

20. There is the same perpetual collision between the collectors of the revenue and the landholders. The troops of the collectors, without discipline and with little and uncertain pay, prey upon the people and depopulate the villages they come near. The Zemindars, on being driven from their strongholds or deprived of their estates, become robbers and murderers.

23. The great landholders have absorbed the greater part of the estates of their weaker neighbours, and employed their increasing rents in maintaining large bands of armed followers and building forts and strongholds, which enable them to withstand the demands of the State. Their weaker neighbours were the proprietors or holders of what are called the Khalsa or allodial lands, four-fifths of which have now been absorbed by the great landholders, (who) have taken their lands either by fraud and collusion with the local authorities, or by open violence, in utter contempt of such authorities. These landholders have converted large quantities of the most fertile lands into jungles around their strongholds, some of them extending over spaces from ten to twenty miles long by from four to eight miles wide, into which no man dares to enter without their permission.

The surface of Oude, with the exception of the belts of jungle above described, is well cultivated, and the soil is richer than in any of our own districts.

APPENDIX II

BRITISH RESPONSIBILITY FOR THE MISGOVERNMENT

EXTRACTS FROM OFFICIAL CORRESPONDENCE

GOVERNOR-GENERAL TO KING OF OUDE. *February* 4, 1855.

THE British Government, influenced by the obligation which many years ago it took upon itself in relation to the people of Oude, can no longer lend its countenance and support to a Government whose existence is the fruitful source of misrule, oppression, and misery to all who live under its control.

The other, and not less important obligation of the treaty, the stipulation, namely, whereby his Excellency bound the sovereigns of Oude to conform ever to the counsels of the British Government, and to establish such a system of administration as should secure the lives and property of his subjects, and be conducive to their prosperity, has from that day to this been utterly and systematically set at nought. The misgovernment of the country continued unabated; the landholders were exposed to the habitual extortions of the farmers of the revenue; the farmers of the revenue were authorized to levy their demands by the most violent and oppressive means; there was no confidence in the integrity of the Government, no security that the fruits of honest industry, whether commercial or agricultural, would be protected, and no assurance whatever that the wrongs and grievances of the people would be, even tardily, redressed.

If the Governor-General permits the continuance of any flagrant system of misgovernment, which by treaty he is empowered to correct, he becomes the participator in abuses which it is his duty to repress. And in this case, no ruler of Oude can expect the Governor-General to incur a responsibility so repugnant to the principles of the British Government, and so odious to the feelings of the British people.

GOVERNOR-GENERAL'S MINUTE. *June* 18, 1855.

47. It is by these aids alone (the countenance of the Government of India and the presence of its troops in his dominions) that the sovereigns of Oude have been enabled for more than half a century to persist in their course of oppression and misrule. . . . Secure of the safety of his person—secure of the stability of his throne—each successive ruler has passed his lifetime careful for nothing but the gratification of his individual passion. . . . Were it not for the support which the Government of India is known to be bound to afford the king against all domestic as well as foreign enemies, were it not for the constant presence of British troops at Lucknow, the people of Oude would speedily work their own deliverance, and would impose upon their ruler that effectual check of general revolt by which Eastern rulers are best controlled. . . . If our troops were withdrawn from Oude, the landholders would, in one month, march over it all and pillage the capital of Lucknow.

APPENDIX III

ON THE LOYALTY OF THE NUWABS OF OUDE

EXTRACTS FROM OFFICIAL CORRESPONDENCE

GENERAL OUTRAM TO GOVERNOR OF INDIA. *March* 15, 1855.

24. I BELIEVE no native sovereigns in India have been better disposed towards the British Government than they (the kings of Oude) have been, or have, in times of difficulty, rendered aid to the extent of their ability with more cordiality or cheerfulness.

MINUTE BY GOVERNOR-GENERAL. *June* 18, 1855.

58. The rulers of Oude . . . . have ever been faithful and true in their adherence to the British power. No wavering friendship has ever been laid to their charge. They have long ackowledged our power, submitted without a murmur to our supremacy, and aided us as best they could in the hour of our utmost need.

NOTE A. OF GENERAL LOW'S MINUTE OF AUGUST 15, 1855.

So much has been published in newspapers respecting real and alleged misrule in Oude during the last thirty years, with no one to write on the opposite side and explain misstatements; and it is, moreover, so frequent a habit on the part of many of my countrymen who have never sojourned in native States, to lay the blame of all acts of violence that may occur in those States on the individual native ruler at the head of it; that it has occasionally happened, to my positive knowledge, that the kings of Oude have been spoken of in

English society as merciless tyrants over their own subjects, and as men who had no feeling of gratitude for the protection or the forbearance of the British Government. Now, that sort of language is positively untrue, as regards every one of the last five kings. They have sadly mismanaged their own affairs, I admit; and I also admit fully that it has become quite necessary to deprive them of all political power, but their general conduct towards us, both as useful public allies of our Government, and as individual princes conducting business in a regular, attentive, courteous, and friendly manner with our public functionaries, has been unusually meritorious and praiseworthy; and we have gained so many solid advantages from that conduct on the part of those kings, that, in my opinion, the present king (if he shall sign the treaty we propose to him), and his heirs and successors after him, are well entitled to most liberal treatment in a pecuniary point of view, after we shall have deprived them of the power, and dignity, and freedom, and wealth which heretofore have belonged to their position as sovereigns of Oude.

It is not only that the kings of Oude have never been hostile to us in their proceedings, and never intrigued against us in any way; they have abstained from every kind of communication with other native potentates, except openly, and through the medium of the British Resident; and during our wars against our enemies they have constantly proved to be *really active* and *most useful* allies to us; they have, again and again, forwarded large supplies of grain or cattle, etc., to our armies, with an alacrity that could not be exceeded by our own British Chiefs of Provinces; and during our wars against the Nepaulese and Burmese, the King of Oude lent us *very* large sums of money—no less than *three* crores of rupees—when we were extremely in want of it, and could not procure it elsewhere; and even so late as in 1842, the grandfather of the present king supplied us with fourteen lakhs of rupees, and his son (the father of the present king) supplied us with thirty-two lakhs of rupees, which were of very great use indeed to Lord Ellenborough's Government, in enabling him to push on and equip General Pollock's army, to retrieve our disasters in Afghanistan.

APPENDIX IV

ALTERNATIVES OF TREATMENT OF OUDE AND ITS DYNASTY ON TAKING OVER ITS GOVERNMENT

MINUTE OF GOVERNOR-GENERAL. *June* 18, 1855.

57. THERE are four modes in which the interposition of the Supreme Government may be proposed—

1st. The king may be required to abdicate the sovereign powers he has abused, and to consent to the incorporation of Oude with the territories of the British Crown.

2nd. He may be permitted to retain his royal titles and position, but may be required to vest the whole civil and military administration of his kingdom in the Government of the East India Company for ever.

3rd. Or for a time only.

4th. He may be invited to place the management of the country in the hands of the Resident, to be carried on by the officers of the king, aided by selected British officers.

MINUTE OF SIR BARNES PEACOCK. *August* 22, 1855.

I would not place the residue of the revenue (of Oude) at the disposal of the East India Company, but would leave it to be disposed of entirely for the benefit of the people of the province.

APPENDIX V

REASONS AND ARTICLES OF THE DRAFT TREATY PROPOSED TO THE NUWAB, FEBRUARY 1856

REASONS.—Whereas in the year 1801, a treaty was concluded between the East India Company and his Excellency the Nuwab Vizier Saadut Ali Khan Bahadur, and whereas the 6th Article of the said treaty requires that the ruler of Oude, always advising with and acting in conformity to the counsel of the officers of the Honourable Company, shall establish in his reserved dominions such a system of administration, to be carried into effect by his own officers, as shall be conducive to the prosperity of his subjects, and be calculated to secure the lives and property of the inhabitants; and whereas the infraction of this essential engagement of the treaty by successive rulers of Oude has been continued and notorious; and whereas its long toleration of such infraction of the treaty on the part of the rulers of Oude has exposed the British Government to the reproach of having failed to fulfil the obligations it assumed towards the people of that country; and whereas it has now become the imperative duty of the British Government to take effectual measures for securing permanently to the people of Oude such a system of just and beneficent administration as the Treaty of 1801 was intended but has failed to provide.

ARTICLES (summary)—

I. The Honourable East India Company takes over sole and exclusive administration of Oude, with full and exclusive right to its revenues, and engages to provide for the due improvement of the province.

II. His Majesty and his heirs male in continual succession shall retain sovereign title of King of Oude.

III. And shall be treated with corresponding honour.

IV. And shall have full jurisdiction in his palace and park at Lucknow.

V. Shall receive twelve [1] lakhs per annum, and also three lakhs more for his palace guard.

VI. The Honourable East India Company takes upon itself maintenance of all collateral members of the Royal Family—heretofore provided for by his Majesty.

[1] Open to increase by three lakhs if desired.

APPENDIX VI

PROCLAMATION TO THE PEOPLE OF OUDE ON ITS ANNEXATION. FEBRUARY 1856

By a treaty concluded in the year 1801, the Honourable East India Company engaged to protect the Sovereign of Oude against every foreign and domestic enemy, while the Sovereign of Oude, upon his part, bound himself to establish "such a system of administration, to be carried into effect by his own officers, as should be conducive to the prosperity of his subjects, and calculated to secure the lives and property of the inhabitants." The obligations which the treaty imposed upon the Honourable East India Company have been observed by it for more than half a century, faithfully, constantly, and completely.

In all that time, though the British Government has itself been engaged in frequent wars, no foreign foe has ever set his foot on the soil of Oude; no rebellion has ever threatened the stability of its throne; British troops have been stationed in close promixity to the king's person, and their aid has never been withheld whenever his power was wrongfully defied.

On the other hand, one chief and vital stipulation of the treaty has been wholly disregarded by every successive ruler of Oude, and the pledge which was given for the establishment of such a system of administration as should secure the lives and property of the people of Oude, and be conducive to their prosperity, has, from first to last, been deliberately and systematically violated.

By reason of this violation of the compact made, the British Government might, long since, have justly declared the treaty void, and might have withdrawn its protection from the rulers of Oude. But it has hitherto been reluctant to have recourse to measures which would be fatal to the power and authority of a royal race who, whatever their faults towards their own subjects, have ever been faithful and true to their friendship with the English nation.

Nevertheless, the British Government has not failed to labour, during all that time, earnestly and perseveringly, for the deliverance of the people of Oude from the grievous oppression and misrule under which they have suffered.

Many years have passed since the Governor-General, Lord William Bentinck, perceiving that every previous endeavour to ameliorate the condition of the people of Oude had been thwarted or evaded, made formal declaration to the court of Lucknow, that it would become necessary that he should proceed to assume the direct management of the Oude territories.

The words and the menace which were then employed by Lord William Bentinck were, eight years ago, repeated in person by Lord Hardinge to the king. The sovereign of Oude was, on that day, solemnly bid remember that, whatever might now happen, "it would be manifest to all the world" that he "had received a friendly and timely warning."

But the friendly intentions of the British Government have been wholly defeated by the obstinacy, or incapacity, or apathy of the viziers and kings of Oude. Disinterested counsel and indignant censure, alternating, through more than fifty years, with repeated warning, remonstrance, and threats, have all proved ineffectual and vain.

The chief condition of the treaty remains unfulfilled, the promises of the king rest unperformed, and the people of Oude are still the victims of incompetency, corruption, and tyranny, without remedy or hope of relief. It is notorious throughout the land that the king, like most of his predecessors, takes no real share in the direction of public affairs.

The powers of government throughout his dominions are for the most part abandoned to worthless favourites of the court, or to violent and corrupt men, unfit for their duties and unworthy of trust.

The collectors of the revenue hold sway over their districts with uncontrolled authority, extorting the utmost payment from the people, without reference to past or present engagements.

The king's troops, with rare exceptions undisciplined and disorganized, and defrauded of their pay by those to whom it is entrusted, are permitted to plunder the villages for their own support, so that they have become a lasting scourge to the country they are employed to protect.

Gangs of freebooters infest the districts. Law and justice are unknown. Armed violence and bloodshed are daily events: and life and property are nowhere secure for an hour.

The time has come when the British Government can no longer tolerate in Oude these evils and abuses, which its position under the treaty serves indirectly to sustain, or continue to the sovereign that protection which alone upholds the power whereby such evils are inflicted.

Fifty years of sad experience have proved that the treaty of 1801 has wholly failed to secure the happiness and prosperity of Oude, and have conclusively shown that no effectual security can be had for the release of the people of that country from the grievous oppression they have long endured, unless the exclusive administration of the territories of Oude shall be permanently transferred to the British Government.

To that end it has been declared, by the special authority and consent of the Honourable Court of Directors, that the treaty of 1801, disregarded and violated by each succeeding sovereign of Oude, is henceforth wholly null and void.

His Majesty Wajid Alee Shah was invited to enter into a new engagement whereby the government of the territories of Oude should be vested, exclusively and for ever, in the Honourable East India Company; while ample provision should be made for the dignity, affluence, and honour of the king and of his family.

But his Majesty the King refused to enter into the amicable agreement which was offered for his acceptance.

Inasmuch, then, as his Majesty Wajid Alee Shah, in common with all his predecessors, has refused or evaded, or neglected to fulfil the obligations of the treaty of 1801, whereby he was bound to establish within his dominions such a system of administration as should be conducive to the prosperity and happiness of his subjects; and inasmuch as the treaty he thereby violated has been declared to be null and void; and inasmuch as his Majesty has refused to enter into other agreements which were offered to him in lieu of such treaty; and inasmuch as the terms of that treaty, if it had been still maintained in force, forbade the employment of British officers in Oude, without which no efficient system of administration could be established there, it is manifest to all that the British Government had but one alternative before it.

Either it must altogether desert the people of Oude, and deliver them up helpless to oppression and tyranny, which acting under the restriction of the treaty it has already too long appeared to countenance; or it must put forth its own great power on behalf of a people for whose happiness it, more than fifty years ago, engaged to interpose, and must at once assume to itself the exclusive and permanent administration of the territories of Oude.

The British Government has had no hesitation in choosing the latter alternative.

Wherefore, proclamation is hereby made that the Government of the territories of Oude is henceforth vested, exclusively and for ever, in the Honourable East India Company.

All Amils, Nazims, Chuckledars, and other servants of the Durbar; all officers, civil and military; the soldiers of the State; and all the inhabitants of Oude, are required to surrender, henceforth, implicit and exclusive obedience to the officers of the British Government.

If any officer of the Durbar—Jageerdar, Zemindar, or other person—shall refuse to render such obedience, if he shall withhold the payment of revenue, or shall otherwise dispute or defy the authority of the British Government, he shall be declared a rebel, his person shall be seized, and his jageers or lands shall be confiscated to the State.

To those who shall, immediately and quietly, submit themselves to the authority of the British Government, whether Amils or public officers, Jageerdars, Zemindars, or other inhabitants of Oude, full assurance is hereby given of protection, consideration, and favour.

The revenue of the districts shall be determined on a fair and settled basis.

The gradual improvement of the Oude territories shall be steadily pursued.

Justice shall be measured out with an equal hand.

Protection shall be given to life and property; and every man shall enjoy, henceforth, his just rights, without fear of molestation.

APPENDIX VII

ON THE FEELING OF OUDE TO THE ENGLISH BEFORE ANNEXATION

MINUTE OF THE GOVERNOR-GENERAL. *June* 18, 1855.

27. THOUGH the British Resident has never been able to secure any substantial and permanent reform in the administration of the Oude Government, he sometimes interposes successfully in individual cases, to relieve suffering and secure redress for wrongs: and the people see that he interferes for no other purposes. . . . The British character is, in consequence of these efforts made by the Resident to secure their protection and redress, respected in the remotest jungles and villages in Oude, and there is no part of India where a European gentleman is received among the people of all classes with more of kindness and of courtesy than in Oude. He is treated with the same respect and courtesy in the most crowded streets of the populous city of Lucknow.

APPENDIX VIII

CONCILIATORY TREATMENT OF PEOPLE ENJOINED ON THE ANNEXATION

GOVERNOR-GENERAL'S MINUTE OF JANUARY 15, 1856.

19. IT is natural to expect that dislike will be felt, and that opposition will be made to the intended transfer of the Government of Oude by officers, nobles, and others of the Court of Lucknow whose personal interests, consideration, and official position are likely to be affected by the change. It must obviously be our policy to conciliate all such opposition.

APPENDIX IX

INSTRUCTIONS RESPECTING THE SETTLEMENT OF LAND REVENUE

LETTER FROM THE GOVERNOR OF INDIA TO GENERAL OUTRAM OF FEBRUARY 4, 1856.

128. OBJECTS in view will be facilitated by the early adoption of measures to conciliate the minds of all persons whose interests or personal consideration may be affected by the dissolution of the existing Government, and you are authorized to use your discretion in giving such assurances and holding out such advantages as (without imposing any undue burden upon the State) will tend to reconcile the minds of influential persons in Oude to the intended transfer of the powers of Government, and you will suggest the amount and the mode of provision which you may consider suitable.

9. Every means should be taken to give employment to the natives of the province, and every encouragement should be held out to them to accept it. Many of them will be found able, no doubt, to undertake the duties which devolve upon the highest classes of native functionaries.

125. You will doubtless recognize the necessity of absorbing in the Oude irregular force and the military and district police, as many of the soldiers of the king's army as may be found fit for the duties that will be required of them.

LETTER FROM THE GOVERNOR OF INDIA TO GENERAL OUTRAM OF FEBRUARY 7, 1856.

14. The (District Officers) must at once proceed to the formation of a summary settlement of the land revenue. The settlement should be made, village by village, with the parties actually in possession, but without any recognition, either formal or indirect, of their proprietary rights. The term of the settlement should be fixed for three years certain. You will take care to impress upon the Financial Commissioner, and through him upon all the officers subject to his authority, the great importance of making the assessments moderate, and, so far as that may be practicable, equable.

21. The administration is to be conducted as nearly as possible in conformity with the system which has been introduced in the Punjab.

38. Government is to show its respect for existing rights by confirming and maintaining all grants for which sufficient authority can be produced and established.

APPENDIX X

LORD STANLEY'S DESPATCH OF OCTOBER 13, 1858, REVIEWING THE TREATMENT OF OUDE AFTER THE ANNEXATION.

TO THE RIGHT HONOURABLE THE GOVERNOR-GENERAL OF INDIA IN COUNCIL.

1. MY LORD,

THE last despatch, addressed to your Government, on the general affairs of Oude, was dated on December 10, 1856. At a subsequent period, a despatch, reviewing considerably in detail all the principal incidents of the administration of the province during the Commissionership of Mr. Coverley Jackson, was under preparation by the Court of Directors of the East India Company, when the disturbances in the North-West Province of India, to which the peculiar circumstances of Oude naturally imparted extraordinary local virulence, rendered many of the remarks, which it was proposed to make on the state of the country and the progress of British rule, altogether unsuited to the altered circumstances of the times.

2. The despatch above noted was written under the not unreasonable hope that the favourable appearances, which were indicated in the earlier months of our administration, would, under the progress of time and circumstances, continue to satisfy the expectation of the British Government. But this hope has been disappointed, and it has now become the duty of that Government to consider in what manner, if at all, the disastrous events of 1857, as far as they were connected with Oude, are to be attributed to, or could have been averted by, the measures of your Government, or the acts of the local officers, during the first year of your administration of the Province.

3. In pursuance of this object, I propose to consider firstly, whether there was any failure to give effect to the benevolent intentions declared in your letter of instructions of February 4, 1856, wherein you insist on the duty of adopting measures to conciliate the minds of all persons, whose interests or personal consideration may be affected by the dissolution of the existing Government; and secondly, whether there was on your part, or on that of the chief local functionaries, any neglect of those wise precautions, which it is necessary to observe, during a period of transition from one system of government to another, when men's minds are naturally unsettled by sudden changes, and designing persons are always ready to take advantage of the imperfect organization which necessarily distinguishes the first introduction of a new administrative system and the employment of a new administrative agency.

4. The position of the former Sovereign of Oude, after his country had been proclaimed a British Province, demands the earliest consideration. In their despatch of December 10, 1856, the Court of Directors confirmed your

proposal to settle upon Wajid Ali, the deposed King of Oude, an annual pension of twelve lakhs of rupees, and to leave him in the enjoyment of the Royal Title for the remainder of his life, with jurisdiction within the Palace and Royal Parks of Lucknow. He refused, however, to enter into any arrangement with your Government, and having fixed his residence in Calcutta, he despatched to England a deputation, consisting of his mother, his son (the "Heir-Apparent"), and his brother, General Secundur Hushmut (with a numerous retinue), and instructed them to endeavour to obtain, in this country, the restitution of his alienated territorial possessions. You assured the king that the members of his family would meet with a respectful reception in England, and it appears that everything, which circumstances permitted, was done by the Court of Directors to justify this assurance.

5. Respecting your subsequent proceedings towards the King of Oude, it is matter of notoriety, that shortly after the outbreak in the North-West Province, you caused Wajid Ali and some of his principal dependants to be arrested and detained prisoners in Fort William. Of this measure no just opinion can be derived from the information which you have forwarded to England. You are desired, therefore, to report with as little delay as possible whether the arrest and confinement of the king have been merely measures of precaution, or whether you were moved to this course by any knowledge, or any reasonsable suspicion, of his having been concerned, either directly or indirectly, with the defection of the native army of Bengal, or with the instigation of revolt in Oude, or in any other province of India.

6. On the departure of the king for Calcutta, a large number of members of the Royal Family of Oude necessarily remained in the different palaces of Lucknow. The utmost consideration was due to the position of these unfortunate persons. Any sudden or violent removal from the asylum in which they dwelt, during the existence of the native Government, would have been more than ungenerous ; it would have been cruel. It is stated, however, by the ex-king of Oude, in a memorial which was forwarded to you, in January 1857, that little or no regard was paid to the situation, even of the ladies of his family, who were rudely driven from their former homes, and, although there is doubtless exaggeration in these statements, it is possible that in the arrangements made for the appropriation of the public buildings of Lucknow to administrative purposes, there may not have been in all cases that consideration shown for the helpless position even of the female members of the Royal Family suddenly deprived of their legitimate protector, that would have become a great and generous nation, after such an assertion of its power over a weaker State.

7. It is only in your letter of June 17 last, received since this despatch was commenced, that you have afforded any information respecting the manner in which the Oude Commission dealt with the stipendiaries of the king, of whom there was a large number in Lucknow, including many members of the Royal Family. It now appears that up to the beginning of March 1857, more than twelve months after the annexation of the province, the stipends had not been paid. During that protracted period, therefore, many influential persons must have been reduced to great pecuniary straits, with all the humiliations attendant on such a state. It is difficult to understand what circumstances can have rendered such a delay in the performance of what was one of the first duties of the British Government, after the removal of the native Sovereign, either an unavoidable or a justifiable omission. Whether the stipends were actually paid before the outbreak at Lucknow, does not appear from the papers received, but even if the adjustment had actually taken place, the previous delay was as

conspicuous for its impolicy as for its injustice, and there is little room to doubt that it did much to embitter the feelings of the upper classes against a Government apparently so neglectful of the welfare and the respectability of those whom circumstances had placed under the immediate protection of the State.

8. In one important respect, however, you appear to have given early consideration to the position of the privileged classes. The attention of the Chief Commissioner and of your Government was directed towards the mode of legal procedure to be adopted towards the members and especially towards the ladies of the Royal Family. Laudably desirous of sparing their feelings, the Judicial Commissioner proposed that an authorized list of persons entitled to claim exemption from ordinary processes on the score of their high rank should be prepared, and that all cases in which such persons were concerned should be tried in a Special Court, presided over by the Town Commissioner, right of appeal being had to the Chief Commissioner. On a full consideration, however, of this proposal, you did not think it advisable to establish a Special Court for privileged classes of the community. But, you directed that, instead of issuing ordinary summonses for the appearance of such persons, letters couched in respectful terms should be addressed to all members of the king's family, and transmitted through the assessment agent to the Governor-General when their attendance might be required in your courts.

9. Besides the numerous members of the Royal Family of Oude, the annexation of the province must have grievously affected the interests of a large number of influential persons connected with the Court, and the public departments. In your letter to the Chief Commissioner of January 23, 1856, you observe—"It is natural to expect that dislike will be felt, and that opposition will be made to the intended transfer of the Government of Oude, by officers, nobles, and others at the Court of Lucknow, whose personal interests, considerations, and official opinion, are likely to be affected by the change. It must obviously be our policy to conciliate all such opposition. The Governor-General in Calcutta requires, therefore that you will use your discretion in giving such assurances and holding out such advantages as (without imposing any undue burden upon the State) will tend to reconcile the minds of influential persons in Oude to the intended transfer of the powers of Government;" and in your letter of February 4 of the same year, you again called the attention of the Chief Commissioner to the duty of "reconciling the minds of influential persons in Oude to the intended transfer of the power of Government."

10. But there is little or nothing in the papers before the Council to lead to the belief that the consideration here spoken of has been shown either for the welfare or for the feelings of the particular classes to which you referred. That many persons holding high offices, and deriving large emoluments from their offices in connection with the Court, and some who were charged with official duties at the capital and in the several districts, must have been suddenly deprived both of the wealth and of the influence appertaining to their position, was one of the immediate necessities of the change. The justice, in such a case, of making liberal provision for all who are suddenly deprived of their offices by the introduction of a new system of government, is not more obvious than the policy of the proceeding. The rules, however, laid down for the granting of pensions and gratuities to the servants of the late Government, were of such a character that the schedule you have forwarded contains the name of only one person entitled to receive a considerable pension under them. And it is stated by the Financial Commissioner

that "a very large number of officers not coming within the rules for pension or gratuity have been excluded altogether." There is too much reason, indeed, to fear that great hardship was inflicted upon, and much natural irritation excited among, the old servants of the Oude Government, who saw themselves everywhere superseded by native officials from the older provinces without any prospect of ever recovering the position they had lost, or of receiving just compensation for their losses. And it is a source of surprise and dissatisfaction that the pensions which were awarded to the Oude functionaries under these rules were so tardily adjusted that many must have despaired of receiving them at all; and it is to be feared that a large number of persons were reduced to absolute want by the delay of your officers in examining and reporting upon their claims. The introduction of a new system of government may have demanded the employment to some extent of a different agency from that which you found existing in the province, but the tardiness with which your officers proceeded to afford relief to those whom the change had deprived of the means of subsistence, there is nothing to justify or to excuse.

11. With the disbanded soldiery of the native Oude Government it was also difficult to deal in such a manner as at once to afford just compensation to them for the loss of their means of subsistence, and to prevent their sudden dispersion from becoming a cause of disorder and of danger. Sixty thousand soldiers in the pay of the late native Government were suddenly disbanded, and in the new Oude levies and police battalions you could find employment only for a small proportion of the number. To some part of the remainder you determined to grant pensions and gratuities, and in accordance with instructions contained in your letter of February 4, 1856, to the Chief Commissioner, military committees assembled at the different large stations to investigate the claims of the disbanded soldiers. These claims were fully examined and reported upon, and dealt with in accordance with the 127th paragraph of the above-mentioned letter of instructions. Taking into consideration the large number of men to whom these pensions and gratuities were to be paid, they were, perhaps, fixed upon as liberal a scale as your finances could bear, but they were scarcely of a nature to satisfy men thus suddenly thrown out of employment. Twenty-five years' service was the minimum period qualifying a soldier to receive even a pension equal to only quarter of his pay. All men having served for a shorter period, not less than seven years, were to receive gratuities ranging between three months' and nine months' pay. Under the discretion allowed to the Chief Commissioner, he properly transgressed in some special cases the general rules submitted for his guidance, by granting higher pensions to deserving old officers, than those fixed by your Government; and he brought another class of claimants, not contemplated in these pension rules, under their operation, by conferring small pensions upon men of short service who had been wounded, or otherwise disabled, in Government employ. Other small concessions were made, showing a disposition on the part of the Chief Commissioner to give a liberal interpretation to your instructions. But, on the whole, it is not to be denied that under the operation of these rules, the compensation must, in most cases, have been inadequate to the amount of injury necessarily inflicted upon the military class, as upon Government servants of other descriptions, and that a very large number of persons trained to the use of arms, and habituated to the commission of acts of lawlessness and violence, must have been let loose upon the country, with the means only of temporary subsistence, and with every disposition to become on the first fitting opportunity the enemies of the State which had deprived them of their employment.

12. A question of a different kind was presented to you in the settlement of the landed revenue of the province. The instructions which you issued to the Chief Commissioner in your letter of February 4, were briefly that a summary settlement should be made with existing occupants for three years, and that the question of determining proprietary rights should, during that time, be held in abeyance. Before, however, these summary settlements were made, the duty of realizing the outstanding balances due to the State devolved upon the local Commissioners. In only one instance was the demand resisted. The Rajah of Toolseepore was in arrears to a large amount, and he refused to attend any summons, or to make any arrangements for the payment of the Government dues.

13. Although this great landed proprietor was the only one of the powerful Talookdars who openly resisted the authority of the British Government on your first assumption of the administration of Oude, he was, in all the general features of his condition, a type of his class. He had been long engaged in a struggle against authority, which had exhausted his finances, and thus impoverished he had not the means of meeting his legitimate engagements with the State. He had a large body of armed retainers, who were in arrears of pay, and were therefore levying contributions upon the surrounding villages. He had failed to contract a loan. His personal property was of little value; and there appeared to you to be no means of realizing the Government dues, except by the sequestration of his estate.

14. The measure was approved by the Chief Commissioner, and Mr. Wingfield, the Commissioner of Baraitch, was authorized to carry it out. His great difficulty consisted in the large number of fighting men in the Rajah's pay, whom there was little hope of dispersing while their master was at large. It was determined, therefore, as a preliminary measure, to seize the person of the Rajah; a detachment of troops was placed at Mr. Wingfield's disposal, and he effected, with great vigour and address, the capture of the Rajah, and carried him a prisoner to Bulrampore. Then the armed followers of the Talookdar tendered their submission, and having received gratuities each according to his respective claims, were quietly dismissed. The Toolseepore estate, comprising 1000 villages, was declared to be sequestrated during the period of the summary settlement, and the greatest readiness to obtain leases was shown. "Such," observed Mr. Wingfield, "is the sense of security now felt."

15. It appeared that a difference of opinion existed between the Judicial and the Financial Commissioners regarding the case of this man, the Judicial Commissioner being of opinion that he could not justly be treated as a defaulter. Whatever opinion might be entertained upon this point, it appears that his inability to meet the demands of the new Government arose out of a state of things antecedent to our assumption of the administration. It was the almost necessary result of the misrule which constituted the grounds of that assumption. It would, therefore, have been sounder policy, as it would have been just in principle, to have taken into consideration the circumstances to which we refer, and to have been lenient towards the pecuniary failures of those whom we found on our assumption of the Government to be without the means of meeting their engagements.

16. The information now before me relating to the summary settlement is scarcely sufficient to enable me to pronounce any decided opinion on its merits. In your letter of February 4, 1856, you instructed the Chief Commissioner to direct the different officers under his superintendence, as soon as they had organized provisional establishments, "at once to proceed to the formation of a summary settlement of the land revenue, and simultaneously the revival and

organization of the village police. The settlement," it was added, "should be made village by village, with the parties actually in possession, but without any recognition, either formal or indirect, of their proprietary right. The terms of the settlement should be fixed for three years certain, and it should be added that it will remain in force and binding on those entering into engagements beyond that period, until another settlement, whether summary or regular, shall be made."

17. Having thus explained the nature of the summary settlement, you proceeded, in very proper terms, to impress upon the Chief Commissioner, and through him upon the district officers, "the great importance of making these assessments moderate, in so far as that may be practicable." "And," you added, "you will require him (the Financial Commissioner) to furnish you, as soon as possible, with a brief statement of these summary settlements, in order to enable the Government to arrive at an approximate estimate of the revenue which the province of Oude may be expected ultimately to yield, as well as of that which will be immediately available for purposes of the administration, and the liquidation of other demands, which will be properly chargeable to it." But it does not appear that, up to the time of the outbreak at Lucknow, any statement regarding the summary settlement had been forwarded to your Government.

18. It is to be gathered, however, from certain minutes of the Financial Commissioner, Mr. Gubbins, forwarded by that officer to the Court of Directors, as well as from a letter received from him, that in many parts of the country the assessments were made, in the first instance, at too high a rate, that he ordered their reduction, and that their reductions had been carried out by the district officers, before the outbreak, to the great satisfaction, as it is alleged, of the people.

19. A question not less important than that of the rate of assessment is that of the parties with whom the settlement was made. The general tendency of the instructions issued to the Chief Commissioner in your letter of February 4, was to impress upon the officers of the Oude Commission the expediency of making the settlement as much as possible in accordance with the system which had "brought the North-West Province to a state of unexampled prosperity," and the Commissioners were especially instructed "to improve and consolidate the popular institutions of the country by maintaining the village Coparcenaries, and adapting our proceedings to the predilections of the people, and the local laws to which they were accustomed." And it appears to me, from such information as I have before me in a scattered fragmentary shape, that the revenue officers in Oude, intent upon giving effect to these instructions, and laudably anxious to promote to the utmost the welfare of the great body of the agricultural classes, were not sufficiently regardful of the interests of the great landed proprietors, or aware of the dissatisfaction with which that class in the North-West Province had been inspired by our proceedings there, but did in many instances ignore their acquired rights, and overlooked them altogether in the three years' summary settlement, although unquestionably persons "actually in possession" at the time of the annexation of the country.

20. This was undoubtedly an error. Many of these large landholders may have obtained possession of these holdings by means of violence and of fraud. But the British Government was not responsible for this, and as, by abstaining from summary interference with the existing state of things, you made no constructive promise to prolong it beyond the period of the summary settlement, it would have been better to tolerate for a time the possible injustice

which you found in existence, than, by the introduction of sudden changes, to incur the risk of originating injustice of your own.

21. On a deliberate survey of all the proceedings above noticed, it is impossible to resist the conviction that the intentions of your Government to conciliate all classes of the community were, especially in respect to the most influential classes, frustrated, partly by the circumstances of our position in Oude, partly by the insufficiency of the means prescribed for the settlement of the country, and partly by the remissness of the agents employed by you to give effect to your measures.

22. It was the natural tendency of the introduction of British rule into the Province of Oude to embitter the feelings of these influential classes against the British Government; firstly, the nobility of Oude; secondly, the public functionaries of the native Government; thirdly, the military classes; fourthly, the territorial aristocracy. But much of this bitterness might have been allayed by a more judicious and considerate course of procedure than that which was adopted, and it is with much regret that I find myself compelled to record my opinion that the Oude Commissioner was in the important instances above-noted injuriously precipitate where caution and deliberation were required, and that where promptitude was demanded there was in some instances culpable delay.

23. It is desirable now to examine the precautionary measures to which you resorted to diminish the dangers of any possible opposition which might be offered to the progress of your rule. It was natural that the very peaceable manner in which the Government was suffered to pass out of the hands of the native sovereigns of Oude should have beguiled you into a belief in the perfect security of your position. Confident that the change would be beneficial to the people, you believed that these benefits would be generally appreciated, and that any large display of military force in the country would be a practical denial of your faith in the blessings conferred upon it by the intervention of the paramount State. You therefore considered a single weak regiment, with one battery of artillery, a sufficient European force for the maintenance of tranquillity in Oude. There was no reason at that time to doubt the fidelity of the native army, and it was not unreasonable to believe that the formation of small movable columns, upon the Punjab system, ready to move from different points at a moment's notice, would meet the requirements of the province far more effectually than more cumbrous bodies of troops without the same facility for prompt operations.

24. If there was a probability at that time of the British troops being engaged in internal warfare, it was for the suppression of some possible rebellion on the part of the great landholders of Oude. You were well aware, on first entering upon the administration of the province, that one of the greatest obstacles to its internal tranquillity, under the native Government, had been the occupation by the great Talookdars and other territorial chiefs of numerous fortified places, and the entertainment by them of large bodies of armed retainers; a condition of things which often enabled them to defy the officers of the native Government. It is stated that in September 1856, the number of fortified places held by the great landholders and other influential persons in Oude amounted to 623, of which 351 were in good repair. Although only a small proportion of these was said to have guns mounted in the embrasures, it was known that many more had been thus defended before our assumption of the Government, and that a considerable number of pieces of ordnance had been buried or otherwise concealed, was a probable conjecture, the truth of which subsequent events have confirmed. The ex-

pediency of levelling these forts, or of otherwise rendering them incapable of resistance, at the earliest possible date, was strongly insisted on by the Judicial Commissioner. In the meanwhile, he recommended that a proclamation should be issued requiring the surrender of all guns and military stores, and declaring that the retention of any such munitions of war after a certain date should be pronounced an offence against the State, punishable as a misdemeanour. The Chief Commissioner concurred in this recommendation, and without previously obtaining the sanction of your Government, issued a proclamation demanding the surrender of all the artillery in the possession of individuals, and declaring the retention of any pieces of ordnance or any military stores, after October 1, to be illegal. In obedience to this order a large number of guns were surrendered (the value of the metal being accounted for as so much revenue paid to the State), and it is not stated that the demand gave offence to the Talookdars. That many guns, however, and probably the most serviceable ones, were still retained in concealment, buried in the earth, bricked up in walls, or concealed in the jungle, until brought out after the disorganization of the country by the military revolt, there is much reason to believe.

25. It is certain that the existence of large bodies of armed retainers, in the precarious pay of the great landholders, must have been very hostile to the general peace and tranquillity of the province. It does not appear, except in the case of the Rajah of Toolseepore adverted to above, that the disbandment of these levies had been effected previous to the outbreak of the revolt. Advantageous, however, as it might have been to break up these corps of undisciplined soldiery, simultaneously with the gradual introduction of some measure to facilitate their employment in peaceful pursuits, it is by no means certain that the sudden dispersion of considerable bodies of armed men would not have been a remedy even worse than the disease. In such a state of society, to discharge a soldier is often to make a bandit, and it would be not unreasonable to expect, that upon the first appearance of a general convulsion, the disbanded retainers of the great landholders, either returning to their old masters, or placing themselves under new leaders, would fight upon the side of our enemies with animosity, strengthened by the remembrances of the injury which they considered had been inflicted upon them by the British Government.

26. Still more important even than this was the question which arose regarding the general disarming of the people. This measure was suggested by the Judicial Commissioner, and the Chief Commissioner, though with some qualification, approved the suggestion. On a subject of so much importance, however, he desired to have the largest amount of information. He invited, therefore, an expression of the opinion of the District Commissioners, and they (with one exception) were adverse to the proposal. Colonel Goldney, whose previous experience in Scinde and the Punjab entitled his opinion to be received with particular respect, indicated in a very forcible manner both the difficulties in the way of the accomplishment of such a measure, and the inherent objections to it if accomplished. On a review of all the opinions expressed, and all the arguments advanced, you came rightly to the conclusion that it would not be desirable to attempt a general disarming of the people. In the Governor-General's minute of September 17, 1856, the arguments which then forced themselves upon his mind are recorded at some length. In the then existing circumstances of the times, they were such as naturally suggested themselves to you. The expediency of disarming the people of the Punjab, and the success which attended that measure, furnished in reality no

argument in favour of a similar measure in Oude. In the Punjab, the warlike habits of the people, and the ambitious character and military talent of some of the chiefs, rendered armed demonstrations on a large scale not improbable events, so long as the benevolent intentions of the new Government and the eventual advantages of the change were imperfectly understood by the Sikh nation. That nation had been in arms against us. It had invited the contest by invading our borders, and had many times met the British army with desperate courage in the field. But Oude had become a province of the British empire, not by armed conquest, but by the peaceful, unresisted assertion of the power of the paramount State. You had reason indeed to believe that the great majority of the people were grateful for their liberation from the insecurity necessarily resulting from continued misrule. No rebellious movement against the new Government had taken place, none was anticipated, and it was considered that the personal affrays and acts of individual violence, which had been so frequent under the native Government of Oude, might be gradually suppressed by some extension of the severity of the ordinary penal enactments, such as a law decreeing transportation beyond the seas, a punishment viewed with mysterious horror by dwellers in an inland province.

27. It was impossible, too, to consider the question of the disarming of the population, without some reference to the fact that Oude had long been the principal nursery of the Bengal army. There was, at that time, no reason to believe that the habitual use of arms by the people, from which so large a number of British recruits were drawn, would do otherwise than contribute to the strength and security of the British Indian empire.

28. On a review of all the opinions expressed by the chief functionaries in Oude, and after full consideration in council of all the arguments adduced by the Governor-General, I do not hesitate to declare my opinion that you were justified by the information then before you, in refusing to sanction either the general disarming of the people or the passing, except with local restrictions, of a law against the carrying of arms; and it is at least doubtful whether any attempt to carry out such a measure would have been attended with general success. Even if no opposition had been offered, and from some classes of the population it was to be expected, concealment would have been so general that the offensive powers of the people in any season of general disturbance would have been but little diminished by the attempt. You had not force readily at your disposal to enable you to carry out such a measure as one of military coercion, and as a mere magisterial enactment it would have been evaded or disobeyed.

29. All the circumstances above enumerated being deliberately weighed, it appears that although the local administration did not succeed in carrying out those measures of conciliation towards all classes of the community which your Government had so wisely and so justly urged upon the Oude Commission, no better results would have been attained, if you had endeavoured to secure the tranquillity of the province by mere rigorous repressive measures. However consistent such measures may be with the policy naturally observed towards a conquered country, or one that has been in rebellion, it cannot but be remembered, that inasmuch as the paramount motive for assuming the Government of Oude was the promotion of the happiness of the people, it was especially the duty of the new administration to recognize existing rights, to be tolerant of ancient usages, and to pay regard to the habits and feelings of all classes of the community, however greatly they might be at variance with our own views, and opposed to the just principles of social polity. To succeed in reforming

the habits of a people it is necessary, at the outset, to be tolerant of much evil, and to trust greatly to the efficiency of time, and the growth of moral influence.

30. The first circumstances of British administration in Oude having thus been brought under review, the policy which it behoves you to adopt on the re-establishment of your authority throughout the province demands most deliberate consideration. The despatch of the Court of Directors of May 5 will have made you acquainted with the spirit in which it is desired that you should address yourselves to the great work of pacification, and it is probable that, on some at least of the points to which your attention is now directed, you will have anticipated my instructions.

31. Your future proceedings towards the ex-king of Oude will be regulated by circumstances, with respect to which the Council are at present in uncertainty. But if the seizure and confinement of Wajid Ali were merely measures of precaution, not influenced by any knowledge or reasonable suspicion of his complicity in the hostile movement against the British Government, it may be concluded that you will adhere to the resolutions already announced, to make a liberal provision for the remainder of the king's life. It is not, however, considered desirable, in the altered circumstances of the times, that the British Government should pledge itself to a continuance of the annual stipend of twelve lakhs, or of any fixed amount to the successors of the present king. Recent events have clearly indicated the expediency of leaving the decision upon this point to the Government of the day, which will act in accordance with the knowledge of the new claimant's character and conduct, and the probability of a large command of money becoming in his hands a blessing or a curse to himself and to others.

32. The perpetuation of the kingly title is still more objectionable. On a former occasion the Court of Directors emphatically declared the grounds of their repugnance to the maintenance of such empty titular sovereignties as the kingship of Delhi. And recent unhappy events have strengthened the impression of the impolicy, and in a large sense of the inhumanity, of prolonging the existence of that which, however shadowy and unreal, is so likely to keep alive delusive hopes, to become a focus of intrigue and a rallying-point of sedition; and thus to involve, not only the titular Sovereign himself, but large numbers of his adherents, in irremediable ruin and disgrace. On the death, therefore, of Wajid Ali Shah, whatever provision you may make for, and whatever privileges you may bestow upon, his successors, the titular sovereignty should cease for ever with the life of the present nominal king.

33. The privileges above adverted to it will be necessary to restrict. Although the experience of half a century had clearly indicated, in the case of the titular kings of Delhi, the inconvenience of permitting them, in consideration of their former power and grandeur, to exercise sovereign dominion within the precincts of the Imperial palace, the Court of Directors were still disinclined, on the deposition of the King of Oude, to depart from the considerate and indulgent policy which had been observed towards the sovereigns of the house of Delhi. You were therefore authorized to concede to the titular King of Oude similar jurisdiction within the palace and royal pleasure-grounds of Lucknow. But the events of the last year have painfully demonstrated, that such a privilege may be abused in a manner even beyond the previous conceptions of the most experienced, and that it would be culpable ever again to place in the hands of a pensioned prince, the power of using the asylum afforded him as a shelter for conspirators and a refuge for traitors of the worst kind. Whilst, therefore, it is right that every consideration consistent

with a wise precaution should be shown for the fallen fortunes of the ex-king of Oude, it is incumbent upon the British Government to withhold the privilege which it was formerly willing to grant, of independent jurisdiction within the precincts of the palace, or rather stated bounds, even though it should appear that Wajid Ali is guiltless of all complicity in the rebellious proceedings which have inflicted so much injury on the country.

34. Towards the members of the Royal Family of Oude you will exercise a becoming liberality. In their last despatch on the affairs of the province, the Court of Directors adverted to that part of the treaty originally proposed, in which it is stipulated that "the Company shall take upon itself the maintenance of all collateral members of the Royal Family, for whom provision is now made by the king," and said they left it to your Government to decide what members of the Royal Family shall be supported out of the hereditary grant of twelve lakhs per annum, and what members shall be brought under the provisions of the above-mentioned article. I see no reason for the withdrawal of these instructions, except where members of the Royal Family are clearly identified with the commission or connivance at some outrage upon humanity. I am willing that their claim should be considered with as much liberality as if the tranquillity of Oude had not been disturbed. Simple hostility is not to be regarded as an offence incurring the forfeiture of all claims upon the favourable consideration of the British Government. In this view of the case, you will doubtless be disposed to act with becoming but discriminating liberality towards these unfortunate persons. With such exceptions as are above noted, the members of the Royal Family may be placed in possession of the legitimate stipends which they *bonâ fide* enjoyed under the Government of the late king, with such arrears as may be found to be due to them. The mode of payment, whether from the revenues of the province or from the pension of the king (should he accept it), may be left for future consideration and adjustment.

35. On the re-organization of the administrative agency, greater regard than heretofore ought to be paid to the expediency of employing the natives of the province in all departments of the executive Government. They may not, in all respects, appear to be the best instruments to give effect to a new system of administration; but it is better for a time to submit to this inconvenience, and either to adapt our system at first to the agents at our disposal, or to wait until the agents can adapt themselves to the system, than that we should perpetually incur the reproach of usurping all the offices of the State, and of taking from the inhabitants of the province the bread which they were in the habit of earning and giving it to strangers. And even as regards the efficiency of the administration, it is not certain that the native officials are more corrupt and more oppressive than those who have been transplanted from the older provinces into Oude; and whether the great object of all administration, the happiness of the people, is more likely to be obtained by the employment of expert native agents from the regulation districts, under a numerous body of European superintendents, than by resorting to the agency which was found in use on the annexation of the province.

36. There are few more delicate questions than that with which you have to deal, when you are called upon to decide in what manner to bring those privileged persons who, under an arbitrary native Government, have been exempt from ordinary legal liability, within the pale of the law, in such a manner as to satisfy the requirements of justice without outraging the feelings of individuals accustomed to the enjoyment of peculiar privileges, undesirable as it is to perpetuate or to prolong the existence of privileged classes, springing

from the stock of extinct dynasties. To the persons thus favoured the intended kindness is often practically injurious. Whilst it is an injustice to the community at large, and a source of embarrassment to the Government, there are nevertheless conjunctures in which it may be wise to incur the risk of these more remote inconveniences, for the sake of conciliating not only the influential few, but the more numerous class of persons who have learnt to venerate the ancient houses, with whose fortunes they have been associated, who identify their own honour and importance with that of their superiors, and who look with jealousy and resentment on every measure which has a tendency to degrade the ancestral reputation of the local nobility. In cases where existing prerogatives and privileges can be continued without any direct injury to humanity, they might perhaps be granted to those who were found, on the annexation of the country, in the enjoyment of special privileges, under a distinct understanding, that after death of the person to whom they had been originally granted, they are either absolutely to cease or to be open to reconsideration. You might expediently take into your consideration the system for the adjudication of suits in which members of the privileged classes were concerned, introduced by the Honourable Mr. Elphinstone into the countries conquered from the Peshwah.

37. It appears, however, that the greatest difficulty with which you will have to contend, in your measures for the general pacification of Oude, will result from the large number of people whom you will find, on the re-assertion of your authority, without any means of honest subsistence ; starving men are desperate men. It is probable that many who have been in arms against the British Government have been incited to hostility simply by the hope of recovering the livelihood which they had lost by the annexation of their country. To provide these people with profitable employment would be to disarm them of their enmity against us. But it is impossible to overrate the difficulty of forming any comprehensive scheme, for the direction into peaceful channels of the energies of 100,000 men, many of whom, lawless in their habits before the outbreak of the rebellion, have been rendered doubly so by a year of rapine and disorder.

38. It is probable that the re-organization of the police of the province may afford you a fitting opportunity of providing for a portion of those who, accustomed to military service, have been thrown out of employment by the disbandment of the Oude army. Whether, during the partial restoration of your authority, it would be found safe to employ in such offices the natives of the province, is, however, open to doubt ; brought into contact and communication with their countrymen, many of them still hostile to the British Government, they would be less likely perhaps to remain true to their employers than strangers from another province. It is probable, therefore, that in the first instance you will be compelled to yield to the necessities of the moment, and form the local police corps chiefly from among the natives of other provinces. But this will doubtless suggest to you the expediency of finding similar employment for the natives of Oude in other parts of the country. It will be sound policy thus, as far as possible, to dissolve the material cohesion of hostile facts resulting from family ties and local interests, and to place men beyond the reach of those influences which are most likely to warp them from their allegiance to the British Government.

39. In any schemes for the pacification of the country, the extension of agriculture, will necessarily enter largely into your consideration, and you will perhaps thus be able to provide honourable and profitable employment for many who are now compelled to earn a precarious subsistence by questionable

means. You will doubtless, on the restoration of your authority throughout Oude, find large tracts of uncultivated land, some covered with forests and jungles, the clearance of which might be encouraged by advantageous grants, and when expedient even by advances of money from the public treasury. Your great object will be to raise the hopes of the people of the soil, to induce all classes of the community to identify the complete restoration of British rule with their own personal interests; a judicious expenditure in this direction will, in the end, prove the truest economy.

40. Towards the Talookdars and other great landholders of Oude you have already entered upon a course of policy which it is to be hoped will, by a fuller recognition of their ancient rights, bring them into allegiance to the British Government. It will be necessary to destroy their fortified places, and to clear the jungles surrounding them, which afford even better defences than the walls of their strongholds. But in doing this, it is desirable that you should induce the landholders so to co-operate with you, as to render the destruction of their fortresses as little as possible a cause of offence or a source of humiliation. You will of course exercise a discriminating clemency or severity towards them, graduated in accordance with your knowledge of the part taken by them in the rebellion; but as a general rule I would prescribe oblivion of past offences as the only guarantee of the cordiality of future relations. You will endeavour by wise and conciliatory personal explanations to make the intentions of your Government clearly understood, and not only by the restoration of their ancient rights, but also by liberal remissions or advances, facilitate the agricultural operations, which must have been greatly obstructed by the recent disorganization of the country.

41. To the general disarming of the province (with such exceptions as circumstances may render expedient) you will doubtless address yourself at an early period. You will have earned the right to deal with Oude as a conquered country, and although there is no reason to consider that the general mass of the population has evinced any hostility to British rule, there is more than enough in the circumstances noted in the despatch to indicate the necessary connection of such a measure with the future tranquillity of the province. It is right, however, that you should take into your consideration the propriety of giving to those who surrender their arms within a certain time adequate compensation for such loss of property. This will at the same time prevent the measure from injuriously affecting the well-disposed, and will appeal to the self-interest of the evil-disposed, who, by delaying the surrender of their arms, will not only forfeit their value, but expose them also to the infliction of such punishment as you may decree for disobedience. As has been before observed, the great practical difficulty with which you have to contend in attempting to give effect to a general measure for the disarming of the people, is their disposition to evade the operation of the law by concealing their weapons. There is a natural unwillingness on the part of men of all descriptions to be deprived of their property, and a sword or a matchlock is not less an article of property than a cooking-pot or a drinking-vessel. But men will often sell what they will not give, and although in some cases the desire to retain their arms may not be dependent on the consideration of their money value, there is little doubt that the promise of compensation will greatly increase the facility, and promote the success of the undertaking.

42. But although the only hope of such a pacification of Oude as can be contemplated with any satisfaction is based upon the adoption of these and similar conciliatory measures, it is to be feared that some time must necessarily elapse before you can dispense with the continual display of your military

power. Moral influences are slow of operation, and we can never conciliate the good feelings of a people with such effect as when we are demonstrably able to chastise their hostility. I am assured, however, that you will endeavour so to stimulate the general confidence of all classes, in the benevolent designs of the British Government, as henceforth to render active demonstrations on a large scale events of improbable occurrence.

Yours truly,

STANLEY.

APPENDIX XI

SIR HENRY LAWRENCE'S ESSAY OF 1843, FORECASTING THE EVENTS OF 1857

ASIA has ever been fruitful in revolutions, and can show many a dynasty overthrown by such small bands as, on November 2, 1841, rose against our force at Cabul; and British India can show how timely energy, as at Vellore, Benares, and Bareilly, has put down much more formidable insurrections. . . . Dissensions among our enemies has raised us from the position of commercial factors to be lords over emperors. Without courage and discipline we could not thus have prevailed; but even these would have availed little had the country been united against us, and would now only defer the day of our discomfiture were there anything like a unanimous revolt. The same causes operated for our first success in both India and Afghanistan, and the errors by which we lost the latter may any day deprive us of the former.

Perhaps our great danger arises from the facility with which these conquests have been made—a facility which in both cases has betrayed us into the neglect of all recognized rules for military occupation. Our sway is that of the sword, yet everywhere our military means are insufficient. There is always some essential lacking at the very moment when troops are wanted for immediate service. If stores are ready, they may rot before carriage is forthcoming. If there are muskets, there is no ammunition. If there are infantry there are no muskets for them. In one place we have guns without a man to serve them; in another we have artillerymen standing comparatively idle, because the guns have been left behind.

To come to examples. Is Delhi or Agra, Bareilly or Kurnaul, Benares or Saugor, or, in short, any one of our important military positions better prepared than Cabul was, should 300 men rise to-morrow and seize the town? Take Delhi more especially as a parallel case. At Cabul we had the treasury and one of the commissariat forts in the town; at Delhi we have the magazine and treasury within the walls.

Now suppose that any morning 300 men were to take possession of these. What would follow if the troops in the cantonment (never more than three regiments) were to keep close to their quarters, merely strengthening the palace guards? The palace at Delhi stands much as did the Bala Hissar with respect to the city, except that the former has not sufficient elevation to command the town, as the latter did. What then would be the result at Delhi, if the palace garrison were to content themselves, as Colonel Shelton did, with a faint and distant cannonade from within their walls; not even effectually supporting the king's bodyguards, who had already sallied into the town, nor even enabling or assisting them to bring off their field-guns when driven back from the city, but should suffer these guns to be abandoned at the very palace gates, and there to lie? Let not a single effort be made to succour or bring off the guards at the magazine or treasury; give up everything for lost; suffer unresistingly the communication between the town and cantonment (almost precisely the same distance in both cases) to be closed; let all this happen in Hindoostan on June 2, instead of among the Afghan mountains on November 2, and does any sane man doubt that twenty-four hours would swell the hundreds of rebels into thousands; and that, if such conduct on our part lasted for a week, every ploughshare in the Delhi States would be turned into a sword? And when a sufficient force had been mustered, by bringing European regiments from the hills and native troops from every quarter (which could not be effected within a month at the very least, or in three at the rate we moved to the succour of Candahar and Jellalabad), should we not then have a more difficult game to play than Clive had at Plassey, or Wellington at Assaye? We should then be literally striking for our existence, at the most inclement season of the year, with the prestige of our name vanished, and the fact before the eyes of imperial Delhi, that the British force, placed not only to protect but to overawe the city, were afraid to enter it.

But the parallel does not end here. Suppose the officer commanding at Meerut, when called on for help, were to reply, "My force is chiefly cavalry and horse artillery, not the sort to be effective within a walled town, where every house is a castle. Besides, Meerut itself, at all times unquiet, is even now in rebellion, and I cannot spare my troops." Suppose that from Agra and Umballa an answer came that they required all the force they had to defend their own posts; and that the reply from Sobathoo and Kussowlee was, "We have not carriage, nor, if we had, could we sacrifice our men by moving them to the plains at this season." All this is less than actually did happen in Afghanistan, when General Sale was recalled, and General Nott was urgently called on for succour; and if all this should occur at Delhi, should we not have to strike anew for our Indian empire?

But who would attribute the calamity to the Civil Commissioner at Delhi? And could not that functionary fairly say to the officer commanding, "I knew very well that there were not only 300 desperate characters in the city, but as many thousands—men having nothing to lose, and everything to gain, by an insurrection. You have let them plunder the magazine and the treasury. They will, doubtless, expect as little resistance elsewhere. A single battalion could have exterminated them the first day, but you let the occasion slip, and the country is now in a blaze, and the game completely out of my hands. I will now give you all the help I can, all the advice you ask, but the Riot Act has been read, and my authority has ceased." Would the civil officer be blamed for thus acting? Could he be held responsible for the way in which the outbreak had been met?

I have endeavoured to put the case fairly. Delhi is nearly as turbulent and unquiet a city as Cabul. It has residing within its walls a king less true to us than was Shah Shoojah. The hot weather of India is more trying to us than the winter of Afghanistan. The ground between the town and cantonment of Delhi, being a long rocky ridge on one side of the road, and the river Jumna on the other, is much more difficult for the action of troops against an insurgent population than anything at Cabul. At Delhi the houses are fully as strong, the streets not less defensible. In short, here as there, we occupy dangerous ground. *Here*, if we act with prudence and intrepidity, we shall, under God's blessing, be safe, as we should have been, with similar conduct, *there*.

But if, under the misfortune that has befallen our arms, we content ourselves with blaming the envoy, or even the military authorities, instead of looking fairly and closely into the foundations of our power, and minutely examining the system that could admit of such conduct as was exhibited in Afghanistan, not in one case, but in many ; then, I say, we are in the fair way of reaping another harvest more terrible than that of Cabul.

The foregoing parallel has been drawn out minutely, perhaps tediously, for I consider it important to show that what was faulty and dangerous in one quarter is not less so in another.

I wish, moreover, to point out that the mode of operation so pertinaciously styled "the Afghan system," and currently linked with the name of the late envoy, as if, with all its errors, it had originated with *him*, is essentially *our Indian system ;* that it existed with all its defects when Sir William Macnaghten was in his cradle, and flourishes in our own provinces now that he is in his grave. Among its errors are—moving with small parties on distant points without support ; inefficient commissariat arrangements ; absolute ignorance on all topographical points ; and reckoning on the attachment of our allies (as if Hindoo or Mahomedan could love his Christian lord, who only comes before him as master or tax-gatherer ; as if it were not absurd to suppose that the chiefs of Burmah, Nepaul, Lahore, and the like could tolerate the power that restrains their rapacious desires and habits, that degrades them in their own and each other's eyes).

Men may differ as to the soundness of our policy, but no one can question its results, as shown in the fact of Hyder Ali twice dictating terms at the gates of Fort St. George (Madras) ; in the disasters that attended the early period of the Nepaul war ; in the long state of siege in which Sir Archibald Campbell was held at Rangoon ; in the frightful mortality at Arracan ; in the surrender of General Matthews ; in the annihilation of Colonel Baillie's detachment ; in the destruction of Colonel Monson's force ; and in the attacks on the Residencies of Poonah and Nagpoor. These are all matters of history, though seldom practically remembered. Still less is it borne in mind how little was wanting to starve General Harris at Seringapatam, General Campbell in Ava, or Sir John Keane in Afghanistan. All these events have been duly recorded, though they have not withheld us, on each occasion, from retracing our old errors. At length a calamity that we had often courted has fallen upon us ; but direful as it is, and wrecked though it has the happiness of numbers, we may yet gather fruit from the thorns, if we learn therefrom how easily an army is paralyzed and panic-stricken, and how fatal such prostration must ever be. If we read the lesson set before us, the wreck of a small army may be the beacon to save large ones.

Our chief danger in India is from within, not from without. The enemy who cannot reach us with his bayonets, can touch us more fatally if he lead us to distrust ourselves, and rouse our subjects to distrust us ; and we shall do his work for him if we show that our former chivalrous bearing is fled, that we pause to count the half-armed rabble opposed to us, and hesitate to act with battalions where a few years before companies would have been deemed sufficient.

The true basis of British power in India is often lost sight of, namely, a well-paid, well-disciplined army, relying, from experience, on the good faith, wisdom, and energy of its leaders.

We forget that our army is composed of men like ourselves, quick-sighted and inquisitive on all matters bearing upon their personal interests ; who, if they can appreciate our points of superiority, are just as capable of detecting our deficiencies, especially any want of military spirit or soldierly bearing.

At Cabul we lost an army, and we lost some character with the surrounding States. But I hold that by far our worst loss was in the confidence of our native soldiery. Better had it been for our fame if our harassed troops had rushed on the enemy and perished to a man, than that surviving Sepoys should be able to tell the tales they can of what they saw at Cabul.

APPENDIX XII

TRANSLATION OF LETTER FROM RAJAH MAUN SINGH TO TALOOKDARS. *Dated July 20, 1857.*

THERE are many who, having become independent by reason of their hereditary estates, have expended their fortune in procuring bodily comforts, and in the enjoyment of sensual pleasures, and are ignorant of the history of former times, and are unacquainted with the misery and ruin which the Mahrattas and Mahomedans inflicted upon India in days gone by.

All such people have become quite careless of the blessings which God has conferred upon every one through the British Government, and are overjoyed at a false hope of increasing their wealth and rank by a change.

In our opinion this change must be for the worse as regards the lives and property of the people of India.

We ought to know how much suffering there was in the times of the Mahrattas and Mussulmans. In those days the proverb originated, "The cultivators till their fields, but their harvest is plunder for those in power."

Those who cultivated their land could not calculate upon enjoying its produce. If they escaped from the Mahratta cavalry, and the plunder and ravage of Sepoys, and succeeded in storing their corn in barns, then only could they hope to enjoy the fruits of their labour.

The jungles in which we find traces of old wells and enclosures were all once thickly populated; these places became jungles by the destruction of the inhabitants, and the country then remained waste for a long time. So many lives were lost in feudal quarrels, that up to this date re-population has not taken place.

The present time is worse than the former one. May God protect us!

My friends, we ought to keep our respect and dignity in our own hands, and wish for the same Government as abolished the tyrannical system of former days, and conferred comfort and peace on the people.

No human being ought to hate that thing which produces comfort, or covet that thing which gives pain and misery.

You can never hope to become rulers by merely assembling bands of armed followers in this time of anarchy, neither can the Telingas[1] ever achieve victory or success.

There are three reasons for this—

1st. Though they are well disciplined, and it is true that by their assistance the British conquered India, still, in reality, they were always kept like a machine which could move or fire a musket on the touch of a spring. They

[1] *Telingas* is a native term for Sepoys.

do not know how to fight, neither do they understand the art of war. The British officers kept this knowledge to themselves. Without those officers they are a machine without a spring, and in the time of need they will neither be able to move nor to fire.

2nd. There used to be twenty or twenty-five British officers to every 1000 men, and these officers were subordinate to one single man, but now-a-days there are 1000 officers, and 1000 kings amongst 1000 men, *i. e.* the men are officers and kings themselves, and when such is the case there are no soldiers to fight. Kings cannot fight alone.

3rd. Life is not a thing which can be given away for nothing. There are three things which make a man careless about sacrificing his life.

1st. Fear.

2nd. Covetousness.

3rd. Shame.

By none of these will the Sepoys be induced to fight.

As they are kings themselves they fear neither imprisonment, corporal punishment, nor dismissal from service.

They have plundered thousands of houses, and they consider every person's property to be their own; therefore they are not likely to covet anything more.

As for shame, every one knows they have none. The worst member of a family used to run away from his parents and enlist in the army.

When they have none of the three inducements above specified, how can they be expected to give their lives in the field and thus deprive themselves of that power for which they have mutinied?

Besides this, when they went into the field under the British Government, they used to be provided with everything, but now they have to provide for themselves, and, finding themselves in want of everything at the time of action, they will be obliged to give up the fight. They must inevitably be defeated. However, even if they were to gain a victory, we cannot but suffer from their hands.

1st. We ought to consider that when they have thrown off the yoke of such a powerful Government from their shoulders, they are not likely to care much for us.

Every person must have observed that one Sepoy of a mutinous regiment can disturb the whole community. What hopes then can we have of our lives from a herd of mutineers?

We should also look back to the Lahore war. How many officers were killed in a very short space of time, and no one expected that the Khalsa troops would leave the British alive. But after all what became of those Khalsa troops? They were all annihilated.

My friends, a paper boat can never float on a bankless river.

2nd. It is also worthy of consideration—that in each of the villages under every Talookdar there cannot be less than ten Telingas, and consequently there will be as many kings in each village.

The Talookdars were dissatisfied and complained enough when only one king (the British) annexed the country, but when they find thousands of kings upon their respective estates, it will be difficult for them to save either their estates or their lives.

3rd. If the Telingas could be reformed and made peaceful subjects, even then we should not be able to manage. They would demand lakhs and lakhs of rupees on account of their pay, and not one of us, but every one of us would have to pay them.

After meeting their exorbitant demands for a short time, we should be reduced to such a state of poverty that not a stitch of cloth to cover our bodies would be left; what reason is there then for us to be happy?

Those who have butchered the children of their masters after eating their salt for ages, will never spare recent acquaintances like us.

It is the custom of this country that when a servant commits himself once, he can never get employment anywhere, and is excluded from society. How then can we with prudence countenance these people?

We should indeed be surprised if any one was to say that we ought to take up the cause of our religion. The Telingas do not fight for religion. They do just the thing which our religion prohibits. They plunder and murder women and children, and no religion admits of such deeds.

People of this sort are called "chundals," or abominably wicked people, and no one who adheres to his religion ought even to salaam to such creatures.

To become their ally is to take part in a sacrilegious deed.

It is also surprising that people should aid and put into power those very Mussulmans who, on invading India, destroyed all our Hindoo temples, forcibly converted the natives to Mahomedanism, massacred whole cities, seized upon Hindoo females and made them concubines, prevented Brahmins from saying prayers, burnt their religious books, and levied taxes upon every Hindoo.

They are those very Mussulmans who prided themselves on calling us infidels, and in subjecting us to all sorts of humiliation.

If any person will reflect on their former deeds, it will make his hair stand on end, cause such disgust that the very sight even of a Mahomedan will be abhorrent.

What is more surprising still, is that the people should consider it a religious deed to kill and destroy those very persons who permitted the re-establishment of the decayed religion, and allowed all temples and places of worship to be rebuilt, and all religious ceremonies to be performed without any hindrance whatever.

We should consider how much we suffered in the time of the Mahomedan kings in Oude.

A short time ago, Moulvie Gholam Hoosein and Ameer Aly did their best to destroy the Hunnooman Gurhee, but it was owing to General Outram that they did not succeed; otherwise all of us would either have lost our lives or our religion, from the oppression of tyrants. The people are forgetting those days, and now not only strive to destroy those who saved our religion, but make their destruction out to be a religious act.

These are the very Telingas who did not consider that taking medicines from the hospitals or biting cartridges with their teeth caused loss of religion, yet now they say that breaking a cartridge by the hand, instead of biting it as formerly, is contrary to their religion.

Is not this all nonsense, a false excuse and mere pretence?

People should reflect and really adopt measures to save their religion, honour, and estates.

They should rest assured they will never be able to cope with that army and people who defeated ten lakhs of Russians in spite of their discipline, wealth, and munitions of war, and finally captured Sebastopol.

Three thousand European soldiers have lately dismayed all the Iranees in Persia.

Have not the English caused the Emperor of China to make good their losses?

There is not a single king in the world who does not fear them.

But if the English were defeated, what good have we to gain? We shall lose our religion, and all our temples and places of worship will be destroyed.

Our people, by supporting Mahomedans, will in fact be instrumental in annihilating their own religion.

In our opinion, to gain the favour of the British is to save religion; to annoy them is a violation of all things sacred.

You may think that the British were always formerly victorious because they treated all with kindness and rendered justice to every one who went to their courts, and that now, as they have forsaken their God and become fearless, they cannot succeed.

It may be true that certain district civil officers, instead of rendering justice as formerly, now strike poor people with rulers, and on a reference to any rule or section of their code, answer that they have all such rules at their fingers' ends. Some may now even hate to see natives, may deprive them of their hereditary rights, and make them consent to do things which are against their religion, and may act contrary to their promise.

And from all this, it may be argued that God therefore made them (the British) instrumental to their own destruction.

But, my friends, this was the folly of the district officers, and they are punished for it. The Supreme Government never intended such things.

Indeed had the Government so intended, God would have been for you, and the British could never have defeated the Nuwab's numerous army with a small force.

Yet you see them conquering on with a handful of men; and still you believe that God is for you—what folly!

God has made kings and governors to rule and cherish their subjects, and to keep them in comfort. But He has also allowed rulers to tax their people.

If kings neglect their duty, they will of course receive punishment from God.

Observe how many kings and rajahs have been ruined by mismanagement. When our rajahs neglected to seek knowledge and to cherish their subjects, they lost their kingdoms and were punished by foreigners.

When the Mahomedan kings neglected their duty, the British came in.

At the first symptoms of the British evincing negligence in discharging their duty, they received a reprimand from God.

Those who have made it a profession to kill people can never hope for mercy.

You see that God inflicted punishment upon individuals, because they used to strike people with rulers, etc. How could He ever dream of restoring the Government to you, from whom He snatched it some 1000 years ago for your unworthiness, finding, as He does, that you are spilling blood in this manner?

If you choose to display loyalty and fidelity to your king (of Oude) still, you should not annoy the British, because your king is in their hands, and if through your wise deeds they were to kill the king, you will be proved disloyal.

If you wish to prove your loyalty to the king, you should assist the British in their bad days. They may then become pleased, release the king, and perhaps give him back his country. If you could effect this, what a name indeed would you get!

You may argue that the king is absent, but his son is present. In that case even, you ought to remain neutral, because it is written by wise men that where there is a female, a boy, many kings, or no king at all to rule, there can be no hope of prosperity.

No one can be prosperous in such a country, and if he escapes with honour he ought to consider himself very lucky. Each of these four things (viz. a female, a boy, many kings, or no kings, to rule) is dangerous to life and honour.

But when you have these four together, what means have you of saving your lives and honour?

If you insist upon having the former times back again, all of you should send in a petition to the Queen of England, desiring that one-fourth of the country be granted in jagheers to those worthless and illiterate people who are generally called in this country Nuwabs and Doolahs, in order that they may pass their time without care or thought, in singing and dancing, perhaps loaded with one or two seers of gold and silver and jewels which, besides the burden of their own bodies, they may desire to carry; that the income of the remaining three-quarters of the country be deposited in the treasury and laid out in bricks and chunam, or be given to buffoons and dancing-girls, or spent on other kingly pomps, or expended on increasing the pay of parasites and sycophants, so that when they die or become useless, their houses may be confiscated, as was done in the time of former kings.

That an order be sent to all the rajahs to select beautiful girls and send them to the prince.

That an order also be sent to the Governor-General, to select from the females of respectable families slave-girls for the Mahul, or, should the Governor-General have no confidence in those appointed to select, he should order a meena bazaar or fancy fair to be held in the Kulan Kothee, and go himself in disguise to pick out the prettiest females.

That, like Nadir Shah and Ahmud Shah Abdallee, her Majesty should order a general massacre, or, like Aurungzebe, should order a general destruction of all the Hindoo temples, and the building of her own in their place.

That European soldiers may be ordered to spit in the faces of all the Hindoos and Mahomedans, and thus convert them to Christianity; that the pensions of all the rajahs, baboos, and nuwabs be stopped, or that they may be killed either by putting out their eyes, or by feeding them upon bread made of equal parts of salt and flour.

That the Government should not pay lakhs of rupees as interest for the money due to bankers, but, like Toghluk Shah, should institute a leather coinage, and thus at once pay off all loans.

That should her Majesty desire to see the sport of a boat sinking, she should, like Surajooddowlah, order the bottom of a ferry-boat to be knocked out in mid-stream, and passengers and all be swamped.

Orders should likewise be solicited that the Pindarees remain idle no longer, but plunder the roads, one-quarter of their loot being the property of Government.

That it should be ordered that the troops receive their pay one or two years in arrears, in order to force them to borrow money from bankers on interest; that when the troops are much in want, they be allowed to plunder the market and to live upon the loot.

That there is no use in fulfilling any engagements with the landholders or the ryots. The Government should extort money from them according to the circumstances of each, press the people to carry the soldiers' baggage on the march, lay a tax on the Zemindars to provide royal pigeons, fighting-cocks, and other amusements.

That the Government need not keep a commissariat department, but make the ryots supply the Government cattle with food. The sugar-canes can be seized from the ryots' fields, and the trees at the gates of people's dwellings felled as fodder for the elephants.

That her Majesty should please her poor subjects by passing her days in pleasure, keeping crores of slaves, God having created them all specially for her benefit.

He will therefore be pleased to steel her heart against any feeling for their inconvenience.

That should the editors of newspapers write anything against her Majesty, an order for their hands to be cut off should assuredly be passed, or, by way of variety, they may with readiness be blown away from guns.

That the people have not run away from their houses for a long time, therefore all the Amils should be ordered to attack them and make them fly.

That no house floors have been dug up for a long time, that orders should therefore be sent out to level a few cities to the ground.

The Governor-General should be ordered to instruct his officers to see every bride before he allows marriage processions to pass.

Two or three sham expeditions should be made to keep the troops up to their trade and support their spirits.

That in order to secure a change every year, her Majesty, like Mahomed of the Deccan, should order five lakhs of Hindoos to be massacred, or by way of variety some well-populated city to be annihilated.

Rely on it, my friends, that if her Majesty does not care for her name, she will sanction all these prayers, and you will gain your desired object without any trouble.

But if you do not like a return to such times, you should strive for peace.

If all of you unite and seek for peace, I am sure the Government will remove all your doubts (of whatever kind), and something better will come out of the future. At any rate we cannot lose anything by the attempt.

(Signed) MAUN SINGH.

APPENDIX XIII

PROCLAMATION, MARCH 1858

THE army of His Excellency the Commander-in-Chief is in possession of Lucknow, and the city lies at the mercy of the British Government, whose authority it has, for nine months, rebelliously defied and resisted.

This resistance, begun by a mutinous soldiery, has found support from the inhabitants of the city, and the province of Oude at large. Many who owed their prosperity to the British Government, as well as those who believed themselves aggrieved by it, have joined in this bad cause, and have ranged themselves with the enemies of the State.

They have been guilty of a great crime, and have subjected themselves to a just retribution.

The capital of their country is now once more in the hands of British troops. From this day it will be held by a force which nothing can withstand, and the authority of the Government will be carried into every corner of the province.

The time, then, has come at which the Right Honourable the Governor-General of India deems it right to make known the mode in which the British Government will deal with the Talookdars, chiefs, and landholders of Oude and their followers.

The first care of the Governor-General will be to reward those who have been steadfast in their allegiance at a time when the authority of the Government was partially overborne, and who have proved this by the support and assistance which they have given to British officers.

Therefore the Right Honourable the Governor-General hereby declares that Drigbiggei Singh, Rajah of Bulrampoor, Koowunt Singh, Rajah of Pudnaha, Rao Kurdeo Buksh Singh of Kutiaree, Kashee Pershad, Talookdar of Sissaindee, Hubr Singh, Zemindar of Gopal Khais, and Chundee Lal, Zemindar of Moraon (Baiswarah), are henceforward the sole hereditary proprietors of the lands which they held when Oude came under British rule, subject only to such moderate assessment as may be imposed upon them; and these loyal men will be further rewarded in such manner and to such extent as, upon consideration of their merits and position, the Governor-General shall determine.

A proportionate measure of reward and honour, according to their deserts, will be conferred upon others, in whose favour like claims may be established to the satisfaction of the Government.

The Governor-General further proclaims to the people of Oude that, with the above-mentioned exceptions, the proprietary right in the soil of the province is confiscated to the British Government, which will dispose of that right in such manner as to it may seem fitting.

To those Talookdars, chiefs, and landowners, with their followers, who shall make immediate submission to the Chief Commissioner of Oude, surrendering their arms and obeying his orders, the Right Honourable the Governor-General promises that their lives and honour shall be safe, provided that their hands are not stained with English blood murderously shed. But as regards any further indulgence which may be extended to them, and the condition in which they may hereafter be placed, they must throw themselves upon the justice and mercy of the British Government. As participation in the murder of English men and English women will exclude those who are guilty of it from all mercy, so will those who have protected English lives be entitled to consideration and leniency.

THE END.

W. & A. K. Johnston, Edinburgh & London.

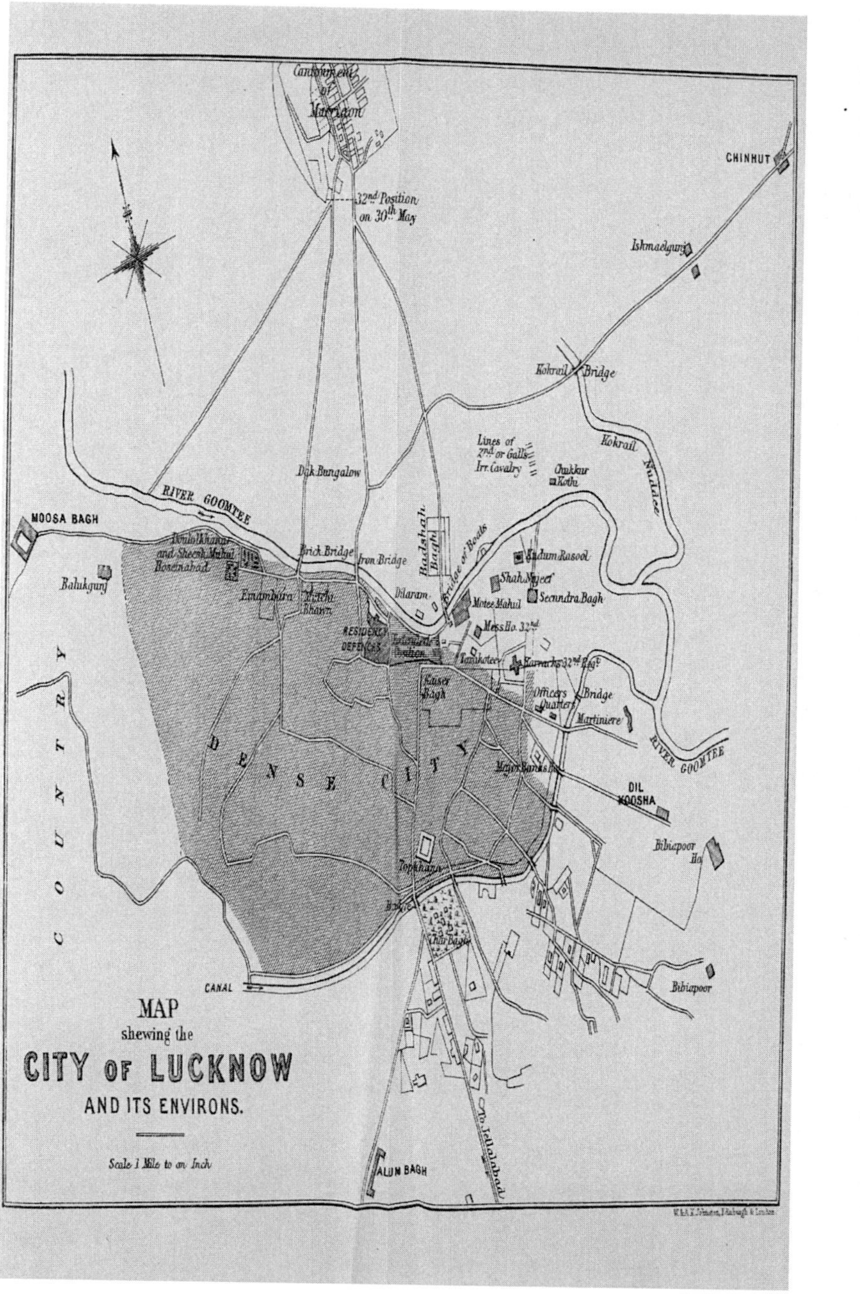
Cantonment of Murriaon
32nd Position on 30th May
CHINHUT
Ishmaelgunj
Kokrail Bridge
Kokrail Nuddee
Lines of 2nd or Galls Irr. Cavalry
Chukkur Kothi
Dak Bungalow
RIVER GOOMTEE
MOOSA BAGH
Balukgunj
Brick Bridge
Iron Bridge
Badshah Baghi
Bridge of Boats
Kudum Rasool
Shah Nujeef
Secundra Bagh
Emambara
Muchi Bhawn
Dilaram
Motee Mahul
RESIDENCY DEFENCES
Mess Ho. 32nd
Tarakotee
Barracks 32nd Regt.
Kaiser Bagh
Officers Quarters
Bridge
Martiniere
RIVER GOOMTEE
DENSE CITY
COUNTRY
Major Banks Ho.
DIL KOOSHA
Bibiapoor Ho.
Topkhana
Bibiapoor
CANAL
To Jellalabad
ALUM BAGH
MAP
shewing the
CITY OF LUCKNOW
AND ITS ENVIRONS.
Scale 1 Mile to an Inch

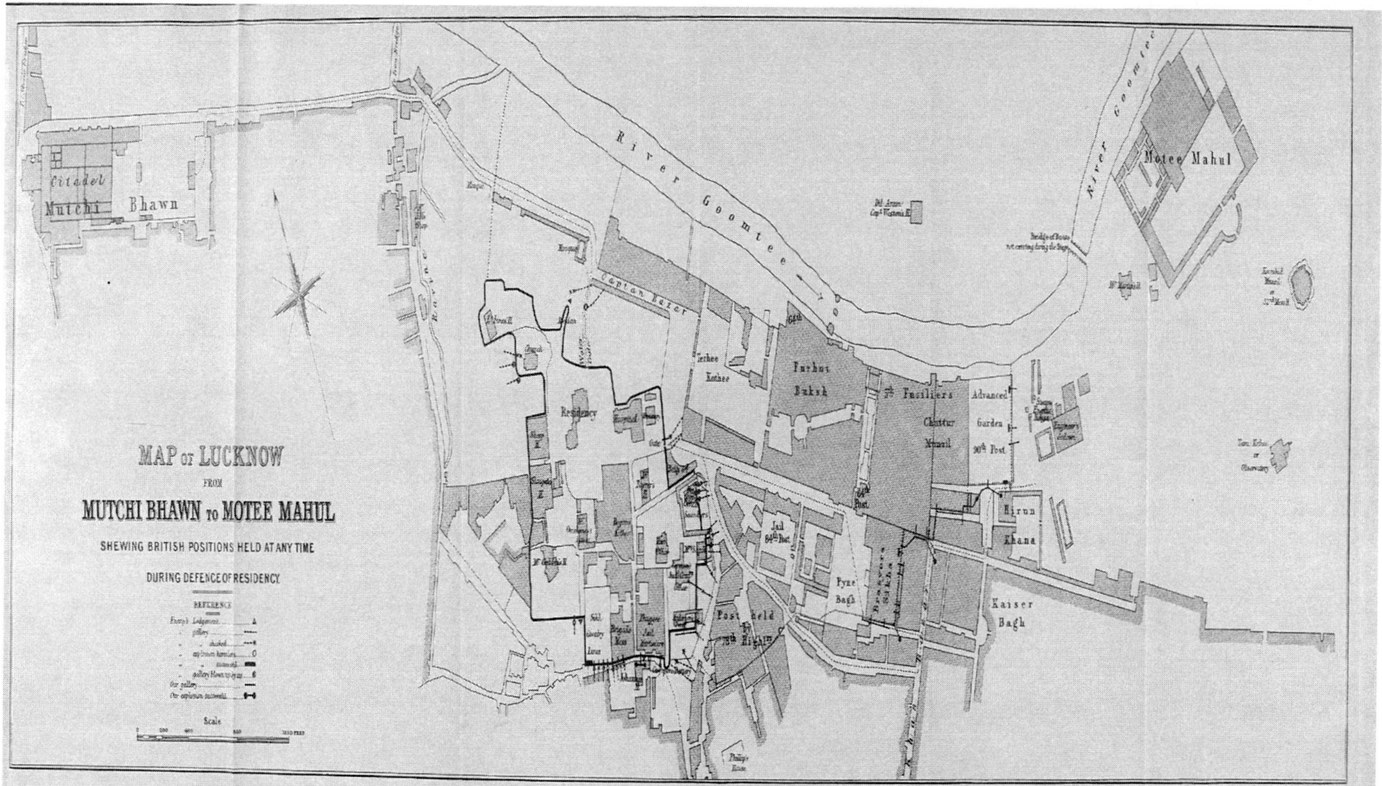
MAP OF LUCKNOW
FROM
MUTCHI BHAWN TO MOTEE MAHUL
SHEWING BRITISH POSITIONS HELD AT ANY TIME
DURING DEFENCE OF RESIDENCY.
REFERENCE
Scale
Citadel
Mutchi Bhawn
River Goomtee
Motee Mahul
Captan Bazar
Residency
Terhee Kothee
Furhut Buksh
Chuttur Munzil
Advanced Garden
90th Post
Jail 84th Post
Pyne Bagh
Post held by 78th Highrs
Hirun Khana
Kaiser Bagh

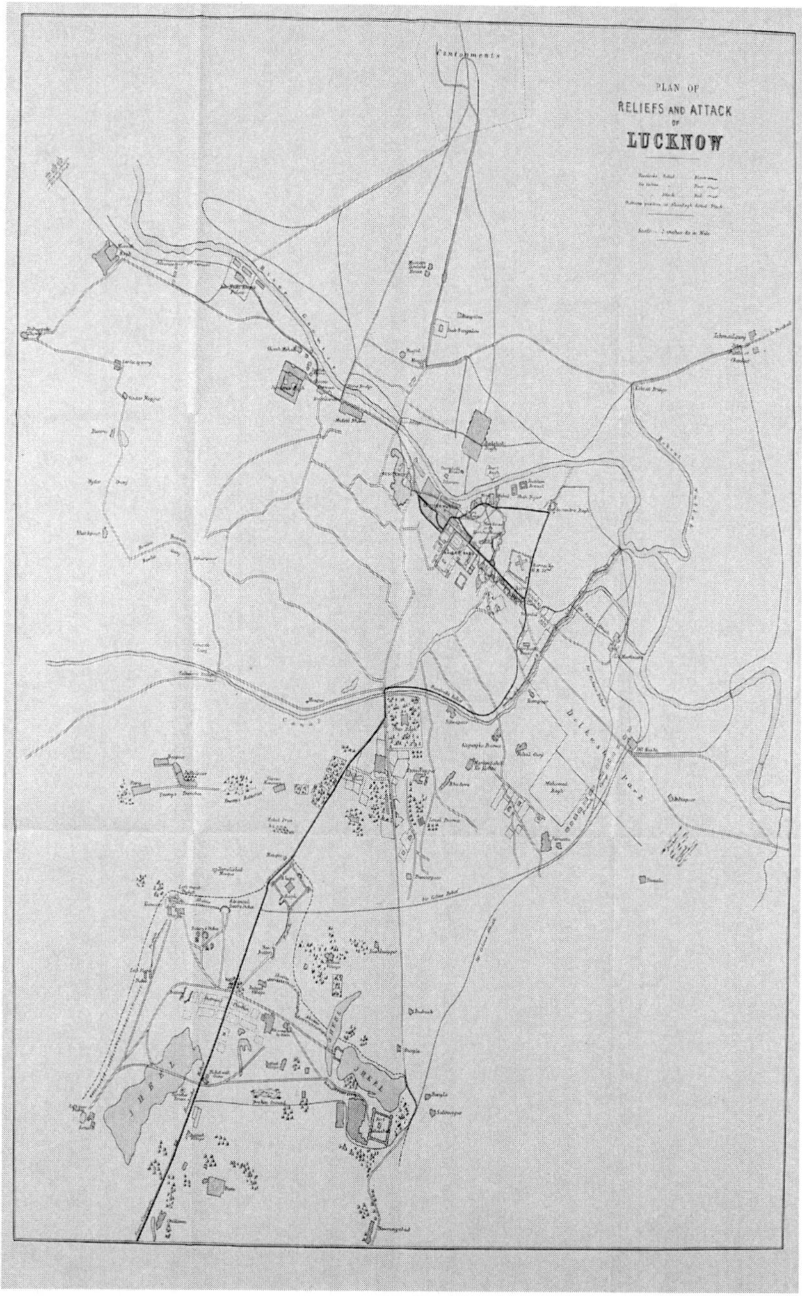
Cantonments
PLAN OF
RELIEFS AND ATTACK
OF
LUCKNOW
Canal